# Popular Modernism and Its Legacies

# Popular Modernism and Its Legacies

## From Pop Literature to Video Games

*Edited by*
*Scott Ortolano*

*With an Afterword by Faye Hammill*

Bloomsbury Academic
An imprint of Bloomsbury Publishing Inc

B L O O M S B U R Y
NEW YORK · LONDON · OXFORD · NEW DELHI · SYDNEY

SVA Library
209 E. 23 St.
New York, N.Y. 10010-3994

**Bloomsbury Academic**
An imprint of Bloomsbury Publishing Inc

1385 Broadway            50 Bedford Square
New York                 London
NY 10018                 WC1B 3DP
USA                      UK

www.bloomsbury.com

**BLOOMSBURY and the Diana logo are trademarks of Bloomsbury Publishing Plc**

First published 2018

© Scott Ortolano and Contributors, 2018

All rights reserved. No part of this publication may be reproduced or transmitted in any form or by any means, electronic or mechanical, including photocopying, recording, or any information storage or retrieval system, without prior permission in writing from the publishers.

No responsibility for loss caused to any individual or organization acting on or refraining from action as a result of the material in this publication can be accepted by Bloomsbury or the editor.

**Library of Congress Cataloging-in-Publication Data**
A catalog record for this book is available from the Library of Congress.

ISBN:   HB:    978-1-5013-2511-3
        ePub:  978-1-5013-2512-0
        ePDF:  978-1-5013-2513-7

Cover design by Emma J. Hardy
Cover image © iStock

Typeset by Fakenham Prepress Solutions, Fakenham, Norfolk NR21 8NN

*For my wife and best friend, Michelle, and my daughter, Lila, who inspire me every day to prove myself worthy of their love.*

# CONTENTS

*List of illustrations* ix
*Acknowledgments* xi

Introduction
Of Titanics, wars, downturns, and Downtons: Popular modernism and its legacies  *Scott Ortolano*  1

## Part 1 New Visions of Popular Modernism

1  *Gentry* modernism: Cultural connoisseurship and midcentury masculinity, 1951–1957  *Marsha Bryant*  19

2  Modernism, operetta, and Ruritania: Ivor Novello's *Glamorous Night*  *Nicholas Daly*  45

3  Fine art on the airwaves: Radio drama and modern(ist) mass culture  *Adam Nemmers*  63

4  "I'm gonna be somebody," 1930: Gangsters and modernist celebrity  *Jonathan Goldman*  79

5  Charlie Chaplin, Walter Benjamin, and the redemption of the city  *Barry J. Faulk*  95

## Part 2 Legacies of Popular Modernism

6  "Catch a wave": Surf noir and modernist nostalgia  *Kirk Curnutt*  113

7  Alien pleasures: Modernism/hybridity/science fiction *Paul March-Russell* 133

8  Josephine Baker's contemporary afterlives: Black female identity, modernist performance, and popular legacies of the Jazz Age *Asimina Ino Nikolopoulou* 149

9  A hitchhiker's guide to modernism: The futuristic Fordisms of Aldous Huxley, Brian O'Nolan, and Douglas Adams *Andrew V. McFeaters* 165

**Part 3 Resonances of Popular Modernism in the Twenty-First Century**

10  Smokescreens to smokestacks: *True Detective* and the American sublime *Caroline Blinder* 183

11  Of modernist second acts and African-American lives: F. Scott Fitzgerald, *The Wire*, and the struggle against lockdown *Walter Bosse* 203

12  Don Draper's identity crisis and *Mad Men*'s modernist masculinity *Camelia Raghinaru* 217

13  A century of reading time: From modernist novels to contemporary comics *Aimee Armande Wilson* 231

14  Hemingway's console: Memory and ethics in the modernist video game *Dustin Anderson* 247

*Afterword, Faye Hammill* 263
*Notes on contributors* 267
*Index* 271

# LIST OF ILLUSTRATIONS

Figure 0.1: Violet Crawley, the Dowager Countess of Grantham, holds up a fan to shield herself from the electric light as her son, Lord Grantham, looks on undisturbed. *Downton Abbey*. Season 1, episode 1. Directed by Brian Percival. Written by Julian Fellowes. Aired September 28, 2010. Carnival Films and Masterpiece, 2010. DVD. 8

Figure 1.1: Cover of *Gentry* with Georges Braque lithograph *Pallas Athene*. *Gentry* 7 (Summer 1953). 20

Figure 1.2: Fabric swatch page from *Gentry* 2 (January 15–April 15, 1952). 23

Figure 1.3: "How Modern is Modern" fold-over from *Gentry* 4 (Fall 1952). 27

Figure 1.4: Advertisement for Alfred of New York, the Varadero, *Gentry* 13 (Winter 1954–5). 32

Figure 1.5: Red velvet and black bengaline host suit in *Gentry* 16, Age of Elegance Number (Fall 1955). 35

Figure 2.1: Anthony Allen and his parents, Act 1. *Play Pictorial* 66, no. 398 (1935). 50

Figure 2.2: Anthony and Militza aboard the *Silver Star*, Act 1. *Play Pictorial* 66, no. 398 (1935). 51

Figure 2.3: The Gypsy Betrothal Ceremony, Act 2. *Play Pictorial* 66, no. 398 (1935). 52

Figure 2.4: Anthony and Militza at the Betrothal Ceremony, Act 2. *Play Pictorial* 66, no. 398 (1935). 52

Figure 5.1: The portrayal of Chaplin in the *Ballet Mécanique*, directed by Fernand Léger (1923–4). 103

Figure 10.1: Richard Misrach. *Pipeline and River Road. Donaldsville, Louisiana*. 2010. © Richard Misrach, courtesy Fraenkel Gallery, San Francisco. 187

**Figure 10.2:** Frank Semyon in the desert. *True Detective.* Season 2, episode 8. Directed by John Crowley. Written by Nic Pizzolatto. Aired August 9, 2015. Home Box Office, 2016. DVD. 188

**Figure 10.3:** Still from *Point Blank.* Directed by John Boorman. 1967. Reissued, Warner Home Video, 2005. DVD. 189

**Figure 10.4:** Detectives Cohle and Hart. *True Detective.* Season 1, episode 8. Directed by Cary Joji Fukunaga. Written by Nic Pizzolatto. Aired March 9, 2014. Home Box Office, 2015. DVD. 190

**Figure 10.5:** Richard Misrach. *Night Releases. Mississippi River Corridor, Louisiana.* 1998. © Richard Misrach, courtesy Fraenkel Gallery, San Francisco. 191

**Figure 10.6:** Image of Detective Hart merged with Richard Misrach's *Night Releases,* from opening credit sequence of *True Detective.* Season 1. Aired January–March 2014. Home Box Office, 2015. DVD. 193

**Figure 10.7:** Image of Detective Cohle, from opening credit sequence of *True Detective.* Season 1. Aired January–March 2014. Home Box Office, 2015. DVD. 194

**Figure 10.8:** David Maisel's *Oblivion 2N* used to introduce *True Detective* series title. From opening credit sequence of *True Detective.* Season 2. Aired June–August 2015. Home Box Office, 2016. DVD. 195

**Figure 10.9:** David Maisel's The Lake Project 1, 200l superimposed on opening credit sequence of True Detective. Season 2. Aired June–August 2015. Home Box Office, 2016. DVD. 195

**Figure 10.10:** First shot from episode 1 of *True Detective.* Season 2. Directed by Justin Lin. Written by Nic Pizzolatto. Aired June 21, 2015. Home Box Office, 2016. DVD. 197

**Figure 11.1:** D'Angelo Barksdale (Lawrence Gilliard, Jr.) offers critical insight about F. Scott Fitzgerald's *The Great Gatsby* during a prisoner-education course. *The Wire.* "All Prologue." Season 2, episode 6. Directed by Steve Shill. Written by David Simon and Ed Burns. Aired July 6, 2003. Home Box Office, 2008. DVD. 209

# ACKNOWLEDGMENTS

First and foremost, I would like to thank the contributors to this collection for believing in and joining the project when it existed only as an emerging idea about the intertwined legacies of modernism and popular culture. I attribute any success that this book may find to the faith, quality, and dedication of the contributors, all of whom made the process both enjoyable and enlightening.

My deepest thanks to Dr. Rebecca Totaro, who read through multiple drafts of the book proposal and offered invaluable guidance throughout the publication process. Without such support, this project would not have been possible. Special thanks also to Dr. Laci Mattison and Dr. Paul Ardoin, both of whom offered encouragement and important advice during critical phases of the book's development. This book would not have been possible without the logistical and financial support of FSW's administration, and I am especially grateful to our College President, Dr. Jeffery S. Allbritten; our Provost and Vice President of Academic Affairs, Dr. Jeff Stewart; our Associate Vice President of Academic Affairs, Dr. Eileen DeLuca; Deans Dr. Martin McClinton and Dr. Emery Alford; and my Department Chair, Prof. Amanda Lehrian. They serve as beacons of light at FSW, encouraging and supporting the research and growth of all faculty at the college. The library staff at Florida SouthWestern State College were also instrumental to this project's success, as they spent multiple academic years acquiring various books, articles, and conference proceedings, often at a moment's notice. I am indebted beyond words to the wonderful editors at Bloomsbury, most notably the remarkable Mary Al-Sayed, for her faith in this project and tireless assistance throughout all stages of its development. Above all, this book and the ideas that underwrite it are part of a long process of exploring and thinking about literature and culture. As such, I would be remiss if I did not take a moment to recognize past professors who have guided me along the way and helped me reflect on many of the issues addressed in this book, particularly Dr. Andrew Epstein, Dr. S. E. Gontarski, Dr. Robin Goodman, Dr. David Ikard, Dr. Barry Faulk, Dr. Maxine Lavon Montgomery, Dr. Myra Mendible, Dr. Rebecca Totaro, Dr. Eric Strahorn, Dr. Daniel J. Vitkus, Dr. Joe Wisdom, Dr. Neil Jumonville, Dr. James Brock, and Dr. Karen Tolchin. Last but certainly not least, I would like to thank my wife and friend, Michelle, and my daughter, Lila, for their continuous love and support.

# Introduction

# Of Titanics, wars, downturns, and Downtons: Popular modernism and its legacies

## Scott Ortolano

*"Before the war, I believed my life had value. I suppose I'd like to feel that again."*
—LORD GRANTHAM, *DOWNTON ABBEY*, SEASON 2, EPISODE 7

The international appeal of *Downton Abbey*, a television series about an aristocratic British household in Edwardian England, has taken many critics by surprise. The series finale drew approximately 10.9 million viewers in Britain and 9.6 million viewers in the United States, and the show has received a number of national and international awards—including twelve Emmys, three golden globes, four Screen Actors Guild Awards, two Producers Guild Awards, and four BAFTAs.[1] Nevertheless, many have dismissed *Downton Abbey* as an escapist melodrama that represents politically regressive strains in the contemporary psyche. *Newsweek* critic Simon Schama categorizes the series as a "servile soap opera" that revels in "cultural necrophilia" as it looks back and romanticizes an oppressive social and economic order.[2] Another bruising assessment from *The Atlantic* argues that the series is "preposterous as history, preposterous as drama," portending only that people are "sentimental and nostalgic" and need avenues to "gratify the[ir] innate conservatism."[3] However, such assessments are so focused on class and aesthetics that they fail to account for *Downton Abbey*'s strategic use of the past, particularly the early twentieth century, as an analogue for the current world. By looking back to an era that Jessica Pressman identifies as "the classical period of our contemporary technological age," the series resonates with viewers ill at ease with their own world.[4] It allows them, in the spirit of Eliot, to shore the fragmented world of Downton against the restructurings of the digital age.

Scholars invested in new modernist studies have identified *Downton Abbey*'s popularity as one facet of a popular wave of interest in people, ideas, and art from the modernist era. In the *Cambridge Companion to Modernist Culture*, Celia Marshik notes that the television series and others like it have "piqued viewers' interest in the culture of the period" and are a testament to modernism's continued ability "to attract scholars while also providing material for contemporary popular culture and literary fiction."[5] Similarly, in "The Contemporaneity of Modernism," Michael D'Arcy and Mathias Nilges claim that the "periodizing effort that underlies the aesthetics" of *Downton Abbey*, along with shows like *Mad Men* and films like *The Hours*, plays upon widespread interest in this era while simultaneously exhibiting "modernism's contemporary relevance."[6] Thus, we might say that the series' success is the result of a strategic invocation of past modernisms to help the audience confront the modernities of our present moment. In the process, the show exemplifies Marshall Berman's prediction that "remembering the modernisms of the nineteenth century ... can help us bring modernism back to its roots, so that it can nourish and renew itself, to confront the adventures and dangers that lie ahead."[7] As Rosalía Baena and Christa Byker explain in an analysis of nostalgia and English identity in *Downton Abbey*, viewers empathize with and gain hope from servants' and aristocrats' struggles to find new ethical and ideological positions as "modernity enters Downton Abbey."[8] The show resonates with viewers' desperate longing for personal and social endurance, for a clean, well-lit space in the darkness. Most importantly, its major plot points serve as doubles to the challenges of the contemporary world and reveal why the currents of modernism have had and continue to maintain such a prominent place in the popular consciousness. In this sense, the show offers a microcosm of the important and underappreciated legacies of popular modernism explored in this collection.

## Popular modernism: Then and now

The "great divide" between modernism and popular culture, to use Andreas Huyssen's famous phrase, once foundational to conceptions of modernism, has fragmented beyond recognition.[9] The dichotomy that Huyssen identifies between art and popular culture emerges from a tradition established by early-twentieth-century critics, perhaps most notably Max Horkheimer and

Theodor Adorno. In *Dialectic of Enlightenment*, Horkheimer and Adorno envision popular culture as a system of ideological and material domination that "impresses the same stamp on everything" and to which conformation can only "mean[] to be rendered powerless, economically and therefore spiritually."[10] Building upon ideas about the avant-garde's relationship to such a spiritually anemic mass culture, particularly as expressed by Peter Bürger's *Theory of the Avant-Garde* and Clement Greenberg's "Avant-Garde and Kitsch,"[11] Huyssen contends that modernist art is "autonomous and totally separate from the realms of mass culture and everyday life."[12] While influential, this categorization of modernism in opposition to mass culture oversimplified the movement to create easy avenues for classifying postmodernism and placing it as a definitively new epoch in the arts.

The shortcomings of Huyssen's thesis have been well documented in recent scholarship, and I offer here only a glimpse of a much broader movement within modernist studies.[13] At their core, all such refutations share a concern with demonstrating the often integral links between modernism and mass culture on the level of aesthetics and content. In the introduction to *High and Low Moderns*, a reassessment of high modernism and popular culture, Maria DiBattista argues that even the most traditional modernist writers "regarded low cultural phenomena and entertainments unique to their times—the popular press, cinema, music hall, and the 'art' of advertising—as an inalienable part of modern life, hence unavoidable subject matter whose forms as well as content might be assimilated or reworked, playfully initiated or seriously criticized, in their own art."[14] Since the last decades of the twentieth century, critics within modernist studies and beyond have called for re-examinations of texts and authors that have been overlooked as a result of the academy's historical dismissal of "low culture." For example, in the influential *The Gender of Modernity*, Rita Felski theorizes the concept of the "popular sublime" as a means of reclaiming sublimity from the "high culture tradition" and challenging "the narrative of modernity as growing disenchantment."[15] This revision effectively expanded the umbrella of modernism by repositioning early-twenty-first-century texts that foreground escapist fantasy and romantic longings as modernist "negation[s] of the everyday" and the "existing social order" that regulated such quotidian realities.[16] This critical shift has produced a two-pronged adjustment within modernist studies as scholars have moved to draw connections between modernism and popular culture and validate the popular in its own right—reclaiming individual authors like Dorothy Parker, broader movements such as the Harlem Renaissance, and popular mediums like radio and television.[17]

In this revised tradition, modernist works, even those in the high modernist canon, are inextricably linked with popular culture—vastly expanding the places one might encounter modernist ideas and aesthetics. Modernism then becomes a series of overlapping and sometimes contradictory attempts to make sense out of and discover meaning within a world in transition, endeavors that frequently used the mediums driving these changes in aesthetically productive ways. As Juan A. Suárez argues in *Pop Modernism: Noise and the Reinvention of the Everyday*, modernism stands as an "urgent aspiration to reinvent the practice of everyday life" by "users" who found themselves "confronted [by] a new, at times overwhelming, material environment."[18] This focus on reinvention, a longing to create something viable in a changing world, present also in Felski's vision of the "popular sublime," is at the core of modernism, popular and otherwise.

*Downton Abbey* follows in this revised tradition of popular modernism. The characters do not merely grapple with a changing status quo but, as *Forbes* contributor Jerry Bowyer notes, themselves are "revolutionary" challenges to cliché archetypes of the aristocracy and lower class because the major characters of both social groups, upper and lower, are positioned as endearing, but flawed human beings.[19] Series creator Julian Fellowes explains that this, and other elements of the show, are designed to argue that it "is possible for us all to get on" during times of great transformation.[20] The characters do not unequivocally triumph over their circumstances but find positions to viably exist within a world that is constantly erecting new truths and new challenges. In America and Britain, societies where cultural factions are often strategically pitted against one another by those at the top of the social-economic order in what Henry Giroux calls a "politics of cynicism and despair,"[21] the show's often unrealistic promises of hope and endurance tap into a deep-seated longing of viewers, one denied to them by the world they inhabit. In this way, the show's rejection of social realities and accepted conventions is an unusual manifestation of aesthetic transgression, or "badness" in the sense of Douglas Mao and Rebecca Walkowitz's theorization of the movement.[22] While this badness has no definitive form, it unites modernism's disparate threads under the logic that "there might be something good about bad artistic behavior" that defies conventions of a given genre, culture, or period.[23]

On yet another level, the order of *Downton*'s world, with its attendant codes and rituals, reflects what scholars like David James have identified as the main reason for the endurance of modernist ideas and aesthetics: the failure of postmodernism to generate anything other than "a futile feedback loop" of "play and parody."[24] Here, the "novels which imitate the form of the Novel, by ... author[s] who imitate[] the role of Author," to appropriate John Barth's words, have proven far less "apocalyptical" than he and other advocates of postmodernism assumed.[25] Instead, the calcification of postmodern thought and art during the late twentieth century has opened a need for an (old) new aesthetic. Speculating on the reasons behind modernism's resurgence, Peter Nicholls contends that modernism offers a much needed solution to this predicament because it continues to "speak to us with an uncanny directness ... [with an] expression of newness [that] can seem more exhilarating than the sceptical novelties of postmodernism."[26] As this book contends, the legacies of popular modernism are not merely relics of the past but powerful tools for understanding the current world. The first half of the twentieth century still calls to us and offers important parallels to our own paradigm.

## Cultural shifts, the Abbey, and contemporary genealogies of popular modernism

The resurgence of modernist ideas and aesthetics in our contemporary moment is a result of the cultural anxieties of the post-9/11 age, and *Downton Abbey* offers an ideal lens for seeing why the legacies of modernism have found such fertile ground in the twenty-first century. The series opens with the sinking of the Titanic, a culturally traumatic event that would prove to be but the first of a number of tremors. The opening lines belong not to the servants or rulers of Downton, but to telegraph operators who receive the news and can only astonishingly remark, "Oh my God! That's impossible."[27] This inability to apprehend the catastrophe continues at Downton where viewers are introduced to the major characters as they wrestle with the loss of the "unsinkable ship." Mrs. Patmore, the head of the kitchen, concludes the servants' reactions and encapsulates the larger significance of the event by morosely reflecting, "Nothing in life is sure."[28] This statement proves far truer than she can yet realize. The loss of the Titanic stands as but one of innumerable shockwaves that Downton and the world will soon face. By the time the series has concluded, it will be all too apparent that no ship or culture is unsinkable, no place beyond assault.

Contemporary viewers will immediately empathize with the show's foregrounding of a shocked reaction to a sudden and seemingly unimaginable catastrophe that shakes a culture to its foundations and forces a reexamination of previously accepted truths. In the *9/11 Commission Report*, the National Commission on Terrorist Attacks upon the United States identifies September 11 as being above all a "failure of imagination."[29] The Commission contends that the "mixture of relief and satisfaction" that followed the end of the Cold War quickly became an unquestioned cultural hubris, a blind spot that prevented Americans from perceiving the global dangers around them.[30] The report further argues that this effectively "created a kind of cultural asymmetry. To us, Afghanistan seemed very far away. To members of al Qaeda, America seemed very close."[31] For Americans and the inhabitants of Downton, such innocence will never again be possible.

The cultural mourning that follows large-scale catastrophes and the recognition that any previous sense of security had been illusory provides a deep connection between our own time and the modernist period. Madelyn Detloff discusses these correspondences in *The Persistence of Modernism*. She draws parallels between cultural shocks experienced when modernism was at its height—two world wars, large-scale revolutions, ethnic and cultural genocides, two atomic bombs, and the fragmentation of historic nation-states—and the post-9/11 world, arguing that modernism offers invaluable "models for writing about devastation and loss."[32] Taking her cue from Virginia Woolf's "Thoughts on Peace in an Air Raid" (1940), she surmises that modernism teaches contemporary audiences that "freedom, means ... 'thinking against the current, not with it.' ... And this type of thinking entails a commitment to end the ideologies of domination, wherever they manifest themselves."[33] For Detloff, the great failure to do this in the wake of 9/11, when the West as a whole allowed itself to be coopted by ideologies of fear to justify imperial excesses in the Middle East, makes modernism valuable as a means of coping with and critiquing the traumatic legacies of September 11 and the War on Terror as well as charting a new path forward.

War and the propaganda that upholds it also binds *Downton Abbey* with the contemporary world. The show's second season jumps to 1916, a time when the easy patriotism of 1914 has faded and the fabric of Edwardian England is quickly unravelling. Characters find themselves troubled by the toll of the First World War as loved ones continue to perish, the wounded return home, and the early rhetoric of the war rings increasingly hollow. Amid reflections on the dead and maimed, a dejected Lord Grantham, who began the season in formal military attire and eager to get to the front, rhetorically asks, "Do you ever wonder what it was all for?"[34] This creeping doubt, about war and the ideas used to support it, becomes one of the lasting legacies of the First World War in the show and in our world. Military historian Robert Doughty laments that the War on Terror itself is an effect of our failure to learn from the legacy of the early twentieth century: "Those who believe that wars can be surgical, that they can be won with 'shock and awe,' or that they can be directed toward a precise endgame or end state know little about the Great War."[35] The inability to accurately read events during the war haunts the characters in the years that follow its conclusion. Similarly, Mao and Walkowitz identify modernism's skepticism of official language and sanitized narratives of life as one of the main drivers of resurgent interest in the movement during our current "crisis of information," when news sources have amplified their means of disseminating information and become inundated with and coopted by political and business interests.[36] In such a context, modernist themes of disillusionment, skepticism, and resistance have especially compelling power—whether for *Downton*'s outmoded ideals or the current 24-hour news cycle.

The technologies driving the cultures' propaganda machines are but small parts of much larger technological revolutions, and this is perhaps the strongest link between the early twentieth century and our own world. As previously noted, critics such as Jessica Pressman have identified the early twentieth century as "the classical period of our digital age" and argued that the rapidity of technological innovation has placed us in a similar position to the early modernists, making modernist "aesthetic practices, principles, and texts" all the more valid for negotiating our own modern landscape.[37] In *Beautiful Circuits: Modernism and the Mediated Life*, Mark Goble similarly argues that modernism is a movement born out of the rapid emergence of new mediums, and at their core, modernists were not simply reactionaries to new technologies but "desired communication and the many forms it took" because "this power was already modernism's own," offering a means by which intellectuals and artists could "make it new."[38] For Goble, our own knotted relationships with technology tie us closely with modernists. New technologies in many ways become us, and our ethos, on an individual and social level, "takes shape as a network of desires for more intimate, material, and affecting relations with technologies."[39] When the characters of *Downton Abbey* express fear, surprise, and hope at the number of new technologies that they encounter—a nearly endless process of large and small innovations, including electric lights, telephones, home radios, cars, tractors, electric blenders, and hair dryers—they reflect the audience's own sometimes knotted but always intimate ties to the technologies they encounter. With each encounter, characters move from being marveled by a new technological gadget to becoming comfortably dependent on it at an almost unimaginable pace.

Like the specter of cultural cataclysms, emergent technologies are foregrounded in the show. The installation of electricity at the Abbey is one of the first pieces of evidence to greet the audience—following shortly upon news of the Titanic and preceding the introduction of the Crawley family. In this opening scene, two housemaids chasten Daisy, the kitchen maid, for being afraid to turn on the lights in the room she's working in, joking that "it's electricity, not the Devil's handiwork" and cautioning that she will "have to get used to it sooner or later."[40] This scene is accompanied by many other instances of people remarking upon the new technology in ways that provoke humor *and* empathy. Just as the viewer laughs as Violet Crawley, the Dowager Countess of Grantham, holds up her fan to shield herself from the electric light, remarking that there is "such a glare" that she feels "as if I were on stage,"[41] they also sympathize with her incomprehensible relation to a technology that her children have already adapted to. As Goble explains, "It is not just that many forms of desire were in communication with technology in the first decades of the twentieth century, but that technology itself gives shape and character to experiences of sexuality, racial identity, class, and history."[42] In other words, technology is not something that we use. It uses and transforms us and remediates how we understand ourselves and our world. *Downton Abbey* connects to viewers'

FIGURE 0.1 *Violet Crawley, the Dowager Countess of Grantham, holds up a fan to shield herself from the electric light as her son, Lord Grantham, looks on undisturbed. Downton Abbey. Season 1, episode 1. Directed by Brian Percival. Written by Julian Fellowes. Aired September 28, 2010. Carnival Films and Masterpiece, 2010. DVD.*

own excitement and anxieties about the technological shifts of our time. They too experience these emotional reactions to new technologies and have similar levels of incommensurability with older relatives who are less able to adapt to new technologies as well as with younger individuals who seem much too at home with change.

Technology (or rapid technological transformation) thus offers a throughline for popular modernism, a touchstone connecting the contemporary era to the past. As Marshall McLuhan famously postulated, "All media work us over completely. They are so pervasive ... that they leave no part of us untouched, unaffected, unaltered."[43] The technological innovations of the modernist era and digital age create the environmental backdrops that the cultural cataclysms are (and were) projected against and perceived through. While the digital age prepares to usher in new modes of production and communication and as global events threaten the status quo established during the previous century, we look back to an age that provides a double to our own. The aesthetic and ideological innovations of that era provide a means through which our anxieties can be expressed and the present can be explored, if not understood.

Through a new modernist lens then, the international success of *Downton Abbey* should come as no surprise. The show encapsulates the hopes and anxieties of a world no longer sure of itself and struggling to regain a purpose. Its run has followed the slow recovery from the Great Recession and the troubled legacy of the War on Terror. Viewers did not merely tune in for the opulence, as some critics have claimed, but because they recognized much of themselves in the characters and the era being represented. While clearly not a modernist work itself, the show's invocation of modernist themes and their surprising resonance with audiences who would not normally be taken with British television is a strong testament to the continued relevance of modernism. The show also speaks to the extent to which decidedly modernist concepts and anxieties exist within the broader culture—both in today's world and when the movement was first coming of age. Ultimately, modernism's sense of experimentation, engagement with new technologies, and paradoxical relationships with the past and future have always been in conversation with—and a driver of—mass culture. It is to this important but often unappreciated truth that the chapters in this collection are dedicated, and our collective hope is that they bring more attention to the many legacies of popular modernism, past and present.

## Popular modernism: A user's guide

The legacies of popular modernism cannot be constrained within any single era or methodology. To account for this, the book is divided into three individualized yet overlapping sections, each of which focuses on specific chronological ranges and engages a diversity of mediums and geographic spaces. Collectively, these sections provide an open, kaleidoscopic vision of the popular modernisms that compose our past and present.

Part 1, "New Visions of Popular Modernism," considers popular modernism in periods historically associated with the movement, discovering hidden connections between modernism and popular culture that move beyond traditional forms of literature to provide a multidimensional view of the movement. Marsha Bryant starts the section by uncovering the modernist aesthetics of *Gentry*, an important but overlooked midcentury men's magazine, adding a significant text to the canon of magazine modernism. Nicholas Daly begins the move into other artistic mediums by investigating the musical theater of Ivor Novello, particularly how the operetta *Glamorous Night* combines the conventions of musical theater and television to produce a wholly new aesthetic. Adam Nemmers continues the push into popular forms of communication by exploring the ways in which midcentury radio dramas blended high modernist aesthetics with the conventions of mainstream radio to create an underappreciated form of popular modernism. Next, Jonathan Goldman considers how 1930s Hollywood gangster films invoked modernist principles to engage and remake popular notions of identity, fame, and success during the Great Depression. In the final chapter of the section, Barry Faulk reverses the perspective of the other chapters by focusing on modernist intellectuals' response to the work of Charlie Chaplin. In the process, Faulk challenges conventional ideas about the relationship between modernist intellectuals and popular culture, arguing that modernist commentary on Chaplin, both Anglo-American and continental, set Chaplin in direct relation to modernist notions of the global metropolis. Collectively these chapters demonstrate the critical importance of popular modernism in the past by rediscovering previously overlooked texts, genres, mediums, and artists.

Part 2, "Legacies of Popular Modernism," traces modernist genealogies from the past to the contemporary era. This section specifically looks at texts that are especially popular or beloved to reveal the vast range of people and works indebted to particular modernist texts, figures, and tenets. Kirk Curnutt begins the section by detailing how modernist nostalgia structures works of surf noir from the 1950s to the present day—discussing artists as diverse as Dashiell Hammett, The Beach Boys, and Thomas Pynchon. Paul March-Russell then examines the links between modernism and popular works of science fiction, using modernist science fiction novels from the end of the Second World War to the present to resituate hybridity as a modernist concept that challenges the presumptions of literary realism and its categorization of peoples, cultures, and places. Shifting from genre studies to individual legacies, Asimina Ino Nikolopoulou describes how Jazz Age performer and international celebrity Josephine Baker used her performances to challenge, destabilize, and refashion restrictive conventions about women of color, in America and abroad—establishing a tradition of liberative aesthetics that continues to be invoked by contemporary music artists like Beyoncé Knowles. Andrew McFeaters concludes the section by tracing modernist anxiety about Fordist discourses of efficiency and progress, identifying a powerful continuum that runs through Aldous Huxley's *Brave New World*, Brian O'Nolan's eclectic prose, and Douglas Adams's *The Hitchhiker's Guide to the Galaxy*. The lineages identified in this section are a testament to the surprising ways that modernist aesthetics and ideals continue to endure and shape our world.

Part 3, "Resonances of Popular Modernism in the Twenty-First Century," focuses on works that have significant cultural capital in the twenty-first century but would rarely appear in academic books or be put into conversation with modernism. Importantly, this section does not argue that such works are inherently modernist but rather discovers how they invoke modernist techniques, texts, and artists to engage social and existential quandaries in the contemporary world. Caroline Blinder begins the section by delving into the HBO series *True Detective*, a show that uses the American landscape in ways that critique both the economics of post-industrialization and its attendant psychological malaise. Blinder contends that the success of *True Detective* demonstrates the continuing currency of crime narrative as a way to render the intersections between internal fear and external power.

Walter Bosse follows by explaining how *The Wire* uses F. Scott Fitzgerald's *The Great Gatsby* to critique the American justice system, particularly the ways in which it plays on black inmates' longing to remake their identities and simultaneously dooms such a second act to failure. Camelia Raghinaru authors the last chapter on a television series, discussing *Mad Men*'s strategic commemoration of a particular manifestation of 1960s upper-middle-class white masculinity. Focusing on protagonist and quintessential adman Don Draper, she offers a critical reading of Draper's masculinity and contextualizes the show's anxiety about femininity within the broader gender politics of modernism. The section then shifts to the emerging field of comic studies as Aimee Armande Wilson analyzes modernist time in Alan Moore and Kevin O'Neill's *The League of Extraordinary Gentlemen*, ultimately revealing the comic book form as an addition to the panoply of modernist techniques that interrupt the linear progression of clock time with time as felt by the individual. In the final chapter, Dustin Anderson explores how popular non-linear video games like *Call of Duty: Modern Warfare*, *Red Dead Redemption*, and *Mass Effect* utilize a particular type of modernist ethics and aesthetics to create an open, ergodic text and a compelling playing experience. Importantly, all of the chapters in this section strategically engage non-academic texts that have a prominent place in the popular consciousness to illustrate the significant ways that popular modernism exists at the heart of our present moment.

It bears mentioning that this book stands on the shoulders of other collections that have helped to redefine and push the boundaries of modernism and the movement's relationship with popular culture, especially *High and Low Moderns: Literature and Culture, 1889–1939* (1996), *Bad Modernisms* (2006), and *Regarding the Popular: Modernism, the Avant-Garde, and High and Low Culture* (2011). These collections successfully challenged limited constructions of modernism by promoting interdisciplinarity and shattering boundaries between "high" and "low" texts. This volume builds upon them by embracing contemporary works (which are largely absent from the above collections) and more thoroughly investing in popular authors, mediums, and concepts that hold popular sway but struggle for validation within the academy. *The Contemporaneity of Modernism: Literature, Media, Culture* (2015), a collection that emerged as this book was in the midst of finding a publisher, does make important contributions toward these goals by widely expanding the range of texts under analysis and grounding itself in the contemporary moment. However, formal definitions of modernism (as a movement, aesthetic, and critical practice) remain rigid within the collection. While this creates a powerful and incisive theoretical framework, it also circumscribes the collection to texts that possess the necessary criteria to be works of modernism. In contrast, this collection contends that many of modernism's most important legacies are observable in works that themselves are not modernist, and it is only by embracing all aspects of modernism's many legacies that we can come to appreciate the movement itself and the myriad lessons it offers today. We envision this project as yet another expansion of new modernist studies, one that will open new avenues for future growth. Because while the modernist period itself may have faded into history, the legacies of popular modernism have not died, or, for that matter, ever really passed.

# Notes

1. Neil Midgley, "From Downton to Sherlock: Who Won the TV Battle for Christmas? Habits are Changing but Broadcasters Still Crave the Top Spot at Christmas," *Guardian*, January 11, 2016, 33; Jennifer Rankin Byrne, "PBS Stations Draw 9.6 Million Viewers to Bid Farewell to 'Downton Abbey' on Masterpiece," *Business Wire*, March 8, 2016, http://www.businesswire.com/news/home/20160308006338/en/.
2. Simon Schama, "No Downers in 'Downton,'" *Newsweek*, January 23, 2012, 12.
3. James Parker, "Brideshead Regurgitated: The Ludicrous Charms of *Downton Abbey*, TV's Reigning Aristo-soap," *Atlantic*, January 1, 2013, 37.
4. Jessica Pressman, *Digital Modernism: Making It New in New Media* (Oxford: Oxford University Press, 2014).
5. Celia Marshik, *The Cambridge Companion to Modernist Culture* (New York: Cambridge University Press, 2015), 11.
6. Michael D'Arcy and Mathias Nilges, "The Contemporaneity of Modernism," in *The Contemporaneity of Modernism: Literature, Media, Culture*, eds. Michael D'Arcy and Mathias Nilges (New York: Routledge, 2015), 1.
7. Marshall Berman, *All that is Solid Melts into Air: The Experience of Modernity* (1982; repr., New York: Penguin Books, 1988), 36.
8. Rosalía Baena and Christa Byker, "Dialects of Nostalgia: *Downton Abbey* and English Identity," *National Identities* 17, no. 2 (2015): 267, 262. Readers should note that Baena and Byker are specifically discussing viewers in the United Kingdom, but I would maintain that the show provides much the same existential function for all Western audiences.
9. Andreas Huyssen, *After the Great Divide: Modernism, Mass Culture, Postmodernism* (Bloomington: Indiana University Press, 1986).
10. Max Horkheimer and Theodor W. Adorno, *Dialectic of Enlightenment*, trans. John Cumming (1944; repr., New York: Continuum, 1994), 120, 133.
11. Peter Bürger, *Theory of the Avant-Garde*, trans. Michael Shaw (1974; repr., Minneapolis: University of Minnesota Press, 1984); Clement Greenberg, "Avant-Garde and Kitsch," in *Clement Greenberg: The Collected Essays and Criticism*, vol. 1, ed. John O'Brian (1939; repr., Chicago: University of Chicago Press, 1986), 5–22.

12  Huyssen, *After the Great Divide*, 53.
13  Those interested in tracing the evolution of modernism as a concept and field should consult Sean Latham and Gayle Rogers's *Modernism: Evolution of an Idea* (London: Bloomsbury Academic, 2015).
14  Maria DiBattista, "Introduction," in *High and Low Moderns: Literature and Culture, 1889–1939*, eds. Maria DiBattista and Lucy McDiarmid (New York: Oxford University Press, 1996), 4–5.
15  Rita Felski, *The Gender of Modernity* (Cambridge: Harvard University Press, 1995), 120–1.
16  Ibid., 121.
17  Readers interested in reading further about the case for placing Dorothy Parker as a modernist author should consult Rhonda S. Pettit's *A Gendered Collision: Sentimentalism and Modernism in Dorothy Parker's Poetry and Fiction* (Madison, NJ: Fairleigh Dickinson University Press, 2000); more about modernism and the Harlem Renaissance can be found in Houston A. Baker's landmark *Modernism and the Harlem Renaissance* (Chicago: University of Chicago Press, 1987); and the connections among mass media technologies and modernism are thoroughly discussed in Mark Goble's *Beautiful Circuits: Modernism and the Mediated Life* (New York: Columbia University Press, 2010).
18  Juan A. Suárez, *Pop Modernism: Noise and the Reinvention of the Everyday* (Urbana: University of Illinois Press, 2007), 5.
19  Jerry Bowyer, "Down on Downton: Why the Left is Torching *Downton Abbey*," *Forbes*, February 14, 2013, http://www.forbes.com/sites/jerrybowyer/2013/02/14/down-on-downton-why-the-left-is-torching-downton-abbey/#17fa33d27e7e.
20  Raymond Zhong, "The Weekend Interview with Julian Fellowes: The Anti-Snobbery of 'Downton Abbey,'" *Wall Street Journal*, February 2, 2013, A.13.
21  Henry Giroux, *Zombie Politics and Culture in the Age of Casino Capitalism* (New York: Peter Lang, 2011), 2.
22  Douglas Mao and Rebecca L. Walkowitz, "Introduction: Modernisms Bad and New," in *Bad Modernisms*, eds. Douglas Mao and Rebecca Walkowitz (Durham: Duke University Press, 2006), 2.
23  Ibid.
24  David James, *Modernist Futures: Innovation and Inheritance in the Contemporary Novel* (Cambridge: Cambridge University Press, 2012), 15.
25  John Barth, "The Literature of Exhaustion," in *The Friday Book: Essays and Other Non-Fiction* (London: The John Hopkins University Press, 1984), 72.
26  Yubraj Aryal, "On New Modernist Studies," An Interview with Peter Nicholls, *Journal of Philosophy* 4, no. 10 (2009): 58.
27  *Downton Abbey*, season 1, episode 1, directed by Brian Percival, written by

Julian Fellowes, aired September 28, 2010 (Carnival Films and Masterpiece, 2010), DVD.
28 Ibid.
29 National Commission on Terrorist Attacks Upon the United States, *The 9/11 Commission Report: Final Report of the National Commission on Terrorist Attacks Upon the United States*, authorized edn (New York: W. W. Norton & Co., 2004), 339–40.
30 Ibid., 340.
31 Ibid.
32 Madelyn Detloff, *The Persistence of Modernism: Loss and Mourning in the Twentieth Century* (Cambridge: Cambridge University Press, 2009), 80.
33 Ibid., 175.
34 *Downton Abbey*, season 2, episode 7, directed by James Strong, written by Julian Fellowes, aired October 30, 2011 (Carnival Films and Masterpiece, 2011), DVD.
35 Robert A. Doughty, *Pyrrhic Victory: French Strategy and Operations in the Great War* (Cambridge: Harvard University Press, 2005), 3.
36 Douglas Mao and Rebecca L. Walkowitz, "The New Modernist Studies," *PMLA* 123, no. 3 (2008): 746.
37 Pressman, *Digital Modernism*, 4, 2.
38 Goble, *Beautiful Circuits*, 3.
39 Ibid., 19.
40 *Downton Abbey*, season 1, episode 1.
41 Ibid.
42 Goble, *Beautiful Circuits*, 19.
43 Marshall McLuhan and Quentin Fiore, *The Medium is the Massage*, prod. Jerome Angel (1967; repr., Berkeley, CA: Gingko Press, 2001), 26.

# Bibliography

Aryal, Yubraj. "On New Modernist Studies," An Interview with Peter Nicholls. *Journal of Philosophy* 4, no. 10 (2009): 56–9.
Baena, Rosalía and Christa Byker. "Dialects of Nostalgia: *Downton Abbey* and English Identity." *National Identities* 17, no. 2 (2015): 259–69.
Barth, John. "The Literature of Exhaustion." In *The Friday Book: Essays and Other Non-Fiction*, 62–76. London: The John Hopkins University Press, 1984.
Berman, Marshall. *All that is Solid Melts into Air: The Experience of Modernity*. 1982. Reprint, New York: Penguin Books, 1988.
Bowyer, Jerry. "Down on Downton: Why the Left is Torching *Downton Abbey*." *Forbes*, February 14, 2013. Available online: http://www.forbes.com/sites/

jerrybowyer/2013/02/14/down-on-downton-why-the-left-is-torching-downton-abbey/#17fa33d27e7e.
Bru, Sascha, Laurence Nuijs, Benedikt Hjartarson, Peter Nicholls, Tania Ørum, and Hubert van den Berg, eds. *Regarding the Popular: Modernism, the Avant-Garde and High and Low Culture*. Berlin: Walter de Gruyter, 2011.
Bürger, Peter. *Theory of the Avant-Garde*, translated by Michael Shaw. 1974. Reprint, Minneapolis: University of Minnesota Press, 1984.
Byrne, Jennifer Rankin. "PBS Stations Draw 9.6 Million Viewers to Bid Farewell to 'Downton Abbey' on Masterpiece." *Business Wire*, March 8, 2016. Available online: http://www.businesswire.com/news/home/20160308006338/en/.
D'Arcy, Michael and Mathias Nilges. "The Contemporaneity of Modernism." In *The Contemporaneity of Modernism: Literature, Media, Culture*, edited by Michael D'Arcy and Mathias Nilges, 1–14. New York: Routledge, 2015.
Detloff, Madelyn. *The Persistence of Modernism: Loss and Mourning in the Twentieth Century*. Cambridge: Cambridge University Press, 2009.
DiBattista, Maria. "Introduction." In *High and Low Moderns: Literature and Culture, 1889–1939*, edited by Maria DiBattista and Lucy McDiarmid, 3–19. New York: Oxford University Press, 1996.
Doughty, Robert A. *Pyrrhic Victory: French Strategy and Operations in the Great War*. Cambridge: Harvard University Press, 2005.
*Downton Abbey*. Season 1, episode 1. Directed by Brian Percival. Written by Julian Fellowes. Aired September 28, 2010. Carnival Films and Masterpiece, 2010. DVD.
*Downton Abbey*. Season 2, episode 7. Directed by James Strong. Written by Julian Fellowes. Aired October 30, 2011. Carnival Films and Masterpiece, 2011. DVD.
Felski, Rita. *The Gender of Modernity*. Cambridge: Harvard University Press, 1995.
Giroux, Henry. *Zombie Politics and Culture in the Age of Casino Capitalism*. New York: Peter Lang, 2011.
Goble, Mark. *Beautiful Circuits: Modernism and the Mediated Life* (New York: Columbia University Press, 2010).
Greenberg, Clement. "Avant-Garde and Kitsch." In *Clement Greenberg: The Collected Essays and Criticism*, vol. 1, edited by John O'Brian 5–22. 1939. Reprint. Chicago: University of Chicago Press, 1986.
Horkheimer, Max and Theodor W. Adorno. *Dialectic of Enlightenment*, translated by John Cumming. 1944. Reprint, New York: Continuum, 1994.
Huyssen, Andreas. *After the Great Divide: Modernism, Mass Culture, Postmodernism*. Bloomington: Indiana University Press, 1986.
James, David. *Modernist Futures: Innovation and Inheritance in the Contemporary Novel*. Cambridge: Cambridge University Press, 2012.
Latham, Sean and Gayle Rogers. *Modernism: Evolution of an Idea*. London: Bloomsbury Academic, 2015.
Mao, Douglas and Rebecca L. Walkowitz. "Introduction: Modernisms Bad and New." In *Bad Modernisms*, edited by Douglas Mao and Rebecca Walkowitz, 1–17. Durham: Duke University Press, 2006.
Mao, Douglas and Rebecca L. Walkowitz. "The New Modernist Studies." *PMLA* 123, no. 3 (2008): 737–48.

Marshik, Celia. *The Cambridge Companion to Modernist Culture*. New York: Cambridge University Press, 2015.
McLuhan, Marshall and Quentin Fiore. *The Medium is the Massage*, produced by Jerome Angel. 1967. Reprint, Berkeley, CA: Gingko Press, 2001.
Midgley, Neil. "From Downton to Sherlock: Who Won the TV Battle for Christmas? Habits are Changing but Broadcasters Still Crave the Top Spot at Christmas." *Guardian*, January 11, 2016, 33.
National Commission on Terrorist Attacks Upon the United States. *The 9/11 Commission Report: Final Report of the National Commission on Terrorist Attacks Upon the United States*. Authorized edition. New York: W. W. Norton & Co., 2004.
Parker, James. "Brideshead Regurgitated: The Ludicrous Charms of Downton Abbey, TV's Reigning Aristo-soap." *Atlantic*, January 1, 2013, 36–7.
Pressman, Jessica. *Digital Modernism: Making It New in New Media*. Oxford: Oxford University Press, 2014.
Schama, Simon. "No Downers in 'Downton.'" *Newsweek*, January 23, 2012, 12.
Suárez, Juan A. *Pop Modernism: Noise and the Reinvention of the Everyday*. Urbana: University of Illinois Press, 2007.
Zhong, Raymond. "The Weekend Interview with Julian Fellowes: The Anti-Snobbery of 'Downton Abbey.'" *Wall Street Journal*, February 2, 2013, A.13.

# PART ONE

# New Visions of Popular Modernism

# 1

# *Gentry* modernism: Cultural connoisseurship and midcentury masculinity, 1951–1957

## Marsha Bryant

Tucked between fashion ads and fabric swatches in a largely forgotten men's magazine, modernism in *Gentry* circulated as cultural capital for American men of means in the 1950s. But not just for *any* affluent men. Gentlemanly jet-setters, *Gentry* men liked cubism with their cocktails and Goethe with their gabardine. They were refined, yet fashion-forward. And their magazine of choice offered sumptuous pages suitable for framing. One subscriber enthused: "Your impeccable taste and high artistic standards combine to make *Gentry* the *ne plus ultra* of current publications."[1] A hybrid form, the magazine was part style guide, part lifestyle manual, part art book. Today, the *Gentry* collector acquires literary selections and reproductions of artworks along with manufacturer's samples of fine woolen, silk, cotton, and synthetic fabrics.

Georges Braque's *Pallas Athene* graced the cover of Number 7, which included features on Alfred Stieglitz, travel wardrobes, and basset hounds. In this number, the magazine's slogan was "The Finest in Art, Sports, Living, Fashions, and Literature." Number 21 had cover art from Henri Matisse's *Jazz* series, a poem by Vachel Lindsay, a feature on snow skiing, W. Somerset Maugham's essay on Henry James, and Thomas Jefferson's Christmas menu. Sharing space with such materials, modernism was refashioned in *Gentry*. Modernism itself had become mainstream by the time the magazine debuted in 1951, and by the end of 1957 (*Gentry*'s final year), *Arts Magazine* had published Clement Greenberg's "Picasso at Seventy-Five."

FIGURE 1.1 *Cover of* Gentry *with Georges Braque lithograph* Pallas Athene. *Gentry 7 (Summer 1953)*.

While modernism was no longer new in the 1950s, modernist art, design, and literature made *something else* new in the pages of *Gentry*.

My chapter recovers this elegant men's magazine in the contexts of midcentury modernism, masculinity studies, and popular culture. Hal Rubenstein, *InStyle*'s fashion director, brought recent attention to *Gentry* with his anthology of excerpts, *The* Gentry *Man: A Guide for the Civilized Male* (2012). That same year, the magazine's stylish covers anchored the exhibition "Pattern and Palette in Print: *Gentry* Magazine and a New Generation of Trendsetters" at the Georgia Museum of Art.[2] Yet critical conversations about magazines and modernism haven't included *Gentry*, which defies standard classifications as much as it defied mainstream masculinity. *Gentry* was much more than a swatch-filled fashion magazine, although some of its sartorial splendor recalls the upscale trade magazine *Apparel Arts* (1931–50), which became *Gentleman's Quarterly*. Like *Esquire*, which debuted in 1933, *Gentry* functioned as a "venue for male consumption based on travel, fashion, and leisure," as David Earle puts it.[3] But *Gentry* was not so commercial; in fact, its debut editorial refused to "be all things to all men."[4] *Gentry* entered culture right before the explosion of American men's magazines that ran across the 1950s, which Earle groups into bachelor, celebrity, and adventure categories.[5] *Gentry* fits into none of these. Indeed, *Gentry* occupied a space between contemporary magazines with fashions more splendid than *Esquire*'s, domestic accoutrements more luxurious than *Playboy*'s, and literature more timeless than the *New Yorker*'s.

*Gentry* also troubles boundaries between minority and mass magazines as well as between cultural and commercial magazines. A subscription quarterly with an estimated readership of "approximately 200,000" in 1954, it was "not casually obtainable at newsstands," as the editors noted in their reader survey report. The majority of *Gentry* subscribers acquired a subscription card from someone else's copy or through word-of-mouth endorsements, the survey revealed.[6] New readers could also find the magazine in select menswear shops across the United States. *Gentry* was a bespoke magazine. It falls outside the modernist "periodical field" that Andrew Thacker sketches in the American volume of *The Oxford Critical and Cultural History of Modernist Magazines*. Like *Smart Set* this magazine mixes "modernism and the culturally modern with a distinctively American sense of taste and 'sophistication,'" but *Gentry* was not "a Magazine of Cleverness."[7] Nor was it a metropolitan magazine. Less text-heavy than literary and mostly literary magazines, *Gentry* offered literary selections that usually proved more establishment than cutting edge.

The magazine offered detailed instructions for appreciating design in visual art and fashion, transferring midcentury modernism's New Critical methods to men's high fashion and gracious living. In doing so, *Gentry* carved out an alternative identity for American men who rejected gray flannel suits—and the mundane minds that came with them. As Rubenstein puts it, "the *Gentry* man's exuberance for the unexpected and sometimes the extraordinary" signals his rejection of suburbia and "domesticated bliss."[8] Indeed, he might fancy himself a better-suited surrealist—with a country estate instead of a bohemian atelier. Like its presentation of modernism, *Gentry*'s sartorial swagger asserted the manly vitality of high style. And as much as its usable past contained European paintings and Edwardian waistcoats, *Gentry* fashioned new cultural relations through American dandyism and post-war aesthetic brinksmanship.

## A debonair debut

Self-made millionaire William Segal founded *Gentry* in 1951 after a successful run of the trade publications *American Fabrics* and *Men's Reporter*. A painter and philosopher as well as an editor–publisher, Segal lived a cosmopolitan life in New York and Paris. He traveled widely, studied Zen Buddhism, and exhibited his paintings. Segal endorsed a cruise that *Gentry* sponsored in Number 13, and produced a travel piece on Japan for Number 16. In short, the magazine's publisher embodied the *Gentry* man it promoted. And his unprecedented magazine displayed this debonair identity with sumptuous aplomb.

What kind of men's magazine was this? And how did *Gentry* call mainstream masculinity into question as it parsed the art of being an American gentleman? The debut number offers a few clues. Printed on buff cardstock, its cover design presented a Polyclitus sculpture in close-up—highlighting the curves of a youthful man's face in a soft black-and-white photograph. Merging the hard body of post-war muscle magazines with high modernist Hellenism (and high production values), *Gentry* fashioned an iconic manhood. The cover image also fronted the first Gentry Fashions portfolio, which featured new takes on the classic country jacket as well as a "revolutionary concept" in dinner jackets ("slanting jetted pockets" and piped cuffs).[9] In some of the later numbers, a smaller version of the Polyclitus image appeared as a frontispiece that signified the magazine itself, neatly distilling a key point in Segal's editorial on timelessness: "*Gentry* brings you, in short, visual and literary fare which has a contemporary flavor, but still possesses the enduring element which characterizes all things of quality."[10]

The magazine's very first page made another debonair impression: a vibrantly colorful ad for upscale leisure shirts by Alfred of New York, with a tipped-on fabric swatch of yellow gabardine. A distinctive feature of *Gentry* until the USPO prohibited their distribution by mail, swatches of natural and synthetic materials appeared throughout the magazine's first ten numbers—glued on one side so readers could feel the fabric.

GENTRY MODERNISM 23

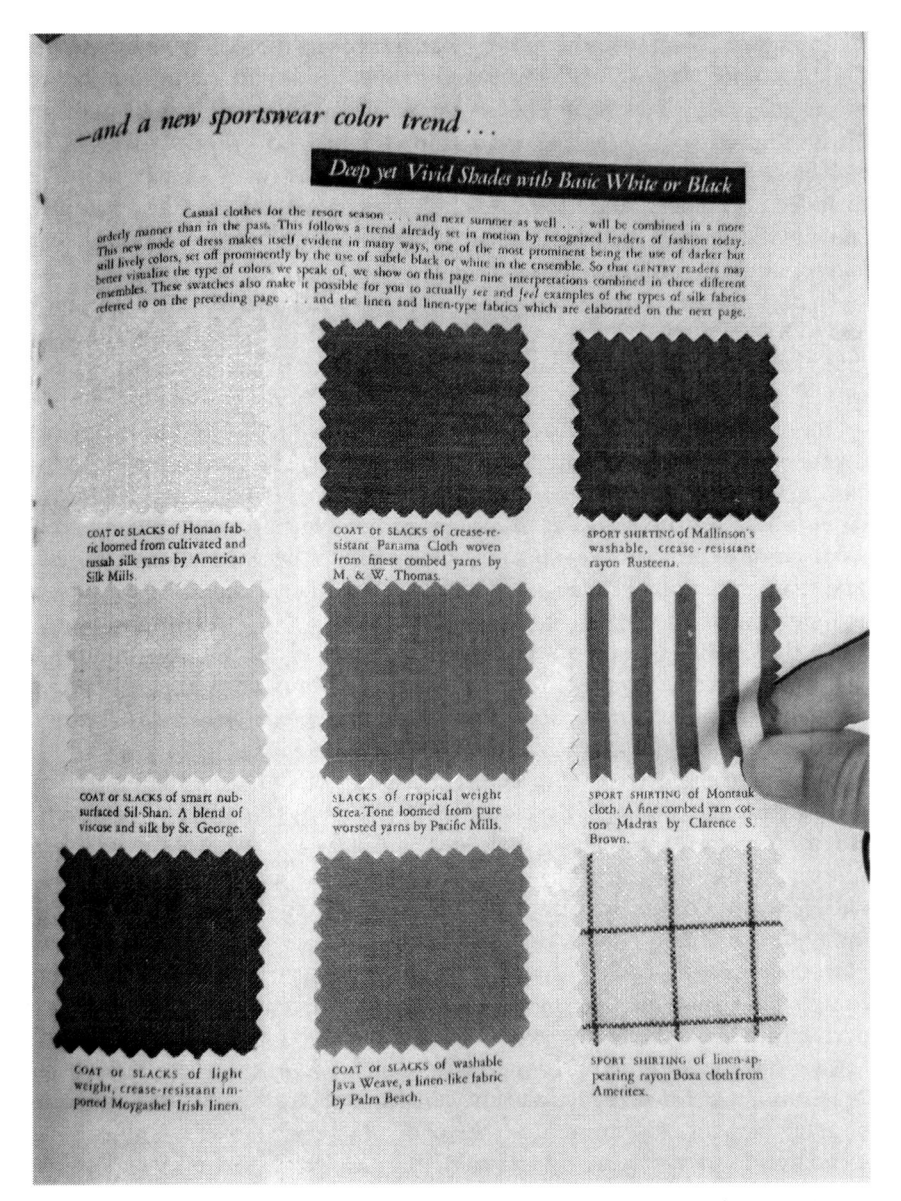

...*and a new sportswear color trend*...

*Deep yet Vivid Shades with Basic White or Black*

Casual clothes for the resort season... and next summer as well... will be combined in a more orderly manner than in the past. This follows a trend already set in motion by recognized leaders of fashion today. This new mode of dress makes itself evident in many ways, one of the most prominent being the use of darker but will lively colors, set off prominently by the use of subtle black or white in the ensemble. So that GENTRY readers may better visualize the type of colors we speak of, we show on this page nine interpretations combined in three different ensembles. These swatches also make it possible for you to actually *see* and *feel* examples of the types of silk fabrics referred to on the preceding page... and the linen and linen-type fabrics which are elaborated on the next page.

COAT or SLACKS of Honan fabric loomed from cultivated and tussah silk yarns by American Silk Mills.

COAT or SLACKS of crease-resistant Panama Cloth woven from finest combed yarns by M. & W. Thomas.

SPORT SHIRTING of Mallinson's washable, crease-resistant rayon Rusteena.

COAT or SLACKS of smart nub-surfaced Sil-Shan. A blend of viscose and silk by St. George.

SLACKS of tropical weight Strea-Tone loomed from pure worsted yarns by Pacific Mills.

SPORT SHIRTING of Montauk cloth. A fine combed yarn cotton Madras by Clarence S. Brown.

COAT or SLACKS of light weight, crease-resistant imported Moygashel Irish linen.

COAT or SLACKS of washable Java Weave, a linen-like fabric by Palm Beach.

SPORT SHIRTING of linen-appearing rayon Boxa cloth from Ameritex.

FIGURE 1.2  *Fabric swatch page from* Gentry 2 *(January 15–April 15, 1952).*

As Figure 1.2 shows, the fabric swatches brought a collage aesthetic to the magazine's pages. Readers reacted to this newfound tactility in letters to the editors. A man from D.C. enthused about reading the first number "from *swatch* to *swatch*"; a man from Kalamazoo quipped that "in a few more issues, we should have enough swatches for a Gentry quilt!"[11] Included so readers could take them to their tailors, these fabric samples contributed to the magazine's distinctive look and texture. (Indeed, the *Gentry* collector will find most of them intact.)

*Gentry* ran an eclectic smorgasbord of features, reflecting the publisher's aim to free his board of editors to "do the kind of articles and presentations they like and are able to execute."[12] Highlights from the debut number range from the luxuriously impractical ("How to Build Your Own Finnish Bath") to the recreational (horseback riding, sports fishing), the art historical (features on Rembrandt and "Japanese versus Chinese Viewpoint in Art"), and the spiritual (features on Buddhism and Zen). If the blueprint in the Finnish bath feature winks at suburban men's DIY endeavors, the pieces on Asian cultures present a gentlemanly alternative to the Beats' Eastward turn. The inaugural number also introduced a "Gentry Gleanings" section—a shopping guide to singular items for the gentleman's wardrobe and home. Later, the Gleanings took on the form of a miscellany of literary quotations that ran the gamut from Aristotle to Simone de Beauvoir. Aiming to civilize the upscale American man, Segal's magazine presented a mash-up of luxury and literature, manors and museums, sports and style.

*Gentry* emerged two years before *Playboy* promoted its alternative to mainstream masculinity for men of the 1950s. Targeting middle-class men, Hugh Hefner created a new identity for American bachelors in his first editorial: "We enjoy mixing up cocktails and an hors d'oeuvre or two, putting a little mood music on the phonograph, and inviting in a female for a quiet discussion on Picasso, Nietzsche, jazz, sex."[13] Surely this famous *Playboy* preamble took a swipe at Segal's publication a few lines later, complaining that the few men's magazines geared toward city dwellers overemphasized travel and fashion, even going so far as a "'how-to-do-it'" feature on "building your own steam bath."[14] *Gentry* did not seek to be "entertainment for men," it did not court middle-class men, and its mode of gracious living did not require the company of women. By Number 13, *Gentry* had a new slogan: "America's Fabulous Magazine for Men."

An outlier, *Gentry* troubles the categories that later critics would use to plot masculinity across the modernist and midcentury periods. Natalya Lusty highlights the rhetoric of crisis that attaches itself to "masculinity and the masculine" in modernist culture, deploying tropes of "vulnerability, anxiety, and even extinction."[15] James Gilbert assesses post-war crises of American masculinity that drew defensive maneuvers from intellectuals beset with "the accusation that elite culture, or high culture as they preferred to call it, was the province of the effete scholar."[16] In both scenarios, the price of refinement is a perceived loss of masculinity. Yet the *Gentry* man's affluence in an expansionist economy shielded him from extinction, and his discriminating taste outflanked the elite/effete dichotomy that burdened so many American men in the 1950s.

Even so, the magazine reflects midcentury inquiries into a newly expansive masculinity that the Kinsey report had opened for exploration. Readers found especially compelling the number's central feature, "What Does it Mean to be a Man?" Framed with the provocative question of who "deserves" to be called a Man, this unattributed piece measures masculinity with "contemporary and age-old standards." In addition to art reproductions and literary quotations, the editors offered sidebar lists of "becoming" and "unbecoming" traits in a man—as well as checklists for gauging one's ability to control body, feelings, and mind. Ideally, men attained "a harmonious balance" like a well-wrought artwork.[17] As Segal and his editorial team wrote in their inaugural piece, the *Gentry* man aimed to move beyond 3-M masculinity, disputing a culture that "places so much stock in money, medals, and muscles."[18]

Over fifty years later, Rubenstein characterized the *Gentry* man as one who "openly lusted for a painting by Paul Klee, had unapologetic fantasies about bullfighting, confessed to yearning to learn more about Eastern philosophy."[19] This mostly spot-on portrait captures the interplay of expected and unexpected passions that powered *Gentry* masculinity. The magazine did, in fact, run a feature on bullfighting in Number 10. Yet Lawrence Chrow's refined piece emphasized ancient religions and artistic images as much as famous matadors' signature styles, and many of the accompanying photographs highlight the richly embroidered fabrics in their costumes.[20] (Chrow served on the magazine's editorial board.) Hemingway is conspicuous by his absence; after all, his was a different brand of masculinity. If the *Gentry* man dreamed about matadors, it was because of their sheer elegance as much as their bravery and prowess. In his debonair shoes, he neatly stepped over dividing lines between gender conformity and nonconformity.

## Layouts, cubism, and cut-outs

The magazine's initial readers applauded the "superb production" of "this luxury type of magazine," pointing out its variety of fine paper stocks and finding individual pages "suitable for framing."[21] Paul Lewis declares that all of Segal's magazines "were characterized by sophisticated layout and high-quality artwork to which he brought the eye of a trained artist and accomplished painter."[22] But *Gentry* was the most beautiful and distinctive of all—from its elegant Garamond typeface to its color reproductions of paintings. Readers began viewing the magazine as a collector's item, and it remains so on Modernism101.com—specialists in "rare and unusual design books and periodicals."[23] While *Gentry* was not, technically speaking, the kind of artists' magazine that Gwen Allen has assessed, its editors clearly saw "the potential of the magazine as a new kind of artistic medium and exhibition space."[24] A Father's Day promotion from Number 6 (Spring 1953) highlights *Gentry*'s rich materiality with humor, assuming the voice of a subscriber's dog: "I like a magazine I can get my teeth in ... Gentry is crammed with things I like—beautiful tip-on pictures ready to be taken out and framed, packaged seeds, sheet music, leather, fabrics."[25] (Periodically, the editors assured readers that "Yes, *Gentry* tip-ons are done by hand," offering as proof photographs of women bent over their office tables with brushes and glue pots.) A well-wrought magazine, *Gentry* created rich contrasts of sensory textures and high-cultural allusions "presented in the *Gentry* manner," as the editors put it. Even the listings of contents assumed aesthetic forms: each appeared opposite a page of visual thumbnails for individual features, with tipped-on fabrics and fine colored papers enhancing the arrangement of black-and-white images. Like the swatches in Figure 1.2, these pages took on properties of collage.

Through his signature magazine's content and design, Segal promoted an aesthetic of innovative timelessness. For example, the magazine's editors created a tipped-on triptych of artworks for Number 11, placing color reproductions of Picasso's "Still Life with Bull's Head" (1938) and Francisco de Goya's "Portrait of a Lady" (1824) alongside a black-and-white photograph of the Temple of Athena Nike.[26] In the *Gentry* gallery, such comparisons conveyed continuity, not juxtapositions. Cubism's status here takes on a key trait of what Greg Barnhisel terms Cold War modernism: "the sense of being belated within a cultural tradition."[27] Picasso had become a household word by the 1950s, but he still had the power to provoke. Prompted by the mere mention of his name in a feature on custom cars, a *Gentry* reader from Chicago wrote the editors that "there is no room in good modern art for the cruelly disfeatured figures of Pablo Picasso."[28] The magazine never ran a feature on Picasso, but Number 4 allotted a page to the *She-Goat* sculpture he cast in 1952—printing a black-and-white photograph on muted gray paper. Although the caption states that the sculpture "created a sensation" in Paris that year, the *mise-en-page* softens Picasso's edginess.[29] For *Gentry* placed the cubist revolution within the evolution of "Man, the Aesthetic Animal," to borrow *Gentry* editor Joseph Pijoan's phrase.[30]

Modernism itself became *Gentry*-fied in a large, folded tip-on that pointedly asked "how modern is modern?"; it also appeared in Number 4. The gray fold-over had square and rectangular holes of assorted sizes, revealing colorful patterns underneath. If readers turned the magazine sideways, they could see the small captions: *contemporary design? a sky by*

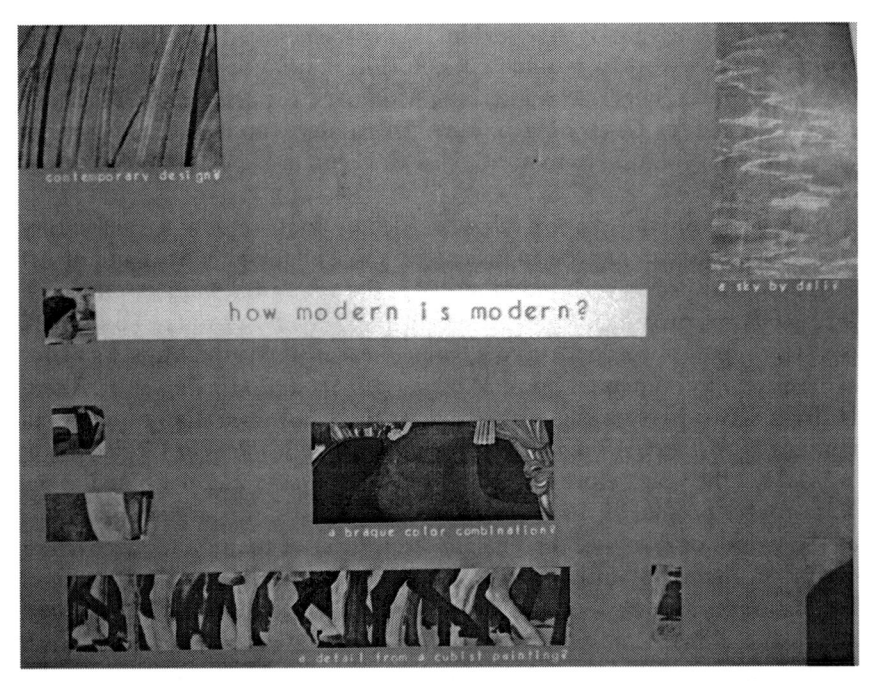

FIGURE 1.3 *"How Modern is Modern" fold-over from* Gentry 4 *(Fall 1952).*

*dali? a braque color combination? a detail from a cubist painting?* Framed in this manner, some of the decontextualized images do indeed take on the look of modernist art and modern design. Opening the flap reveals the temporal *trompe l'oeil*: a partial reproduction of Piero della Francesca's 1558 fresco depicting the Battle of Constantine. The text under the flap, signed *Gentry*, depicts this innovative layout as a form of masking "the approaches which have inspired a variety of recent art movements." So were modernist painting and midcentury design faking it new? Was cubism disguising something classic and customary? According to *Gentry*, organically-derived artistic expression "retains its soundness and causes time in art to be boundless"—the embedded rhyme highlights the magazine's position that the best art does not make a clean break from the past.[31] (In parallel fashion, *Gentry*'s literary gleanings embedded modernist writers with Wordsworth, Shelley, Arnold, and Pater.)

We see this principle at work in Number 13, which included a short assessment of Matisse signed "W. L." (most likely W. Lully, listed among the magazine's art department). Grounding the artist's contemporary influence in his "capacity to synthesize," the piece presents him as an aesthetic time traveler who "stands close to the great artists of the past, to the Greek vase painters, the Byzantine mosaic artists, the artists of the High Renaissance—as well as to future greats." If Picasso was a male Muse for the magazine's innovative layout, Matisse embodied key aspects of its sensibility. His work was intensely colorful; it bridged art and design; it presented vibrantly gracious interiors. Moreover, the artist himself became a fitting model for *Gentry* masculinity. "A painter who has passed through virtuosity to revolution to maturity," as W. L. put it. He was not a maverick like Picasso.[32]

Eighty-two in the year of *Gentry*'s debut, Matisse saw a midcentury revival of American interest in his career. The Philadelphia Museum of Art staged a retrospective exhibition in 1948, the year after Matisse published *Jazz*—a book of prints from his recent work with cut-outs. The artist's post-war reputation experienced a banner year in 1951: the MoMA's major exhibition, its companion book *Matisse, His Art and His Public* by Alfred H. Barr, a two-part profile in the *New Yorker*, and several appearances in that year's *Artnews Annual*. Greenberg published his Pocket Library book on Matisse the year before his death in 1954. As Janet Flanner noted in the *New Yorker* profile, by 1951 the United States had "the largest collections of the works of Matisse, the biggest proportion of them, and the liveliest market in them."[33] Matisse's renewed status also shaped popular culture. For example, the first of a television series on understanding modern art featured his 1935 painting "Pink Nude." Gordon B. Washburn's commentary for this program appeared in *Gentry*'s final issue, along with a reproduction of Matisse's artwork. (At the time, Washburn was the Carnegie Institute's Director of the Department of Fine Arts.[34]) Matisse's most prominent appearance in *Gentry* was on the striking cover to issue 21: a vertically-oriented reproduction of "The Lagoon" cut-out from *Jazz*. Allotted much more space than Picasso's, artworks by Matisse appeared in eight issues. By the end of the magazine's run, in fact, Matisse had become part of the *Gentry* brand.

Equally at home in the art museum or gracious abode, Matisse's drawings, paintings, and cut-outs contributed to the magazine's distinctive layout. In the debut issue, an untitled portrait drawing decorates the back fold of the Finnish bath blueprint—its burnt sienna lines complementing the pale blue tissue paper. Appearing opposite the frontispiece page for the feature "Drawing: The Most Masculine Branch of Art," Matisse's artwork functions as ornament and emblem at once. *Still Life with Oysters* (1940) enlivened issue 14 with its intense hues, appearing on the backside of a glossy page fronted by blue-toned men's sports shirts. The magazine's caption for this painting highlights its geometric layout and "severe architectural rhythm," praising Matisse's dynamic use of bold and subtle colors.[35] In the Age of Elegance number (Fall 1955), a detail from a 1948 still life drawing functions as frontispiece and embellishment to the portfolio on "Elegance in the Modern Country Home and in the Gentleman's Apartment in Town." Evacuated of its female nude, the enlarged detail equates modernist aesthetics with midcentury interior design—a fitting editorial rearrangement to preface designer William Pahlmann's opening text: "Elegance is a cultivated state of mind; the expression of a fine individual taste. It is not intrinsic in any particular period, but is vested in people of any age who have taste and learn to give expression to it."[36] In Number 4, Matisse's contemporary cut-out "Sorrows of the King" had appeared in Pijoan's feature on ancient philosophy and classic artworks.[37]

While the painter himself never appeared in *Gentry*, Matisse became a figure of refined manhood for the magazine's readers. This is hardly surprising for a magazine of the American 1950s. After all, the artist saw his ideal audience in the educated businessman. Longstanding consensus views Matisse as bourgeois, not bohemian. Yet for *Gentry* readers, who occupied neither position, there was something more to Matisse: he displayed sartorial elegance into his later years. Marcia Brennan notes that by this decade, "the American popular press repeatedly cultivated an image of Matisse as a respectable gentleman," pointing to *Time* magazine's 1948 characterization of him as "a meticulous dandy" who "wears a light tweed jacket and tie when he is painting."[38] Flanner's later profile for the *New Yorker* details how, even as an invalid, the artist maintained an impeccable appearance at home. She draws attention to "the drapery of his pale silk painting jacket" and his "carefully tended" hands.[39] One might say that Matisse was the *Gentry* man among the reigning modernists at midcentury.

Indeed, the magazine offered its readers a "special *Gentry* Edition" of *Henri Matisse: Fifty Years of His Graphic Art*, with text by MoMA's own William S. Lieberman.[40] Number 21 included a pull-out sample of the forthcoming book, produced in partnership with George Braziller, Inc. This promotional material highlighted the materiality of Matisse's cut-outs, which he created with paper patterns, tailor's shears, and pins. The artist's process intersects with a fine clothes maker's, tailoring compositions that "willfully blur the differences between fine art and decoration," as Peter Schjeldahl writes of the cut-outs.[41] Moreover, these aesthetic objects manifest a signature style that remains vested in their creator, a quality more in line with *Gentry*'s humanistic approach to art and literature. Tradition and the individual tailor, in short. If "mechanization becomes the text's author" in William S. Burrough's cut-ups, which convey an "anti-author(ity)" that S. Alexander Reed links with industrial music,[42] Matisse maintains authority in his cut-outs. For *Gentry* and other midcentury arbiters of culture, they continued the career of distinctive artistic expression he had achieved with paint and brush. The magazine's publisher and editors saw a similar process at work in the design of *Gentry* itself.

## A tale of two Alfreds

In *Gentry* modernism, the father of modern photography and a designer of fine shirts become interconnected signifiers of stylistic and technological innovation in vanguard New York. Like the makers of *Gentry*, Alfred Stieglitz and Alfred Shapiro benchmarked their work with European art to promote a new American aesthetic. The magazine featured Stieglitz as a pioneering artist: the first to take photographs in night lighting, in snow, in rain.[43] Alfred of New York was an advertising mainstay for *Gentry*, reinventing menswear with signature touches such as the convertible collar, cuffed sleeves, and the slash pocket. Each innovator pushed past presumed limitations of his material, transforming perceptions of mechanical production with artistry. If Stieglitz wrested photography from painterly expectations, Alfred of New York rescued the men's leisure shirt from banality. Curating these dashing figures within their makeover of midcentury masculinity, *Gentry*'s editors bridged the modernist legacy of gallery 291 with New York's "Men's Fashion Miracle Mile."[44]

Picasso was the magazine's touchstone for cubism, and Stieglitz was its standout photographer. In fact, Stieglitz was the first featured modernist artist in *Gentry*, appearing between the Braque cover and Fashion Portfolio of Number 7 (Summer 1953). The editors chose Henri Cartier-Bresson's portrait "Alfred Stieglitz, New York" (1946) for the frontispiece, and Robert W. Marks's essay makes the maverick photographer America's stateside impresario of transatlantic modernism. Praising Stieglitz and his Photo-Secession group for bringing the work of Picasso and Matisse to American audiences, Marks places "photography side by side with its correlatives sculpture and painting."[45] The magazine layout reflects this aesthetic equity, flanking a Matisse drawing, a Paul Strand photograph, and a Georgia O'Keefe painting with reproductions of Stieglitz's "Spring Shower" and "The Terminal." Along with Strand's iconic "Wall Street," these Stieglitz photographs highlight New York's pivotal role in shaping metropolitan modernism. After all, Strand and Charles Sheeler's city symphony film, *Manhatta* (1921), had preceded Eliot's London-based literary landmark, *The Waste Land*. Here *Gentry* participates in the aesthetic brinksmanship that Barnhisel discusses; Cold War modernism championed American-made art, asserted equality with European art, and rerouted modernism's development through the United States.[46]

Stieglitz's lifelong commitment to innovation made him an exemplar of revolutionary style, while his post-war prominence rendered him contemporary for *Gentry* readers. (MoMA had staged a major Stieglitz exhibition in 1947.) In Marks's characterization, Stieglitz's stylistic directness carries forward Pound's Imagism: "He made straight-forward, honest, pictorial shots of everyday life," assiduously avoiding painterly fuzziness. Exploding the laboratory analogies that expatriates Pound and Eliot employed to promote modernist poetry, Marks claims that Stieglitz's effect is "very much what the new atom-smashing machines are to modern chemistry,"[47] reflecting the new technological prowess of the United States. Modern American photography would hold special status in *Gentry* across its midcentury run. The editors ran features on Clarence White (whom Stieglitz launched), Clarence John Laughlin, Peter Fink, Harry Callahan, Edward Weston, and Thomas Eakins. Emphasizing the latter's "prescient experiments," the magazine's editors back-dated the beginnings of American modernist art to the 1880s.[48]

Marks also sees Stieglitz as "father to modern advertising photography,"[49] and no advertiser in *Gentry* rivaled the photographic impact that Alfred of New York made on the page. Branding the fine leisure shirt with a poetics of unabashed personality, these ads gave each design a distinctive name: the Corsican, the Revere, the Ribbonaire, the Gentry. In these sumptuous ads, image and text fashion a debonair masculinity, retailoring old Continental elegance with new American-engineered fabrics such as Dacron®, Orlon®, and Sir Ultra®. If Eliot's tailor neatly distilled the poet's style as "nothing ever quite in excess,"[50] the Alfred man was cut from richer cloth. Flamboyant, cultured, and fashion-forward, his leisure shirts were works of manufactured art in the age of midcentury modernism. And Alfred himself reigned over this lavish gallery as artist in his own right. Fittingly, the Ribbonaire ad features American muralist Lumen Winter in his studio, standing before his portrait of Alfred with a palette and brush.[51]

Many Alfred ads allude to canonized artists from Europe's past, giving their leisure shirts the aura of future museum objects. For example, the "hand-detailed color accents" on the Varadero are as distinctive as "a Cezanne still life,"[52] while the Revere's form proves "as ageless as a Rembrandt."[53] In a Father's Day portfolio, the Revel shirt's "visual perfection" makes it a "masterpiece" on a par with Michelangelo.[54] The ad for the Balmoral even equates its distinctive design with an artist's signature: "An art connoisseur, looking at a collection of unsigned canvasses, will suddenly exclaim 'It's a Degas or a Matisse' ... Same with an Alfred shirt."[55] These ads also draw from the literary canon, quoting Goethe, Poe, Dr. Johnson, and Shakespeare. Like the ideal *Gentry* reader, the Alfred man was culturally literate as well as finely dressed.

Most spectacular of all was the penultimate number's "Alfredorama in Six Acts," which followed a cover image by Matisse. Tapping the theatrics of the decade's widescreen epic films, this elaborate photo spread outfitted the *Gentry* man—and the national character—with signature verve and American ingenuity. It featured color plates of models standing alongside and atop the skyscrapers of New York. Each panoramic page pushes the frame with its culminating copy, written like voice-over narration and signed ALFRED (a nod to fellow auteur Alfred Hitchcock, perhaps?). Arranged on

32  POPULAR MODERNISM AND ITS LEGACIES

FIGURE 1.4 *Advertisement for Alfred of New York, the Varadero, Gentry 13 (Winter 1954–5).*

the terrace of Lever House, a midcentury glass-box skyscraper, the fifteen men modeling the Socialite attest to the "practicality" undergirding its fashion "flourish."[56] Surrounded by skyscrapers in The Skyline panel, two young men atop the RCA building gaze upward—Alfred's new Continental collar alongside Manhattan's monuments of American modernism. The Alfredorama narration proclaims that Americans are "forever looking for new horizons."[57] If the man in the Hathaway shirt traveled the world in an eye patch to show his sophistication, the Alfred man showed his by wearing fine leisure shirts in New York. In the pages of *Gentry*, their maker found a stylish home with Stieglitz and other modernist masters.

This tale of two Alfreds reflects a hybrid historical sense that refashioned transatlantic modernism into an urban scene of refined *flânerie* and luxury shopping. Stepping neatly over the gendered cultural divide inflecting modernism's early decades, the *Gentry* man could partake in the pleasures of consumption without taking on the feminized taint of mass culture. Neither Baudelaire's *flâneur*-connoisseur of urban squalor nor a window-shopping *flâneuse*, the *Gentry* Man was metropolitan yet not alienated, observant yet not obsessed, flamboyant yet not effeminate. If *Playboy* assured middle-class, straight men "there was nothing queer" about artiness and "indoor pleasures," as Barbara Ehrenreich contends,[58] *America's fabulous magazine for men* gave elite men license to attain masculine elegance through the stuff that *women's* magazines were made of: fashion and shopping. For by applying the same discriminating eye to clothes as he applied to art and literature, the *Gentry* man found the fitting form and defining detail that distinguished his style.

## American dandies and revolutionary gentlemen

From its debut number, *Gentry* invited its readers to remake their wardrobes and boldly wear where no American man had worn before. Rubenstein applauds the "explosion of color, texture, and pattern, technological innovation, precision tailoring, and daring" that characterized *Gentry* style, reflecting the magazine's "joyous immersion in sartorial splendor."[59] Declaring independence from Savile Row, Segal's publication promoted a revolutionary refinement with *flair*. After all, American designers were retailoring iconic English fashions for American men—updating the London host coat, Edwardian waistcoat, and Norfolk jacket with new synthetic fabrics and innovative blends. Adjudicating men's clothing was serious business for *Gentry*. The magazine listed the Ten Best Dressed American Gentlemen of 1955 in its Age of Elegance number; here Segal invoked Walter Pater to proclaim higher forms of "gracious living" in the

United States on a par with "bygone ages of elegance."[60] *Gentry* ushered in a midcentury dandy revival. Velvet jackets and bow-tied shoes vied with carved cufflinks and dashing hats for the reader's attention in the magazine's lavish fashion portfolios. Vibrant photographs displayed fine clothing in red, purple, paisleys, and stripes. In a fashion editorial "Why Not Color in Evening Wear?" the editors decried the default setting of "funereally garbed" men at social occasions.[61] *Gentry* men were peacocks, not Prufrocks.

The magazine tapped the genealogy of American dandyism that ran from Yankee Doodle to the *New Yorker*'s Eustace Tilley, benchmarking it with Beau Brummell and Oscar Wilde. At first glance, the figure of the dandy may seem unfitting for American men in a time of post-war expansion. Traditionally, dandyism signifies European cultural decline, marking a sartorial fall from Brummell's Regency refinement to Wilde's Decadent foppery. (Like Brummell's bankruptcy and exile, Wilde's imprisonment serves as a cautionary tale for men of the finer cloth.) Black-clad Baudelaire, the most modernist of dandies, deployed his style as an extended act of mourning a world that embraced mediocrity and vulgarity. The *Gentry* man maintained Baudelaire's insistence on originality, and he turned to paintings for aesthetic instruction. But he was a jet-setter, not an exile, and he did not shun high society (although he preferred those with a taste for singularity). As Elisa Glick insists, the dandy has always been a paradoxical figure, both "a privileged emblem of the modern and ... a dissident in revolt against modern society."[62] The *Gentry* man continued this tradition with his higher form of gracious living and disdain for poor taste.

The *Gentry* man also straddled Brummell's and Wilde's revolutions in style through his impeccable flamboyance and singular sensibility. In 1956 the magazine placed the dueling dandies in proximity. Number 19 defended the Beau from charges of foppery in its unattributed feature "Beau Brummell: A New Look at an Old Fallacy." Prompted by MGM's 1954 release of *Beau Brummell*, the piece praised Stewart Granger's redemption of the Regency dandy as "a synonym for sartorial splendor," eschewing the overdone styles that John Barrymore and Clyde Fitch donned in their earlier portrayals. The piece ends with Max Beerbohm's insistence that Brummell was "an *artist* ... in the utmost sense of the word" because of the "fastidiousness" and "harmoniousness" with which he *wore* his exquisitely-tailored clothes.[63] Thus the Beau is traditional and modern at once, a fitting forebear of *Gentry* style. Number 20 published "An Alphabet of Uncommon Sense," the editors' collection of twenty-six Wilde witticisms—including this pithy gem: "No civilized man ever regrets a pleasure, and no uncivilized man ever knows what a pleasure is."[64] But the magazine showed its fullest Wilde side in the sumptuous Host attire that graced the fashion portfolios.

Surely the Decadents' ultimate dandy would relish the "At-Home Elegance" of this Host Coat's red velvet fabric with black bengaline lapels

**FIGURE 1.5** *Red velvet and black bengaline host suit in* Gentry 16, Age of Elegance Number *(Fall 1955).*

and cuffs, luxuriously complementing the black bengaline trousers with red velvet striping—"the mark of a *bon vivant.*"[65] *Gentry* even advertised red plush containers for storing the magazines. The magazine's dandy revival offered a Queer eye for the post-war guy. Like Brummell, Wilde had renewed cultural currency in midcentury America. Two British films (*An Ideal Husband* [1947] and *The Importance of Being Earnest* [1952]) screened in the United States. And in 1958, the American TV Western *Have Gun—Will Travel* aired its "Ballad of Oscar Wilde" episode. Dressed in dandy accoutrements, carrying an international itinerary, the *Gentry* man was the culmination of Segal's project of refashioning American manhood.

Ellen Moers reminds us that the word *dandy* has American roots in the Revolutionary War: English troops belittled American soldiers for their inferior costume, dubbing them "Yankee Doodle dandies."[66] Founding fathers George Washington and Thomas Jefferson receive a midcentury makeover in issue number 21, sharing space with the Matisse feature and "Alfredorama." Homegrown forebears for the *Gentry* man, these revolutionary gentlemen minded their manners (and manors). Indeed, excerpts from Washington's "Rules of Civility and Decent Behaviour" render him an etiquette expert at the tender age of fifteen: "Be not forward, but friendly and courteous, the first to salute, hear, and answer, and be not pensive when it is time to converse."[67] The first President would prove his gentlemanly prowess as Mt. Vernon's owner, expanding and embellishing the manor with flourishes such as the dining room's carved mantelpiece.[68] Washington offers an image of timeless civility in *Gentry*, which advertised a set of Wedgewood cufflinks embellished with his profile.[69]

Jefferson was progenitor of the gracious living that *Gentry* promoted, arguably our first dandy president. The magazine's contents page gave Jefferson a garland of epithets: "statesman, architect, author, educator, horticulturist, musician, country gentleman, and gourmet."[70] *Gentry* even bestowed an anachronistic invitation to "Christmas Dinner at Th: Jefferson's," a multicourse affair of Monticello dishes starting with pigeon cream and pumpkin soups, and ending with sugared pancakes.[71] Jefferson and Washington embody the Genteel Patriarch ideal that Michael Kimmel finds central to American masculinity; displaying the "well-rounded character, with exquisite tastes and manners and refined sensibilities" that distinguished the early American gentry.[72] Ultimately, Revolutionary refinement becomes a foundational aspect of the national character for *Gentry*—one that its exclusive readers could reclaim. The magazine's final issue printed verse by John Quincy Adams, Abraham Lincoln, and Calvin Coolidge: "Our Poetical Presidents."[73] Such presentations of cultured American statesmen were fitting in the age of Eisenhower, a proponent of cultural diplomacy who was also an amateur painter and *Gentry* subscriber.[74]

# The returns of *Gentry* modernism

In the post-war years, Barnhisel reminds us, many European intellectuals derided American culture "for what they perceived as its lack of intellectual or artistic achievement"—as well as for the economic and military power of the United States.[75] *Gentry* pushed back against this perception, and its portrayals of modernist art intersect with the Cold War modernism that Barnhisel assesses. Yet the magazine aimed higher than the middle classes in domesticating European modernism and claiming cultural maturity. Moreover, it reclaimed a Wilde West for the American gentry, who now measured up their European forebears. *Gentry* promoted an "aesthetic of intelligently executed affluence," as Rubenstein puts it.[76] Segal saw his target readers as a cut above the merely wealthy—the better minds of their generations. The magazine claimed among its readers "Ambassadors, Congressmen, the heads of many of the nation's largest industrial empires, and important figures in the fields of the arts, the sciences, and the professions."[77]

Mapping modernism and little magazines before the Second World War, Suzanne W. Churchill and Adam McKible locate the most experimental writing in the more aesthetically-minded publications, those maintaining "higher artistic and intellectual standards than their commercial counterparts."[78] *Gentry* modernism also defied the mainstream, but without embracing the extreme. It advertised New Directions books, and it promoted new directions in men's fashion. This singular magazine brought finer materials to modernist material culture—literally hand-pasting them onto the page. *Gentry*'s readers appreciated its exceptional form and exclusive content. Indeed, one charter subscriber could not contain his refined enthusiasm: "In *Gentry* I have, at last, found versions that do not conceal from the inquisitive soul; descriptions that reveal the perceptive mind; illustrations that appeal to the discriminating eye."[79] *Gentry* represented a respectable elitism, a rarified sensibility. Revisiting *Gentry* opens up more spaces for modernist studies, which has expanded outward to include the Decadent 1890s and the Cold War 1950s. And it requires us to retailor our conceptions of men's magazines.

Where do we locate the traces of *Gentry* modernism—and *Gentry* masculinity—in our own cultural moment? Like the magazine itself, they can appear in unusual forms and unexpected places. For example:

- In the 1990s filmmaker Ken Burns made three short films about Segal, whom he'd met at a drawing workshop in the 1970s. More lyrical and luminous than Burns's popular documentaries, they distill Segal's quest for *another relation to reality* through art and philosophy. Burns intended them for a coterie audience. Two of the films aired on PBS in 2010, and the entire trilogy is now available on DVD.[80]

- In 2013 Nathaniel Adams and Rose Callahan's splendid volume *I Am Dandy: The Return of the Elegant Gentleman* reclaimed masculine high style for a new century. Epigraphs from Nietzsche and Epictetus front the prefatory essays, and sumptuous host shoes enliven Callahan's lavish photographs.[81]
- Sold individually and in batches, *Gentry* still appears on Ebay as a collectible men's magazine. As this essay is going to press, Modernism101.com offers *a complete set* for $1,750—assuring potential buyers that a tipped-in Ty Cobb baseball card remains intact in number 20.

These sightings and circulations reveal a *Gentry* effect that can embellish our understanding of modernism and popular culture. If we fashion more extraordinary critical apparel, we can parse their dynamic relations with style.

# Acknowledgments

I would like to thank my UF colleague Melanie Davis, Interlibrary Loan Program Coordinator for UF Smathers Libraries, for giving me access to the full run of *Gentry* for my research. I'm also grateful to my former student Jill Pruett for putting *Gentry* on my radar through the wonders of Ebay.

# Notes

1 "Letters to the Editors," *Gentry* 4 (Fall 1952): 2.
2 "Pattern and Palette in Print: *Gentry* Magazine and a New Generation of Trendsetters," exhibition, Georgia Museum of Art (Athens, GA, 2012), https://georgiamuseum.org/art/exhibitions/past/pattern-and-palette-in-print.
3 David Earle, *All Man! Hemingway, 1950s Men's Magazines, and the Masculine Persona* (Kent, OH: Kent State University Press, 2009), 109.
4 "Most Readers Will Skip This Page," Editorial, *Gentry* 1 (Winter 1951): 46.
5 Earle, *All Man!*, 2.
6 "About You—The People Who Read *Gentry*," *Gentry* 10 (Spring 1954): 28.
7 Andrew Thacker, "General Introduction: 'Magazines, Magazines, Magazines!,'" in *The Oxford Critical and Cultural History of Modernist Magazines, Vol 2: North America 1894–1960*, eds. Peter Brooker and Andrew Thacker (Oxford: Oxford University Press, 2012), 16.
8 Hal Rubenstein, *The Gentry Man: A Guide for the Civilized Male* (New York: Harper Design, 2012), 7.

9 "Gentry Fashions," *Gentry* 1 (Winter 1951): 128.
10 William Segal, "Can the Element of Timelessness Be Achieved by a Contemporary Magazine?," Editorial, *Gentry* 17 (Winter 1955–6), 40.
11 "Letters to the Editors," *Gentry* 2 (January 15–April 15,1952): 15; "Letters to the Editors," *Gentry* 3 (May 1–August 1, 1952): 3.
12 "Most Readers," 46.
13 Editorial attributed to Hugh Hefner, *Playboy* (January 1953): 3.
14 Ibid.
15 Natalya Lusty, "Introduction: Modernism and Its Masculinities," in *Modernism and Masculinity*, eds. Natalya Lusty and Julian Murphet (New York: Cambridge University Press, 2014), 1.
16 James M. Gilbert, *Men in the Middle: Searching for Masculinity in the 1950s* (Chicago: University of Chicago Press, 2005), 189.
17 "What Does It Mean to Be a Man?," *Gentry* 1 (Winter 1951): 73–82.
18 "Most Readers," 46.
19 Rubenstein, *The Gentry Man*, 7.
20 Lawrence Chrow, "At the Sign of Taurus," *Gentry* 10 (Spring 1954): 39–61.
21 "Letters to the Editors," *Gentry* 3 (May 1–August 1, 1952): 3; "Letters to the Editors," *Gentry* 2 (January 15–April 15, 1952): 15.
22 Paul Lewis, "Obituary for William Segal," *New York Times*, May 22, 2000, http://www.nytimes.com/2000/05/22/arts/william-segal-95-publisher-who-painted-self-portraits.html.
23 See http:/www.modernism101.com.
24 Gwen Allen, *Artists' Magazines: An Alternative Space for Art* (Cambridge, MA: MIT Press, 2015): 43.
25 "His Master's Choice," *Gentry* 6 (Spring 1953): 26.
26 These images appear on pages 40–1.
27 Greg Barnhisel, *Cold War Modernists: Art, Literature, and American Cultural Diplomacy* (New York: Columbia University Press, 2015), 3.
28 "Letters to the Editors," *Gentry* 5 (Holiday Issue 1952): 2.
29 Picasso, *She-Goat* (reproduction), *Gentry* 4 (Fall 1952), 33.
30 Joseph Pijoan, "On the Subject of Art," *Gentry* 4 (Fall 1952): 29, 29–32.
31 "How Modern Is Modern?" *Gentry* 4 (Fall 1952): 123.
32 W. L., "The Art of Matisse," *Gentry* 13 (Winter 1954–5): 124.
33 Janet Flanner, "Profiles—King of the Wild Beasts—I," *New Yorker* (December 22, 1951): 31.
34 See "Looking at Pictures," *Gentry* 22 (Spring 1957): 41–2, 45–8.
35 See *Gentry* (Spring 1955): 84.
36 "*Gentry* Presents the Age of Elegance in the Modern Country Home and in the Gentleman's Apartment in Town," *Gentry* 16 (Fall 1955): 48.

37 Pijoan "On the Subject of Art," 31.
38 Marcia Brennan, *Modernism's Masculine Subjects: Matisse, the New York School, and Post-Painterly Abstraction* (Cambridge, MA: MIT Press, 2004), 10, 31.
39 Flanner, "Profiles—King of the Wild Beasts—I," 34.
40 Promotion for Gentry Edition of *Henri Matisse: Fifty Years of His Graphic Art. Gentry* 21 (Winter 1956-7): 148.
41 Peter Schjeldahl, "Shapes of Things: The Radicalism of Matisse's Cutouts," *New Yorker* (October 20, 2014): 102.
42 S. Alexander Reed, *Assimilate: A Critical History of Industrial Music* (New York: Oxford University Press, 2013): 33-4.
43 Robert W. Marks, "Alfred Stieglitz," *Gentry* 7 (Summer 1953): 67.
44 *Gentry* Number 15 offered a map of this shopping district, centered along a block of Fifth Avenue. See pages 88-9.
45 Ibid., 68.
46 Barnhisel, *Cold War Modernists*, 3. See esp. Ch. 2, "'Advancing American Art': Modernist Painting and Public–Private Partnerships."
47 Marks, "Alfred Stieglitz," 68, 72.
48 "Eakins," *Gentry* 20 (Fall 1956): 65.
49 Marks, "Alfred Stieglitz," 67.
50 Hugh Kenner, "Elements of Style: The Possum's Tailor," *GQ* (September 1985): 30.
51 Alfred of New York Advertisement, "Ribbonaire," *Gentry* 17 (Winter 1955-6): 20.
52 Alfred of New York Advertisement, "Varadero," *Gentry* 13 (Winter 1954-5): 15.
53 Alfred of New York Advertisement, "Revere," *Gentry* 13 (Winter 1954-5): 16.
54 Alfred of New York Advertisement, "Revel," *Gentry* 15 (Summer 1955): 14.
55 Alfred of New York Advertisement, "Balmoral," *Gentry* 15 (Summer 1955): 17.
56 Alfred of New York Advertisement, "The Socialite," *Gentry* 21 (Winter 1956-7): 12.
57 Alfred of New York Advertisement, "Alfredorama in Six Acts," *Gentry* 21 (Winter 1956-7): 9-15.
58 Barbara Ehrenreich, *The Hearts of Men: American Dreams and the Flight from Commitment* (Garden City, NY: Anchor/Doubleday, 1983), 51.
59 Rubenstein, *The Gentry Man*, 8.
60 William Segal, "On Gracious Living," Editorial, *Gentry* 16 (Fall 1955): 44.
61 "Why Not Color in Evening Wear?," Editorial, *Gentry* 2 (January 15–April 15, 1952): 76.

62 Elisa Glick, *Materializing Queer Desire: Oscar Wilde to Andy Warhol* (Albany: State University of New York Press, 2009), 17.
63 "Beau Brummell: A New Look at an Old Fallacy," *Gentry* 19 (Summer 1956): 77, 80.
64 "An Alphabet of Uncommon Sense from the Works of Oscar Wilde," *Gentry* 20 (Fall 1956): 37.
65 "At-Home Elegance: The Host Suit," *Gentry* Fashion Portfolio, *Gentry* 16 (Fall 1955): 95.
66 Ellen Moers, *The Dandy: Brummell to Beerbohm* (New York: Viking, 1960), 11.
67 George Washington, "Rules of Civility and Decent Behaviour," *Gentry* 21 (Winter 1956–7): 77–8.
68 Readers interested in learning more about Mt. Vernon (and Washington's life there) should see the estate's official website at http://www.mountvernon.org/.
69 This advertisement appeared in *Gentry* 13 (Winter 1954–5): 159.
70 "In This Issue," *Gentry* 21 (Winter 1956–7): 33.
71 "Christmas Dinner at Th: Jefferson's," *Gentry* 21 (Winter 1956–7): 73–6.
72 Michael Kimmel, *Manhood in America: A Cultural History*, 3rd edn (New York: Oxford University Press, 2012), 13.
73 "Our Poetical Presidents," *Gentry* 22 (Spring 1957): 9.
74 The magazine's editors refer to Eisenhower's subscription in "About You— The People Who Read *Gentry*," 8.
75 Barnhisel, *Cold War Modernists*, 20.
76 Rubenstein, *The Gentry Man*, 8.
77 "About You," 28.
78 Suzanne W. Churchill and Adam McKible, Introduction to *Little Magazines & Modernism: New Approaches* (Burlington, VT: Ashgate, 2007): 6.
79 "Letters to the Editors," *Gentry* 4 (Fall 1952): 4.
80 *Seeing, Searching, Being: William Segal, Three Films by Ken Burns*, Dir. Ken Burns, with Buddy Squires and Roger Sherman (William Segal Films, PBS Distribution, 2010), DVD.
81 Nathaniel Adams and Rose Callahan, *I Am Dandy: The Return of the Elegant Gentleman* (Berlin: Gestalten, 2013).

# Bibliography

"About You—The People Who Read Gentry." *Gentry* 10 (Spring 1954): 28.
Adams, Nathaniel and Rose Callahan. *I Am Dandy: The Return of the Elegant Gentleman*. Berlin: Gestalten, 2013.
Alfred of New York Advertisement. "Revere." *Gentry* 13 (Winter 1954–5): 16.
Alfred of New York Advertisement. "Varadero." *Gentry* 13 (Winter 1954–5): 15.

Alfred of New York Advertisement. "Balmoral." *Gentry* 15 (Summer 1955): 17.
Alfred of New York Advertisement. "Revel." *Gentry* 15 (Summer 1955): 14.
Alfred of New York Advertisement. "Ribbonaire." *Gentry* 17 (Winter 1955–6): 20.
Alfred of New York Advertisement. "Alfredorama in Six Acts." *Gentry* 21 (Winter 1956–7): 9–15.
Alfred of New York Advertisement. "The Socialite." *Gentry* 21 (Winter 1956–7): 12.
Allen, Gwen. *Artists' Magazines: An Alternative Space for Art*. Cambridge, MA: MIT Press, 2015.
"An Alphabet of Uncommon Sense from the Works of Oscar Wilde." *Gentry* 20 (Fall 1956): 36–7.
"At-Home Elegance: The Host Suit." *Gentry* Fashion Portfolio. *Gentry* 16 (Fall 1955): 95.
Barnhisel, Greg. *Cold War Modernists: Art, Literature, and American Cultural Diplomacy*. New York: Columbia University Press, 2015.
"Beau Brummell: A New Look at an Old Fallacy." *Gentry* 19 (Summer 1956): 76–80.
Brennan, Marcia. *Modernism's Masculine Subjects: Matisse, the New York School, and Post-Painterly Abstraction*. Cambridge, MA: MIT Press, 2004.
"Christmas Dinner at Th: Jefferson's." *Gentry* 21 (Winter 1956–7): 73–6.
Chrow, Lawrence. "At the Sign of Taurus." *Gentry* 10 (Spring 1954): 39–61.
Churchill, Suzanne W. and Adam McKible. "Introduction." In *Little Magazines & Modernism: New Approaches*, 1–18. Burlington, VT: Ashgate, 2007.
"Eakins." *Gentry* 20 (Fall 1956): 65–72.
Earle, David. *All Man! Hemingway, 1950s Men's Magazines, and the Masculine Persona*. Kent, OH: Kent State University Press, 2009.
Ehrenreich, Barbara. *The Hearts of Men: American Dreams and the Flight from Commitment*. Garden City, NY: Anchor/Doubleday, 1983.
Flanner, Janet. "Profiles—King of the Wild Beasts—I." *New Yorker* (December 22, 1951): 30–2, 34–8, 43–6.
"Gentry Fashions." *Gentry* 1 (Winter 1951): 123–30.
"*Gentry* Presents the Age of Elegance in the Modern Country Home and in the Gentleman's Apartment in Town," *Gentry* 16 (Fall 1955): 46–57.
Gilbert, James M. *Men in the Middle: Searching for Masculinity in the 1950s*. Chicago: University of Chicago Press, 2005.
Glick, Elisa. *Materializing Queer Desire: Oscar Wilde to Andy Warhol*. Albany: State University of New York Press, 2009.
"How Modern Is Modern?" *Gentry* 4 (Fall 1952): 123.
"In This Issue." *Gentry* 21 (Winter 1956–7): 33.
Kenner, Hugh. "Elements of Style: The Possum's Tailor." *GQ* (September 1985): 27, 30.
Kimmel, Michael. *Manhood in America: A Cultural History*, 3rd edn. New York: Oxford University Press, 2012.
"Letters to the Editors." *Gentry* 2 (January 15–April 15, 1952): 15, 133.
"Letters to the Editors." *Gentry* 3 (May 1–August 1, 1952): 3–4.
"Letters to the Editors." *Gentry* 4 (Fall 1952): 2, 4.
Lewis, Paul. Obituary for William Segal, *New York Times*, May 22, 2000.

Available online: http://www.nytimes.com/2000/05/22/arts/william-segal-95-publisher-who-painted-self-portraits.html.
Lusty, Natalya. "Introduction: Modernism and Its Masculinities." In *Modernism and Masculinity*, edited by Natalya Lusty and Julian Murphet, 1–15. New York: Cambridge University Press, 2014.
Marks, Robert W. "Alfred Stieglitz." *Gentry* 7 (Summer 1953): 65–72.
Moers, Ellen. *The Dandy: Brummell to Beerbohm*. New York: Viking, 1960.
"Most Readers Will Skip This Page." Editorial. *Gentry* 1 (Winter 1951): 46.
"Our Poetical Presidents." *Gentry* 22 (Spring 1957): 9.
"Pattern and Palette in Print: *Gentry* Magazine and a New Generation of Trendsetters." Exhibition. Georgia Museum of Art. Athens, GA, 2012. Available online: https://georgiamuseum.org/art/exhibitions/past/pattern-and-palette-in-print.
Picasso, *She-Goat* (reproduction). *Gentry* 4 (Fall 1952): 33.
Pijoan, Joseph. "On the Subject of Art." *Gentry* 4 (Fall 1952): 29–32.
Reed, S. Alexander. *Assimilate: A Critical History of Industrial Music*. New York: Oxford University Press, 2013.
Rubenstein, Hal. *The Gentry Man: A Guide for the Civilized Male*. New York: Harper Design, 2012.
*Seeing, Searching, Being: William Segal. Three Films by Ken Burns*. Dir. Ken Burns, with Buddy Squires and Roger Sherman. William Segal Films, PBS Distribution, 2010. DVD.
Segal, William. "Can the Element of Timelessness Be Achieved by a Contemporary Magazine?" Editorial. *Gentry* 17 (Winter 1955–6): 40.
Segal, William. "On Gracious Living." Editorial. *Gentry* 16 (Fall 1955): 44.
Schjeldahl, Peter. "Shapes of Things: The Radicalism of Matisse's Cutouts." *New Yorker* (October 20, 2014): 102–3.
"Socialite," *Gentry* 21 (Winter 1956–7): 12.
Thacker, Andrew. "General Introduction: 'Magazines, Magazines, Magazines!'" In *The Oxford Critical and Cultural History of Modernist Magazines, Vol. 2: North America 1894–1960*, edited by Peter Brooker and Andrew Thacker, 1–28. Oxford: Oxford University Press, 2012.
W. L. "The Art of Matisse." *Gentry* 13 (Winter 1954–5): 124.
Washington, George. "Rules of Civility and Decent Behaviour." *Gentry* 21 (Winter 1956–7): 77–8.
"What Does It Mean to Be a Man?" *Gentry* 1 (Winter 1951): 73–82.
"Why Not Color in Evening Wear?" Editorial. *Gentry* 2 (January 15–April 15, 1952): 76.

# 2

# Modernism, operetta, and Ruritania: Ivor Novello's *Glamorous Night*

## Nicholas Daly

We do not often think about operetta and modernism together, except, perhaps, as opposites. Franz Lehár's *The Merry Widow* (1907), for example, with its syrupy signature waltz seems like the kind of thing that the modernists longed to kill off. Futurist Luigi Russolo expresses just such a view in *The Art of Noise* (1913), in which he argues, echoing Filippo Tommaso Marinetti, that "the noises of trams, backfiring motors, carriages, and bawling crowds" are a more likely source for the music of the future than the synchronized "mewing" of violins.[1] The music that George Antheil composed for Fernand Léger and Dudley Murphy's film *Ballet Mécanique* (1924) suggests what Russolo had in mind: a syncopated, atonal score, using the sounds of sirens, propellers, and player-pianos alongside more conventional instruments. I hope to show, however, that the relations of operetta and modernism are a little more complicated.

Beginning on the side of modernism, it would be possible to argue that some of Kurt Weill's work falls into the category of modernist operetta. *The Firebrand of Florence* (1944), for instance, Weill's collaboration with Ira Gershwin, is usually categorized as a two-act operetta; and the more familiar *Threepenny Opera* (1928) has operetta elements. What Weill meant by combining the two in the latter work is, of course, debatable, though Theodor Adorno asserted that the work's combination of opera and operetta "captures the little ghosts of the bourgeois world, and reduces them to ashes by exposing them to the harsh light of active memory."[2] That is to say, Weill's work conjures up the spirits of the operetta of the 1880s and 1890s in order to exorcize them. Mewing violins are out, replaced by syncopated rhythms and jazz-influenced orchestration.

But we might also start from the side of operetta, and that is what I want do here. In particular I wish to argue that in the crowd-pleasing operettas of Welsh composer Ivor Novello we can find a strain of the popular modernism that this edited collection wishes to spotlight. Novello himself is an extraordinary figure, whose contributions to twentieth-century popular culture range from the sentimental First World War anthem, "Keep the Home-Fires Burning" (1914), to collaboration with Alfred Hitchcock, to the line "Me Tarzan, You Jane" in the film *Tarzan the Ape Man* (1932). The operetta I will focus on in this essay, *Glamorous Night* (1935), is a "Ruritanian operetta," a subgenre involving political and romantic intrigue and pageantry in tiny, imaginary, mittel-European principalities. (The term "Ruritania" itself comes from the setting of Anthony Hope's popular adventure novel of 1894, *The Prisoner of Zenda*.) Novello adds to the usual confection a plot that features the recent invention of television and the rise of fascism and a score that contains jazz songs as well as arias.

## Operetta: A pocket history

To understand Novello's work we need a Ruritanian-sized history of operetta. Operetta combines operatic singing, spoken dialogue, and often dance; its plots are comic and usually romantic. It is now a largely moribund form, and it has been one for some time. Yet from the middle of the nineteenth century until after the Second World War it enjoyed immense popularity. As late as the 1950s, lavish screen versions of such earlier stage productions as Sigmund Romberg's *The Student Prince* (1924; dir. Richard Thorpe, 1954) could still attract huge audiences, and formally-trained singers like Kathryn Grayson and Mario Lanza were major film stars. Operetta's origins as a musical form are complex and beyond the scope of this essay since, as Richard Traubner describes, among its ancestors are French *opéra comique* and vaudeville (short comic sketches with songs), English ballad operas, and German *Singspiel*.[3] Its more proximate origins lie in the short, farcical musical plays that began to appear in Paris in the 1840s in the theaters of the boulevard du Temple. Hervé's *Don Quichotte et Sancho Panza*, which appeared at the Théâtre National in 1848, is sometimes cited as the first real operetta.[4] At his theater on the Champs-Élysées, Jacques (Jakob) Offenbach developed operetta into a whole evening's entertainment in such popular successes as *Orphée aux enfers* (1858) and *La belle Hélène* (1864). Writing in the 1930s, Siegfried

Kracauer argued that the appearance of operetta at this time and place was due to an affinity between the new cultural form and the phantasmagoric world of the Second Empire, which he saw as "living in a dreamworld" and driven by pomp and spectacle, not unlike, perhaps, the Germany of the 1930s.[5] The topical and risqué operettas of Offenbach had been eclipsed by the end of the nineteenth century by Viennese operetta; Johann Strauss II's *Die Fledermaus* (1874) is a well-known instance. In the early twentieth century, waltz-driven Viennese operetta continued in favor, but it also began to converge to some extent with musical comedy.[6] Romantic love plots dominated, and elaborate sets and costumes were the norm.

It is in this period that the "Ruritanian" strain really develops, and a whole string of operettas followed Hope's *Prisoner of Zenda* in featuring political intrigue in Germanic, semi-feudal principalities, with plots often turning on mistaken identities. Ruritanian operetta became a highly flexible form that not only offered scope for spectacle and pageantry, but for exploring a variety of contemporary themes, including the competing pulls of the nation and the self, duty and pleasure, tradition and modernity. In the greatest operetta success of the Edwardian years, for instance, Franz Lehár's 1905 *The Merry Widow* (*Die lustige Witwe*), Ruritania is the place left behind: we are introduced to, but never see, the backward land of Marsovia, where marriages are arranged, and women are kept in their place.[7] This operetta's vision of émigré Ruritanians leaving behind their joyless upbringing to quaff champagne and cut capers among the fleshpots of Paris charmed a generation of Europeans and Americans who felt themselves to be kicking over the traces of their Victorian past. In Britain alone, some 200,000 copies of the sheet music were sold, and more than 1 million people went to see it; in New York it ran for 416 performances. Countless women bought into its glamour by wearing versions of the elaborate "Merry Widow hat" worn by Sonia. Even Leopold Bloom imagines Mrs. Cunningham wearing one in 1904 in the Circe episode of *Ulysses* (1922), a year too early.

## Novello: Reinventing operetta

Surprisingly, perhaps, given lingering anti-German feeling, and stiff competition from other cultural forms, including cinema and jazz reviews, the post-war years saw another blossoming of Ruritanian operetta, with Austro-Hungarian composer Sigmund Romberg's *The Student Prince* (1924), *Princess Flavia* (1925, a version of *The Prisoner of Zenda*), and *Rosalie* (1928), co-written with George Gershwin.[8] By the mid-1930s operetta was losing ground, but it continued to attract large audiences.[9] At this point our main subject enters the scene, the Cardiff-born composer who made the Ruritanian strand into something new: David Ivor Davies (1893–1951), better known to the world as Ivor Novello, and to the theatrical community as just Ivor.[10] (He had long used the surname Novello professionally and adopted it as his legal name in 1927.) Once enormously successful, a rival to his friend Noël Coward, he is now largely remembered not so much for his own work as for the Ivor Novello Awards for composition and songwriting. Of his own vast output as a composer only a handful of songs are still familiar, including two of his sentimental war songs: "Keep the Home Fires Burning" (1914), a veritable national anthem during the First World War; and "We'll Gather Lilacs" (1945), which performed a similar role in the Second World War. His hit musical plays have followed the path of most other operettas into deep obscurity. Once voted Britain's favorite film actor, his films too are forgotten outside specialist circles. It is a curious fate for someone who enjoyed extraordinary popularity across four decades as a composer, actor, and playwright.

Buoyed by the enormous vogue of "Keep the Home Fires Burning," Ivor worked as a composer through the 1910s and 1920s, contributing steadily to popular musicals and revues. But his matinée idol looks also helped to make him a much sought-after actor, on screen and then on stage. Spotted first by the pioneering French director Louis Mercanton, he went on to work with that other great popular modernist, Alfred Hitchcock, starring in *The Lodger* (1926) and *Downhill* (1927), the latter adapted from Ivor's stage play. This was quite lucrative work: his role in the 1928 screen version of Margaret Kennedy's *The Constant Nymph* paid for his country house, Redroofs, where he lived with his partner, actor Bobbie Andrews. (That Novello was gay was a fairly open secret.[11]) Under the name E. S. Davidson, Ivor wrote the comedy *The Truth Game* (1928), and the Broadway success of this comedy, in which he also starred, led to an offer to come to Hollywood, where he worked on, *inter alia*, the dialogue for *Tarzan the Ape Man* (1932). Johnny Weissmuller's famous line "Me Tarzan, you Jane" was apparently written by him.[12] But primitivism was not really Ivor's thing; he decided to return to London, where he began to write the musical plays that brought him fresh fame.

His first great success in this line was the production I want to focus on for the rest of this chapter: *Glamorous Night*, a romantic Ruritanian extravaganza, which opened at Drury Lane on May 2, 1935. Lavishly staged, it combined, as Peter Noble puts it, "the thrills of the old Drury Lane melodramas ... with a romantic operetta framework."[13] Novello had grown up on *The Merry Widow*, and other rich Edwardian fare, his bedroom decorated with pictures of Lily Elsie as Sonia. While his version of Ruritania is something new, it was also clearly a nostalgia project, an attempt to recapture the spell of the musical theater of his Edwardian youth on the capacious Drury Lane stage; the heroine, Militza, even borrows her name from another musical hit of that era, *The King of Cadonia*.[14] There would be scope for mittel-European royal pageantry, romance a-plenty, and affect-freighted arias; there would, in short, be glamour, something that Depression-era audiences expected on a night out.

Novello's version of Ruritania is Krasnia, which is ruled by the weak King Stefan (Barry Jones) and his more formidable prima donna lover, Militza Hajos (Ellis), who is of Gypsy origin. However, before we ever get to Krasnia we meet our English hero, Anthony Allen (Novello himself in a non-singing role), the son of an electrician, who has invented "a system of television which can bring any desired scene before the eyes of the public."[15] Offered £500 and two months leave by his employer, Lord Radio (Clifford Heatherley), to develop his new device—or possibly to suppress it,[16] Allen heads for Krasnia, where in the best Ruritanian fashion he becomes embroiled in national affairs. The prime minister, Baron Lydyeff (Lyn Harding), a regular Drury Lane villain, is anxious to seize power for himself and plotting against King Stefan. He first plans to get rid of Militza, in whom he recognizes the power behind the throne. Militza, meanwhile, is rehearsing an old-fashioned operetta, also called *Glamorous Night*, in which a king spends a night with a shepherdess only to discover that she is really the princess that he is engaged to marry. Allen saves Militza from being assassinated outside the opera house and is handsomely rewarded by the King. In a happy coincidence Militza and Allen end up taking a voyage aboard the same ship, and after he saves her from another attempt on her life, they fall in love. Lydyeff's men blow up the ship, but Militza and Allen survive, and ashore they go through a sort of Gypsy betrothal ceremony. However, Militza realizes that she also has a duty to her king and country, and she rallies her people to help the King, who has fallen into Lydyeff's clutches. In (another) climactic scene, Allen shoots Lydyeff as he threatens to kill the King. After he has been saved, King Stefan will only reign with Militza at his side, and the lovers must part, despite their Gypsy vows. The King rewards Allen for his services with financial backing for his invention, and he returns home to London to perfect the technology in the Actual Vision studio. Sore of heart, he watches his first broadcast, which shows the wedding of the King and Militza.

Part of Novello's charm for his contemporaries was that he revitalized formulae with which they were already more than familiar. This plot-heavy production featured a large cast and show-stopping, spectacular scenes, including the operetta within the operetta, the attempted assassination at the Krasnian opera house, the dramatic sinking of the *Silver Star* and the Gypsy wedding. In terms of *mise en scène* and characterization, Novello plays around quite self-consciously with the Ruritanian formulas he has inherited. The action opens on an ordinary suburban London street, complete with a Wall's Ice Cream tricycle, and our hero is a suburban man. As Joyce democratizes epic in *Ulysses* (1922), Novello replaces the aristocratic ethos of operetta with something more quotidian.

FIGURE 2.1 *Anthony Allen and his parents, Act 1.* Play Pictorial 66, *no. 398 (1935).*

FIGURE 2.2 *Anthony and Militza aboard the* Silver Star, *Act 1.* Play Pictorial 66, no. 398 (1935).

**FIGURE 2.3** *The Gypsy Betrothal Ceremony*, Act 2. Play Pictorial 66, no. 398 (1935).

**FIGURE 2.4** *Anthony and Militza at the Betrothal Ceremony*, Act 2. Play Pictorial 66, no. 398 (1935).

The next scene takes us to the modernist interior of Lord Radio's office in Superhet House, before we are finally whisked off to a more recognizable Ruritania for most of the rest of the action.[17] But even there surprises abound—sinking ships are not part of the usual Ruritanian menu, most such territories being landlocked; this is, one presumes, Novello's little joke. The scene at the end recalls the renunciation at the end of Anthony Hope's novel, returning us to the hero's everyday world, in which he contemplates what might have been. But this too is updated: we see distant Krasnia through Allen's television invention, a genuine stage innovation, presumably accomplished using a projector and scrim.[18]

How do we read Novello's *Glamorous Night* as popular modernism? While it hardly belongs to a politically-engaged "intermodernism," despite its evident escapism it is a piece that processes the social and political transformations of the interwar years.[19] Allen, as we have seen, is a democratized Ruritanian hero, a suburban man with technical training, not the aristo-military hero of an earlier era. The Ruritanian setting, Krasnia, is also tweaked in interesting ways. In many ways it is a typically heterochronous Ruritanian land in which uniforms are dazzling, passions run high, the peasants are fickle, and political scheming is rife. With its court scenes, and the operetta within an operetta, Novello was giving audiences "glamour," one of the "words of power" of the period, as W. Macqueen-Pope points out.[20] But Novello was in his way a painter of modern life, and through the King and Militza he was presenting audiences with a version, however anamorphic, of contemporary European politics, including its political violence.

The plot of his extravaganza derives from stories of the "playboy King," Carol II of Romania (1893–1953) and his lover, Elena, or Helena, Lupescu (1895–1977), known in the press of the time as Magda Lupescu.[21] Son of the internationally popular Queen Marie, and a great-grandson of Queen Victoria, Carol was colorful enough to elicit a biography by romance writer Barbara Cartland, *The Scandalous Life of King Carol* (1957).[22] When they met, before his marriage to Princess Helen of Denmark and Greece, Elena Lupescu was Elena Tampeanu, the Titian-haired wife of a Romanian army officer, but by 1925 she was divorced; she became Carol's public consort, and the source of much media interest, as well as of hostility among Romania's ruling families.[23] That Lupescu's father had been Jewish made her an easy target in a country in which anti-Semitism was rife. Outmaneuvered, and in the face of a media storm, Carol was forced from his position as Crown Prince, and lived in exile as Mr. Carol Caraiman in France with Lupescu; he divorced Princess Helen in 1928. By this point Carol and Lupescu were media figures, pursued by international reporters, and usually depicted as living a life of hedonism.[24] But in 1930, three years after the death of King Ferdinand, he flew back to Romania from Munich, and returned to power, replacing his own young son, Mihai (1921–), on the throne to become King Carol II.[25] Skywriting planes wrote "Carol" over Bucharest.[26] In the early years the playboy king, who had been quietly joined by Lupescu, was acclaimed as something of a modernizer, promoting education, youth movements (the *Straja Țării*), agricultural reform, and air links to the rest of the world, while retaining a taste for Ruritanian uniforms and royal pageantry.[27]

Importantly, there was nothing very operetta-like about Romania in these years. The country's traditional alignment with France was increasingly undermined as Germany extended its sphere of influence in the region, Romanian oil and grain making it a very desirable satellite. This became clearer in the years after *Glamorous Night*: by 1938 Carol was in effect a royal dictator, presiding over anti-Semitic policies while also violently suppressing the Iron Guard, the main fascist opposition. But the Guard, backed by Hitler, were not so easily suppressed. By 1940, orchestrated mobs were besieging the Royal Palace, shouting "Death to Lupescu" and "Death to the Jewess."[28] Carol and Elena fled Romania in September of that year, bringing with them three poodles, two Pekingese, and Carol's stamp collection—as well as, presumably, a considerable quantity of money.[29] For a period, at least, Carol plotted another return to Romania, but he died in Estoril, Portugal in 1953 and was buried in the Church of St. Vincent in Lisbon; Elena lived on until 1977.

In *Glamorous Night*, then, we see an artfully refracted version of Romania in the early 1930s. King Stefan and Militza are, like King Carol and Elena Lupescu, on the cusp between a traditional world in which the prestige of royalty was more or less taken for granted, and one in which the crown has to contend with democratic and fascistic forces. Lydyeff, with his black military uniform, is some kind of proto-fascist, perhaps based on the Iron Guard leader, Codreanu. Here, however, the exotic Militza, rather than being a target for anti-Semitic fascist hostility, like Elena Lupescu, is the conduit between King Stefan and the people, and she forsakes her own true love to stand by him.

It is worth bearing in mind, of course, that the play may also be modeling events a little closer to home. Among those who came to see the glittering but unhappy land of Krasnia was one of King Carol's distant cousins, King George, who attended with Queen Mary, a reminder that as with other versions of the Ruritanian formula, Krasnia is at once an exotic land, a location for exciting adventures, and a refracted image of England itself. Soon England would have its own Militza in the form of Wallis Simpson. *Glamorous Night* had just prematurely finished its long run when King George died; Edward VIII was crowned on January 20, 1936. He would abdicate that December when it became apparent that the political establishment would not tolerate the twice-divorced American as his consort. This may be pure happenstance, but it is also quite likely that Ivor, with his wide circle of well-connected friends, had some inkling of Prince Edward's relationship with Simpson, which had begun in 1934.

Molding the stuff of the newspapers, Pathé newsreels, and elite gossip into its plot, Novello's operetta also absorbs the modern at the level of form. In visual terms, for example, Lord Radio's office at "Superhet House" was presented, according to the *Daily Mail* review, as a piece of pure Futurism. And in keeping with the uneven modernity of its settings, *Glamorous Night* is musically eclectic, drawing on the present as well as the past.[30] As Traubner notes, the device of the operetta within a more contemporary musical play allowed him to "have his Schmaltz-covered cake and eat it too"—the more sentimental operetta numbers could be cordoned off, and enjoyed by the audience at one remove.[31] After something old, we get something blue: the song that follows soon after is "Far Away in Shanty Town," sung by African-American singer Elisabeth Welch, who plays a "stowaway," Cleo Wellington, aboard the *Silver Star*. "Far away in Shanty Town" owes little to operetta, and is much closer to the modern, blues-influenced "folk," musical of *Show Boat* (1927). Novello is here attempting to absorb the very popular vernacular influences that had overtaken Edwardian operetta and would in the end consign his own work to the musical attic.

Bringing together the operetta's historical content and its formal side is Anthony Allen's television invention. At one level *Glamorous Night* is presciently exploring a new broadcast technology that would eventually transform popular entertainment, remediating—or cannibalizing—older cultural forms as it developed. (Television broadcasting did not begin in Britain until the following year, but Logie Baird had been demonstrating his new technology since 1926, and by 1930 he was able to screen large-scale images in a London cinema.) Incorporating television into the play's plot, as well as making it the closing spectacle, Novello was tapping into popular interest in the new medium; consciously or not, he was also greeting the entertainment technology that would radically reshape popular audiences. But the content of the television broadcast that closes *Glamorous Night* is also worth considering. The royal wedding that Allen magically broadcasts is both a reminder of the lingering power of aristocratic pageantry and a shrewd recognition that the nature of royalty would change in an increasingly media-saturated age. Royal events had been captured on the screen as early as Victoria's reign, and Pathé newsreels fed cinema audiences a steady diet of royal material in the 1930s, including the arrival of King Carol in Bucharest in 1930. But the invention of radio and television would change things significantly. King George V's radio-broadcast 1932 Christmas message inaugurated a new intimacy between Britain's rulers and the nation, allowing their voices to resonate through individual homes. A device that could bring royal pageantry directly into the living room would be powerful indeed. Of course, as King Carol had discovered, a media-saturated age also meant that royalty were under scrutiny as never before, and retaining the public's favor meant to some extent pandering to that media scrutiny—being a "playboy King," had become a tricky business.

A final aspect of the popular modernism of *Glamorous Night* is its knowingness. The more general political context of Europe in the 1930s, which was making Ruritanian escapism harder to imagine, is both acknowledged and dismissed in the opening Guards' chorus:

> We hear in Krasnia
> Of war-like song and dance
> Up in Berlin:
> But for us
> There's never need to fuss,
> There's not the slightest chance
> Of joining in![32]

The audience is reassured by such self-reflexivity that whatever might happen in their on-stage Ruritania, it will not involve any commentary on real politics. As we have seen, of course, this is somewhat disingenuous, given the resemblance of King Stefan and Militza to Carol and Elena. The same generic self-awareness carries over into the dialogue, as in this exchange between Militza and Anthony Allen:

> **Anthony:** Aren't these things [sc. assassination attempts] always happening in this little musical comedy country?
> **Militza:** Musical comedy? Aren't you being rather insolent?
> **Anthony:** I don't mean to be. But it is, let's face it. Pure musical comedy, and as such completely out of date.[33]

Ivor was happy to acknowledge his own belatedness, and even, with a nod and a wink to the audience, make a virtue of it.

A film version of *Glamorous Night* appeared in 1937, though by then Ruritanian and Vienna-waltz films were out of fashion, not least because mittel-Europe's place in the political imaginary was rapidly changing.[34] Directed by Brian Desmond Hurst, it featured Otto Kruger as the King, Victor Jory as the Prime Minister, Barry Mackay as Anthony Allan (*sic*), and Mary Ellis in a reprise of her leading role as Melitza (*sic*) with the veteran Maire O'Neill (Molly Allgood, one-time fiancée of John Millington Synge) playing her servant, Phoebe. The action of the stage play is changed around considerably, and the rising tensions of the 1930s, including the pre-war struggle to control oil resources, feed more obviously into Krasnia: the gypsies live on a potential oilfield ("Oil means war," notes Melitza) and Prime Minister Lyadeff (*sic*) is explicitly presented as the leader of a black-shirt fascist group. Once again royal families closer to home are evoked.

*Variety* noted that the recent abdication gave it a certain "timeliness": when it appeared at Drury Lane "it bore a resemblance to the story of King Carol of Rumania and Mme Lupescu, but present-day audiences will conjure up the later romance."[35] The film also shares the operetta's awareness of the power of new media combined with old prestige: in a key scene King Stefan makes a radio broadcast to his people, urging them to stand up to the fascist Lyadeff.

One might have assumed that the war would finally quench the appetite for Ruritanian fare on stage, but in 1949 Novello returned to the formula in *King's Rhapsody* (Palace Theatre, September 15, 1949), another piece that seems to echo the life of the Duke of Windsor as well as that of Carol of Romania.[36] This time our protagonist is Nikki (Novello), the exiled heir to the Muranian throne, who is supposed to have given up all claim to it because of his love for an actress, Marta Karillos (Phyllis Dare). *King's Rhapsody* was a major success, running for 841 performances, and outliving Novello himself. It was clearly seen by the critics as Britain's answer to the increasing hegemony of the American musical: Ivor Brown in the *Observer* opined that Novello "can with his tranquility stand up to all the bounding Oklahomans and Brigadooners in the world," while Harold Hobson in the *Sunday Times* viewed it as "a better musical than *South Pacific*" (Noble 259–60).[37] In his final musical, *Gay's the Word* (Palace Theatre, Manchester, October 17, 1950), Novello offers his last respects to Ruritanian operetta by making Ruritania the title of a flop show, his trademark operetta within an operetta. He died on March 6, 1951, mourned by enormous crowds of fans—his funeral was even covered by Pathé news.

Ivor's particular brand of Ruritanian whimsy and escapism seems to have held its power only while he was on stage himself to bring it to life: the film versions of *Glamorous Night* (1937) and *King's Rhapsody* (1955) failed to please, even though the latter deployed the lingering star power of Errol Flynn. *Glamorous Night* was last revived briefly in 1975, and *King's Rhapsody* in 1988; neither resembled the big-budget originals, and neither was a success. I have attempted here to give some sense of the political and technological shifts that Novello absorbed into his old-fashioned Ruritania. But I do not wish to downplay the extent to which his operettas were also out of time, vehicles for utopian longings. In a late interview Novello claimed that he would like to write a realistic play, but found he could not: "Prewar is forgotten, the war years are too miserable, the present is so dreary. Escape lies in imagination and romance."[38] But the same could be said of *Glamorous Night* in the 1930s: his Ruritania was always clearly a more technicolor heterotopia of Britain itself. However saturated it was in the social and political changes of its time, his work also offered a glimpse of something better, a brighter and more melodic reality. It is doubtful that Russolo or Adorno would have approved of his frothy musical cocktail of the traditional and the modern, but Novello was in his way as attuned to the spirit of the times as Weill, and the seismic historical changes of the period register at the level of form as well as content in his work. Most importantly, perhaps, as John Raymond, noted in the *Daily Graphic* in 1949 "he made the people sing."[39]

## Notes

1 Luigi Russolo, "The Art of Noises" (1913; reprinted in *The Art of Noise: Destruction of Music by Futurist Machines*, Sun Vision Press, 2012), 58.
2 Theodor Wiesengrund Adorno, "The Threepenny Opera," in *Kurt Weill, The Threepenny Opera*, ed. and trans. Stephen Hinton (Cambridge: Cambridge University Press, 1990), 131.
3 For a detailed account, see Traubner, *Operetta: A Theatrical History* (London: Victor Gollancz, 1983).
4 Traubner, *Operetta*, 20. Hervé was born Louis-Auguste-Florimond Ronger. For more on early operetta in Paris see James Harding, *Folies de Paris: The Rise and Fall of French Operetta* (London: Chapell/Elm Tree Books, 1979).
5 Quoted in Graeme Gilloch, "The Word on the Street: Charles Baudelaire, Jacques Offenbach, and the Paris of their Time," in *Manifestoes and Transformations in the Early Modernist City*, ed. Christian Hermansen Cordua (Farnham: Ashgate, 2010), 68.
6 See, for instance, William A. Everett and Paul R. Laird, eds., *The Cambridge Companion to the Musical* (Cambridge: Cambridge University Press, 2002).
7 In its original production as *Die lustige Witwe* (Vienna 1905, with scenario and lyrics by Leo Stein and Victor Leon), Pontevedro is the name of the fictional territory, one of a number of hints that Montenegro is its model. The first English adaptation was by Edward Morton, with lyrics by Adrian Ross, though Basil Hood was later brought in to make further changes.
8 William A. Everett, *Sigmund Romberg* (New Haven and London: Yale University Press, 2007), 151.
9 See Barry Keith Grant, *The Hollywood Musical* (Oxford: Wiley-Blackwell, 2012), 14.
10 The stage name was borrowed from his mother's middle name, which was in turn taken from the soprano Clara Novello. For further reading on Novello's life and work, see W. Macqueen-Pope, *Ivor: Story of an Achievement* (London: W. H. Allen, 1951); Peter Noble, *Ivor Novello, Man of the Theatre, with a foreword by Noël Coward* (1951; repr., London: White Lion, 1975); and James Harding, *Ivor Novello: A Biography* (1987; repr., Cardiff: Welsh Academic Press, 1997). For production photographs from *Glamorous Night*, see David Slattery-Christy's *In Search of Ruritania* (Milton Keynes: AuthorHouse, 2008).

11  In this light his playful work, which delights in artifice, seems a good candidate for analysis in terms of the "middlebrow camp" that Nicola Humble describes in "The Queer Pleasures of Reading: Camp and the Middlebrow." See Erica Brown and Mary Grover, eds., *Middlebrow Literary Cultures: The Battle of the Brows, 1920–1960* (Houndmills: Palgrave, 2012), 218–30.

12  Noble, *Ivor Novello*, 154.

13  Ibid., 199.

14  Harding, *Ivor Novello*, 37.

15  "Glamorous Night," *Play Pictorial* 66, no. 398 (1935): 3–9. The article provides a lavishly-illustrated summary.

16  This aspect of the plot seems to have confused reviewers: some accounts describe Lord Radio as having bought off Allen and his invention.

17  Maurice Willson Disher's review in the *Daily Mail* describes Lord Radio's office as "a futurist setting." Cited in Noble, *Ivor Novello*, 203. The superheterodyne, or "superhet," was a type of radio receiver, an improvement on the heterodyne.

18  For additional photographs of the original sets, see *Glamorous Night: A Romantic Play With Music by Ivor Novello, Lyrics by Christopher Hassall, Amateur Version Prepared by Sydney Box and Conrad C. Carter, Under the Supervision of the Author* (London: Samuel French, 1939).

19  For more on "intermodernism," see Kristin Bluemel, ed., *Intermodernism: Literary Culture in Mid-Twentieth-Century Britain* (Edinburgh: Edinburgh University Press, 2009).

20  Macqueen-Pope, *Ivor*, 315.

21  A. L. Easterman claims that the name Magda was coined by the Italian press, who assumed that Elena was short for Magdalena. See his *King Carol, Hitler, and Lupescu* (London: Victor Gollancz, 1942), 75.

22  Barbara Cartland, *The Scandalous Life of King Carol* (London: Muller, 1957). For contemporary views, see Hector Bolitho, *Roumania Under King Carol* (London: Eyre and Spottiswoode, 1939) and Easterman, *King Carol*. An authorized biography by the Baroness Helena van der Hoven, *King Carol of Romania*, appeared in 1940; Madame Lupescu is barely mentioned. For a recent account, see Maria Bucur, "King Carol II of Romania," in *Balkan Strongmen: Dictators and Authoritarian Rulers of Southeast Europe*, ed. Bernd Fischer (London: Hurst and Company, 2007), 87–117.

23  Easterman suggests that the British press in this period uncritically reprinted tales circulated by Carol's Romanian enemies about his "promiscuous philanderings, champagne bibbings [and] gambling orgies," *King Carol*, 43.

24  Easterman reproduces, for instance, an *Evening Standard* cartoon of King Carol, which shows the King torn between Helen and Lupescu.

25  In May 1928, the British press was full of reports that Carol was sequestered in Godstone, Surrey, planning a secret flight to Romania to recapture the

throne; eventually he was forced to leave Britain under police escort. Buchan's *Castle Gay* is loosely based on this episode.
26  "Carol's Crown," *Time*, June 16, 1930.
27  "Playboy into Statesman," *Time*, November 13, 1939. For a fictional—and enthusiastic—representation of Carol's *Straja Țării*, a sort of scouting movement, see John Buchan's *House of the Four Winds* (1935).
28  Easterman, *King Carol, Hitler, and Lupescu*, 12.
29  Richard Cavendish, "Death of Carol II of Romania," *History Today*, April 2003.
30  Cited in Noble, *Ivor Novello*, 204.
31  Traubner, *Operetta*, 349.
32  *Glamorous Night*, Act 1.1.
33  *Glamorous Night*, Act 2.1.
34  John Mundy, "Britain," in *The International Film Musical*, eds. Corey K. Creekmur and Linda Y. Mokdad (Edinburgh: Edinburgh University Press, 2012), 18.
35  "Film Reviews: *Glamorous Night*," *Variety*, May 19, 1937, 23. On its American prospects, see also the *Motion Picture Review Digest* entry for *Glamorous Night*, January–December, 1938, 37.
36  *King's Rhapsody: A Musical Romance, Devised, Written and Composed by Ivor Novello, Lyrics by Christopher Hassall* (London: Samuel French, 1955).
37  See Noble, *Ivor Novello*, 259–60.
38  Adrian Wright, *A Tanner's Worth of Tune: Rediscovering the Post-war British Musical* (Woodbridge, Suffolk: Boydell Press, 2010), 38.
39  John Raymond in *Daily Graphic*, September 25, 1949, cited in Noble, *Ivor Novello*, 13.

# Bibliography

Adorno, Theodor Wiesengrund. *The Threepenny Opera*. 1929. Reprinted in *Kurt Weill, The Threepenny Opera*, edited and translated by Stephen Hinton, 129–34. Cambridge: Cambridge University Press, 1990.
Bluemel, Kristin, ed. *Intermodernism: Literary Culture in Mid-Twentieth-Century Britain*. Edinburgh: Edinburgh University Press, 2009.
Bolitho, Hector. *Roumania Under King Carol*. London: Eyre and Spottiswoode, 1939.
Bucur, Maria. "King Carol II of Romania." In *Balkan Strongmen: Dictators and Authoritarian Rulers of Southeast Europe*, edited by Bernd Fischer, 87–117. London: Hurst and Co. 2007.
"Carol's Crown." *Time*, June 16, 1930.
Cartland, Barbara. *The Scandalous Life of King Carol*. London: Muller, 1957.
Cavendish, Richard. "Death of Carol II of Romania." *History Today*, April 2003.

Easterman, A. L. *King Carol, Hitler, and Lupescu*. London: Victor Gollancz, 1942.
Everett, William A. *Sigmund Romberg*. New Haven and London: Yale University Press, 2007.
Everett, William A. and Paul R. Laird, eds. *The Cambridge Companion to the Musical*. Cambridge: Cambridge University Press, 2002.
"Film Reviews: Glamorous Night." *Variety*, May 19, 1937, 23.
Gilloch, Graeme. "The Word on the Street: Charles Baudelaire, Jacques Offenbach, and the Paris of their Time." In *Manifestoes and Transformations in the Early Modernist City*, edited by Christian Hermansen Cordua, 59–76. Farnham: Ashgate, 2010.
"Glamorous Night." *Motion Picture Review Digest*, January–December, 1938, 37.
"Glamorous Night." *Play Pictorial* 66, no. 398 (1935): 3–9.
Grant, Barry Keith. *The Hollywood Musical*. Oxford: Wiley-Blackwell, 2012.
Harding, James. *Folies de Paris: The Rise and Fall of French Operetta*. London: Chapell/Elm Tree Books, 1979.
Harding, James. *Ivor Novello: A Biography*. 1987. Reprint, Cardiff: Welsh Academic Press, 1997.
Humble, Nicola. "The Queer Pleasures of Reading: Camp and the Middlebrow." In *Middlebrow Literary Cultures: The Battle of the Brows, 1920–1960*, edited by Erica Brown and Mary Grover, 218–30. Houndmills: Palgrave, 2012.
Macqueen-Pope, W. *Ivor: Story of an Achievement*. London: W. H. Allen, 1951.
Mundy, John. "Britain." In *The International Film Musical*, edited by Corey K. Creekmur and Linda Y. Mokdad, 1–28. Edinburgh: Edinburgh University Press, 2012.
Noble, Peter. *Ivor Novello, Man of the Theatre, With a Foreword by Noël Coward*. 1951. Reprint, London: White Lion, 1975.
Novello, Ivor. *King's Rhapsody: A Musical Romance, Devised, Written and Composed by Ivor Novello, Lyrics by Christopher Hassall*. London: Samuel French, 1955.
Novello, Ivor and Christopher Hassall. *Glamorous Night: A Romantic Play With Music by Ivor Novello, Lyrics by Christopher Hassall. Amateur Version Prepared by Sydney Box and Conrad C. Carter, Under the Supervision of the Author*. London: Samuel French, 1939.
"Playboy into Statesman," *Time*, November 13, 1939.
Russolo, Luigi. "The Art of Noises." 1913. Reprinted in *The Art of Noise: Destruction of Music by Futurist Machines*. Sun Vision Press, 2012.
Slattery-Christy, David. *In Search of Ruritania*. Milton Keynes: AuthorHouse, 2008.
Traubner, Richard. *Operetta: A Theatrical History*. London: Victor Gollancz, 1983.
Wright, Adrian. *A Tanner's Worth of Tune: Rediscovering the Post-war British Musical*. Woodbridge: Boydell Press, 2010.

# 3

# Fine art on the airwaves: Radio drama and modern(ist) mass culture

## Adam Nemmers

In a period rife with manifestos, *The Radia* stands alone for its quixotic confidence in the potential of technology. Authors F. T. Marinetti and Pino Masnata were veterans of the form, having previously composed the 1908 Futurist Manifesto, which called for the rejuvenation and modernization of Italy through danger, speed, and complex machinery. Their 1933 *Radia* was remarkable in its specific application of ideology to technology, as Marinetti and Masnata posit the nascent medium of the radio as central to the success of the Futurist movement and humankind. In the manifesto's preface they envision Futurists creating influential radio programs, simultaneously destined to "multiply a hundredfold the creative genius of the Italian race" as well as "abolish the old nostalgic rage of distances and ... impose everywhere words-in-freedom as its logical and natural mode of expression."[1] The authors termed their movement's medium not as the accustomed "radio," but instead the "radia," "a new art form particular to radio transmission" and distinct from theater ("because radio has killed the theater"); film ("because the filmmaker is already on his deathbed"); and print ("because the book bears the blame for having made humanity myopic").[2] According to the manifesto, the radia would be a radically transformational genre, abolishing "space or any required scenery," "time," "unity of action," and "the dramatic character," and offering, among other qualities, "freedom from any point of contact with literary and artistic traditions"; "an art without time or space without yesterday and tomorrow"; and "the characteristic life of every noise and an infinite variety of the concrete-and-abstract and the done-and-dreamed by means of a populace of noises."[3] In all, radia is proposed as the primary medium by which Futurists might overcome such obstacles as "patriotism," "chemistry," "war and revolution," "the machine," "the earth," and even "death."[4] Extended to its utmost power, the radia would catalyze a future in which radio users could transmit thoughts and vibrations at light-speed, solely by the power of their mind.

While Futurist visions of the radia were extreme, even considering the interwar ideological climate, their manifesto is indicative of modernists' fantastic belief in the power of radio to transform society, humanity, and the arts. According to theorist Douglas Kahn, such associations were shared among the avant-garde of the 1910s and 1920s, a generation for which radio was "coterminous with a range of mythological, theological, and literary instances where communication at a distance produced compensatory and exaggerated relationships among objects and bodies."[5] Because radio allowed people to listen to disembodied voices speaking from thousands of miles away, many believed that radio waves held limitless possibility: contact with alien life forms, communication with persons from the future and past, and transportation of color, image, taste, and odors. In his clairvoyant "The Radio of the Future," Russian Futurist Velimir Khlebnikov even foretold of "long-distance synesthetic healing without medicine and the transmission of an anthem of strength in production," explaining that "certain notes like 'la' and 'ti' are able to increase muscular capacity ... During periods of intense hard work like summer harvests or during the construction of great buildings, these sounds can be broadcast by Radio over the entire country, increasing its collective strength enormously."[6]

Nearly a century has passed since the popularization of the radio, and such prophesies seem absurd in retrospect, stymied by, as the Futurists termed it, "a realism albeit fleeting that is still to be overcome."[7] Yet the profound and lasting impact of radio as a modernist art form is just now attracting scholarly attention, as a number of recent books—*Radio Modernism* (2006), *Broadcasting Modernism* (2009), *Broadcasting in the Modernist Era* (2014), *Modernism at the Microphone* (2015)—stand to testify. Such titles have uniquely positioned radio at the intersection of mass culture and modernism, characterized by novelty, innovation, and ephemerality, capable of instantaneous broadcast communication to an audience both mass and individual. Moreover, as the only art form born and matured during the modernist period, radio drama is a genre *sui generis*. Unlike modernist works exhibited in literary periodicals and cosmopolitan art galleries, radio broadcasts were free, immediate, accessible, and widely available, all democratizing factors that allowed listeners an easy and simultaneous consumption, making it the most popular form of mass entertainment during the interwar period. At the same time, radio dramas relied upon methods endemic to "high" modernism, including polyvocal narration, stream of consciousness, and internal monologues, in addition to the innovative experimentation with time, perspective, and form that have become a hallmark of modernist study in other mediums. Because these dramas were performed live and over the air, directly consumed and rarely recorded, many remain aesthetic artifacts lost to time, a blend of high and low art and one of the few forms that can be truly classified as "popular modernism."

## "Science's gift to poetry and poetic drama"

The dawn of the Radio Age was as impactful as it was sudden. In *Radio Modernism*, Todd Avery reports that on the night of November 14, 1922, the "*annus mirabilis* of literary modernism, the character of human communication changed irrevocably in Britain" when "for the first time and in the comfort of their own home, anyone with a radio receiver that was switched on and properly tuned" could listen to a BBC broadcast from London's 2LO station.[8] Radio had a similarly spectacular emergence in the United States—KDKA's coverage of the Presidential election on November 4, 1920 is widely recognized as the nation's first scheduled radio broadcast[9]—and indeed proved popular around the world, where sundry cottage industries had exploded into mainstream consumption by the end of that year. The rapidity with which radio was adopted and popularized testified to the essential democracy and portability of the medium. Early broadcasts crossed national boundaries, and early practitioners could both transmit and receive communication from those at home and abroad. Thus from the beginning of popular adoption, radio was marked by experimentation and cosmopolitanism, functioning as a global network of independent broadcasters seeking connection with fellow humans, however remote or removed they might be.

"Wireless," as it was initially called, had begun as a method of point-to-point communication akin to the telegraph, with amateur operators transmitting on unassigned wavelengths. In the United States, the ad hoc system of American radio was a tangle of business interests, amateur broadcasts, and naval communications, unregulated until Congress passed the Radio Act of 1912, which appropriated the airwaves as public property, to be temporarily allocated to individuals or corporations through a licensing regime.[10] Radio use was further curtailed by the advent of the Great War, when Woodrow Wilson placed all private radio stations under the control of the navy, which "ordered amateurs to cease operations and to dismantle their sets, beginning a period of enforced silence that would last until September 1919."[11] The improvement of technology during the war years, coupled with the material prosperity of the nation following Armistice, catalyzed an explosion of broadcasting energy in the 1920s, inviting private investment into a form with seemingly limitless potential. In the UK, by contrast, the state-run British Broadcasting Corporation was not founded until after the war (October 18, 1920), and its small, local stations were centrally connected through telephone link to London. As opposed to the nakedly commercial American model, British public broadcasting was funded not by advertisements, but instead by listeners' purchase of a compulsory radio license, an edict that lasted until 1971.

Radio programming initially featured news reports and sporting events, consigned to relay the same information that had once been delivered via telegraph. Broadcasting music was a simple and natural addition, as programming required only placing a microphone near a live orchestra or band. In short order, broadcasters realized radio was a more expansive medium that could be used to deliver original programming to audiences at home. Historians of the radio drama consider Eugene Walter's *The Wolf*, adapted from the stage and broadcast on WGY in August 1922, as the first "on air" drama;[12] the first play written for radio was *A Comedy of Danger* by Richard Hughes, which was transmitted in the UK on January 15, 1924.[13] Radio made steady gains in popularity throughout the interwar period, peaking in the late 1930s, when by one reckoning, American radio put five million shows on the air.[14] These were usually half-hour or hour-long programs broadcast according to a weekly schedule and sponsored by various products and corporations. After the Second World War radio entered a period of gradual decline corresponding with the advent of television, culminating on November 25, 1960—"the day radio drama died"—when the major American networks ceased their broadcast of prime time programming.[15] In all, radio drama enjoyed a twenty-five-year prime amidst its nearly forty-year life span, during which it was the predominant form of mass media entertainment.

The first radio dramas were little more than stage plays adapted and read aloud, without elaboration or sound effect. As radio was considered a "blind" medium, many producers employed a metaphorical darkness to level the experience of players and listeners—for instance, the balcony scene from *Cyrano* was broadcast in semi-darkness with virtually stationary players as a BBC experiment in 1922. Even those dramas written specifically for radio used the fiction of darkness to "blind" players and place the audience on equal sensory footing. The aforementioned *Comedy of Danger*, for example, is set in a Welsh coal mine; its opening exchange of dialogue features an unexpected power outage, ushering in a darkness that lasts for the duration of the play. As Richard Hand and Mary Traynor explain in their *Radio Drama Handbook*, by utilizing this and similar constraints, early radio writers "relegated the visual dimension—the most pre-eminently important aspect in the theatre and the cinema—into ...

irrelevancy,"[16] conveying strictly the listening experience of a blind person attending a stage play.

Radio drama quickly evolved, however, both in technique and complexity. In particular, the use of sound effects and acoustic techniques enabled programs to render a fuller auditory experience that mimicked narrative devices used by other forms, from scenery to atmosphere, distance to chronology. The innovative *Mercury Theater*, according to Neil Verma, introduced a "code of amplitude in which direct present-tense narration [was] denuded of effects and miked more closely than past-tense sound," coloring the present as a "state in which sound reveals nothing about location, while the past is a dynamic state in which sound is replete with detailed information."[17] Background audio—sounds of the harbor, receding footsteps, and woodland ambiance—functioned as shorthand "establishing shots" akin to those used by film, while the use of volume could establish perspective: louder noises were nearer and those fainter more distant. To this end critic W. J. T. Mitchell has suggested that sound effects "are a form of ekphrasis, 'verbalizing' an unavailable picture without using words, but relying instead on properties of iconicity, metonymy and 'customary contiguity.'"[18]

The most ambitious radio dramas, such as *The Columbia Workshop*'s 1937 "The Fall of the City," combined sound effects, technical acumen, and advanced dramatic technique to deliver vibrant and original programing— in this case a trenchant allegory on the rise of fascism. Epic in scale and complexity, the drama featured an all-star cast (including the young Orson Welles) and 200 extras, broadcast live from the drill hall of the Seventh Regiment Armory in New York. An unsigned contemporary review in *Time* noted, "Aside from the beauty of its speech and the power of its story, 'The Fall of the City' proved to most listeners that the radio, which conveys only sound, is science's gift to poetry and poetic drama, that 30 minutes is an ideal time for a verse play, that artistically radio is ready to come of age, for in the hands of a master a $10 receiving set can become a living theatre, its loudspeaker a national proscenium."[19] Scarcely fifteen years after its commercial debut, radio had come of age, a "living theatre" and "science's gift to poetry and poetic drama."

## "Part and parcel of his way of life"

Radio drama was inherently broadcast to a dual audience: both group and individual, public and private. Because radio waves cut through doors and windows and walls, the reach of programming was unparalleled. Listeners could tune in individually, eavesdrop upon others' sets, or gravitate to stores, squares, and public parks where a radio might be playing. Radio accordingly inducted a radical shift in the notion of the public, producing a new body of consumers characterized by Gillian Beer as "more intermixed, promiscuous, and democratic than the book could cater for."[20] The oral nature of the medium flattened access to news and knowledge as well, revolutionizing "dynamics of mass media," which had previously been predicated upon print culture, and becoming "the first medium to provide information to people who were non-literate."[21] The democratization of access across geography and class created a new kind of mass audience, connecting disparate citizens into a contiguous public. As Hand and Traynor explain, the advent of radio meant "isolated communities could at last be 'in the loop'; news of current affairs and other events could be spread instantaneously; thousands of miles and disparate voices could be connected in an instant."[22] The immediacy of radio broadcasting additionally lent the listener a sense of inclusion, of participation in the same act at the same moment, the sense that "everything had the potential to be 'dramatic' not just the obviously dramatic genres."[23] This palpable sense of dramatic immediacy surely contributed to moments such as the 1939 "War of the Worlds" hoax/fiasco, in which the fictional report of alien invasion induced mass pandemonium across the United States.

Even in purportedly "private" homes, radio-listening, unlike the reading of novels, newspapers, and magazines, was an inherently communal activity. As Ray Barfield explains, "the location of domestic radios was typically 'averaged out' ... sometimes the radio was located at the bottom of a staircase or near a heating vent so that its sounds would carry through several rooms, perhaps the entire house."[24] Such central placement allowed an entire household of individuals to listen together, even while apart. At the same time, like a book or magazine a radio drama could be consumed by oneself, and indeed, for many listeners the radio set became a constant companion. As late as 1951, David R. Mackey reported in *Drama on the Air* that "the average person in America spends more time each day listening to the radio than on any other activities except sleeping and working. To him a radio is not merely an instrument of culture, a method of receiving news, a source of pleasure or gratification, a provider of entertainment. Radio to him is part and parcel of his way of life."[25] Thus radio listeners engaged in both active and passive listening, with "culture," "news," "pleasure," and "gratification" becoming a backdrop for citizens' everyday lives.

At the individual level, radio drama relied upon the listener's imagination to craft a distinct and dramatic experience. Extensively marketed as the "Theater of the Mind"—a performance occurring in the brain-space of each listener—radio programs sought to provide a skeletal narrative structure while leaving room for listeners to "fill in the gaps." Indeed, during the height of radio's Golden Age, psychology professor T. H. Pear concluded that listening to the radio was "a process of thinking," and therefore "an individual as opposed to group activity."[26] As an active, individual act of thinking and processing, radio-listening is a uniquely provocative and interactive medium; even among a large group of listeners, the nature of radio broadcast creates an audience of one. *The Radio Drama Handbook*, a guide for aspiring radio dramatists, advises that "it is the act of listening which creates the drama. The writer and the production team provide stimuli, but the conversion of that information into drama is entirely dependent on the imagination of the listener."[27] Though the radio program may provide the stimulus, it is the listener's imagination that provides the response.

Thus, while broadcast via an immensely popular and public medium, radio drama was (and is) an intimate and individual genre, through which meaning was created dialectically between the program and audience. Its lack of transmitted imagery, ostensibly a weakness rendering it "blind," was instead a benefit, allowing the radio broadcast to "infiltrate the mind, to unleash the most powerful dramatic weapon of all: the imagination of the listener."[28] Listening to a radio drama was an experience akin to reading a novel—if there were millions of others reading the same page at the same moment. As Marinetti and Masnata realized when composing *The Radia*, this immense collective power could be harnessed both for entertainment and for political purposes, a strategy that Benito Mussolini, Adolf Hitler, and Franklin Delano Roosevelt each employed during the 1920s and 1930s. Given radio's ability to reach mass audiences at the individual level, "it is no accident," as Philip Cannistraro observes, "that the birth of the totalitarian state coincided with the appearances of modern techniques of mass communications."[29] Thus the many-tentacled medium of radio reached popular audiences home and abroad, delivering information, entertainment, and propaganda in real time while also making way for the development of radio-specific art forms.

# The art of radio

It is no accident, either, that the rise of the wireless dovetailed with the emergence of modernist writing, a synchronic development that *Broadcasting Modernism* argues is "significantly intertwined."[30] Though radio drama was a massively popular form of mass entertainment during the interwar period, it was also, as indicated by this chapter title, a form of fine art broadcast on the airwaves. More specifically, radio drama was a modernist art genre, born in and of the modernist period, and promulgated not only by avant-gardes like the Futurists, but also by "mainstream" modernists such as Gertrude Stein, Ezra Pound, Virginia Woolf, and Berthold Brecht. The impact of radio drama, which extended modernism vertically within the usual aesthetic-class structure, as well as horizontally across nations and continents, was recognized even by conservative types like E. B. White, who in a 1938 column for the *New Yorker* asserted that "radio has immensely accelerated culture in that it has brought to millions of people, in torrential measure, the distant and often adulterated sounds of art and life."[31] To append the study of radio drama to that of literature, cinema, and the visual arts is to further reassess the traditional conception of modernism—especially "high" modernism—which is usually drawn in opposition to the notion of mass culture and reserved for the erudite and elite: subscribers to "little" magazines and literary salons; cosmopolitan aesthetes in metropoles such as Paris, London, and New York; and those with the wealth, access, and acumen to consume "difficult" cinema, literature, and art. In contrast, radio drama was free and widely available to anyone with a set and an ear to listen, and even those who could not read well or at all could hear and understand radio drama programming.

It was through radio, not literature or art, that most persons were exposed to the precepts of modernism—though they may not have recognized characteristics of the abstract and abstruse movement as such. In addition, because radio drama had no set history or genre conventions, and because it required little capital to produce a broadcast, the form was ripe for experimentation, inviting innovative practitioners of the form to take to the airwaves without barriers or boundaries. As Masnata explained in an unpublished gloss to *The Radia*:

> We writers for radio, not beholden to a visual scene, are instead free of the oppressive nightmare of always situating the actors in the same place. We are pleased that the scene can change with every cue; it can be external, internal, real, unreal, points in space, small, large, universal ... Scenic space will reach its maximum expansion with radia; the infinite (to use the word in its true sense) scene will open out to a listening audience of infinite dimensions.[32]

Masnata's conception of the "infinite" is an appropriate metaphor, for radio waves literally expanded, in all directions, into infinite space (even now, SETI intercepts and transmits radio waves in an attempt to communicate with those from other worlds). Freed from technical considerations and the tyranny of the "visual scene," radio drama could venture anywhere within the human imagination. Thus, while radio drama straddles the dichotomy of public/private spheres, the genre was simultaneously of the masses and of modernism. As Avery argues, "To read modernism through the lens offered by radio—in other words, to see, or hear, modernism as in significant part a radio phenomenon—is to gesture toward a reconceptualization of modernism itself in relation to the masses and mass culture."[33] Radio, as a form inherently popular and "modernist," eliminated the "reified disjunction" between the two, demonstrating that modernism could be fully popular, and that a work of art might appeal to both the masses and elite.

One of the primary modernist methods employed by radio drama is the use of polyvocal and non-linear narrative. The default voice in radio is the all-encompassing and authoritative narrator, and simple radio programs often featured small casts with repeated use of names as personal markers. Yet more complex pieces disobeyed or subverted these conventions, introducing a number of players with interrelated or overlapping perspectives: episodes such as Morse's "Tropics Don't Call It Murder" routinely used seven voices; "The Thing That Cries in the Night" occasionally had eight; and "The Pirate Loot of Skull Island" could feature up to thirteen speaking characters. The properties of sound transmission, moreover, allowed radio to transcend the necessarily univocal qualities of print, which must relay events sequentially, no matter how transposed or immediate. On the radio several voices (and sounds) could occur simultaneously, and not just in concept, as they did on the page. Other radio dramas used the skeleton of the authoritative news report to open up the form, capitalizing on listeners' credulity to play with conceptions of authority and reality. The German radio dramatist Frederich Wolf, for instance, used the dramatic device of the messenger in his *SoS Rao-Rao-Foyn* (1928) to "imitate a live broadcast of a rescue attempt by the crew of the Krassin."[34] A similar feature was used to devastating effect in the infamous "War of the Worlds" broadcast (1939), which mimicked the conventions of radio newscasting in reporting the invasion of a Martian army. As literature and art utilized fragmentation, collage, and bricolage to produce a multifarious sensation, so too could radio drama render voice-over, dialogue, and sound effects simultaneously, achieving a polyvocal narration that both represented reality and destabilized notions of authority and truth.

When radio drama featured a single narrator or protagonist, it often did so using modernist techniques of stream of consciousness and interior monologue to provide a more introspective representation of reality. Radio, as an aural medium without accompanying images, was able to proximate the current of human thinking, allowing individual listeners to attend closely to the mind-space of radio characters. The American dramatist Wyllis Cooper popularized such a technique in his horror program *Lights Out* (1934–47), most notably in the 1935 episode "After Five O'clock," which follows a businessman's thoughts as he cheats on his wife during a day at the office. Prominent examples of extensive interiorization include *Skyscraper* (1931), which transmits the final thoughts and memories of a man falling to his death, and even later, postmodern plays such as Samuel Beckett's *Cascando* (1961), which according to R. J. Gray centered on a character who "opened and closed the never-ending stream of words of the other characters on the one hand, and on the other, produced an unending spring of individual musical phrases and motifs composed in a 'stream of consciousness' style."[35] Paradoxically benefitting from its exclusion of other senses, the "blind" medium of radio could replicate the aural quality of the human mind, achieving a natural stream of consciousness painstakingly fashioned by artists in other forms.

Beyond the modernist practices adopted across artistic mediums, radio drama often employed experimental techniques endemic to the audio genre itself. Radio, unlike any form before it, was broadcast live and at regular intervals, and therefore well-suited for collaborative and dialectic audience participation. As Donald McWhinnie observes in *The Art of Radio*, when listening to radio each listener is obligated to "translate the sound-pattern he hears into his own mental language; he must apply his imagination to it and transform it," a "collaboration which makes radio drama special; we are part of the creative act, rather than party to it."[36] An illustrative example of radio collaboration is Bertolt Brecht's 1929 radio play, *The Flight Across the Ocean*, which relies upon the intervention of listeners to chronicle Charles Lindbergh's famous transatlantic feat. As Mark E. Cory reports in "Soundplay: The Polyphonous Tradition of German Radio Art," Brecht envisioned his play as a collective work of art, structuring the action in two parts, whereby "the listeners would collectively play the part of Lindbergh and the radio would fill in the dialogue and noises of meteorological characters such as the fog and the snowstorm. The radio would also play the parts of a variety of antagonists, including Lindbergh's environmental enemy, the sea, and his human enemy, sleep."[37] Rather than spoken by a voice actor, Lindbergh's part was supplied by listeners' "collective-I-singing ('the collective singing of notes and reading out loud of the text')," performed en masse and at home, aligning the play's formal qualities with the content Brecht wished to convey.[38] While not a true two-way communication system, such prompted participation invited the audience to act as chorus for broadcasts, situating each listener at the individual, group, and community levels, further indicating the interactive possibilities of the form.

Perhaps the most innovative early dramatist was Hans Flesch, founder of the *Berlin Radio Hour* and director of "Magic on the Air: Attempt at a Radio Grotesque" (1924), widely credited as the first German radio play. Flesch's highly inventive piece features a mélange of characters—the announcer, the fairy tale lady, a bandleader, artistic director, violinist, and "strong voice," as well as the titular magician—all of whom vie for control of the airwaves. At the same time, the human action is interrupted by a variety of instruments, objects, sounds, and effects: a violin, piano, telephone, and typewriter; a song called "Silence"; shattered glass, a kettlebell, and a siren. "Magic" is characterized by malfunction and personification: errant reception, mechanical breakdown, a stubborn microphone and animated player piano, with the Artistic Director struggling to enforce order amidst the maelstrom.[39] The protracted contest over the broadcast can be seen as sublimation of radio medium binaries such as sound/voice, order/chaos, and art/magic, with the station's director occupying a liminal position in between. On another level, Lecia Rosenthal argues, "such tensions are a kind of modernist standard, an articulation of a perhaps generic conflict, at once technological, aesthetic, and historical, between the established and the new, the dominant and the emergent, the predictably programmatic and the somehow still discordant, unruly, or unexpected."[40] "Magic" survives as early evidence that modernist radio programs were not only comprised of sound, but composed *about* sound, exploring how the radio medium might be controlled, ordered, and transmitted for public reception.

Radio dramatists could even use purposeful silence to shape the delivery of a narrative—just as visual poets had begun to use white space on the printed page to shape perception of the written word. As Margaret Fisher reports, another of Ferrieri's manifestos, "Radio as a Creative Force" (1931), "introduced the seminal idea that the source of radio's true, paradoxical power derives from silence."[41] In this context, radio silence is the default of the medium, the state from which a broadcast emerged and to which it would return, lurking behind and between every sound. Ferrieri believed that the time in between sounds "has a prime geometric quality: length. In addition, we can have variable depths of silence and variable volume ... Silences in radia, naturally, will have other lengths, depths, volumes, diverse values. People still need to understand how to create these [silences]."[42] The concept of silence as a "creation" rather than a negation was a crucial breakthrough for the development of radio drama, utilized in horror, suspense, or other dramatic situations that came to rely on "deep" silences to inject tension and emotion. Just as they used sound to alter the tenor and cadence of their programs, radio dramatists began to use variable and diverse forms of silence, confirming McWhinnie's contention that "silence, as a calculated device ... can be more expressive than words."[43]

## "Evanescence of the now"

The very term "modernism," of course, is inherently tied to immediacy, deriving from the Latin *modo*: "just now, the present." As Kevin Dettmar details in the Blackwell *Companion to Modernist Literature and Culture*, "for the loosely affiliated group of writers and artists who first described themselves by the term *modern*, and who were later labeled *modernists* by others, the evanescence of the now, the present, 'this moment,' would prove a recurrent challenge."[44] For modernist radio dramatists, however, capturing the present proved no challenge, for their work was modern in every sense of the word. The phrase "evanescence of the now" does well to capture the medium of radio, which was both completely now—live and instantaneous communication—and completely evanescent, its sound disappearing into the ether as soon it was heard. Radio dramatists did not have to "make it new," for nearly everything produced on the radio was novel and without precedent from which to depart or subvert. For radio audiences, too, the experience was immediate and meaningful. Shawn VanCour posits the act of listening as a "modernist practice," arguing that radio's modernness "derived from the modes of aural experience it invited and their connections to larger structural and perceptual transformations of twentieth-century modern life."[45]

Radio did indeed transform the mode of public and private life, offering immediacy and access, fine art and entertainment, and interpersonal connection across time and space. Yet it is a central paradox that a century from its popular introduction, radio is not an emblem of the dynamic future, but of the static past. Radio drama lacks an archive; few tangible "texts" or artifacts survive; there are no famous sites or markers of cultural memory. While the book, magazine, cinema, and television still exist in largely the same form as they did in their heyday, radio drama is all but defunct, and radio sets themselves have largely disappeared from households. Thus the entire enterprise and apparatus of radio drama has proven evanescent as well, having departed from this earth, save for sporadic "Old Time Radio" broadcasts and treatment in essays like this. That the future envisioned by Marinetti and Masnata never came to fruition is not merely a sign of radio's quixotic nature, but also evidence of its enduring status—in its immediacy, experimentation, and transience—as an essentially modernist medium.

# Notes

1 F. T. Marinetti and Pino Masnata, "The Radia: Futurist Manifesto," in *Futurism: An Anthology*, eds. Lawrence Rainey, Christine Poggi, and Laura Wittman (New Haven: Yale University Press, 2009), 292.
2 Ibid., 293.
3 Ibid., 293–4.
4 Ibid., 293.
5 Douglas Kahn, "Introduction: Histories of Sound Once Removed," in *Wireless Imagination: Sound, Radio, and the Avant-Garde*, eds. Douglas Kahn and Gregory Whitehead (Cambridge, MA: MIT Press, 1992), 21.
6 Ibid.
7 Marinetti and Masnata, "The Radia," 293.
8 Todd Avery, *Radio Modernism: Literature, Ethics, and the BBC, 1922–1933* (Burlington, VT: Ashgate, 2006), 1.
9 Douglas Craig, *Fireside Politics* (Baltimore: Johns Hopkins University Press, 2003), 8.
10 Ibid., 5.
11 Ibid., 7.

12  Richard Hand and Mary Traynor, *The Radio Drama Handbook: Audio Drama in Context and Practice* (New York: Bloomsbury Academic, 2011), 15.
13  Tim Crook, *Radio Drama: Theory and Practice* (New York: Routledge, 1999), 6.
14  Neil Verma, *Theater of the Mind* (Chicago: University of Chicago Press, 2012), 4.
15  Jim Cox, *Say Goodnight, Gracie: The Last Years of Network Radio* (Jefferson, NC: McFarland & Co., 2002), 2.
16  Hand and Traynor, *The Radio Drama Handbook*, 16.
17  Verma, *Theater of the Mind*, 61.
18  Ibid., 33.
19  "Fall of the City," *Time*, April 19, 1937, 60.
20  Gillian Beer, "'Wireless': Popular Physics, Radio and Modernism," in *Cultural Babbage: Technology, Time, and Invention*, eds. Francis Spufford and Jennifer S. Uglow (Boston: Faber and Faber, 1996), 150.
21  Crook, *Radio Drama*, 110.
22  Hand and Traynor, *The Radio Drama Handbook*, 9.
23  Ibid.
24  Ray Barfield, *Listening to Radio, 1920–1950* (Westport, CT: Praeger, 1996), 40.
25  David R. Mackey, *Drama on the Air* (New York: Prentice-Hall, 1951), 17.
26  Crook, *Radio Drama*, 60.
27  Hand and Traynor, *The Radio Drama Handbook*, 34.
28  Ibid.
29  Quoted in Matthew Feldman, Henry Mead, and Erik Tonning, introduction to *Broadcasting in the Modernist Era*, eds. Matthew Feldman, Henry Mead, and Erik Tonning (New York: Bloomsbury Academic, 2014), 5.
30  Ibid.
31  Debra Rae Cohen, Michael Coyle, and Jane Lewty, "Signing On," in *Broadcasting Modernism*, eds. Debra Rae Cohen, Michael Coyle, and Jane Lewty (Gainesville, FL: University of Florida Press, 2009), 1.
32  Fisher, "The Art of Radia," 164.
33  Avery, *Radio Modernism*, 139.
34  Verma, *Theater of the Mind*, 36.
35  R. J. Gray, "French Radio Drama from the Interwar to the Postwar Period (1922–1973)," (master's thesis, University of Texas at Austin, 2006), 193.
36  Donald McWhinnie, *The Art of Radio* (Faber and Faber: London, 1959), 25.
37  Melissa Dinsman, *Modernism at the Microphone: Radio, Propaganda, and Literary Aesthetics during World War II* (Bloomsbury Academic: London, 2015), 10.

38  Ibid., 9.
39  Mark E. Cory, "Soundplay: The Polyphonous Tradition of German Radio Art," in *Wireless Imagination: Sound, Radio, and the Avant-Garde*, eds. Douglas Kahn and Gregory Whitehead (Cambridge, MA: MIT Press, 1992), 336.
40  Lecia Rosenthal, "Introduction," "Magic on the Air: Attempt at a Radio Grotesque," written by Hans Flesch, Lisa Harries Schumann, and Lecia Rosenthal, *Cultural Critique* 91, no. 1 (2015): 15.
41  Margaret Fisher, "'The Art of Radia': Pino Masnata's Unpublished Gloss to the Futurist Radio Manifesto Introduction," *Modernism/modernity* 19, no. 1 (2012): 156.
42  Ibid., 169.
43  McWhinnie, *The Art of Radio*, 88.
44  Kevin J. H. Dettmar, "Introduction," *A Companion to Modernist Literature and Culture*, eds. David Bradshaw and Kevin J. H. Dettmar (Malden, MA: Blackwell Publishing, 2006), 1.
45  Shawn VanCour, "Early Radio Listening as a Modernist Practice: Ambient Radio and the Aesthetic of Distraction," *Modernist Cultures* 10, no. 1 (2015): 7.

# Bibliography

Avery, Todd. *Radio Modernism: Literature, Ethics, and the BBC, 1922–1933*. Burlington, VT: Ashgate, 2006.
Barfield, Ray. *Listening to Radio, 1920–1950*. Westport, CT: Praeger, 1996.
Beer, Gillian. "'Wireless': Popular Physics, Radio and Modernism." In *Cultural Babbage: Technology, Time, and Invention*, edited by Francis Spufford and Jennifer S. Uglow, 149–66. Boston: Faber and Faber, 1996.
Cohen, Debra Rae, Michael Coyle and Jane Lewty. "Signing On." In *Broadcasting Modernism*, edited by Debra Rae Cohen, Michael Coyle, and Jane Lewty, 1–7. Gainesville, FL: University of Florida Press, 2009.
Cory, Mark E. "Soundplay: The Polyphonous Tradition of German Radio Art." In *Wireless Imagination: Sound, Radio, and the Avant-Garde*, edited by Douglas Kahn and Gregory Whitehead, 331–72. Cambridge, MA: MIT Press, 1992.
Cox, Jim. *Say Goodnight, Gracie: The Last Years of Network Radio*. Jefferson, NC: McFarland & Co., 2002.
Craig, Douglas. *Fireside Politics: Radio and Political Culture in the United States, 1920–1940*. Baltimore: Johns Hopkins University Press, 2000.
Crook, Tim. *Radio Drama: Theory and Practice*. New York: Routledge, 1999.
Dettmar, Kevin J. H. "Introduction." In *A Companion to Modernist Literature and Culture*, edited by David Bradshaw and Kevin J. H. Dettmar, 1–5. Malden, MA: Blackwell Publishing, 2006.
Dinsman, Melissa. *Modernism at the Microphone: Radio, Propaganda, and*

*Literary Aesthetics during World War II*. London: Bloomsbury Academic, 2015.

"Fall of the City." *Time*, April 19, 1937, 60.

Feldman, Matthew, Henry Mead, and Erik Tonning. "Introduction." In *Broadcasting in the Modernist Era*, edited by Matthew Feldman, Henry Mead, and Erik Tonning, 1–22. New York: Bloomsbury Academic, 2014.

Fisher, Margaret. "'The Art of Radia': Pino Masnata's Unpublished Gloss to the Futurist Radio Manifesto Introduction." *Modernism/modernity* 19, no.1 (2012): 155–8.

Flesch, Hans, Lisa Harries Schumann, and Lecia Rosenthal. "Magic on the Air: Attempt at a Radio Grotesque." *Cultural Critique* 91, no. 1 (2015): 14–31.

Gray, R. J. "French Radio Drama from the Interwar to the Postwar Period (1922–1973)." Master's thesis, University of Texas at Austin, 2006.

Hand, Richard and Mary Traynor. *The Radio Drama Handbook: Audio Drama in Context and Practice*. New York: Bloomsbury Academic, 2011.

Kahn, Douglas. "Introduction: Histories of Sound Once Removed." In *Wireless Imagination: Sound, Radio, and the Avant-Garde*, edited by Douglas Kahn and Gregory Whitehead, 1–30. Cambridge, MA: MIT Press, 1992.

Kahn, Douglas and Gregory Whitehead, eds. *Wireless Imagination: Sound, Radio, and the Avant-Garde*. Cambridge, MA: MIT Press, 1992.

Mackey, David R. *Drama on the Air*. New York: Prentice-Hall, 1951.

Marinetti, F. T. and Pino Masnata. "The Radia: Futurist Manifesto." 1908. Reprinted in *Futurism: An Anthology*, edited by Lawrence Rainey, Christine Poggi, and Laura Wittman, 292–4. New Haven: Yale University Press, 2009.

McWhinnie, Donald. *The Art of Radio*. Faber and Faber: London, 1959.

Rosenthal, Lecia. "Introduction." In "Magic on the Air: Attempt at a Radio Grotesque." Written by Hans Flesch, Lisa Harries Schumann and Lecia Rosenthal. *Cultural Critique* 91, no. 1 (2015): 14–17.

VanCour, Shawn. "Early Radio Listening as a Modernist Practice: Ambient Radio and the Aesthetic of Distraction." *Modernist Cultures* 10, no. 1 (2015): 6–25.

Verma, Neil. *Theater of the Mind*. Chicago: University of Chicago Press, 2012.

ns and
# 4

# "I'm gonna be somebody," 1930: Gangsters and modernist celebrity

*Jonathan Goldman*

## The notorious Rico

The first great talking gangster flick, *Little Caesar* (1930), invokes a version of celebrity that is a major component of literary modernism as a way of negotiating the uneasy entangling of crime, success and individuality during the United States' Great Depression. It does so almost immediately after the film begins, in its inaugural dialogue. The eponymous protagonist, a.k.a. Rico (budding star Edward G. Robinson), a small-time crook who has pulled off a small-town heist, finds himself face to face with his ideal: the famous Diamond Jim Montana, being fêted by fellow gangsters at a lavish Chicago celebration. But Rico's ideal seems far away: the face appears in a photograph, and the photograph appears in a newspaper, and the newspaper appears on the counter of a dingy diner somewhere in the anonymous Midwest. Rico gazes lustfully at the image and declares that, like Diamond Jim, he will "be somebody."[1] What Rico knows, what the scene announces, is that to "be somebody" is not merely to be successful, but to be publicly acknowledged as such, to be a celebrity—and that to be celebrity is to be not merely publicly known, but, moreover, publicly reproduced, embodied textually, in images. Rico's desire to "be somebody" encompasses, for sure, some obvious and transhistorical aspects of fame that relate to social power: a rise in rank, financial circumstances, geography, sartorial sense, and renown. But Rico's sense of celebrity also entails an abstraction of the self, a transformation from flesh-and-blood to a more idealized version of the individual.

This desire to self-textualize the subject is how celebrity links early 1930s Hollywood to literary modernism in its 1920s high modernist incarnation. As Aaron Jaffe writes, "like the star image, the textual imprimatur is a metonym for its subject, a metonym that represents it as an object of cultural production."[2] Jaffe distinguishes cinema stardom from the parallel machinations of modernist celebrity, which is "not intrinsically image-based but predicated instead on a distinctive textual mark of authorship."[3] Leaning on Jaffe's work, I have written that such authorial textualizing operates as a fantasy of insulating the subject from materiality. The text, authorial style, formal strategies and idiosyncrasies, become the bearers of individuality. This fantasy, *Little Caesar* shows us, can operate via images as well: Rico's desire for celebrity corresponds to a desire to transcend the desolate material conditions of 1930s America.

That it does so as part of Rico's origin story, the psychological explanation for his ensuing actions, and here at a formative moment in the first major talking gangster film, underscores the significant degree to which the gangster cycle relies on a modernist notion of self-objectification.[4] It is often noted that the 1930s Hollywood gangster cycle specifically, and that the gangster genre generally, chronicles a distorted version of the American dream. What has received less comment is that the complicated but ultimate de-legitimation of the gangster's illegal pursuit of success produces the legitimation of what emerges as its corollary: the pursuit of success via the entertainment industry. In this chapter I will argue that the gangster film views both through celebrity culture. My readings will focus on the exemplary *Little Caesar* and its successor gangster films *The Public Enemy* (1931), and *Scarface: Shame of a Nation* (1932). These, the first major talking gangster movies, pose a simple question: is it acceptable to work outside of legal institutions in order to pursue the American dream? The answer arrives just as simply: no, it is not; do that and you will die. However, the films cannot rationalize censuring the act of trying to work outside of a broken system, which, by January of 1931, had already thrown 8 million people out of work.[5] After all, products of popular culture, as Frederic Jameson writes, "cannot manipulate unless they offer some genuine shred of content as a fantasy bribe to the public about to be manipulated."[6] In other words, without something transgressive, popular culture wouldn't be popular. Performing this principle, the gangster genre, instead of condemning criminals for seeking a viable if illegal route to American success, takes the question of crime and re-writes it as a question of celebrity. These films depict the gangsters striving for and achieving aspects of celebrity, and it kills them off for this reason. The 1930s gangster cycle, in this way, both constitutes a case study in how popular texts incorporate the logic of celebrity into their very narratives, and draws attention to the cultural force that celebrity of the modernist variety had become in the United States, as it remains.

## The out-of-body experience of celebrity

It might not be immediately apparent why the logic of celebrity is clearly legible within the narrative of Depression-era film, although Charles Eckert and others have crafted convincing arguments with just such an approach.[7] But celebrity as we know it is a phenomenon of the early twentieth century, and, as we shall see, makes perfect sense as discourse threading through popular 1930s texts. Critical writings over the last decades, from literary and cultural studies as well as from sociology, while nuancing our sense of what celebrity is, have generally concurred about the idea that twentieth-century celebrity appears distinct from previous incarnations. Film historian Richard Schickel summarizes a popular view when he throws down this particular gauntlet, claiming that "there was no such thing as celebrity prior to the beginning of the twentieth century."[8] Earlier forms of fame and renown, he explains, neither went by the word celebrity nor possessed the qualities of our recent version of it.

To U.S. cultural historians, the advent of modern celebrity corresponds to how the idea of the individual itself transformed in a nation culturally dominated by mass industrial society. Warren Susman has theorized this change most thoroughly, naming it a transition from "a culture of character" to a "culture of personality," the first an inner identification with moral values, the second a public performance of individualism.[9] He writes:

> [S]tarting somewhere in the middle of the first decade of the twentieth century, there rapidly developed another vision of self, another vision of self-development and mastery, another method of the self in society ... To be somebody one must be oneself ... The importance of being different, special, unusual, of standing out in a crowd—all of this is emphasized ...[10]

These claims are predicated on the notion of a nation in transition "from a producer to a consumer society."[11] The new celebrity, with its emphasis on the unique stamp of the individual, is understood to be a product of new economic conditions in which the cultural imperative is consumption.

Through the prism of Susman's claims, one can easily see how the economically influenced shifts in individual identity and achievement map on to changing notions of celebrity. In the early twentieth century, celebrity becomes a commodified form of the individual, something that, as Leonard Leff puts it, can "like gas engines or soda crackers or other consumer goods, be mass manufactured."[12] This instant production is in opposition to a supposed more organic form of fame that attaches itself to the figures who earn it more gradually, and via traditional forms of achievement. The new form of celebrity is predicated on new figures of celebrity, often if not largely comprising the new stars produced in Hollywood. In 1943, social researcher Leo Lowenthal surveyed biographies published in the United States from the beginning of the twentieth century and identified a dramatic change in the subjects represented, which he describes as a "considerable decrease of people from the serious and important professions and a corresponding increase of entertainers."[13] These entertainers he invokes clearly correspond to the film industry. Writing of the same period, P. David Marshall claims, "The nascent focus on the persona became the economic motor force of film production from 1910 onward, essentially paralleling the maturation of the movie industry."[14] As Marshall points out here, and as his writings generally argue, the stars function as commodities: celebrity is "an effective means for the commodification of the self."[15] Back in 1935 this was clear to Walter Benjamin, who would directly associate the willful manufacture of the celebrity qua commodity with the film industry. He writes of "the artificial build-up of the 'personality' outside the studio," and observes that "the cult of the movie star, fostered by the money of the film industry, preserves not the unique aura of the person but the 'spell of the personality,' the phony spell of a commodity."[16] Pejorative aside, Benjamin represents the easy correlation of Hollywood stardom with the dynamics of celebrity, dynamics that treat individuals as commodities.

But to turn people into commodities entails more than simply considering human beings to be objects that are marketable in an economic realm. In Marx's understanding of the commodity fetish, the commodity's value becomes separate from what inheres in the object. Marx writes, "in [the commodity] the social character of men's labor appears as an objective character stamped upon the product of that labor ... the existence of things *quâ* commodities, and the value-relation between the products of labor which stamps them as commodities, have absolutely no connection with their physical properties."[17] The act of exchange imposes a value on the commodity, one only arbitrarily linked to the object's materiality. That is, value derives from circulation, not from something essential in the object. The object disappears, replaced by mediating images that convert "every product into a social hieroglyph."[18] In other words, the hieroglyph acts as a sign that will only refer to the commodity's value in a system of exchange, rather than point to any innate value of the object. In fact, by this process, Marx is saying, we no longer perceive the object, but only see the commodity, an image that signifies a relationally determined value.

Similar to Marx's analysis, celebrity logic of the twentieth century turns its objects into commodities by identifying the celebrated person only in relation to others—Susman's "standing out in a crowd." This identity is embodied not by the object, but by the image, the sign that distinguishes this celebrity from all other images circulating in the marketplace. Aaron Jaffe has termed this sign the "imprimatur," and has pointed out that it may be constituted by a star image as well as by the distinct textual style of the modernist author. If the desire for celebrity is also a desire for commodification of the self, then it is a desire for a process that vexes the relationship between the object (the body of the celebrity) and its value. This is the crux of twentieth-century celebrity. Celebrity comprises a process by which identity departs from the body and is turned into an idea wrapped in an image: an instantly-identifiable formula, a signature, a text.

And this is what Rico wants as well. Amid the dingy environs of the diner, Rico lifts a newspaper off the counter and, as the camera holds still on the front page, jealously reads out its headline: "Underworld pays respects to Diamond Pete Montana." He says to Joe: "And look at us. Just a couple of nobodies, nothing." The nobody has no name, no brand, is the un-commodity. Meanwhile, Montana gets a party and his own flashy title, Diamond Pete, the name here signaling the distinct personality. In the very next scene, in which Rico's first crime boss christens him "Little Caesar" and Rico visibly brightens. Back in the diner, though, Rico can only gaze at a photograph from the mass-produced medium of print journalism. When his partner Joe Massara (Douglas Fairbanks Jr.) asks, "Is that what you want, Rico? A party like that for you?" Rico announces that he is more deserving of Montana's success: "I could do all the things that fella does and more. Only I never got my chance." Rico's desire embraces not only Montana's position but also this commodification, this existence as an idealized entity.

## Crime doesn't play

Depression-era Hollywood had a problem. The gangster proved an obvious and irresistible narrative choice for the movies, providing the dynamism of transgression with easily adaptable narrative arcs. Yet Hollywood was beset by public concern and censorship, primarily embodied by the hostile office of Will Hays, who had been hired by a nervous industry to direct its censorship group, Motion Picture Producers and Distributors of America.[19] Hays's power, in fact, is on display in *Scarface*, the ending of which had to be re-shot, and which contains an absurd interlude, inserted after the film was supposed to be finished, depicting city officials and concerned citizens arguing about what to do about the gangster scourge.

(It ends with a newspaper editor turning to the camera and basically exhorting the audience members to write their congressman.) To compound Hollywood's vexations, the non-filmic gangsters constituted real rivals for public attention, a shadowy mirror of the Hollywood star system. Gerald Horne has noted that "by the early 1930s there were entire magazines" devoted to the gangsters and their culture.[20] The gangster was very much part of the tapestry of the new celebrity, and the Hollywood studios had been anxious of their public reputation ever since the 1921 Fatty Arbuckle sexual assault scandal. This atmosphere explains why gangster films needed to disavow their protagonists.

But in gangster films made against the backdrop of the Depression, organized crime constituted one way by which Americans could dutifully work toward a life of success, thereby putting themselves in a position to become dutiful consumers. Consider: when Rico reads off the headline featuring Diamond Jim, the initial response from Joe Massara is to ask, "What's that got to do with the price of eggs?" His question is both a popular aphorism and a reminder that these characters live every day with the financial concerns plaguing a nation. "Plenty," answers Rico, an astute response whether he intends to say "everything" or "bounty." The film means both. Gangsterdom means a way to both avoid material hardship and acquire wealth. As Bergman writes:

> That only gangsters could make upward mobility believable tells much about how legitimate institutions had failed—but that mobility was still at the core of what Americans held to be the American dream ... Unloosed in the 1870s, Rico could have cornered wheat, built railroads, cheated farmers on freight rates, paid off legislators, and thus achieved a legitimate success. *Little Caesar* was a very old story in America. Rico's nation demanded achievement, wanted it accomplished individually, and, in 1930, lacked the lawful means to bring it off.[21]

Bergman highlights the American ethos that one should make a perseverant attempt to raise one's position, in the tradition of Horatio Alger's fictions and Andrew Carnegie's advice books. It is an ethos contradicted in the 1930s by the American system's failure to provide realistic, legal means to do so. So when Rico complains, "I never got my chance," his frustrated desires are clearly a nod to working-class America for whom upward mobility seemed remote, only achievable in the movies.

Or, perhaps, via the movies: the face of Fairbanks Jr. in this scene announces Hollywood's presence within the cinematic narrative. The image of Joe Massara connotes Hollywood royalty. His waspishly handsome features recall those of his famous father, as immediately as they and his vocal intonations contrast with the less leading-man-ish appearance and vocal intonations of Robinson/Rico. In 1930, Fairbanks père, not yet a victim of the transition to synchronized sound, would have been one of the most revered figures in Hollywood, equally famous for his perpetual success as a swashbuckling star and for his marriage to America's sweetheart Mary Pickford. His significance was such that Schickel theorizes celebrity by using Fairbanks as case study.

The 1929 W. R. Burnett novel from which *Little Caesar* is adapted describes Joe Massara in terms referring to another Hollywood star. Casting Fairbanks Jr. in the role of Joe is the best way that *Little Caesar*'s filmmakers could translate the novel's description of Joe as "vain of his resemblance to the late Rudolph Valentino," given the absence of a son of Valentino to enlist.[22] Valentino, who had died in 1924, was, of course, an über-celebrity, a starting point for Miriam Hansen's theory that "the presence of the star actually undercuts [a film's] apparent primacy, unity, and closure.[23] Hansen refers to a way of reading a film that simultaneously accounts for the character within the narrative and the star performing it, with all the semiotic connotations (created through both previous performances and fan magazines, public appearances, etc.) of that star. So it is particularly appropriate that the Joe Massara character, via Fairbanks Jr.'s celluloid face, constitutes the ghostly presence of the Hollywood star machine at Rico's elbow. The inclusion within this scene of this emblem of Hollywood provides an immediate negative comment on and counterpoint to Rico's desire for celebrity.

In addition to recalling his celebrity father, Joe Massara will constitute a foil for Rico vocationally, sexually, and sartorially. Mostly, Joe represents a resistance to the life of crime. Throughout the movie Joe will continually try to go straight, but every time he tries to get out, Rico pulls him back in. Persuaded to tread the straight and narrow by his paramour and performance partner Olga, Joe finally rats Rico out and causes his fall from power. However, the irresolute Joe constitutes less the moral center for the film than its constant reminder of Hollywood; Joe's career choice has implications beyond their legal legitimacy. Joe represents the other way to achieve celebrity: show business. Back in the diner, Joe, imagining life in the big city, says that if he were to succeed in crime then he would change professions: "I'd go back to dancing, like I used to before I met you." At this Rico shoots Joe a look that communicates both disdain and astonishment. He repeats the word "dancing"—as well he might, for within the context the possibility seems less than remote. This exchange commences the comparison between performance and crime that permeates the film. Joe will indeed become a dancer, and though his rise is less meteoric than Rico's, he indeed becomes "somebody." The film's final moments highlight Joe's success; they take place underneath a billboard advertising Joe and Olga's act, the word "success" underneath their illustration.

The billboard, an advertisement and a reproducible image visible to all those anonymous people who might drive past, constitutes an abstraction of Joe. It is Joe who has achieved Rico's desire and become abstracted from himself, a commodity, a celebrity. The film firmly sets Rico and Joe in high relief here. First Rico, who has been living destitute in a flophouse, trudges past the billboard, which dwarfs him. When the police arrive they gun Rico down through the billboard. The bullet holes literally underline the sign's printed words: "Laughing Dancing Singing Success." The gangster's death occurs behind the billboard, invisible to the road, though visible on screen. The moment clearly sets the illegitimacy of Rico's pursuit against the success of Joe the entertainer. Rico's famous and oft-parodied dying question—"Is this the end of Rico?"—further removes Rico from celebrity status. Visible on screen is a tattered tramp, while his words allude to a media sensation. As Robert Warshow notes, Rico "speaks in the third person because what has been brought low is not the undifferentiated *man*, but the individual with a name, the gangster, the success."[24] Rico has, in fact, been trapped by the police through their repeatedly planting his name in derogatory press items, a distortion of Rico's initial desire to get his name in the newspapers. Neither this ruse nor the billboard is taken from Burnett's novel. They emerge in the filmic text that concerns itself with stripping the gangster of the right to achieve celebrity.

The billboard, with its two stars facing one another in profile, suggests nothing so much as a movie advertisement, a one-sheet. Thus the giant billboard, a visual representation of the celebrity, aligns Joe again with Hollywood; Joe has been conferred the Hollywood happy ending (codified well prior to 1930): social and economic resolution plus appropriate bourgeois heterosexual coupling. At this moment *Little Caesar* uses the generic conventions of American cinema to castigate the gangster. Joe and Olga's union contrasts with Rico's complete lack of heterosexual desire and the intensely homoerotic undertones of his obsession with keeping Joe in the gang.[25] The codified resolution is granted to the figures working in the entertainment industry.

The films released in *Little Caesar*'s wake also follow this pattern. *Public Enemy* and *Scarface* both articulate the failure of the gangsters by making it clear that they will not be granted the domestic resolution one hopes to achieve in Hollywood. In *Public Enemy*, the famous grapefruit-to-the-face misogyny of Tommy Powers (Jimmy Cagney) gives way to celibacy; he seems unable to consummate with Gwen (starlet Jean Harlow). The audience becomes privy to this secret in a hotel room scene when Tommy says, "You know all my friends think that—that things are different between us than they are." Tommy's secret shame is that, either because of a surname-belying impotence or some other reason, he is not getting any of this kind of action. *Scarface* makes the gangster's sexuality even more of an issue, injecting Tony Cramonte (Paul Muni) with suggestions of miscegenation and incest. Muni uses posture and intonation to portray Tony as ethnic beyond stereotype, in fact somewhat monstrous. In an early scene in Johnny Lovo's apartment, the film foregrounds, literally, the miscegenetic quality of Tony's desire for the ultra-blonde Poppy. Director Howard Hawks bathes the preening moll in soft white light that contrasts sharply with the shadowy portion of the room where the gangsters conduct their shady business. Repelled by Tony, Poppy complains. "You have an office for this, Johnny, why don't you use it?" Tony's obsession with his sister Cesca eventually interferes with both the miscegenistic couple and also the film's sanctioned domestic pairing of Cesca and Guino, whose marriage lasts one day before an enraged Tony shoots his sister's husband. Thus Tony's problematic sexual desires announce the disjuncture between *Scarface* and Hollywood convention. The denying of sexual union further severs the gangsters from success, in that they will not be reproducing themselves. There will be no little Little Caesar, no new Powers, and no baby Cramonte. The gangsters' sexuality, preventing cinematic climax, constitutes another sign that these movies use their medium and industry to de-legitimate the gangsters. Early in *Little Caesar*, as their relationship gets underway, Joe says to Olga, "Perhaps we're beginning to ... mean something." The consonance between the phrases "means something" and "be somebody" highlight how depriving the gangsters of domestic couplings is an extension of the concern with not crime but celebrity.

## Spectacular failure

The failure to achieve Hollywood resolution undermines attempts to see the gangster genre as an oppositional one by brushing aside the gangsters' unhappy endings. Lawrence Levine writes that as audiences are "privy to the entire film and not simply at the mercy of formulaic endings, which were often in stark contrast to what had preceded them,"[26] the 1930s gangster cycle constitutes a political critique. To this Jonathan Munby adds that the gangster films popularized "a critical disposition toward the law."[27] From this position the gangsters' deaths matter less than their colorful lives. I would contend, however, that their deaths are very much part of their lives. The conventions of the 1930s gangster film are present from the outset; the knowledge that the hero will meet a bad end is a working dynamic throughout. The foreknowledge of ultimate punishment is part of the cinematic experience.

By keeping in mind the films' enlisting of celebrity as a primary de-authorizing device, the thrill of the gangsters' transgressions can themselves be bracketed within a space embodied by the star, rather than the character. For example, *Scarface* audiences familiar with Muni would recognize from the moment he appears as a gangster that this is emphatically not the handsome leading man of *I am a Fugitive from a Chain Gang*, in which he portrays a sympathetic, upright victim of economic ills; in *Scarface* he hunches his shoulders menacingly and juts out his jaw a lot. Similarly, Bergman reports that the attempt by Paramount to deny that *The Public Enemy* glorifies gangsterdom was "shattered the moment Cagney strolled across the screen."[28] The fixation is on the star beyond the narrative, not the character within. We can thrill at the actor because the character is condemned. Bergman cites Lincoln Kirsten, who calls Cagney "the American hero, whom ordinary men and boys recognize as themselves."[29] The American hero is now a Hollywood commodity.

The stars playing the gangsters, in fact, most emphatically transcend their roles in exactly the scene of conclusion, often a spectacular instance of punishment. Such moments resonate with Thom Gunning's approach to early cinema, which he terms "the cinema of attractions." This aesthetic "directly solicits spectator attention, inciting visual curiosity, and supplying pleasure through an exciting spectacle."[30] In Gunning's various writings, he establishes the opposition between early cinema's "theatrical display" and classical (Hollywood, narrative) cinema's "narrative absorption."[31] While the concept emerges from pre-Hollywood film, attractions appear residually in classical cinema, via displays of jokes, musical numbers, or violence. Violence constitutes the attraction that disrupts the absorbing narrative within the gangster cycle. The protagonists' deaths are foregone conclusions, after all. Therefore the films imprint visually memorable conclusions that freeze narrative into a spectacle. *Little Caesar*'s finale cuts from Rico's dying words to the Joe Massara/Olga billboard, punctured with police bullets. Tony's death in *Scarface* is staged, after a prolonged siege, at the hands of a massive strike force assembled in front of his *nouveau riche* home, his steel-shuttered bunker of an apartment.

Tommy Powers's end is perhaps most unforgettable, combining spectacle with the disruption of the domestic space. Tommy's mother, happy to hear reports that the hospitalized Tommy is ready to return home, starts preparing his bedroom as the phonograph plays throughout her house. When the doorbell rings it is Tommy's brother Mike, the First World War vet, the narrative foil, the good son, the trolley operator and night school student whom Tommy had sneered was "learning to be poor." The doorway frames Cagney, now portraying Tommy's fresh, bandaged corpse, eyes wide open; rival gangsters have murdered him in the hospital and left the body leaning on the doorstep. The body teeters briefly before crashing forward to the floor. The film then intercuts shots of the phonograph, its needle skipping repeatedly at the record's end, shots of the oblivious Mrs. Powers, and Mike's response to Tommy's arrival. Mike leans over the lifeless body and turns a grim gaze from Tommy to the camera. This final shot, and the stuck needle, emphasize the "attractions" aspect of the moment, mobilizing the kind of "direct look" that breaks narrative continuity.[32] Thus Tommy's dramatic death, a momentous attraction, the sheer spectacle of which is further dramatized by his brother's direct look at the audience, decries in the strongest possible terms the gangster's ill-gotten gains, while maintaining that the body on display, the visibility of the gangster, is the cause of his spectacular failure—as we knew it would be all along.

In addition to the spectacular nature of such moments, the deaths of the protagonists suggest a consideration of the personality beyond the narrative; after all, there is no moment that reminds us that actors are acting as much as the moment that they are playing dead. Indeed, their gangster roles proved to be formative in these actors' careers, particularly in the case of Robinson, who, like Humphrey Bogart after him, would have a difficult time escaping the shadow of his gangster performance; he would be soon transformed into "Edward G. Robbinsome" in a Warner Brothers cartoon reel called *Thugs With Dirty Mugs*. It is by considering the actors playing the gangsters, specifically their ethnic backgrounds—Robinson and Muni were immigrant Jews, Cagney was Irish-Catholic—that Munby concludes that a "collusion of real and cinematic identity had everything to do with the refinement of the gangster as an 'authentic' American type."[33] That is, audiences are supposed to perceive the stars' ethnicity alongside that of the characters. We might take this approach further and say that this doubling of character and actor keeps the critique and punishment of the gangsters from becoming a simple narrative about suppressing the ethnic Other. The separation of actor from character at the moment of death complicates the reading that the dominant culture has just killed off an ethnic intruder by highlighting the star turns of non-Anglo-Saxon Protestants, products of New York's Lower East Side vaudeville circuits.

## Fameful employment

In F. Scott Fitzgerald's *The Great Gatsby*, published five years before *Little Caesar* was released, a fictional gangster who accrues many of the characteristics of celebrity suffers violent punishment for his transgressions. Hollywood gangsters, in fact, may be said to derive from such characters as Fitzgerald's Gatsby and, to a lesser extent, Marcellus of Willa Cather's *The Professor's House*—characters with problematic ethnic and business associations, who appear in 1920s American novels that worried over nativism. I have hardly touched upon much of the semiotic material the gangster cycle uses to condemn its protagonists, such as their vexed relationships to consumption, their suspicious abstemiousness when it comes to alcohol, their *nouveau riche* sartorial tastes, their manners, and their ethnicity, but these characteristics compel the comparison to the 1920s literary precursors, particularly to the eponymous Gatsby. Gatsby, whose mysterious business involves bootlegging, throws lavish celebrations like Rico, and, like Tony, boasts of a large collection of shirts and a large house in his attempts to earn a woman's affection. Gatsby, whose ethnic connections are decidedly suspect, achieves renown and notoriety, and is reproved with death for his transgressions.

But Gatsby's textual relationship to his vocation is markedly different from the gangsters of the 1930s. In *Gatsby*, the criminal is never seen acting criminally. His business is kept hidden from the masses who flock to his gatherings, from Nick the narrator, and thus from the audience. Gatsby's illegal operating is never on display. He occasionally disappears to the telephone, a motif that underscores the fact that his work is invisible, off-camera. In fact, the one moment when Nick, and Daisy too, overhear his phone conversation, what they get is an absurd rendition of the organized crime boss:

"I can't talk now, old sport ... I said a *small* town ... He must know what a small town is ... Well, he's no use to us if Detroit is his idea of a small town ... " He rang off.[34] (Ellipses and emphasis in the original)

Replete with Gatsby's Oxford affectation ("old sport"), this one side of a gangster conversation registers as harmless, humorous, stuff, criminals debating geographical semantics, a Tarantino scene before its time. To similar effect, Nick's one casual attempt to ascertain Gatsby's vocation is met with strangeness. "When I asked him what business he was in he answered 'That's my affair,' before realizing that it wasn't an appropriate reply."[35] When Daisy ultimately hears the source of Gatsby's wealth she turns cold: "with every word she was drawing further and further into herself."[36] In the 1925 text, Gatsby's true work is unacceptable to the extent that it must stay off screen in order for the narrative to make sense. When revealed, it destroys the romantic plot at the novel's core.

It seems obvious to say: the gangster films of the 1930s comprised sequential images of criminals working. Of course, there was little legal employment to be had during the Great Depression, a fact that underwrites the narratives of disparate Hollywood movies, the plots of which often start with the question of a job and end by turning the unemployed into entertainers. Think of *King Kong* (1933), in which Faye Wray needs work and eventually winds up on stage, and *Modern Times* (1936), in which Charlie Chaplin and Paulette Goddard need work and eventually wind up on stage. In fact, the film that consciously tries to consolidate and summarize all of the major tropes of the gangster cycle, Raul Walsh's *The Roaring Twenties* (1939), argues that the unavailability of gainful employment created gangsterdom. Commencing with the First World War and set over the years of the Prohibition decade, the movie clearly reads like a Depression-era text; its premise is that the gangster (Cagney again plays the lead, Eddie Bartlett) might have stayed straight had he been able to find an honest job upon his return from war. Eddie, a mechanic before the war, continually returns to his vocation, cars, throughout the film. The way the 1930s altered its gangster inheritance is clear: it put work on camera, visible to the audience.

The display of work is what aligns the gangsters with celebrity and justifies their condemnation. The continual placement of work front and center in these texts underscores what I have been arguing all along: that the gangsters' sins are not their illegal business but their illegitimate grab for celebrity power. A text like *Gatsby* could use Nick's snobbish disdain and Daisy's prudish horror to condemn Gatsby's criminality, but when the institutions of state have so unraveled that there are no jobs, you cannot recriminate those who look elsewhere to achieve success. Thus Hollywood, under fire and unnerved by its proximity to gangsterdom, turned to celebrity to de-legitimate its other.

In the 1930s, before film noir turned the genre into an existential celebration of moral ambiguity, the gangster movies could be read with the simplicity of fables and Shakespearian tragedies, punishing cultural transgressors, however celebrated. Jameson has expressed a view of mass culture as "transformational work on social or political anxieties and fantasies which must then have some effective presence in the mass cultural text in order to be subsequently 'managed' or repressed."[37] That is, a popular narrative must generate a solution to a problem plaguing the populace by portraying fantasies and changing them into something else. The gangster film cycle, then, promises the thrill of working outside of the system to rise through the American economic ranks, but condemns that figure when it strives to be somebody above the plebian through such means. Thus gangster films not only enlisted but also furthered the aspects of celebrity distinct to fame in the twentieth century (and, perhaps, also the early twenty-first). The gangster cycle exacerbated and disseminated the understanding of celebrity as an idealization of the individual that circulates as an image. The material hardships of the Depression would certainly make the idea of abstraction attractive; its films reserve such a privilege for the chosen few. The gangster cycle made use of that desire for celebrity to rationalize punishing protagonists for taking on the only work available to them.

# Notes

1   Rico's words are so resonant that Warren Susman would use them to summarize the aspirations of one generation (in *Culture as History*) and Marlon Brando would invoke them to characterize the disappointments of another (in Elia Kazan's 1957 *On the Waterfront*).

2   Aaron Jaffe, *Modernism and the Culture of Celebrity* (Cambridge: Cambridge University Press, 2005), 1.
3   Ibid.
4   In treating these films together I am following the lead of Munby, who writes: "The term 'cycle' (which was also the contemporaneous term adopted to describe the gangster films of the time) does justice to the idea that while these films shared generic conventions, they were part of a socially viable formula in flux," *Public Enemies, Public Heroes* (Chicago: University of Chicago Press, 1999), 4.
5   Andrew Bergman, *We're in the Money: Depression America and Its Films* (New York: Harper Colophon Books, 1971), 9.
6   Frederic Jameson, "Reification and Utopia," *Social Text* 1, no. 1 (1979): 144.
7   Eckert provides a strong model for understanding how celebrity can be written into the cinematic narrative. He argues that Depression-era movies starring Shirley Temple posit her affection and charm as an acceptable substitute for money—when she was, as it was widely known, a valuable commodity to her family, and her studio.
8   Richard Schickel, *Intimate Strangers* (New York: Fromm International Publishing Company, 1986), 33.
9   Warren I. Susman, *Culture as History* (New York: Pantheon Books, 1973), 277.
10  Ibid., 275–7.
11  Ibid., 277.
12  Leonard J. Leff, *Hemingway and His Conspirators* (Lanham: Rowman & Littlefield Publishers, 1997), xiii.
13  Leo Lowenthal, *Literature, Popular Culture, and Society* (Englewood Cliffs, NJ: Prentice-Hall, 1961), 11.
14  P. David Marshall, *Celebrity and Power* (Minneapolis: University of Minnesota Press, 1997), 111.
15  Ibid., 26.
16  Walter Benjamin, "The Work of Art in the Age of Mechanical Reproduction," in *Illuminations*, trans. Harry Zohn (New York: Schocken Books, 1968), 231.
17  Karl Marx, *Capital, Volume One: A Critique of Political Economy*, ed. Friedrich Engels, trans. Samuel Moore and Edward Aveling (1867; repr., Cambridge: Dover Publications, 2011), 83.
18  Ibid., 85.
19  Bergman, *We're in the Money*, 3–4.
20  Gerald Horne, *Class Struggle in Hollywood, 1930–1950* (Austin: University of Texas Press, 2001), 100.
21  Bergman, *We're in the Money*, 7–9.
22  W. R. Burnett, *Little Caesar* (New York: The Literary Guild of America, 1929), 6.

23  Miriam Hansen, *Babel and Babylon* (Cambridge: Harvard University Press, 1991), 246.
24  Robert Warshow, *The Immediate Experience* (1946; repr., Cambridge: Harvard University Press, 2001), 103.
25  This is yet another aspect of the film altered from Burnett's novel, in which Rico does indeed engage with women, however cautiously.
26  Lawrence W. Levine, "The Folklore of Industrial Society: Popular Culture and Its Audiences," *American Historical Review*, 97, no. 5 (1992): 1392.
27  Munby, *Public Enemies, Public Heroes*, 44.
28  Bergman, *We're in the Money*, 11.
29  Quoted in Bergman, *We're in the Money*, 11.
30  Thom Gunning, "The Cinema of Attractions: Early Film, Its Spectator, and the Avant-Garde," in *Early Cinema: Space Frame Narrative*, ed. Thomas Elsaessar (London: BFI Publishing, 1990), 58.
31  Ibid., 59.
32  Hansen, *Babel and Babylon*, 37.
33  Munby, *Public Enemies, Public Heroes*, 39–40.
34  F. Scott Fitzgerald, *The Great Gatsby* (1925; repr., New York: Scribner, 2004), 93.
35  Ibid., 90.
36  Ibid., 134.
37  Jameson, "Reification and Utopia," 141.

# Bibliography

Benjamin, Walter. "The Work of Art in the Age of Mechanical Reproduction." In *Illuminations*, translated by Harry Zohn, 217–51. New York: Schocken Books, 1968.
Bergman, Andrew. *We're in the Money: Depression America and Its Films*. New York: Harper Colophon Books, 1971.
Braudy, Leo. *The Frenzy of Renown*. New York: Vintage, 1986.
Burnett, W. R. *Little Caesar*. New York: The Literary Guild of America, 1929.
Eckert, Charles. "Shirley Temple and the House of Rockefeller." In *American Media and Mass Culture*, edited by Donald Lazare, 164–77. Berkeley: University of California Press, 1987.
Fitzgerald, F. Scott. *The Great Gatsby*. 1925. Reprint, New York: Scribner, 2004.
Gunning, Thom. "The Cinema of Attractions: Early Film, Its Spectator, and the Avant-Garde." In *Early Cinema: Space Frame Narrative*, ed. Thomas Elsaessar, 56–62. London: BFI Publishing, 1990.
Hansen, Miriam. *Babel and Babylon*. Cambridge: Harvard University Press, 1991.
Horne, Gerald. *Class Struggle in Hollywood, 1930–1950*. Austin: University of Texas Press, 2001.

Jaffe, Aaron. *Modernism and the Culture of Celebrity*. Cambridge: Cambridge University Press, 2005.
Jameson, Frederic. "Reification and Utopia." *Social Text* 1, no. 1 (1979): 130–48.
Leff, Leonard J. *Hemingway and His Conspirators*. Lanham: Rowman & Littlefield Publishers, 1997.
Levine, Lawrence W. "The Folklore of Industrial Society: Popular Culture and Its Audiences." *American Historical Review*, 97, no. 5 (1992): 1369–99.
*Little Caesar*. Directed by Mervyn LeRoy. Warner Brothers Pictures, 1930.
Lowenthal, Leo. *Literature, Popular Culture, and Society*. Englewood Cliffs, NJ: Prentice-Hall, 1961.
Marshall, P. David. *Celebrity and Power*. Minneapolis: University of Minnesota Press, 1997.
Marx, Karl. *Capital, Volume One: A Critique of Political Economy*, edited by Friedrich Engels, translated by Samuel Moore and Edward Aveling. 1867. Reprint, Cambridge: Dover Publications, 2011.
Munby, Jonathan. *Public Enemies, Public Heroes*. Chicago: University of Chicago Press, 1999.
*Scarface: Shame of a Nation*. Dir. Howard Hawks. Universal Pictures, 1932.
Schickel, Richard. *Intimate Strangers*. New York: Fromm International Publishing Company, 1986.
Susman, Warren I. *Culture as History*. New York: Pantheon Books, 1973.
*The Public Enemy*. Directed by William Wellman. Warner Brothers Pictures, 1931.
*The Roaring Twenties*. Directed by Raoul Walsh. Warner Brothers Pictures, 1939.
Warshow, Robert. *The Immediate Experience*. 1946. Reprint, Cambridge: Harvard University Press, 2001.

# 5

# Charlie Chaplin, Walter Benjamin, and the redemption of the city

*Barry J. Faulk*

## Chaplin and modernism

As a popular figure around the globe, Chaplin offers an ideal example of the "popular modernism" explored in this collection, in that he was embraced by a global audience that included many modernist writers. In his excellent study of modernism and movies, David Trotter remarks that "mainstream cinema mattered, to Joyce, Eliot, and Woolf" and "Chaplin's films help us to understand why."[1] This chapter follows Trotter's path-breaking study in focusing on how mainstream Hollywood cinema in the form of Charlie Chaplin exercised the imagination of modernist writers. My focus here is not on Chaplin's films per se, but on a common feature in how the silent film comedian was constructed in modernist commentary. This commentary inevitably turned to another topic of immense importance to literary modernism: the central role played by the metropolis in modern art. The writers that I discuss here emphasize how the Tramp and his knowing way in the city represents a significant new mode of being modern. Chaplin's artistry as a filmmaker is attributed to his unique ability to utilize the materials of street life to fashion his art form.

Specifically, modernist critics credited Chaplin's artistry to the unique skill set that he had acquired over the course of his life and career. These critics insisted that the "secret" behind his success as a filmmaker was his expert knowledge of the city itself. The comedian was known to have come from working class London, and his London background was believed to explain his uncanny skill at visualizing and representing urban types. His films were hailed as the modern-day equivalent to the "botanizing on the asphalt" famously described by Walter Benjamin in his landmark study of the Paris Arcades. For clarity, I divide my account of modernist commentary on Chaplin into sections dealing first with Continental and then Anglo-American writers. There are, however, marked continuities between the two groups; both share the premise that Chaplin represented a unique artist hero figure whose mastery of his art comes from his extensive knowledge of the metropolis.

## The failed *flâneur*

I begin my study of the modernist construction of Chaplin in what would seem to be an unpromising place: in an essay by Walter Benjamin that nowhere mentions the comedian, "Some Motifs of Baudelaire" (1939). That essay places Charles Baudelaire and many other French writers in the context of the structural transformation of Paris in the nineteenth century into a world city. While not mentioned by name in the essay, Chaplin and his art are a powerful shadow presence within it.

"Some Motifs of Baudelaire" is the culmination of Benjamin's twenty-year meditation on the poet, dating back to 1922. The essay builds on arguments that Benjamin developed in his proposal for his major study of the Paris Arcades, begun in the late 1930s and never completed. For this reason, my argument about Chaplin must begin here, in Benjamin's essay/prospectus for the Arcades Project, "The Paris of the Second Empire in Baudelaire" (1938). That essay is an extended treatment of the many different urban types that populated Paris in the 1850s and 60s, most famously the mysterious figure of the *flâneur*, the alienated, inquisitive, and implicitly male street loiterer. Benjamin's survey covers a vast range of peripatetics in a thoroughgoing endeavor to historicize French literature of the period, and make the case for the exemplary "modernity" of the greatest poet of the age, Charles Baudelaire.

Both "The Paris of the Second Empire" and the "Some Motifs" essays paint on an exceptionally large canvas, and present a wide-ranging portrait of *flânerie*. Benjamin represents Baudelaire as a heroic artist, but a failed *flâneur*. Although Baudelaire longs to escape from himself in the crowd, Benjamin suggests that the poet finds more pain than solace in his chosen refuge. This point is emphasized by Benjamin's comparison of Baudelaire with the *flâneur* narrators of Edgar Allen Poe's "The Man of the Crowd" and E. T. A Hoffmann's "The Cousin's Corner Window." Like Baudelaire, the narrators in these stories pay "rapt attention ... [to] the spectacle of the crowd."[2] However, unlike the poet, these spectators maintain their equanimity before what they survey. They "[view] the crowd with great circumspection" in the case of Hoffmann's narrator, or in Poe's storyteller, exercise a "penetrating gaze." These fictional versions of the *flâneur* assume a privileged position to the crowd, refusing to "forego the life of a gentleman of leisure" even in the hurly burly of the streets.[3] Hoffman's narrator adopts a superior attitude to the multitude, fancifully constructing "principles of the art of seeing" from his secure observation post. Benjamin presents this sanguine view of the crowd as a stark contrast with the image of the streets represented in Baudelaire's poetry. Behind the prose poem "A Lost Halo," Baudelaire's fanciful account of meeting a fellow writer who has lost his metaphorical "halo" while mingling with the crowd, Benjamin senses—or projects—an intensely personal pain: "Of all the experiences which made his life what it was, Baudelaire singled out his having been jostled by the crowd." Baudelaire, Benjamin concludes, primarily encountered the crowd through its "meanness."[4]

"Paris in the Second Empire," the first "draft" of "Some Motifs," is primarily a dark, extended meditation on the transformation of the city of Paris into a capitalist inferno.[5] However, the seeds of Benjamin's dialectical view of history, balanced between critique and revolutionary hope, are already present in the long expose for the Arcades Project. Even in the midst of hell, he hints, there are utopian possibilities.

For Benjamin, one surprising source of hope lies in the urban physiology, the literature of street life written for Parisian newspapers in the 1840s. The physiologue was a literary descriptive sketch of city dwellers that, as Benjamin explains, "investigated the human types that a person taking a look at the marketplace might encounter."[6] Benjamin shows a measure of respect and esteem for the genre as a unique and distinctive interface between literature and social practice. Along with the panorama, richly detailed pictures of city life created for museum exhibition, Benjamin suggests that the physiologue, a chief example of what he dubs "panoramic literature," is "marked by certain peculiarities which, upon closer inspection, reveal aspects of social forces of such power and hidden depth that we may count them among those which alone are capable of covering both a subtle and a profound effect upon artistic production."[7]

Yet at the same time, Benjamin also criticizes the physiologue for being a completely "petty-bourgeois genre."[8] Such writing presents the dislocations of urban modernity in its most beguiling, but also most deceptive aspects, as something "harmless and perfectly affable." Baudelaire stresses the pain that accompanies the attempt to merge with the crowd; the physiologue imagines the effortless assimilation of the individual within the collective. In this fashion, the genre provides the reading public with the false sense that "everyone could make out the profession, character, and background, and lifestyle of passers-by." The false promises of the physiologue lead Benjamin to conclude that the genre "constituted, so to speak, the blinkers of 'the narrow minded city animal' that Marx wrote about."[9]

As I have already noted, Benjamin categorized the physiologue among the various so-called panoramic arts that proliferated in the nineteenth century, along with the visual technologies of the stereoscope, the diorama, and the panorama. The aim of all these inventions was to extend the range of human perception, providing the citizen-spectator with a unique and highly detailed perception of the urban world of which they were a part. Although an implacable critic of liberal notions of unilinear progress, Benjamin's account of nineteenth century Paris nonetheless has an element of technological determinism. In the narrative he provides in the Arcades Project, the late Victorian invention of cinema is cast not only as the inheritor, but the culmination of the burgeoning panoramic arts. Technology, he writes, "has subjected the human sensorium to a complex kind of training," concluding that "there came a day when a new and urgent need for stimuli was met by *the film.*"[10] The advantage of cinema, unlike these earlier media, lies in the unique capacity to be put to collective use and thus to socialist purposes. The "Some Motifs" essay emphasizes the utopian possibilities of cinema, its capacity to transform the urban environment from the alien to the hospitable and to represent urban life for the first time without the ideological alibis and mystifications provided by the street sketch and the panorama.

The radical potential of film is closely linked in Benjamin's imagination to the prospect of a revolutionary refashioning of the *flâneur*-poet. Benjamin argues in "Some Motifs" that Baudelaire's poetry both suggests the poet's passionate desire to lose himself in the crowd, and famously, that the crowd itself constitutes the great absent center of his poetry, what the lyric poem cannot represent.[11] For Benjamin, Baudelaire's true greatness lies in this poetic "unconscious," which bears powerful witness to the shock of modernity. "If [Baudelaire] succumbed to the force by which he was drawn to [the crowd]," he writes, "he was nevertheless unable to rid himself of a sense of their essentially inhuman makeup."[12]

This amounts to saying that Baudelaire's poetry wears its modernity like a scar. He represents the artist overwhelmed: a heroic failure as a *flâneur*, beleaguered by the massive transformations in the capital city to which his poetry bears witness. However, from the dialectical point of view assumed in the Arcades Project, oscillating between the Infernal Present and Future Deliverance, Baudelaire's heroic martyrdom to his art also suggests that Redemption is imminent. The poet's own failure carries with it the possibility—the necessity for the dialectical thinker—of a Future Artist capable of succeeding where he failed, capable of imagining the crowd as his collaborator in the act of artistic creation.

Consistent with the technological determinism that distinguishes both "Some Motifs" and Benjamin's fullest treatment of film, "The Work of

Art in the Age of Mechanical Reproduction" (1936), Benjamin suggests that science itself will redeem the artist of the future, who is tasked with representing the life of the urban collective. The urban masses, educated by the many stimuli of urban life, culminating in cinema, await their representative artist. Although Baudelaire himself is unable to achieve a balance between his art form and the needs of the urban collective, Benjamin notes that the poet caught a glimpse of the Artist of the Future who might succeed where he failed, or at least recognized the tools that the future Artist would require. Baudelaire regarded the American writer Edgar Allen Poe as a visionary, and pledged full allegiance to Poe's schemes for a literature based on scientific principles. Here Benjamin continues and furthers Baudelaire's appreciation of Poe:

> Poe was one of the greatest technicians of modern literature. As Valéry pointed out, he was the first to attempt the scientific story, the modern cosmogony, and the description of pathological phenomena. These genres he regarded as exact products of a method for which he claimed universal validity.
>
> Baudelaire sided with him on this point and in Poe's spirit he wrote: "The time is approaching when it will be understood that a literature which refuses to proceed in brotherly concord with science and philosophy is a murderous and suicidal literature."[13]

The heroic example of Baudelaire finds fulfillment in a messianic figure able to transform urban experience in their own practice, thus reintegrating aesthetic form and social function. In "Some Motifs," Benjamin treats cinema as a utopian technology that by means of entertainment also equips spectators for urban living. Can the overpowering stimulus offered by the city inspire art, so that what Baudelaire registered as traumatic shock instead becomes the basis of a new art form?[14] Can the poet be assimilated to the collective in the manner of the writer of the Paris feuilleton, who combined work and everyday life in their ceaseless participant-observation of life on the boulevards? For Benjamin, cinema answered these questions in the affirmative, and, in "Some Motifs," Benjamin's last words on Baudelaire, film represents both the final redemption of the city-sketch and the city-dweller.

## Chaplin and the continental modernists

Benjamin tested out versions of these arguments about the artist and the metropolis in his critical writing on Chaplin in the late 1920s. He followed the French surrealist movement closely throughout the decade, and their writing had a considerable impact on his reflections on cinema. Benjamin's essay "Chaplin in Retrospect" was written in 1929, the same year that he published a major essay on the surrealist movement. Tellingly, the subtitle of the latter essay—"The Last Snapshot of the European Intelligentsia"— equates the critical gaze with the camera eye.

Benjamin's unique understanding of cinema as an evolutionary development of nineteenth century forms is already evident in his writing on Chaplin in the late 1920s. His notes toward a review of *The Circus* (1928) represent his first engagement with the English comedian. Benjamin's description of the Tramp's studied aloofness recalls the figure of the *flâneur*: "The chase is set in a maze; his unexpected appearance would astonish a magician; the mask of noninvolvement turns him into a fairground marionette."[15] Throughout Benjamin's film synopsis, he highlights the Tramp's mobility, equating the Tramp's image, and the camera itself, with the restless motion of the aimless *flâneur*. The closing scenes leave him spellbound: "Then you think the end is absolutely unavoidable, but then he gets up and you see him from behind, walking further and further away, with that gait peculiar to Charlie Chaplin; he is his own walking trademark, just like the company trademark you see at the end of the other films. And now, at the only point where there's no break and you'd like to be able to follow him with your gaze forever—the film ends!"[16] Benjamin's phrase "walking trademark" equates the Tramp with the commodity: the walking man is also the Walking Brand. Benjamin's précis of the closing shots of the film evoke a street scene, with the Tramp coming into our line of vision, only to disappear into the crowd. The Tramp's constant movement provides the only continuity in the succession of screen shots.

"Chaplin in Retrospect" both treats *The Circus* and assesses Chaplin's accomplishments thus far as a filmmaker. To Benjamin, Chaplin's personal history as a Londoner becomes especially clear from this vantage point. He equates the English comic actor's mastery of his medium to this historical fact. Here Benjamin acknowledges the influence of French surrealist poet and novelist Philippe Soupault, the author of several influential appreciations of Chaplin that in his words, "[contain] a number of ideas around which a definitive picture of the great artist one day may be able to crystallize."[17] Benjamin places special emphasis on Soupault's central insight into "the territorial origins of [Chaplin's] art," which lie "in the metropolis of London." From this perspective, a film from the late twenties like *The Circus* is in essential continuity with the rest of his work in that they all can be interpreted as expressions of Chaplin's foundational experience of the city. A substantial portion of the essay is taken up by this remarkable quote from Soupault:

> In his endless walks through the London streets, with their black and red houses, Chaplin trained himself to observe. He himself has told us

that the idea of creating his stock character—the fellow with the bowler hat, jerky walk, little toothbrush moustache, and walking stick—first occurred to him on seeing other workers walking along the Strand. What he saw in their bearing and dress was the attitude of a person who takes some pride in himself. But the same can be said of the other characters that surround him in his films. They, too, originate in London: the shy, young, winsome girl; the burly lout who is always ready to use his fists and then to take to his heels when he sees that people aren't afraid of him; the arrogant gentleman who can be recognized by his top hat.

In the manner of the "Some Motifs" essay, Soupault links the content of Chaplin films to everyday street scenes of the sort depicted in the physiologue. Significantly, neither Benjamin nor Soupault treat Chaplin as a *Hollywood* filmmaker; what matters instead are the "territorial origins" of his cinematic art.[18]

For Benjamin, these London roots, rather than Hollywood, explain why Chaplin is a global force in cinema: "With his art, Chaplin confirms the old insight that only an imaginative world that is firmly grounded in a society, a nation, and a place will succeed in evoking the great, uninterrupted, yet highly differentiated resonance that exists between nations."[19] Having explained to his satisfaction the reasons for Chaplin's artistic success, Benjamin goes on to clarify why Chaplin's pioneering films represent the antithesis of the Hollywood system. It has to do with the impositions of the Hollywood studio system, specifically budget restrictions, and how they limit the director's autonomy. "When we learn that 125,000 meters of film were shot for this 3,000-meter work," Benjamin observes, "we get some idea of the capital that this man requires, and that is at least as necessary to him as to a Nansen or an Amundsen if he is to make his voyages of discovery to the poles of the art of film. We must share Soupault's concern that Chaplin's productivity may be paralyzed by ... the ruthless competition of the American trusts." The obvious conclusion of this line of argumentation is that Chaplin's origins in London are more important to his art than the comedian's place within the Hollywood system.[20]

Benjamin's intellectual dialogue with surrealism is well known; the specific influence of Soupault on his understanding of Chaplin less so, but it is nonetheless crucial. Like Benjamin, Soupault the surrealist sees Chaplin through the lens of the dialectic, "where the present illuminates the past in a lighting flash."[21] The two writers also share a conception of the metropolis that is both materialist and mystical. In the long quote above, Soupault's Chaplin resembles a character from a Dickens novel, or perhaps Dickens himself, capable of turning observations of the urban scene into artful narrative. Soupault will conflate the two figures, Dickens and Chaplin, in his London reverie in "Westwego" (1917–1922) as well as in the scholarly essay on Chaplin that Benjamin references in "Chaplin in Retrospect."[22]

Soupault would render Paris in magical realist fashion in his novel *The Last Nights of Paris*, but London also held an equally important place in Soupault's imagination. He visited London as a child, with his family, and images of the Docks and Whitechapel, London's working class areas, stayed with him and would reverberate throughout all of his writing.[23] Soupault regarded these localities as enchanted spaces, where artists, criminals and other social outcasts lived together outside of the law. Soupault associated Chaplin himself with this magical—and highly romanticized—vision of London.[24] His 1931 narrative, *Charlot*, relates the adventures of an anonymous wanderer obviously modeled on Chaplin, with plot lines taken directly from Chaplin films, including *The Gold Rush* (1925), *The Circus*, and *City Lights* (1931). Soupault provides what might be seen as the *flâneur*'s mission statement in this remark about his Charlot: "Everything advises him (Charlot) not to remain motionless, and he refuses to listen to the people and things that suggest he should stop."[25]

The notion that Chaplin's genius was the product of his urban upbringing inspires both Benjamin and Soupault to invent their own version of "auteur" theory (ironically, given the immense value that Benjamin places on cinema as a collective art in his other commentary on film). Much film criticism of Chaplin in the 1920s struggled with the issue of what made Chaplin's movies so distinctive. For the Russian formalist critic Viktor Shklovsky, Chaplin's singularity was explained by the comedian's innovations as a film actor; he praises Chaplin for having "broken finally and completely with theatre and for that reason ... [gaining] the right to the title of the first film actor."[26] Prompted by Soupault's theory of Chaplin's metropolitan savvy, Benjamin goes beyond Shklovsky in "Chaplin in Retrospect." Decades before Alexandre Astruc and François Truffaut articulated their Auteur Theory, Benjamin would make a clear distinction between the work done by Chaplin the Actor and Chaplin the Director, and stress the greater importance of the latter. In "Chaplin in Retrospect," Benjamin develops the comparison Soupault would draw between Chaplin as actor and director to William Shakespeare's dual labor as actor and playwright, adding this detailed gloss: "What is meant by this is of course *not* that Chaplin is the 'author' of his film *scripts*. Rather, he is simply the author of his own films—that is to say, their director. Soupault has realized that Chaplin was the first (and the Russians have followed his example) to construct a film with a theme and variations—in short, with the element of composition—and that all this stands in complete opposition to films based on action and suspense."[27] Although Benjamin and Soupault make a unique contribution to Chaplin criticism, we shall see that they are not alone in equating cinema with the city, or in placing Chaplin films within this particular matrix.

## Chaplin and Anglo-American modernism

As singular as the continental view of Chaplin the film *flâneur* was, there are nonetheless important parallels between these observations and the Anglo-American modernist discourse of on Chaplin. We have seen that Benjamin imagined the coming of a cinematic *flâneur* who would redeem urban alienation by artistic means. Anglo-American film writing also makes unambiguous connections between Chaplin, cinema, and the metropolis. These writers insist that the city is at the core of Chaplin's artistic identity and more relevant than his place within the current Hollywood studio system. In many instances, the keywords of their critical discourse echo Benjamin and Soupault's notions of Chaplin's film *flânerie*.

As Laura Marcus observes, French avant-garde film criticism of the late 1910s and 1920s invented "a syllogism ... which could be expressed as 'cinema=movement, Chaplin=movement, therefore Chaplin=cinema.'"[28] The notion of cinematic movement carried significant weight in the film criticism of Fernand Léger, French film director Louis Delluc, and surrealist Louis Aragon. The term also historicizes "movement," specifically aligning it with the motions of the machine. French film theory generally, and the

FIGURE 5.1 *The portrayal of Chaplin in the* Ballet Mécanique, *directed by Fernand Léger (1923–4).*

surrealists in particular, saw Cinema as the ultimate product of the Machine Age, which in turn they associated with American industrial modernity.

These sentiments are given eloquent expression by Matthew Josephson, in his article "Made in America" (1923), published in *Broom*, a journal of the international avant-garde edited by Josephson and another American, Harold Loeb. Josephson explicitly links the special genius of the nation with industrial production; as he memorably puts it, "The machine is our magnificent slave, our fraternal genius. We are a new and hardier race, friend to the sky-scraper and the subterranean railway as well."[29] Appropriately enough, Fernand Léger's woodcuts representing Chaplin "as a fragmented, mechanical body," images that would later frame Léger's own avant-garde cinematic experiment, *Ballet Mecanique* (1924), were also featured in *Broom*. Chaplin the Tramp suggested a walking trademark to Benjamin, but for the French avant-garde, the figure also represented a version of what we would now call the Post-Human, and thus a weapon that could be wielded against humanist tradition. Laura Marcus nicely summarizes the complex set of relations between cinema, form, and the machine age developed in this strand of film criticism, noting that "Léger, (Yvan) Goll, and Gertrude Stein found in the early Chaplin films forms of rhythm, repetition, and automatization which they saw as performances of the essence of the cinematic machine and of modernity itself, and as profoundly at odds with the movements of plot and story," the latter deemed the mere detritus of a humanist culture made obsolete by Chaplin films.[30]

The Josephson essay also makes explicit how these notions of industrial movement could slip into an argument about the aesthetic superiority of American film. In sharp contrast to Benjamin and Soupault, Chaplin and his films bear the burden of American exceptionalism in Josephson. In the same article, Josephson immediately pivots from praise of the superiority of American "naïve profound film" over "artistic or literary German cinemas" to pay tribute to the primacy of the American city over all others. He singles out Chaplin as the filmmaker who best represents the "panorama" of the American city: "No cities will quite equal what New York or Chicago or Tulsa have ... Reacting to purely American sources, to the at once bewildering and astounding panorama, which only Chaplin and a few earnest unsung film-directors have mirrored, we may yet amass a new folk-lore out of the domesticated miracles of our time."[31]

Like Josephson, the American Gilbert Seldes was also living in Paris in 1923 when he wrote his pioneering and widely read defense of American popular culture, *The Seven Lively Arts*. Seldes shared the enthusiasm of Josephson and the French avant-garde for film as an art form, and also maintained that cinema was uniquely American. Chaplin plays a significant role in *The Seven Lively Arts*; the comedian legitimates the central claim of the book that cinema represents an artistic endeavor on a par with the so-called great arts of painting, writing, etc. The Tramp, Seldes writes, represents an aesthetic invention only possible in cinema: "The little figure ... is always a complete creation; it is not Chaplin and it is not a new combination of characteristics Chaplin has seen in other comedies; it is a whole separate thing, living by its own energies."[32]

Seldes's Chaplin, like Benjamin and Soupault's, escapes categorization as a Hollywood filmmaker. In fact, his image of the Tramp harkens back to the nineteenth anatomies of urban life that Benjamin chronicles in *The Arcades Project*. In this striking passage, the masks of the Tramp suggest various urban types, uncannily echoing the taxonomy of city dwellers—ragpickers, *flâneurs*, gamblers, and revolutionary conspirators—that Walter Benjamin presents in "The Paris of the Second Empire in Baudelaire." As a modern-day *flâneur* figure, Seldes imagines the Tramp has mastered all the various possibilities of disguise that might facilitate his untrammeled movement. Again, the code words of "movement" and "motion" are used in ways that suggest the urban context as the clear referent:

> Like every artist in whatever medium, Charlie has created the mask of himself—many masks, in fact—and the first of these, the wanderer, came in the Keystone comedies. It was there that he first detached himself from life and began to live in another world, with a specific rhythm of his own ... He created then that trajectory across the screen which is absolutely his own line of movement. No matter what the actual facts are, the curve he plots is always the same. It is of one who seems to enter from the corner of the screen, becomes entangled or involved in a force greater than himself as he advances upward and to the centre ... He wanders in, a stranger, an imposter, an anarchist, and passes again, buffeted but unchanged.[33]

Seldes's description of the Tramp anticipates Benjamin's reading of *The Circus*; both writers equate the motions of the Tramp with the movements of the camera and thus with the apparatus of film. The screen shot replaces the street as the field of vision, and the Tramp's activity on screen suggests the passage of a city dweller weaving in and out of the crowd, all the while maintaining his poise and aloofness from the scene.

Seldes's description of Chaplin introduces another significant keyword in the 1920s discourse on the comedian, "rhythm," in order to describe the Tramp's on-screen image. T. S. Eliot relies on the same word to describe Chaplin's unique features in the 1923 essay, "Dramatis Personae," where he offers the comedian this reluctant praise: "The egregious merit of Chaplin," he observes, "is that he has escaped in his own way from the realism of the cinema and invented a rhythm. Of course the unexplored opportunities of the cinema for eluding realism must be very great."[34] In his excellent study of cinema and modernism, David Trotter suggests Eliot's remarks have a largely instrumental function: praise for Chaplin doubles as advocacy for the experimental, anti-realistic aesthetic of modernism. Eliot's admiration of Chaplin for "being modern without being anti-mimetic" in his film art simultaneously affirms the value of Eliot's own literary work.[35]

However, Eliot's other references to Chaplin in the early twenties seem less occupied with modernist polemics; moreover, they provide striking parallels with the Benjamin–Soupault school of Chaplin criticism. In the ambitiously titled "The Romantic Englishman, The Comic Spirit and the Function of Criticism" (published in 1921), Eliot presents an alternative view of Chaplin that is more historical than aesthetic. The essay details a long view of English comedy, from Shakespeare through Dickens and beyond, to newspaper cartoons and contemporary theater. Chaplin is a contemporary addition to this august list of great comedians, and although Eliot emphasizes the comic's universal appeal—"Charlie Chaplin is not English, or American but a universal figure, feeding the idealism of hungry millions in Czechoslovakia and Peru"—it can hardly be an accident that Chaplin is included in Eliot's survey of English comedy, which is itself preoccupied with London life.[36] The suggestion seems to be that Chaplin is "not English, or American" because he is so obviously a Londoner, a figure of the global metropolis. Eliot's remarks here anticipate Benjamin's observation in "Chaplin in Retrospect" that the comedian's stature as an international star is the specific result of the comedian's London upbringing. As with Benjamin, the image of the Tramp is conflated with urban modernity, and the global reach of this image suggests the ubiquity of urbanization.

In recent scholarship, Gertrude Stein's remarks to Chaplin upon meeting the filmmaker have become an important component of the modernist reception of the filmmaker. According to Chaplin in his *Autobiography*, Stein held forth at their meeting, in David Trotter's words, on "the feebleness of [his] film plots."[37] In Chaplin's recollection: "She would like to see me in a movie just walking up the street and turning a corner, then another corner, and another."[38] Trotter compares Stein's remarks with T. S. Eliot's praise of the rhythmic movement of Chaplin on screen, and as yet another manifesto in brief for modernist aesthetics. In Trotter's words, "Stein [wished] to convert an occasional event or gesture into an abstract rhythm, into modernist anti-mimesis."[39] In Stein's polemical reading, Chaplin films are mechanisms both in their mode of production and in their single-minded subversion of narrative. Stein's ideal Chaplin film would jettison narrative structure altogether, replacing it with the *jouissance* of the urban scene, represented by the autonomous but highly situated movements of the Tramp on screen.

Trotter provides a compelling reading of Stein's remarks, but they shouldn't overshadow what seems to be her primary point: the complete and total identification of the Tramp with the urban scene. Stein's comments underscore the centrality of the street scene for Chaplin and his movies, equating the Tramp's comic walk with urban modernity. On this point, Stein and Eliot would seem to agree. For Eliot, the image of Chaplin on screen is the distilled essence of London. For Stein, the Tramp on the street represents the ur-Chaplin film in its purest form. And Stein and Eliot are at one with Walter Benjamin in holding that London finally matters more to Chaplin's artistry than the Hollywood studio system, or for that matter, America itself.

## Comic redemption

All these various appreciations of Chaplin, especially Benjamin's, presume that Chaplin films both represent technological modernity and somehow offer redemption from it. In Benjamin's essay "Theses on the Philosophy of History," written the year after "Some Motifs of Baudelaire," in the final year of his life, Benjamin would make the idea of redemption a necessary prerequisite for historical understanding. "The idea of happiness is indissolubly bound up with the idea of redemption," he writes, observing that "[t]he past carries with it a temporal index by which it is referred to redemption."[40] For Benjamin, understanding the relation between Chaplin's movies and his "territorial roots" in London is not simply a critical insight; it is a salutary reminder of the necessity of revolution, the only means to redemption. Benjamin's faith in revolution provides the context for his shocking observation at the close of "Chaplin in Retrospect": "In his films, Chaplin appeals both to the most international and the most revolutionary emotion of the masses: their laughter."[41] Benjamin allows Soupault the final word, in a flourish that brings his essay, and mine, to a close: "Chaplin merely makes people laugh. But aside from the fact that this is the hardest thing to do, it is socially the most important."[42]

## Notes

1  David Trotter, *Cinema and Modernism* (Malden, MA: Blackwell Publishing, 2007), 182.
2  Walter Benjamin, "The Paris of the Second Empire in Baudelaire," in *The Writer of Modern Life: Essays on Charles Baudelaire*, ed. Michael W. Jennings, trans. Howard Eiland, Edmund Jephcott, Rodney Livingston, and Harry Zohn (Cambridge: MA: Harvard University Press, 2006), 80.
3  Walter Benjamin, "Some Motifs of Baudelaire," in *Illuminations: Essays and Reflections*, ed. Hannah Arendt, trans. Harry Zohn (New York: Schocken Books, 1969), 173.
4  Ibid., 193.

5 "Some Motifs" is dated 1940 by the Harvard editors of Benjamin's writings and included among essays categorized under the heading "Materialist Theology."
6 Benjamin, "Paris," 67.
7 Benjamin, "Some Motifs," 170.
8 Benjamin, "Paris," 69.
9 Ibid., 70.
10 Benjamin, "Some Motifs," 175.
11 Cf. Benjamin's reading of the "absent" crowd in Baudelaire's "À Une Passante," from *Le Fleurs du Mal*, in "Some Motifs," 168.
12 Benjamin, "Some Motifs," 172.
13 Benjamin, "Paris," 74.
14 "Experience" is an important keyword in "Some Motifs," absent from "The Paris of the Second Empire in Baudelaire." In "Some Motifs," the term signifies a body of knowledge that has been slowly accumulated and passed down by the folk, and it is opposed to both "information" and "sensation." Following sociologist Georg Simmel, Benjamin understands urban life to be a decisive rupture with the past. Benjamin expresses the hope that cinema could restore a kind of shared wisdom based on experience for urbanites in "Some Motifs."
15 Walter Benjamin, "Chaplin: A Fragment," in *Selected Writings*, vol. 2, *1927–1934* (Cambridge, MA: Harvard University Press, 1999), 199.
16 Ibid., 200.
17 Benjamin, "Chaplin in Retrospect," in *Selected Writings*, vol. 2, *1927–1934*, 222.
18 John Kraniauskas expands on Benjamin's insights here on film as an international experience in "Laughing at Americanism: Benjamin, Mariátegui, Chaplin," in *Walter Benjamin: Critical Evaluations in Cultural Theory*, vol. 3, *Appropriations*, ed. Peter Osborne, (Routledge: London, 2005), 368–77.
19 Ibid., 223.
20 Again, Benjamin closely follows Soupault's lead throughout "Chaplin in Retrospect." See, for instance, Soupault's "Charlie Chaplin": "London had a tremendous influence on Charlie. Let's not forget; isn't it undoubtedly the only city in the world where both the most beautiful miracles and the greatest crimes can happen? ... It is London again that influenced his film scripts, always more British than American." In Soupault, "Charlie Chaplin," *Europe: Revue Mensuelle*, November 18, 1928, 380. (My gratitude to Manfa Sanogo for the translation.)
21 Walter Benjamin, "On the Concept of History," in *Selected Writings*, vol. 4, *1938–1940*, eds. Michael Jennings, Howard Eiland, and Gary Smith, trans. *Gesammelte Schriften* (Cambridge, MA: Harvard University Press, 2003), 390.
22 Keith Aspley, *The Life and Works of Surrealist Philippe Soupault: Parallel Lives* (Lewiston, PA: Edwin Mellon Press, 2001), 95.

23  Ibid., 13.
24  Soupault's "Ode to the Bombed London," written during the London Blitz, also reflects the surrealist's romantic view of the city: "Now we follow her good old ghosts, / Thomas Dekker gliding from tavern to tavern / And Thomas de Quincey drinking the sad, sweet poison of opium / To his poor Anne, on his dreamy way / Tonight when London is being bombed for the hundredth time" (*Ode to the Bombed London*, trans. Norman Cameron [Algiers: E. Charlot, 1944], 11). Soupault's vision of wartime London as a city haunted by the presence of its social outcasts, including its renegade artists, anticipates the spectral city that would later feature in the work of Iain Sinclair, headquartered in modern day Hackney.
25  Aspley, *the Life and Works*, 233.
26  Quoted in Laura Marcus, *The Tenth Muse: Writing About Cinema in the Modernist Period* (Oxford: Oxford University Press, 2007), 227.
27  Benjamin, "Chaplin in Retrospect," 222–3.
28  Quoted in Marcus, *The Tenth Muse*, 227.
29  Ibid., 228–9.
30  Ibid., 229.
31  Ibid., 229.
32  Ibid., 227.
33  Ibid., 232.
34  T. S. Eliot, "Dramatis Personae," in *The Complete Prose of T. S. Eliot*, vol. 2, *The Critical Edition, The Perfect Critic, 1919–1926*, eds. Anthony Cuda and Ronald Schuchard (Baltimore: Johns Hopkins University Press, 2014), Project Muse e-book, 438.
35  Trotter, *Cinema and Modernism*, 193.
36  T. S. Eliot, "The Romantic Englishman, The Comic Spirit, and the Function of Criticism," in *The Complete Prose of T. S. Eliot: The Critical Edition*, vol. 2, *The Perfect Critic, 1919–1926*, eds. Anthony Cuda and Ronald Schuchard (Baltimore: Johns Hopkins University Press, 2014), Project Muse e-book, 303.
37  Trotter, *Cinema and Modernism*, 198.
38  Charles Chaplin, *My Autobiography* (New York: Simon and Shuster, 1964), 306.
39  Trotter, *Cinema and Modernism*, 198.
40  Walter Benjamin, "Theses on the Philosophy of History," in *Illuminations: Essays and Reflections*, ed. Hannah Arendt, trans. Harry Zohn (New York: Schocken Books, 1969), 254.
41  Benjamin, "Chaplin in Retrospect," 224.
42  Ibid.

# Bibliography

Aspley, Keith. *The Life and Works of Surrealist Philippe Soupault: Parallel Lives*. Lewiston, PA: Edwin Mellon Press, 2001.
Benjamin, Walter. *Illuminations: Essays and Reflections*, edited by Hannah Arendt, translated by Harry Zohn. New York: Schocken Books, 1969.
Benjamin, Walter. *The Writer of Modern Life: Essays on Charles Baudelaire*, edited by Michael W. Jennings, translated by Howard Eiland, Edmund Jephcott, Rodney Livingstone, and Harry Zohn. Cambridge: MA: Harvard University Press, 2006.
Benjamin, Walter. *Selected Writings*, edited by Michael Jennings, Howard Eiland, and Gary Smith, translated by *Gesammelte Schriften*. 4 vols. *1913–1940*. Cambridge, MA: Harvard University Press, 1999.
Chaplin, Charles. *My Autobiography*. New York: Simon and Shuster, 1964.
Eliot, T. S. "Dramatis Personae." In *The Complete Prose of T. S. Eliot: The Critical Edition: The Perfect Critic, 1919–1926*, edited by Anthony Cuda and Ronald Schuchard. Baltimore: Johns Hopkins University Press, 2014. Project Muse e-book.
Eliot, T. S. "The Romantic Englishman, The Comic Spirit, and the Function of Criticism," in *The Complete Prose of T. S. Eliot: The Critical Edition. The Perfect Critic, 1919–1926*, edited by Anthony Cuda and Ronald Schuchard. Baltimore: Johns Hopkins University Press, 2014. Project Muse e-book.
Kraniauskas, John. "Laughing At Americanism: Benjamin, Mariátegui, Chaplin." In *Walter Benjamin: Critical Evaluations in Cultural Theory*, vol. 3, *Appropriations*, edited by Peter Osborne, 368–77. Routledge: London, 2005.
Marcus, Laura. *The Tenth Muse: Writing About Cinema in the Modernist Period*. Oxford: Oxford University Press, 2007.
North, Michael. *Reading 1922: A Return to the Scene of the Modern*. Oxford: Oxford University Press, 1999.
Soupault, Philippe. "Charlie Chaplin." *Europe: Revue Mensuelle*, November 18, 1928, 379–402.
Soupault, Philippe. *Ode to the Bombed London*, translated by Norman Cameron. Algiers: E. Charlot, 1944.
Trotter, David. *Cinema and Modernism*. Malden, MA: Blackwell Publishing, 2007.

PART TWO

# Legacies of Popular Modernism

# 6

# "Catch a wave": Surf noir and modernist nostalgia

## Kirk Curnutt

Hardboiled crime fiction, despite its mass-market popularity, is at heart a modernist genre. Its 1920s nascence was influenced by moderns out to "make it new" (Ernest Hemingway) before it in turn inspired many of them (William Faulkner, Gertrude Stein, Hemingway himself) to emulate its form and style.[1] Like modernist literature, the "tough-guy" school often resists resolution. Cases may be closed and culprits revealed, but hermeneutic puzzles remain unsolved, with contradictory clues dramatizing what Ernest Lockridge calls "the modernist predicament," the paralyzing awareness "that it is impossible to see or know anything absolutely."[2] Mining concerns over cultural decay and alienation, both genres shield their vulnerabilities behind an armature of tight-lipped masculinity that, at worst, gives way to masochistic nihilism or, at best, projects a "hardboiled sentimentality" that soothes despair by embodying personal standards of "grace under pressure" integrity.[3] Although modernism became a museum piece circa 1960, its defeatist sensibility remains the distinguishing tone of highbrow art: "Real literature," Umberto Eco insisted shortly before his 2015 death, "is about losers."[4] Similarly, despite the near-century since hardboiled crime fiction emerged from the pulp pages of *Black Mask Magazine*, the genre has changed remarkably little. It may have diversified into subcategories (procedurals, thrillers, noir), but its standard inability to redeem justice from social corruption, or even to believe in truth, continues. Whether Philip Marlowe, Lew Archer, Hieronymus "Harry" Bosch, Easy Rawlins, or Kinsey Milhone, the crime-solver remains a version of T. S. Eliot's impotent Fisher King, a knight errant unable to set the mean streets in order.[5]

Two additional consanguinities stand out. First, as John Scaggs notes, the setting for modernism and hardboiled crime fiction alike is usually an urban environment so rife with "artifice, insubstantiality, fakery, and façades" that the metropolis—personified through its governing institutions, history, lifestyle, or even geography—becomes a veritable character in the drama.[6] Second, the inhabitants of these "unreal cities," as Eliot would call them, express nostalgia for their locales' prelapsarian past. From *The Big Sleep* (1939) to *Playback* (1958), for example, Raymond Chandler depicted Los Angeles—the most famous hardboiled-crime setting—as a fallen paradise infested with avarice and concupiscence. "I used to like this town," Chandler's Marlowe sighs in *The Little Sister* (1949). "A long time ago ... Los Angeles was just a big dry sunny place with ugly homes and no style, but goodhearted and peaceful."[7]

Such quotes will sound familiar to aficionados of L.A. crime fiction, some of whose notions of its modernist disgruntlement may be complicated by revisionary studies such as Mike Davis's *City of Quartz* (1992) or documentaries like Thom Andersen's *Los Angeles Plays Itself* (2003).[8] Yet for all the scholarly attention lavished upon hardboiled writers' obsession with the City of Angels, one local subgenre remains relatively unexplored. Admittedly, the category of *surf noir* is numerically small. The term tends to be applied to a single author: Kem Nunn (1948–), a Pomona-born television writer/producer best known for *Tapping the Source*, a 1984 cult novel often cited as the basis for Kathryn Bigelow's 1990 surfer-crime flick *Point Break*, starring Patrick Swayze and Keanu Reeves. Although that attribution is incorrect, *Source* and several comparable crime novels do explore the rise, corruption, and ultimate legacy of the surf-pop culture that boomed along the beaches of Southern California between roughly 1957 and 1966.[9] Surfing both predated and survived this period, of course, but the first half of the 1960s is the era in which the L.A. beach scene was most obviously transformed into a fad, its lifestyle appropriated by music, fashion, and—yes—even quality literature.[10] For hardboiled novelists of the period like Ross Macdonald, the surf world represents a dangerous youth culture that, as an embodiment of anomie, sparks the private detective's nostalgia for parental authority and family cohesion.

Yet in the work of Nunn and other contemporary authors—including Thomas Pynchon in *Inherent Vice* (2009)—surf culture is *the object* of that nostalgia, symbolic of the passing of baby-boomer innocence into the tumult of the late 1960s and 1970s. Apropos of Macdonald, the ultimate cause of the subculture's corruption are broken family relationships, which allow corrupt mentor figures, many of them either explicitly or allusively connected to Charles Manson, to exert a nefarious influence and destroy the beach ethos. What makes the nostalgia that compensates for this breakdown modernistic is the figure of the surfer, who functions as the consummate craftsman who stands outside the commodification of art (or sport) to commit to the purity of aesthetic ideals. For Pynchon, the surfer-as-artist has a surprising coeval in one real-life musical figure who originally came to fame for exploiting the surf scene as a musical fad but went on to be heralded as a visionary whose Icarus-like rise and fall, itself precipitated by familial abuse, has become its own touchstone of nostalgia: Brian Wilson, the chief songwriter and producer for the Beach Boys.

## Let's go surfing now

As historians note, early glimpses of surfing appear in Herman Melville's *Mardi, or a Voyage Thither* (1848), Mark Twain's *Roughing It* (1872), and Jack London's "Surfing: A Royal Sport" (1907).[11] Migrating to California thanks to Second World War servicemen who discovered the hobby in Polynesian outposts, the sport became a popular youth pastime in the 1950s. Its pop-culture appropriation began in 1957 with Frederick Kohner's novel *Gidget: the Little Girl with Big Ideas*. Gidget was based on Kohner's fifteen-year-old daughter, Kathy (b. 1941), who befriended several Malibu surfers, most significantly Terry-Michael "Tubesteak" Tracy (1935–2012) and Miklos "Miki" Dora, later known as "Da Cat" (1934–2002). As *Vanity Fair* noted in 2006, *Gidget* predated Jack Kerouac's *On the Road* by only a few months and far outsold that Beat Generation totem, with a half-million copies in print by the decade's end.[12]

Pop-culture aficionados likely associate Gidget—a portmanteau of "girl" and "midget"—with the quaintly virginal star of the 1959 film adaptation, Sandra Dee, or perhaps with the cherubic Sally Field of the 1965–6 TV show. The novel's treatment of youth culture is racier, however, paralleling Kerouac's. Much as *On the Road* popularized beatnik slang, *Gidget* introduced surf argot to the wider world—it is thanks to Kohner that the word "bitchen" entered common usage.[13] *Gidget* is also surprisingly frank on teen sexuality. Most importantly, as Kristin Lawler notes, the novel portrays Tracy and Dora's lightly fictionalized clique as sharing the Beat Generation's bohemian rejection of professional advancement, bourgeois prosperity, and consumerism. "Tubesteak" Terry lived in a shack improvised from telephone poles and palm fronds that so rankled authorities they tore it down—a hipster-vs.-squares conflict that loosely forms the climax of *Gidget*.[14] In effect, Hollywood adaptations of Kohner's novel did to "beachniks" what *Mad Magazine* and Maynard G. Krebs on CBS-TV's *The Many Loves of Dobie Gillis* (1959–63) did to beatniks: they contained the rebellious threat the subculture posed by rendering the character of the "surf bum" ridiculous. The depiction hardly stopped kids from flocking to the ocean, though. One surfing enthusiast, sixteen-year-old Dennis Wilson of the inland L.A. suburb Hawthorne, returned from a day at Manhattan

Beach Pier in 1961 to encourage his older brother, Brian, to write a song about the lifestyle.[15] Thus was born the Beach Boys' first single, "Surfin'," which led in quick succession to "Surfin' Safari," "Surfin' USA," "Surfer Girl," "Catch a Wave," "Girls on the Beach," "California Girls," and a host of songs that nationalized California beach life into an idyllic paradise where summer never waned.

As Lawler demonstrates, adults rarely embraced surf culture as the utopian lark that rock historians now celebrate "Surfin' USA" or Jan and Dean's "Surf City" as. Instead, the subculture prompted "great concern on the part of parents, property owners, teachers, police, and community leaders that the new and growing crop of 'surf bums' was an increasing threat to the law and order they were enforcing."[16] This threat explains the earliest appearance of the rebel surfer in crime fiction. Published in November 1962, barely a week before the Beach Boys' first album, *Surfin' Safari*, broke onto the music charts, *The Zebra-Striped Hearse* is the tenth entry in Ross Macdonald's Lew Archer series. As Michael Kreyling notes, it is the first Macdonald novel to examine "the downside of youth culture." The titular vehicle belongs to "a nomadic band of surfers, whom Archer meets at first accidentally and a second time by intent."[17] The ominousness of youth cruising the coast in a retro-fitted chariot of death hardly seems accidental considering the car most associated with surfers was not a hearse but the wood-paneled station wagons dubbed "woodies"—as in "We're loadin' up our woodies with our boards inside / So if you're coming get ready to go."[18]

As Kreyling argues, Macdonald's "directionless youth" symbolize "radical estrangement in the Promised Land." The boys have long hair, the girls short, and in their indistinctness they don't act as individuals but move "in unison like a platoon."[19] On several occasions Archer refers to them as a "tribe." Only one girl, Mona, encourages the "comitatus" to assist Archer.[20] The gumshoe ponders the girl's fate among such a disaffected cohort: "As I drove back toward Los Angeles, I wondered what Mona was doing on the beach. Maybe if I met her father or her mother I could stop wondering."[21] For Macdonald, the surfers represent a youth culture untethered from adult oversight, left only to its own introversion for moral guidance—a depiction that many real-life habitués of the subculture in time felt rang true.[22]

Macdonald had compelling personal reasons for worrying about youth's unsupervised energies. In 1956 his teenaged daughter, Linda, had killed two thirteen-year-olds in a drunken hit-and-run accident; three years later, she disappeared under mysterious circumstances, prompting a ten-day nationwide search that ended in a bar in Reno. Although Macdonald guiltily believed his daughter's difficulties were retribution for his own seduction at an exceedingly young age of a mentally handicapped girl, he also saw Linda as a harbinger of a generational inability to control its impulses.[23] Yet *The Zebra-Striped Hearse* does not condemn youth. Rather, as Archer's comment about Mona's father and mother suggests, their anomie is the fault of inattentive parents who have allowed the family unit to erode beyond repair, a point reinforced by the novel's main plot. Hired by the imperious Colonel Blackwell to find his missing daughter, Harriet, Lew Archer discovers, in Leonard Cassuto's words, that "her parents have failed her so miserably" that the crimes she eventually confesses to committing are "almost an afterthought." Instead, blame for Harriet's problems lies squarely with the adulterous, hypocritical Colonel, who commits suicide upon realizing how his behavior damaged her. As Cassuto writes, Macdonald was "the first crime novelist to treat the generation gap with sensitivity." As such, his depiction of the surfers reads like a prescient warning to parents about the estrangement that in the later 1960s enabled the rise of dangerous countercultures as tribal substitutes for family.[24]

The year after *The Zebra-Striped Hearse*, surf culture exploded into a national fad before the Summer of Love and the hippie movement supplanted it in 1967. In this four-year timeframe, exploitation novels such as *Surf Broad*, *Surf Safari Nurse*, and *Surfside Sex* cashed in on the scene. These disposable paperbacks are to surf fiction what the Fantastic Baggys' "Tell 'Em I'm Surfin'" is to authentic surf music: transparent cash-ins. (Although the Beach Boys were initially considered appropriators of the subculture, their congenial lyrics, coupled with their breathtaking harmonies, gave voice to surf music, which was previously an instrumental genre.) While few pulp surf novels today merit interest beyond their retro-kitsch pleasures, one example provides a surprising transition between Macdonald's nostalgia and the type found in surf noir from the 1970s on. Between 1969 and 1973, George Snyder published ten entries in his Operation Hang Ten series under the pen name Patrick Morgan. These zesty crime novels chronicle the adventures of Bill Cartwright, a P.I./ government spy who splits his time between catching waves and uncovering criminal conspiracies (when not bedding nubile surfer girls). The series' seventh installment, *The Girl in the Telltale Bikini*, finds Cartwright relocating to Australia's Gold Coast to determine how an imposter has framed him for stealing top-secret documents. Along the way he battles a cult led by a sinister guru with the unlikely name Maha Lon Caffrey. As Cartwright discovers, Caffrey employs the phony surfer impersonating him to seduce beach bunnies into his white-slave ring and sell the stolen intelligence to Middle Eastern governments by secreting the information in his victims' bikinis.[25]

Gurus and cults as fronts for criminal enterprises are nothing new in California crime fiction. Hammett's *The Dain Curse* (1929) finds his Continental Op foiling an Aleister Crowley-like cult, while Macdonald's first Archer mystery, *The Moving Target* (1949), features a crooked spiritual leader suspected of kidnapping a missing millionaire. Both the cover imagery and promotional text on *The Girl in the Telltale Bikini*, however, link Maha Lon Caffrey to one real-life cult leader whose conviction for L.A.'s most infamous murder spree occurred the same year as the book's publication: Charles Manson. Manson's connection to surf culture is tenuous but tantalizing. A year before the murders of actress Sharon Tate and six others on August 9 and 10, 1969, he and the itinerant band of dropouts and runaways he dubbed "The Family" resided at the Sunset Strip home of the same Dennis Wilson who inspired the Beach Boys to sing surfing songs at the decade's outset.[26] (Dennis was the lone true surfer in the band.) Thanks to the historical notoriety of the Manson/Wilson link, surf noir from the 1970s on warns against the influence of older mentor figures who exploit youth culture for nefarious purposes, much the way that Morgan's phony Cartwright uses his athletic prowess on the waves to bedazzle beach kids and recruit them into Caffrey's cult.

As it turns out, this concern long predated Manson. A striking aspect of the *Gidget*-era beach culture was the age disparity among its denizens. The surf bums young Kathy Kohner hung out with were not teenagers but in some cases nearly a decade older. By September 1961 when *Life Magazine* published its oft-analyzed essay "The Mad Happy Surfers," its three featured enthusiasts were disciples of Miki Dora, remembered today as *the* quintessential surfer, the subject of several biographies and rumored movie biopics.[27] Dora's status is as much a tribute to his iconoclasm as to his incontestable athletic grace. As one of *Life*'s subjects, Larry Shaw, recalled to *Vanity Fair* forty-five years after the pictorial, "Malibu was a counterculture before the counterculture ... And there was Miki ... this Fagin-like character who was 10 years older than us but was just as adolescent as we were." When not at the beach, Dora survived as a scammer and cat burglar, infiltrating Beverly Hills parties and spiriting off cash, food, jewelry, and cars. "He did it all for a simple reason: freedom," another acolyte recalled. "Every guy on that beach wanted to do nothing but surf all day, but only Miki had found a way to do it."[28]

Dora's legend grew long after the pop-surf boom subsided. In 1973 he fled the U.S. to avoid fraud charges, only returning after eight years on the lam to serve a prison sentence. Unlike another charismatic surfer-turned-felon, Jack "Murph the Surf" Murphy (1938–), Dora was never accused of murder, so it may seem inappropriate to call him a proto-Manson figure. And yet intriguing connections between the pair encourage just such a linkage: Dora and Manson purportedly met through Dennis Wilson in 1968; a decade and a half later, Dora re-encountered the cult leader while incarcerated at the same Vacaville, California, prison.[29] Thanks to this contiguity, the Pied Piper-like sway both men exerted over their followers has served respectively as a cautionary tale about youth's naiveté and the corruption of adolescents' tribal instincts by mentors serving as surrogate parent figures. In Kem Nunn's surf noir, this corruption excites a nostalgia for the supposed innocence of original surf culture, which Nunn scripts into a devotion of the aesthetics of the sport.

## Kem Nunn and the surfer as modernist artist

Dora is explicitly cited as a paragon of authenticity in two of Nunn's three surf noir novels, *The Dogs of Winter* (1997) and *Tijuana Straits* (2004). As Sam Fahey, the ex-con protagonist of *Tijuana Straits* explains, "[Dora] had this riff about riding a wave, above the lip of the wave, the parts that's throwing out over your shoulder. That stuff in the lip, that's everything that's out to get you—cops, teachers, priests, bureaucrats, everything that would say your life has to be this or that ... it's all going by, and you just keep on riding, keep tapping that source, 'cause that's where it's at ... life in the moment."[30] In his dedication to aesthetics, Dora represents for Nunn a version of the modernist artist, the genius who creates new forms and techniques while resisting the corruptions of the marketplace. Surfers throughout Nunn's triptych struggle with the market appropriations Dora railed against in the mid-1960s: *Tapping the Source* condemns surf competitions and surf shops for commercializing the sport; *Dogs* depicts surf photography as encouraging hot-dogging for fame; and *Straits* regrets the ecological impact of its popularity. Amid their crime plots, the novels appeal to what Lawler calls the key "recurring theme in surf nostalgia," the belief that there is a firm "separation between 'real,' 'authentic' surf culture and surfers, of which Dora is clearly canonized as one, and the phony surf image" popularized through beach-party movies and derivative surf music.[31]

Despite his reverence for Dora's artistry, Nunn never denies the contradiction in "Da Cat's" reputation as "a great surfer and a beguiling sociopath," as *Vanity Fair* put it.[32] Instead, the novelist incorporates this dualism into his plots to question the role of mentors in forming youth's morality. If Lew Archer laments the absence of strong parent figures and familial cohesion, Nunn's triptych asks how the mad happy surfers coming of age in the mid-1960s were supposed to know which idols were benign and which were lethal. The issue is the dramatic crux of *Tapping the Source*, which effectively splits the competing sides of Dora's personality into two diametrical characters: the surfer-philosopher vs. the surfing Fagin-figure. As naïve narrator Ike Tucker searches early 1980s Huntington Beach for his missing sister, Ellen, he befriends two estranged surfers from the 1960s, Preston March and Hound Adams. Like Miki the purist, Preston has renounced the beach scene, including the successful surf shop he and Hound co-founded. Like Miki the scammer, Hound uses surfing as a front for illicit activities, including drug pushing and pornography.

The deeper Ike probes Ellen's disappearance, the more he uncovers his mentors' connection to their Manson-like mentor, Milo Trax. While Preston has eluded Trax's clutches by breaking with Hound, Hound himself has become a minion, doing Milo's perverted bidding by feeding beach girls (including Ellen) to members of his sex cult. In this way, Hound resembles the phony Bill Cartwright in *The Telltale Bikini*, even though Nunn's tone is worlds away from Morgan's cartoonish exploitation. In both cases the conduit between the once-innocent beach culture and the false guru is the corrupted surfer who extratextually links Miki Dora to Charles Mason.

For many readers, the climactic appearance of Milo's cult, "decked out ... elaborately in a kind of funky evening dress that seemed to Ike to be more costume than anything else," nearly ruins *Tapping the Source* by evoking the Satanist hysteria that Manson, with his glib references to himself as both Jesus Christ and the Devil, at once stoked and parodied.[33] (The cult's costume even resembles the corny outfits that Maha Lon Caffrey's disciples sport on the cover of *Telltale Bikini*.) Nevertheless, Nunn's message is not dissimilar from Ross Macdonald's: youth's belief in "life in the moment," epitomized by surfing, leads to moral isolation as much as moral freedom. After a bloody shootout in which Preston and Hound mortally confront each other, "while the invisible surf pounded below them, the last heartbeat of a dream gone bad," Ike realizes that his heroes' deaths represent the failure of youth tribalism when bereft of proper adult influence. As it turns out, both Preston and Hound sowed the seeds of their destruction by compromising the purity of surfing when at their athletic peak they named their shop Tapping the Source: the image referred not to the sport's spiritual essence but to an inside joke about the drug running the pair fell into as a sideline, leading them to Milo.[34]

Rather than denounce the catchphrase, the novel ends with Ike trying to redeem it as nostalgic ideal by reproducing the logo Preston and Hound created when they opened their store, drawing the image in colored wax on the brick wall of the pair's now-abandoned surf shop atop several layers of paint where the original once glowed. Doing so, Ike himself becomes a version of the modernist artist, devoted to "speak[ing] in some secret voice of a secret thing": "For the first time [Ike] was not inclined to run. Because that secret was what there was, he thought. And the pursuit of it was all that mattered."[35] Revivifying the secret, pure idea of "tapping the source" is the aim of the heroes of *The Dogs of Winter* and *Tijuana Straits*, too. As such, Nunn leverages nostalgia for the sport's innocence against the defeatism in which noir often revels.

## The beached boy: Brian Wilson and familial nostalgia in *Inherent Vice*

Miki Dora is not explicitly named in Pynchon's *Inherent Vice*, but Charles Manson certainly is. Set in 1970 on the eve of the Manson trials, this shambolic pastiche—in which Pynchon pokes fun at the disjunction between the classic tropes of detective fiction and the counterculture era with which he remains enamored—leads pot-smoking P.I. Doc Sportello through an L.A. paranoid over the Tate-LaBianca murders. Doc's nemesis, LAPD detective Bigfoot Bjornsen, coins an adjective to convey the state of being over the hippie homicide spree: "Mansonoid."[36] For Pynchon, Manson symbolizes the random "hand" that will "reach terribly out of the darkness and reclaim [an era], easy as taking a joint from a doper and stubbing it out for good," extinguishing "this little parenthesis of light" that the "Psychedelic Sixties" represent for the writer.[37] Against this darkness, *Inherent Vice* seeks to cling to lightness, both in its slapstick tone and in its choice of countervailing imagery. As one such point of light, Pynchon even depicts his most Doraesque character, an incorruptible surfing purist called St. Flip of Lawndale, as a Christ figure who embodies what one reviewer calls the "incarnational hopefulness of California dreaming."[38]

St. Flip is a minor character, however. A subplot depicting a more developed source of "incarnational hopefulness" focuses on a surf-music performer instead of a surfer. As Doc investigates various conspiratorially connected cases, he learns about the disappearance of Coy Harlingen, a saxophonist for a leading surf band called the Boards. Coy has supposedly died of a heroin overdose, although his widow, Hope, refuses to believe the rumor. As Doc discovers, the musician faked his death to escape celebrity and cure his addiction but at the price of becoming an unwilling agent provocateur for "different antisubversive outfits." Because Coy's shadowy handlers forbid him from contacting Hope and their daughter, Amethyst, Doc must bargain for his freedom to reunite the family.[39]

In many respects, Coy Harlingen seems designed to recall the Beach Boys' Brian Wilson, whose withdrawal from the public eye in the period in which *Inherent Vice* is set after masterminding his band's popular and groundbreaking hits from 1962–7 remains one of rock 'n' roll's most enduring legends. Like the Beach Boys, the Boards are described as blossoming from a garage band into musical "pioneers," having founded a "subgenre they called 'surfadelic'" that blends dissonance, sound effects, and vocal harmonies into a form far more inventive than the standard blues progressions surf hits were based on.[40] In 1966, Wilson wrote, produced, and arranged *Pet Sounds*, one of rock's most influential and progressive albums, as well as the single "Good Vibrations," a psychedelic collage that broke pop music's rigid, repetitive structure. He was famously at work on a conceptual tour de force called *Smile* when, overwhelmed by group resistance and drug abuse, he retreated to his bedroom to spend the 1970s as the "Howard Hughes of rock," as famous for his reclusiveness as for his musical accomplishments. The connection between the Boards' rumored masterwork and *Smile* is cemented by Pynchon's description of a *Rolling Stone* article that insists "the Boards' new album will make Jimi Hendrix *want* to listen to surf music again."[41] After Wilson abandoned *Smile* in 1967 and the Beach Boys plunged precipitously from the pop-music charts, the guitar virtuoso ended his song "Third Stone from the Sun" with the words "You'll never have to listen to surf music again," a line widely interpreted as dismissing the Beach Boys as has-beens.[42]

To be sure, enough differences distinguish Harlingen from Wilson to prevent *Inherent Vice* from being a *roman-à-clef*. As previously noted, Harlingen is a saxophonist, not a songwriter and singer with an achingly vulnerable falsetto. Pynchon also wisely avoids labeling him a "genius," a honorific that has both sustained Wilson's legend in rock criticism (to the point of becoming a cliché) and served as a code word for the mental illness for which only three decades later in the 1990s would he finally receive proper treatment.[43] Nevertheless, when Coy steps out of the shadows of the Club Asiatique looking bedraggled, his rumored "death and its other side effects [having] destroyed any fashion sense [he] might have had," his description recalls the oft-republished photo that Annie Leibovitz captured of a forlorn and dazed Wilson for *Rolling Stone* (c. 1971) dressed in a bathrobe and tennis shoes, manning the floor of a health-food store called the Radiant Radish he briefly operated in L.A.[44]

Similarly, the scene in which Doc journeys to the Boards' communal home in Topanga Canyon, encountering Coy with "a look on his face so desperate, so longing, and way too nervous," recalls the weird domestic atmosphere depicted in the two-part article that the Leibovitz photo illustrates, Tom Nolan's "The Beach Boys: A California Saga."[45] The profile captures to an uncomfortable degree the environment at Wilson's Beverly Hills mansion as family and entourage deny his crumbling mental state while insisting his musical gifts are intact. (Not insignificantly, thirty years later Nolan would pen the definitive Ross Macdonald biography.) Doc's trip to meet Coy goes bad: thanks to smoking "mystery weed," the P.I. has a nightmarish vision of partygoers as zombies, sending him "fleeing through the corridors of the creepy old mansion with uncertain numbers of flesh-eating creatures behind him."[46] For Pynchon, the scene may have personal relevance. In an anecdote well known to fans of both Wilson and Pynchon, the pair were introduced in 1966 by mutual friend Jules Siegel, a journalist then writing the definitive account of *Smile*'s conception and abandonment, "Goodbye Surfing, Hello God: The Religious Conversion of Brian Wilson." Siegel invited the twenty-nine-year-old author of the recently published *The Crying of Lot 49* to meet the twenty-four-year-old auteur behind the recently released *Pet Sounds* at the latter's home. The duo smoked hashish in an Arabian tent erected in Wilson's living room, but instead of a meeting of the minds, the artists retreated into stoned, paranoid silence, "one of the strangest scenes I'd ever seen in my life," as Siegel told Wilson biographer Peter Ames Carlin.[47]

Significantly, although alluding to the chief Beach Boy's withdrawal, Pynchon does not depict Coy Harlingen as a victim of record-industry exploitation as Wilson frequently is, pressured both by the business and his family to grind out surf hits instead of chasing artistic innovation. ("Don't fuck with the formula," lead singer Mike Love supposedly commanded Wilson while recording the avant-garde *Pet Sounds*.[48]) Rather, the light that Wilson's story represents is channeled through the drama of Coy's reunion with Hope and Amethyst. As Geoffrey O'Brien has noted, for many baby-boomer admirers of Brian Wilson throughout the 1970s, both his music and the story of his decline and withdrawal served as a "talisman against suffering, or else a talisman designed to induce a suffering that, it was hoped, would lead to the same kind of aesthetic satori."[49] The empathetic touchstone of this anguish was parental abuse and betrayal. Nolan's "California Saga" was the first article to document the macabre punishments and humiliations that Wilson and his brothers (including Dennis and the youngest sibling, Carl, who was barely fifteen when the Beach Boys broke onto the charts) suffered at the hands of their controlling father, Murry (1917–73), their original manager. Among those abuses, none startled more than the rumor reported by Nolan that in Brian's infancy Murry had struck him hard enough to cause nearly 95 percent deafness in his right ear, a disability that makes his accomplishments as a songwriter and producer all the more astonishing. Despite a denial from Murry, Nolan's article explained why the Beach Boys' music, for all its sunny advocacy of surfing and beach culture, was beneath the surface profoundly melancholy.[50]

Pynchon's decision to commit both Doc and Coy to the value of family by returning the missing musician to Hope and Amethyst seems an effort to correct such parental failings and assert family as a core value of the psychedelic generation. "You saved your life, Coy," Doc tells the saxophonist in their final phone conversation as the father sentimentally coos over his daughter. "Now you get to live it."[51] As an essential component of the light, Coy's love, Pynchon implies, will protect Amethyst from seeking out that need for parental affection from corrupting older influences like a Manson. It also seems an effort to revise the Shakespearean extremes of the Wilson family's own irrevocably sad story, whose tragedies would continue to mount well into the 1980s (when an alcoholic Dennis drowned during an ocean swim) and 1990s (when Brian would battle for freedom from psychologist Eugene E. Landy, who overtook his estate and overmedicated him nearly to the point of catatonia, and when Carl would die at fifty-one of brain cancer). In this way, perhaps the Harlingens' happy ending is Pynchon's own "Save a Rock 'n' Roller Program," the outreach effort that an undercover Doc claims to represent while interviewing a drug dealer named Pepe: "You know how many musicians have been overdosing in recent years, it's an epidemic. I've noticed it especially in my own area, surf music ... ." Pepe can only agree: "Too many needless losses."[52] If surf noir tends to pine for authentic, nurturing mentor figures committed to preserving surfing's spiritual/aesthetic values, *Inherent Vice* insists that the beach-culture ethos is a vehicle of the "light" because it is dedicated to preserving communal ties and upholding humanistic values instead of indulging in dangerous hedonism.

A reader need not agree that Pynchon fictionalizes the Brian Wilson legend in the story of Coy Harlingen to appreciate how for the writer both the Beach Boys and surf music in general are instruments of the light in *Inherent Vice*. The novel's closing paragraphs find Doc zooming into the California night to the radio strains of the *Pet Sounds* classic "God Only Knows," arguably the Beach Boys' most incandescent love song. This "last song playing on the car radio AM, a spectral voice by the edge of the mighty Pacific ... crooned in all psychedelic innocence" reassures readers that "paranoia does not reign [as] globally supreme" as Pynchon's tangled plot webs would otherwise have us believe, and that "the production of vice is not inherent in the system."[53] In the Pynchon oeuvre the ending of *Inherent Vice* stands out as atypically sentimental, which is why it is not entirely accepted by critics dubious of the author's nostalgia for the psychedelic era. Nevertheless the unexpected appearance of "God Only Knows" offers an opportunity to discuss the ultimate limits of hardboiled crime fiction's dependency on modernist defeatism and nostalgia.

For this reader, Pynchon's mention of the song recalls a comment in Greil Marcus's seminal *Mystery Train: Images of America in Rock Music* (1975, and updated through six editions, most recently in 2015). In a discussion of hardboiled depictions of L.A., Marcus makes an interesting contrast between Raymond Chandler, Nathanael West, and the Beach Boys:

> Because the [noir] vision of L.A. pushed Chandler and West into a queer sort of Puritanism, they never noticed something else that matters about Southern California: its incredible exuberance ... Put the Beach Boys of the early sixties up against West, and *he* sounds hysterical; there isn't a hint of their warmth or friendliness in [these writers'] definitive book[s] ... Empty, tired, desperate, stupid, and even as insane as they were through the next decades, [the Beach Boys] nevertheless performed life as [joyfully] as some people lived it. Their pleasures, as opposed to those of such latter-day inheritors as the Eagles, always radiated affection—perhaps because those pleasures were rooted in friendship, its memory, or its fantasy.[54]

Whether that affection can shine in noir is debatable: the pleasure of hardboiled crime literature is masochistic, the pleasure of ennobled defeat. Yet too often we confer depth for depth's sake to that darkness, the literary investment in modernist bleakness leading us to forget, perhaps, the counterbalancing value of "exuberant warmth and friendliness."

In the end, 1960s' surf culture appeals to authors of L.A. noir not simply because the fad's passing offers such an irresistible symbol of the erosion of that era's youth culture into the historical chaos that Manson so viciously emblematizes. It also appeals because of the nostalgia the surf-pop boom evokes for lost warmth and friendliness, the pleasure of "radiating affection" that seems all the more poignant because we cannot determine the boundaries between "its memory, or its fantasy." Yet just because art can only evoke, not institute, the prelapsarian purity of the "California dreaming" ideal that the 1960s' surf culture came retrospectively to epitomize does not mean crime fiction must dismiss its pleasures as irrecoverable. However fallen L.A. noir insists the City of Angels is (and always was), the naked vulnerability and absolute lack of guile in a Beach Boys song such as "God Only Knows" represents something we ought to keep in mind—even if, as we stab at the Mansonoid darkness with our steely knives, we just cannot kill the beast:

We ought to enjoy our dreams at least as much as we enjoy being disappointed by them.

# Notes

1  For three modernist treatments of hardboiled fiction, see William Faulkner's *Sanctuary* (New York: Cape and Smith, 1931), Gertrude Stein's *Blood on the Dining-Room Floor* (written in 1933 but unpublished until 1948 [Pawlett, VT: Banyan Press]), and Ernest Hemingway's *To Have and Have Not* (New York: Scribner, 1937).

2  Ernest Lockridge, "F. Scott Fitzgerald's *Trompe l'Oeil* and *The Great Gatsby*'s Buried Plot," *The Journal of Narrative Technique* 17, no. 2 (1987): 178–9.

3  For recent explorations of these themes, see Sean McCann, *Gumshoe America: Hard-Boiled Crime Fiction and the Rise and Fall of New Deal Liberalism* (Durham, NC: Duke University Press, 2000); Christopher Breu, *Hard-Boiled Masculinities* (Minneapolis: University of Minnesota Press, 2005); Leonard Cassuto, *Hard-Boiled Sentimentality: The Secret History of American Crime Stories* (New York: Columbia University Press, 2009).

4  Umberto Eco, "Real Literature is for Losers," *Guardian*, November 12, 2015. http://www.theguardian.com/books/booksblog/2015/nov/12/umberto-eco-real-literature-is-about-losers.

5  For discussions of this defeatism in hardboiled fiction, see Carl Daryl Malmgren, *Anatomy of Murder: Mystery, Detective, and Crime Fiction*

(Bowling Green, OH: Bowling Green State University Popular Press, 2001), 7–8; Richard B. Schwartz, *Nice and Noir: Contemporary American Crime Fiction* (Columbia: University of Missouri Press, 2002), 15–23; Richard Bradford, *Crime Fiction: A Very Short Introduction* (Oxford: Oxford University Press, 2015), 32–4.

6   John Scaggs, *Crime Fiction* (London and New York: Routledge University Press, 2005), 70–1.

7   Raymond Chandler, *The Little Sister* (New York: Knopf, 1949), 357.

8   Mike Davis, *City of Quartz: Excavating the Future in Los Angeles* (New York: Vintage, 1992); *Los Angeles Plays Itself*, directed by Thom Andersen (Los Angeles: Thom Andersen Productions/Submarine Entertainment, 2003), DVD.

9   Nunn's publisher, Simon and Schuster, advertises the current trade paperback edition of *Source*, which was nominated for the National Book Award in 1984, as the inspiration for the movie, but the movie itself does not credit the novel. A script for a potential movie version of *Source* supposedly floated around Hollywood throughout the late 1980s and may have been associated through movie-production osmosis with another project called *Johnny Utah*, *Point Break*'s original title, about an FBI agent infiltrating a hyper-masculine band of surfing bank robbers. Other than surfing, the similarities are modest.

10   For an illustrative history of 1960s' surf culture and its influence on pop trends, see Brian Chidester and Domenic Priore, *Pop Surf Culture: Music, Design, Film, and Fashion from the Bohemian Surf Boom* (Santa Monica CA: Santa Monica Press, 2008).

11   For an appreciation of the variety of literary treatments of surfing, see Matt Warshaw, ed., *Zero Break: An Illustrated Collection of Surf Writing, 1778–2004* (New York: Harvest Books, 2004). The collection includes several of the texts discussed in this essay as well as one significant one that is not: Tom Wolfe's "The Pump House Gang," which first appeared in the *New York Herald Tribune* on February 13 and 20, 1966 and was subsequently republished as the lead essay in *The Pump House Gang* (New York: Farrar, Strauss and Giroux, 1968), 17–39.

12   Frederick Kohner, *Gidget: The Little Girl with Big Ideas* (New York: Putnam's, 1957); Sheila Weller, "Malibu's Lost Boys," *Vanity Fair*, August 2006. http://www.vanityfair.com/news/2006/08/malibu-surf-scene-200608.

13   Ibid., 4.

14   Kristin Lawler, *The American Surfer: Radical Culture and Capitalism* (London and New York: Routledge, 2010), 100.

15   Timothy White, *The Nearest Faraway Place: Brian Wilson, the Beach Boys, and the Southern California Experience* (New York: Henry Holt, 1995), 132.

16   Lawler, *The American Surfer*, 113.

17   Michael Kreyling, *The Novels of Ross Macdonald* (Columbia: University of South Carolina Press, 2005), 108.

18 The Beach Boys, "Surfin' Safari," *Surfin' Safari*, LP, Capitol Records, T 1808, 1962.
19 Ross Macdonald, *The Zebra-Striped Hearse* (New York: Knopf, 1962), 32.
20 Ibid., 43.
21 Ibid., 204.
22 Among *The Zebra-Striped Hearse*'s greatest fans was the late singer-songwriter Warren Zevon (1948–2003), who dedicated at least one of his albums to Macdonald after the novelist helped the rock star suffer through Valium withdrawal in 1979. "I was that kid," Zevon told one journalist of Ray Buzzell, the leader of the surf gang. See Tom Nolan, *Ross Macdonald: A Biography* (New York: Scribner, 1999), 375. The album Zevon dedicated to Macdonald (whose real name was Kenneth Millar) was 1981's *Bad Luck Streak in Dancing School*. So, too, Denise Hamilton, author of the Eve Diamond novels and editor of the anthology *Los Angeles Noir* (2007), found the ominousness of Macdonald's depiction of the subculture compelling, claiming "it capture[s] something almost Greek in the primitive atavism ... These pagans gathered around a fire at the edge of the continent, at night. He really captured something about youth tribes." Scott Timberg, "Lew Archer is Back on the Case," *Los Angeles Times*, August 22, 2007, http://www.latimes.com/cl-macdonald-story.html.
23 Nolan, *Ross Macdonald*, 163–7, 203–14.
24 Cassuto, *Hard-Boiled Sentimentality*, 161, 155.
25 Patrick Morgan, *The Girl in the Telltale Bikini* (New York: Fawcett, 1971).
26 For a thorough and recent account of the relationship between Manson, Dennis Wilson, and the Beach Boys, see Jeff Guinn, *Manson: The Life and Times of Charles Manson* (New York: Simon and Schuster, 2013), 148–71.
27 "The Mad Happy Surfers: California 'Hot Doggers' Enjoy a New way of Life on the Wavetops," *Life Magazine*, September 1, 1961, 47–53. The three teenagers featured in the piece—Larry Shaw, Mike Nader, and Duane King—are profiled forty-five years later in Weller, "Malibu's Lost Boys," focusing in particular on their relationship with the mercurial Dora, who is neither mentioned nor pictured in the *Life* photo essay. The problems with abusive and/or absentee parents that drove the young men to escape into L.A. beach culture and Dora's troupe of lost boys parallel Macdonald's critique of familial indifference in *The Zebra-Striped Hearse*. For a biography of Dora, see David Rensin, *All for a Few Perfect Waves: The Audacious Life and Legend of Miki Dora* (New York: Harper, 2009).
28 Weller, "Malibu's Lost Boys."
29 Rensin, *All for a Few Perfect Waves*, 267–8.
30 Kem Nunn, *Tijuana Straits* (New York: Simon and Schuster, 2004), 176. Nunn, it should be noted, is cited in Rensin's biography of Dora. See *All for a Few Perfect Waves*, 18.
31 Lawler, *The American Surfer*, 98.
32 Weller, "Malibu's Lost Boys."

33 Kem Nunn, *Tapping the Source* (New York: Delacorte, 1984), 264–5.
34 Ibid., 296.
35 Ibid., 300.
36 Thomas Pynchon, *Inherent Vice* (New York: Penguin, 2009), 29.
37 Ibid., 254–5. For a discussion of Pynchon's use of light imagery in the novel, see David Cowart, *Thomas Pynchon and the Dark Passage of History* (Athens: University of Georgia Press, 2012), 125–35. For a discussion of the importance of beach culture to the novel, see Hanjo Berressem, "Life on the Beach: The Natural Elements in Pynchon's California Trilogy," *Pynchon's California*, eds. Scott McClintock and John Miller (Iowa City: University of Iowa Press, 2011), 58–64. This section, entitled "The Beach," is preceded by a discussion of beach culture throughout Pynchon's preceding works (35–57).
38 Rob Wilson, "On the Pacific Edge of Catastrophe or Redemption: California Dreaming in Thomas Pynchon's *Inherent Vice*," *boundary 2* 37, no. 2 (2010): 221.
39 Pynchon, *Inherent Vice*, 346.
40 Ibid., 36.
41 Ibid., 37.
42 Jimi Hendrix, "Third Stone from the Sun," Track Records, 1967.
43 For a discussion of the limitations of the various meanings of "genius" that have defined Wilson's legacy, see the introduction to my *Brian Wilson* (London: Equinox Publishing, 2012), 4–20.
44 Pynchon, *Inherent Vice*, 85.
45 Ibid., 131. See also Tom Nolan, "The Beach Boys: A California Saga." 1971. *The Beach Boys Complete*. New York: Amsco, 1973, 24.
46 Pynchon, *Inherent Vice*, 133.
47 Quoted in Carlin, Peter Ames Carlin, *Catch a Wave: The Rise, Fall, and Redemption of the Beach Boys' Brian Wilson* (New York: Rodale, 2006), 103–4. For Siegel's original account of the night, see "Who Is Thomas Pynchon … And Why Did He Take Off with My Wife?" *Playboy* (March 1977). For Siegel's essay on *Smile*, see "Goodbye Surfing, Hello God: The Religious Conversion of Brian Wilson," in *The Rock History Reader*, 2nd edn, ed. Theo Cafetonis (New York and London: Routledge, 2013), 83–94.
48 Carlin, *Catch a Wave*, 84.
49 Geoffrey O'Brien, "The Lonely Sea," in *Sonata for Jukebox: Pop Music, Memory, and the Imagined Life* (New York: Counterpoint, 2004), 246.
50 Nolan, "A California Saga," 22.
51 Pynchon, *Inherent Vice*, 363.
52 Ibid., 267.
53 Wilson, "On the Pacific Edge of Catastrophe or Redemption," 224.
54 Greil Marcus, *Mystery Train: Images of America in Rock 'n' Roll Music*, 6th edn (New York: Plume, 2015), 95–6.

# Bibliography

The Beach Boys. "Surfin' Safari." *Surfin Safari*. LP. Capitol Records, T 1808. 1962.
The Beach Boys. "God Only Knows." *Pet Sounds*. LP. Capitol Records, T 2458. 1966.
Berressem, Hanjo. "Life on the Beach: The Natural Elements in Pynchon's California Trilogy." In *Pynchon's California*, edited by Scott McClintock and John Miller, 35–64. Iowa City: University of Iowa Press, 2011.
Bradford, Richard. *Crime Fiction: A Very Short Introduction*. Oxford: Oxford University Press, 2015.
Breu, Christopher. *Hard-Boiled Masculinities*. Minneapolis: University of Minnesota Press, 2005.
Carlin, Peter Ames. *Catch a Wave: The Rise, Fall, and Redemption of the Beach Boys' Brian Wilson*. New York: Rodale, 2006.
Cassuto, Leonard. *Hard-Boiled Sentimentality: The Secret History of American Crime Stories*. New York: Columbia University Press, 2009.
Chandler, Raymond. *The Little Sister*. New York: Knopf, 1949.
Chidester, Brian and Domenic Priore. *Pop Surf Culture: Music, Design, Film, and Fashion from the Bohemian Surf Boom*. Santa Monica CA: Santa Monica Press, 2008.
Cowart, David. *Thomas Pynchon and the Dark Passage of History*. Athens: University of Georgia Press, 2012.
Curnutt, Kirk. *Brian Wilson*. London: Equinox Publishing, 2012.
Davis, Mike. *City of Quartz: Excavating the Future in Los Angeles*. New York: Vintage, 1992.
Eco, Umberto. "Real Literature is for Losers." *Guardian*, November 12, 2015. Available online: http://www.theguardian.com/books/booksblog/2015/nov/12/umberto-eco-real-literature-is-about-losers.
The Fantastic Baggys. "Tell 'Em I'm Surfin'." *Tell 'Em I'm Surfin'*. LP. Dunhill 12270, 1964.
Faulkner, William. *Sanctuary*. New York: Cape and Smith, 1931.
Guinn, Jeff. *Manson: The Life and Times of Charles Manson*. New York: Simon and Schuster, 2013.
Hammett, Dashiell. *The Dain Curse*. New York: Knopf, 1929.
Hemingway, Ernest. *To Have and Have Not*. New York: Scribner, 1937.
Jimi Hendrix, "Third Stone from the Sun." *Are You Experienced*. LP. Track Records, 612 001. 1967.
Kohner, Frederick. *Gidget: The Little Girl with Big Ideas*. New York: Putnam's, 1957.
Kreyling, Michael. *The Novels of Ross Macdonald*. Columbia: University of South Carolina Press, 2005.
Lawler, Kristin. *The American Surfer: Radical Culture and Capitalism*. London and New York: Routledge, 2010.
Lockridge, Ernest. "F. Scott Fitzgerald's *Trompe l'Oeil* and *The Great Gatsby*'s Buried Plot." *The Journal of Narrative Technique* 17, no. 2 (1987): 178–9.

Los Angeles Plays Itself. Directed by Thom Andersen. Los Angeles: Thom Andersen Productions/Submarine Entertainment, 2003. DVD.
McCann, Sean. *Gumshoe America: Hard-Boiled Crime Fiction and the Rise and Fall of New Deal Liberalism*. Durham, NC: Duke University Press, 2000.
Macdonald, Ross. *The Moving Target*. New York: Knopf, 1949.
Macdonald, Ross. *The Zebra-Striped Hearse*. New York: Knopf, 1962.
"The Mad Happy Surfers: California 'Hot Doggers' Enjoy a New Way of Life on the Wavetops." *Life Magazine*, September 1, 1961, 47–53.
Malmgren, Carl Daryl. *Anatomy of Murder: Mystery, Detective, and Crime Fiction*. Bowling Green, OH: Bowling Green State University Popular Press, 2001.
Marcus, Greil. *Mystery Train: Images of America in Rock 'n' Roll Music*. 6th edn. New York: Plume, 2015.
Morgan, Patrick. *The Girl in the Telltale Bikini*. New York: Fawcett, 1971.
Nolan, Tom. "The Beach Boys: A California Saga." 1971. Reprinted in *The Beach Boys Complete*, 2–24. New York: Amsco, 1973.
Nolan, Tom. *Ross Macdonald: A Biography*. New York: Scribner, 1999.
Nunn, Kem. *The Dogs of Winter*. New York: Scribner, 1997.
Nunn, Kem. *Tapping the Source*. New York: Delacorte, 1984.
Nunn, Kem. *Tijuana Straits*. New York: Simon and Schuster, 2004.
O'Brien, Geoffrey. "The Lonely Sea." In *Sonata for Jukebox: Pop Music, Memory, and the Imagined Life*, 231–54. New York: Counterpoint, 2004.
*Point Break*. Directed by Kathryn Bigelow. Twentieth Century Fox, 1991. DVD.
Pynchon, Thomas. *Inherent Vice*. New York: Penguin, 2009.
Rensin, David. *All For a Few Perfect Waves: The Audacious Life and Legend of Miki Dora*. New York: Harper, 2009.
Scaggs, John. *Crime Fiction*. London and New York: Routledge University Press, 2005.
Schwartz, Richard B. *Nice and Noir: Contemporary American Crime Fiction*. Columbia: University of Missouri Press, 2002.
Siegel, Jules. "Goodbye Surfing, Hello God: The Religious Conversion of Brian Wilson." In *The Rock History Reader*, edited by Theo Cafetonis, 83–94, 2nd edn. New York and London: Routledge, 2013.
Siegel, Jules. "Who Is Thomas Pynchon ... And Why Did He Take Off with My Wife?" *Playboy*, March 1977.
Stein, Gertrude. *Blood on the Dining-Room Floor*. Pawlett, VT: Banyan Press, 1948.
Timberg, Scott. "Lew Archer is Back on the Case." *Los Angeles Times*, August 22, 2007. Available online: http://www.latimes.com/cl-macdonald-story.html.
Warshaw, Matt, ed., *Zero Break: An Illustrated Collection of Surf Writing, 1778–2004*. New York: Harvest Books, 2004.
Weller, Sheila. "Malibu's Lost Boys." *Vanity Fair*, August 2006. Available online: http://www.vanityfair.com/news/2006/08/malibu-surf-scene-200608.
White, Timothy. *The Nearest Faraway Place: Brian Wilson, the Beach Boys, and the Southern California Experience*. New York: Henry Holt, 1995.
Wilson, Rob. "On the Pacific Edge of Catastrophe or Redemption: California Dreaming in Thomas Pynchon's *Inherent Vice*." *boundary 2* 37, no. 2 (2010): 221.

Wolfe, Tom. "The Pump House Gang." *New York Herald Tribune*, February 13 and 20, 1966. Reprinted in *The Pump House Gang*, 17–39. New York: Farrar, Strauss and Giroux, 1968.

Zevon, Warren. *Bad Luck Streak in Dancing School*. LP. Asylum Records, 5E 509. 1980.

# 7

# Alien pleasures: Modernism/ hybridity/science fiction

## *Paul March-Russell*

In seeking to distance his work from the label of postmodernism, the British New Weird author, China Miéville, has argued in conversation with Joan Gordon that "I don't think it's fair that hybridity, uncertainty, blurring identities, fracturing, formal experimentation, or the blurring of high and low culture should be ceded to postmodernism!"[1] Speaking with Tony Venezia seven years later, Miéville added further that there has been a "flattening out of the sharp edges of theory": "if you come across a text which is anyway interested in interstitiality, or marginality, or subalternity, there's a notion that *ipso facto* this can be thought of as a 'postmodern' text."[2] As a Marxist, wedded to the belief that dialectics is "about movement, dynamism, tendencies within an overall, comprehensible, and total system," in which "Modernity, history, is always-already-in-transition,"[3] Miéville sees such concepts as hybridity as already inscribed within the pulp modernisms that he has sought to celebrate in his fiction and criticism.[4] However, whereas Miéville regards this inscription very specifically within the practices of weird fiction writers such as William Hope Hodgson, M. R. James and H. P. Lovecraft, this chapter will argue that it also occurs in the relationship between modernism and its popular counterpart, scientific romance, the British literary precursor to genre SF. In this respect, the chapter will focus upon Naomi Mitchison's *Memoirs of a Spacewoman* (1962), a pioneering work of feminist SF and a late modernist text, its indebtedness to the thematic and narrative structure of Olaf Stapledon's pre-war novels, most notably *Star Maker* (1937), and its comparisons—in terms of hybridity, difference and alienness—with the

Aleutian Trilogy of Gwyneth Jones and Stephen Baxter's Xeelee sequence of novels and stories.[5]

## Hybridity and science fiction

As Jessica Langer has observed, "all postcolonial science fiction—indeed, all postcolonial cultural production—is about hybridity."[6] The concept however, as formulated by Homi Bhabha, needs to be examined. Bhabha regards the hegemony of colonial discourse as resting upon the Freudian (and, before that, Marxist) principle of disavowal: the increasingly desperate denial of the colonial subject as a person in his/her own right. The psychological and political vicissitudes associated with disavowal become the well-spring for the emergence of hybridity: a splitting of "the dominant discourse ... along the axis of its power to be representative, authoritative" so that "the discriminated subject" becomes "the terrifying, exorbitant object of paranoid classification—a disturbing questioning of the images and presences of authority."[7] So for example, to use one of Bhabha's own literary case studies, Joseph Conrad's *Heart of Darkness* (1899), Marlow's increasingly conspicuous use of adjectives to describe the alleged unspeakableness of African rites articulates his own anxiety as a narrator of colonialism. On the one hand, Marlow seeks to deny his human kinship with the Africans, to compartmentalize the cannibals as "fine fellows ... in their place,"[8] whilst on the other hand, he struggles to become aware of their all-too-humanness and of his own complicity in an act of cannibalism: the imperial powers' consumption of Africa for its human and material resources. Hybridity then, according to Bhabha, "creates a crisis for any concept of authority based on a system of recognition: colonial specularity, doubly inscribed, does not produce a mirror where the self apprehends itself; it is always the split screen of the self and its doubling, the hybrid."[9]

This crisis of representation within the discursive and political instruments of colonial power not only contributed to the characteristic ambivalence of modernism's textual strategies but also, according to critics such as John Rieder, the emergence of early SF.[10] The alarming ambiguity of, for instance, H. G. Wells's *The War of the Worlds* (1898) is that the invading Martians are not merely alien and non-identical with the humans—or that by a rhetorical sleight of hand are to be read as an allegorical representation of Western imperial aggression—but that they are Wells's prediction for what humans will evolve into. This kinship, shaped by the seemingly inevitable bonds of natural selection, is what fundamentally shatters the tone of late Victorian complacency with which the novel begins. As Kelly Hurley has argued, one aspect that characterizes the post-Darwinian ethos of Wells and his successors, such as the weird fiction author William Hope Hodgson, is their realization that humans are no more than evolved hybrids of various animal species.[11]

Robert Young, however, has mounted a stringent critique of Bhabha's theoretical position, claiming that it is motivated by a similar principle of disavowal that Bhabha detects within colonial discourse, as one critical orientation is successively supplanted by another. It is worth quoting Young at length:

> Bhabha's claims to describe the conditions of colonial discourse ... seem always offered as static concepts, curiously anthropomorphized so that they possess their own desire, with no reference to the historical provenance of the theoretical material from which such concepts are drawn, or to the theoretical narrative of Bhabha's own work, or to that of the cultures to which they are addressed.[12]

Although Young entertains the possibility that Bhabha is intentionally hybridizing the hegemony of critical theory, what he points to is the "flattening out" that Miéville similarly detects within postmodern thought, so that it appears as if "the concept in question constitutes the condition of colonial discourse itself and would hold good for all historical periods and contexts,"[13] only for it to be displaced within the swerves in Bhabha's critical position. In Young's subsequent work, he traces the historical undercurrents with which the notion of hybridity is freighted where, within the discourse of late nineteenth-century colonialism, it was used as a synonym for miscegenation and as a by-word for cultural degeneration.[14] The context-free usages to which the term is put by Bhabha and by others hardly help to assuage its earlier associations with the racist and imperialist ideologies that postcolonial theory ostensibly seeks to deconstruct.

Young's own critical trajectory—from an advocate of post-structuralism to a revitalized Marxism via his engagement with colonial literature, postcolonial theory and the politics of the independence movements—mirrors Miéville's re-insistence upon the reading of dialectics, "blurred interstices, gray areas, hard cases," within "a social and historical totality" in the hope of understanding better the tensions that both drive and potentially undermine the system.[15] SF, too, in its early appreciation of the interrelatedness between self and Other, due to its application of evolutionary theory to the premise of alien encounter and life on other planets, subjects notions such as hybridity to sustained, albeit idiosyncratic, critique. To understand more clearly this response, I shall turn briefly to Wells's great successor, Olaf Stapledon, before moving on to Stapledon's friend, the prolific author—and sister of the evolutionary biologist J. B. S. Haldane—Naomi Mitchison.

## Hybridity in Stapledon and Mitchison

Like Wells, Stapledon took a Darwinian approach to the future development of humanity and the prospect of alien life in the universe. Although the titular Star Maker is presented as an all-powerful, cosmic creator, Stapledon is at pains for him not to be read as an analogue for the Judeo-Christian God. Instead, he is more like an experimental scientist who tests his conclusions against a series of models:

> Again and again ... the Star Maker learned from his creature, and thereby outgrew his creature, and craved to work upon an ampler plan. Again and again he set aside a finished cosmos and evoked from himself a new creation.[16]

Not only is he dispassionate about his goals—being both the creator and destroyer of worlds—the Star Maker's motivations cannot be understood against human criteria: he "neither loved nor had need of love."[17] For Stapledon's cosmic voyager, it is "more than enough to have been used, to have been the rough sketch of some perfected creation,"[18] a reassuringly utopian and idealistic sentiment that darkens considerably in the post-war novels of Baxter and Jones.

Instead, just as each universe is depicted in a constant state of evolution as part of an overarching desire by the Star Maker for perfection, so too is he "an awakening spirit":[19] "The creature's achievement of perception and of will was seemingly the instrument by which the Star Maker himself, cosmos by cosmos, woke into keener lucidity."[20] Although timeless and eternal, the Star Maker is not static like the Judeo-Christian God; instead, his being is morphological, adapting and refining itself to the universes that are both part and particle of his protean nature. This pantheistic conception of divinity, again heterodox of traditional Judeo-Christianity, permits Stapledon to equate the Star Maker with a Hegelian desire for totality: "the absolute spirit itself, in which all times are present and all being is comprised."[21] The effect not only generates a tense and dynamic model of dialectical change, as practiced by Miéville in such novels as *Perdido Street Station* (2000), but it also produces a narrative form that is curiously decentered. Although the anonymous narrator supplies a measure of focalization, his journey into the depths of time and space is fundamentally that of the picaresque whilst the widening gyres of his quest resembles more of a chronicle rather than a linear narrative grounded in cause and effect.

Writing to Stapledon after the publication of his earlier masterpiece, *Last and First Men* (1930), the literary critic John Dover Wilson declared: "You have invented a new kind of book & the world of Einstein & Jeans is ready for it."[22] Although Stapledon had an ambivalent attitude towards the Bloomsbury Group, despite the admiration of leading members such as Virginia Woolf, the episodic and expansive structures of his fiction produce a modernist narrative that confounds the mimesis of both social and psychological realism. The equivalent to Stapledon's fiction might be Wyndham Lewis's external approach to writing as exhibited by his own foray into Wellsian scientific romance, *The Childermass* (1926), although Stapledon's debt to the speculative essays of Mitchison's brother, Haldane, is more profound. The success, first of *Last and First Men* and then *Star Maker*, brought Stapledon into the ambit of Mitchison's literary and intellectual circles.[23] Although Mitchison's fictional output shifted between social realism (*We Have Been Warned* [1935]), historical romance (*The Corn King and the Spring Queen* [1930]) and epic fantasy (*Travel Light* [1952]), she did not turn to science fiction until the 1960s—but when she did so, the fragmented *Memoirs of a Spacewoman* resembles the narrative structure of Stapledon's fiction.

Mitchison's novel concerns a communications expert, Mary, who has been trained to explore other worlds and make contact with their inhabitants. As with the Darwinian fictions of Stapledon and Wells, the creatures that Mary encounters have evolved in accordance with their own planetary eco-systems and appear to be radically non-identical with *homo sapiens*. Communication therefore entails a gradual and complex process of observation. In *The War of the Worlds*, by contrast, the inability of the humans to communicate with the Martians adds to their frightfulness; the incomprehensible ululations transmitted by their tripods, while resembling a war cry, are in themselves a form of hybridized speech that disrupts the sense-meaning of human expression. Although in *The First Men in the Moon* (1901) contact is achieved between Cavor and the Grand Lunar, the latter's incomprehension at Terran concepts such as war ultimately results in the silencing of Wells's inventor–hero. Instead, in *Star Maker*, Stapledon proposes telepathy as an advanced method of communication between his traveler and the radically divergent species that he encounters: "in time I came to be able to live through the experiences of my host with vividness and accuracy, while yet preserving my own individuality."[24] Not only does telepathy permit Stapledon's protagonist to experience the dramatically alien sensory perceptions of his hosts, in effect, becoming a hybridized being, it also enables him to construct a travelling band of companions: a dramatization of Stapledon's ideal of "personality-in-community."[25] Yet, this union of self and Other is only a microcosm of the unfolding cosmic narrative in which, first, the diverse alien species find a commonwealth through a process of symbiosis, then, the planets reveal themselves to be living organisms, and, finally, the stars execute "perfectly their part in the communal dance, and the desire to press forward to the attainment of full insight into the nature of the cosmos."[26] This Hegelian vision is repeatedly offset against the fascism and imperialism that beset alien cultures at earlier stages of their social and spiritual evolution.

Whereas the basis of Stapledon's telepathy remains shrouded in pseudo-science, Mitchison's protagonist employs an intricate method of emotional empathy, anthropological detail and biological observation. Although such an approach almost inevitably invokes comparisons with the racial assumptions of colonial exploration and post-war anthropology (as for example in the careers of two other Marys, Kingsley and Douglas, respectively), Mitchison stresses the anti-colonialism of her future society. The explorers are governed by a policy of non-interference which, whilst suggesting similarities with the Watchers in Arkady and Boris Strugatsky's *Hard to be a God* (1964) or the Prime Directive of the *Star Trek* franchise, is nuanced by the detachment of Mitchison's scientific education, her experience of the First World War as a volunteer nurse, her campaigning alongside the likes of Stapledon and Wells for world governance and against the Spanish Civil War, and latterly, Mitchison's involvement in Scottish politics where she defended the rights of island communities. The year that *Memoirs of a Spacewoman* was published also marked the first of Mitchison's trips to Botswana, an experience that she recounted in *Return to the Fairy Tree* (1966), and which brought her into contact with both local tribespeople and colonial administrators. Still, as Mary relates in the story of fellow explorer Françoise, who does intervene in a struggle between alien butterflies and caterpillars, killing one of the attacking butterflies and, as a punishment, being confined permanently on Terra, non-interference brings with it unresolved ethical dilemmas.

At the other extreme of non-interference lies the risk of absorption into the mental and emotional life of the observed. This danger befalls Mary on her first exploration where she encounters one of the most unearthly species in the novel: "a radial form, something like a five-armed starfish, itself developing out of a spiral."[27] In particular, perhaps because of their anatomical structure, the radiates have no conception of binary thinking; to understand them, Mary finds her own Western logic becoming "smudged out":

If alternative means, not one of two, but one, two, three or four out of five, then action is complicated and slowed to the kind of tempo and complexity which is appropriate to an organism with many hundreds of what were in evolutionary time fairly simple suckers and graspers, but which in development have adapted themselves for locomotion, food retention, tool-handling, the finer delicacies of touch and probably for other purposes of which I only became partly aware.[28]

Mary compares the loss of her logical self with the sensation of being drugged: as possible options expand, so her actions become more inert, disorientated and sluggish. In effect, she has gone native. While the process prevents Mary from acting upon her sexual attraction to her companion, T'o, there is little condemnation of her temporary transition; instead, it is viewed both by herself and her team as no more than an occupational hazard. In becoming a hybridized psychological entity, she has fulfilled her mission in communicating with the radiates. Communication is more highly prized than anything else; by contrast, Mary makes a worse mistake when initially she misrepresents the radiates' sex life due to her "own anthropomorphizing."[29]

The value with which inter-species communication is viewed contrasts with how it operates in Stapledon's work. Although Mary's intuition borders upon the telepathic, Mitchison does not grant it the pseudo-science that features in *Star Maker*: the mechanics of Mary's training may not be discussed in detail but the reader learns enough that it is a practiced technique with a method, knowledge and rationale behind it. The pragmatic, utilitarian approach that Mary takes towards communication also informs Mitchison's composition of the novel: instead of the transcendent ending to *Star Maker*, in which the telepathic communication between individuals, races, planets and stars forms a series of necessary steps towards the final revelation, in *Memoirs of a Spacewoman* the act of communication itself is enough. Whereas for Stapledon the narrative trajectory is one of outward expansion, for Mitchison the movement is towards intimacy. Consequently, although Mary resumes her interplanetary travel, there is a reciprocal pull back towards Terra, to domesticity and her loved ones. What Mary rejects is the exclusive hold upon her from either direction. This tension between the desires of self and Other also underscores the process of inter-species communication.

The porous sense of psychological boundaries is given physical embodiment, firstly, through Mary's consent to use her body for the growing of alien grafts and, secondly, through the child that she accidentally conceives with the Martian Vly. In the first instance, tissue so alien that it is not recognized by human antibodies is grown on a host body so that it becomes a "whole animal,"[30] lacking obvious sentience but able to perceive. As a consequence, it is theoretically possible to communicate with the graft. Mary demands to be a host body since, in what might be taken as a biologically essentialist statement, "I don't believe this is a man's job. You ought to get a woman to do it."[31] Once the graft has taken, the symptoms it produces in Mary are akin to pregnancy, in addition to a desire for swimming, as if the graft itself wants to be afloat in amniotic fluid. The inexplicability of this feeling is something that Mary can only communicate with the genetically modified dogs and jackals (perhaps an allusion to the super-evolved protagonist of Stapledon's *Sirius* [1944]) who have carried similar grafts; the intimacy of their conversation dramatizes the cyborg identities in both Mary and the animals. In contravention of the admonishment not to anthropomorphize, Mary insists upon naming the graft Ariel and describes it as "flesh of my flesh."[32] The sexualized wanderings of its pseudopodia, "reaching now to my mouth," "delicately" inserted "between my lips and elsewhere," "the peculiar feel and taste on my tongue,"[33] suggest also an exercise in autoeroticism, the pleasure of which none of Mary's lovers can equal. No wonder then, allied to Mary's melancholy at the subsequent death of Ariel, that she agrees towards the end of her memoir to another, near-fatal attempt at grafting.

The only comparable instance is Mary's sexual encounter with Vly. In rescuing the human survivors from the planet Jones 97, the Martians are forced to remove their protective clothing so that they can communicate with the unconscious humans. As Mary explains, the Martians "communicate through the highly educated tactile senses" of their body parts: these can include their tongue, hands, feet and sexual organs.[34] Like the Gethenians in Ursula Le Guin's *The Left Hand of Darkness* (1969), Mitchison's Martians are hermaphroditic; the physical and emotional disaster on Jones 97 shocks Vly into a temporary male sexuality so that, in communicating with Mary's semi-conscious body, he unwittingly stirs her into ovulation. The child which she gives birth to, named Viola, is haploid which is to say that it only has a single set of Mary's chromosomes, effectively a diminutive clone of its mother. Viola's immaculate conception, achieved almost telepathically without sexual penetration and with the inadvertent assistance of an alien Other, violates all manner of taboo colonial desires, in particular the miscegenation—or hybridization—between separate races. As if in a demonstration of self-love, Mary retains special affection for Viola over and above the four children that she conceives within more conventional human relationships. Yet, Mary's love is also a testament to her hybrid desires; a need fulfilled in Viola ultimately achieving the breakthrough in inter-species communication that has previously defeated Mary.

## Hybridity in Jones and Baxter

The radicalism of Mitchison's sexual politics, intersecting First and Second Wave Feminisms, can be measured against Gwyneth Jones's *White Queen*, the first installment in the Aleutian Trilogy that Jones published during the early to mid-1990s (the other volumes being *North Wind* [1994] and *Phoenix Café* [1997]). Whereas Mitchison's deep-space exploration is predicated on some form of gender equality having been established on Earth, as is characteristic of Jones's fiction, *White Queen* is set against the backdrop of global crisis, an apocalyptic moment that resonates with the political urgency that frames Stapledon's *Star Maker*.[35] However, whilst Mitchison and Stapledon ascribe to a belief in historical progress, Jones's view of social change is rooted in the other side of Wellsian SF—in the inevitability of entropy and its catastrophic effects. Taking into account the immediate contexts for the writing of *White Queen*, namely the fall of the Berlin Wall and the collapse of the Soviet Bloc, the novel can also be read as a critique of prevailing theories surrounding "the end of history" and the neo-Hegelian optimism of political thinkers such as Francis Fukuyama. Instead of the onward march of free-market capitalism and liberal democracy, a major earthquake that has destroyed much of Japan has also devastated the global economy. The European Union appears to be paralyzed whilst the United States has collapsed into race-fueled civil war. West Africa, although still impeded by imbalances in power, finance and technology between the First World and the developing nations, senses fresh opportunity and it is here that much of the novel is set. In other words, far from the supposed realism of cyberpunk novels such as Bruce Sterling's *Islands in the Net* (1988), in which Western-style capitalism is exported to the rest of the world, with all of its neo-colonial relations intact, *White Queen* imagines those relations having been hybridized by the effects of natural events outside the anthropocentric logic of Western progress.

Into this confusion arrive Jones's visiting party of Aleutians who, as somewhat opportunistic traders, use their circumstances to seal the basis for world domination. This is no coordinated invasion plan however, as in *The War of the Worlds*, since the small group of Aleutians is vastly outnumbered, they have no advanced military technology like Wells's Martians, and they frequently mistake or misrepresent the actions of their human hosts. For their part, however, the humans appear to be mesmerized by the radical Otherness of the Aleutians, ascribing to them powers of immortality and telepathy that can instead be explained away by the physiological differences of the Aleutians. By contrast, as Brian Attebery explains in his summary of the biological science behind Jones's aliens, each Aleutian "carries a multiplicity of genotypes, only one of which is expressed in the individual":

> It is as if all the recessive genes each of us carries made up a separate potential person to which one might give birth—only multiplied millions of times over. Each Aleutian individual resides, *in potentio*, within the genetic memory of every other and might be reborn at any time, to any parent.[36]

Not only does this method of reproduction obviate the need for sex, gender or genealogy, it also means that there is no concept of Otherness within Aleutian psychology; all Others are merely an extension of self. The lice-like "wanderers" that inhabit their skin are also microcosms of themselves, recording memories and subtle emotional changes, before restoring that data in the collective memory of the Aleutians. Whereas the humans attribute mysterious and unfathomable powers to the Aleutians, rendering them both enigmatic and Other, the visitors regard the humans as slightly odd variants of themselves; they are motivated instead by a desire for self-sameness rather than radical difference.

In presenting the Aleutians as a challenge to the binary opposition of self and Other,[37] Jones also deconstructs the colonial desires of attraction and repulsion by which the West has traditionally represented the indigenous subject. Although Attebery associates Jones's playing with sexual and cultural boundaries with the ironic strategies of postmodernism, her deconstruction of these borders is all of a piece with the popular modernism of Mitchison and Stapledon. The exoticization of the Other which, as it turns out in *White Queen*, disables the perceiver more than the perceived, is given its most scarifying treatment when Johnny, the out-of-work journalist, makes love with the alien Clavel:

> She was such a kid, this alien. Quite harmless. She used his hand as an anchor, and pulled herself into his arms ... She reached into her bodysuit-thing, brought out a hand crawling with blood-coloured lice. They glistened. Johnny stared, too disgusted and fascinated to move a muscle. The arm around his shoulders drew his face down ... It took his hand and buried it to the wrist in a fold that opened along its groin. The chasm inside squirmed with life ... Something slid out of the fold: an everted bag of raw flesh, narrowing to a hooked end. It was enormous. Johnny felt a jolt of horrible arousal ... Clavel's eyes were still fixed on his, *still sweet and child-like*. Suddenly, he lost his nerve completely.[38]

If Johnny fancies himself as the actively sexual male, who will educate this alien into the ways of human lovemaking, the abjection that he experiences hybridizes this illusory sense of sexual and colonial mastery. Instead, it is Johnny who is subjected to the prone position traditionally inhabited within space opera and planetary romance by women and sexually innocent female aliens, whilst Clavel dominates him. This overly neat reversal of sexual and subject positions is destabilized further by Johnny's realization that Clavel is not female but a hermaphrodite—the shifts in this passage from "she" to "it" but also "he" indicating Johnny's inability to comprehend not only Aleutian sexual anatomy but also whether he has been raped or not. In short, like the claw that emerges from Clavel's pouch, Jones forcibly rips apart the assumptions that underwrite the colonial gaze of the humans towards their alien guests.

The contemporaneous novels and stories of Stephen Baxter, known collectively as "the Xeelee sequence"—although these god-like beings only make their presence felt in the second of the novels, *Timelike Infinity*—also cleave to the more pessimistic aspects of Wellsian SF. Baxter's concern, however, is not only the relative insignificance of humanity when faced with the vastness of the cosmos but also its place within the evolutionary and entropic structures that shape the universe. While Baxter's determinism, in contrast with the more chance-ridden narratives of Jones and Mitchison, echoes the transcendent visions of Stapledon and Wells as well as that of their post-war successor, Arthur C. Clarke, it is shaded by an ultimate sense of loss and futility. As the dying physicist Michael Poole observes, projected forwards five million years into the future, there is something tragically heroic about the fate of humanity: "by God it had been a grand conception. To think of finite humans, already long since dust, even daring to challenge these deserts of time."[39] Saved by an entity created by the Xeelee to go backwards in time and modify their evolutionary development, Poole's spirit is converted into "a tight knot of quantum wave functions,"[40] which, like the astral projection of Stapledon's anonymous traveler, enables him to journey throughout the now thinning fabric of space-time.

Unlike the final reconciliation with the Star Maker, Poole only finds broken vestiges of humanity's place in the universe and its ultimately doomed conflict with the Xeelee:

Everywhere he found relics of war. Ruined stars and worlds, squandered energy. But he found no people—no sentience—anywhere.[41]

Like the devastated colossus and its surrounding environment in Percy Bysshe Shelley's poem, "Ozymandias" (1817), these ruins cause the spectator to pause, embodying as they do the waste of time immemorial and the vain, albeit vaunted, ambitions of the human race. Their spectacular melancholy, though, also reflects critically upon the position of Poole, who, through two chances of happenstance, is given the opportunity of witnessing these sites of devastation. The absurd irony of Poole's situation—on the one hand, he has fallen through a series of wormholes accidentally generated in the defeat of humanity's oppressors in the fifty-fifth century, whilst on the other hand, he has been saved minus a body by an entity designed by humanity's ultimate conquerors who themselves have mysteriously disappeared from the cosmos—runs counter to the deterministic pattern of Baxter's vast future history. Not everything can be accommodated into the unfolding teleology of Baxter's cosmic narrative, so that Poole's reappearance long after he should have died calls attention to the limits of even such a capacious discourse.

What begins, in *Timelike Infinity*, as a first-contact narrative, in which humanity painfully learns its lowly place in the grand pecking order of alien species, ends as a last man narrative, an enduring storyline that has its origins within the Romantic sublime of such writers as Lord Byron, Thomas Campbell, and Mary Shelley. Yet, in the same global context that underlines Jones's novel, the last man narrative acquires added resonance: Poole is the revenant that returns at the end of history with a melancholic gaze fixed on the futilities of human progress. This Derridean spin, however, on Baxter's time-traveling narrative does not do full justice to how it responds to the colonialist and expansionist dreams of humanity moving out into the cosmos. Instead, where in the work of Mitchison and Stapledon notions of intuition and telepathy hybridize anthropocentric models of communication so as to build fraternities between alien species, the vision in Baxter's fiction is closer to that of Wells and the unbridgeable gaps in understanding between the humans and the alien inhabitants of the Moon or Mars. Whilst in Jones, the self-sameness of the Aleutians is read as radical alterity by the humans, and vice versa, the Qax—humanity's oppressors for two centuries—achieve their advantage by studying Earth's history and by adapting "methods used by humans to oppress their fellows."[42] As the diplomat Jasoft Parz observes, the Qax are humanity's nemesis: "an externalized embodiment of man's treatment of man, a judgement of history."[43] In other words, despite their alienness, the Qax identify with the worst of human nature just as Wells's Martian invasion is rooted in the real-life atrocities of Western colonialism within Tasmania.

At the same time however, due to the temporal paradoxes of Baxter's narrative, the refugees from Qax domination appear to be almost as alien as the Qax themselves to their already post-human predecessors such as Poole. (It is Poole's achievement in the pre-Qax era to construct a stable wormhole that enables the refugees to escape in the first place.) In other words, although Baxter is even more heavily indebted to the Wellsian tradition than Jones, his vision of the universe and its denizens is inherently hybrid. Characters are locked into conflicts that traverse eons of time and space, in which the fates of individuals are bound up in vast macrocosmic narratives, and not even the Xeelee can master the forces of entropy. Patterns of order and chaos are embedded in one another, mutually diverging and converging, within discreet and dynamic tensions that can only be described as hybrid. Such hybridity, though, is part of the dialectical tension between modernism and SF.

# Notes

1 Joan Gordon, "Revelling in Genre: An Interview with China Miéville," *Science Fiction Studies* 30, no. 3 (2003): 363. See also Gordon's article in the same issue, "Hybridity, Heterotopia, and Mateship in China Miéville's *Perdido Street Station*," 456–77.

2 Tony Venezia, "Weird Fiction: *Dandelion* meets China Miéville," *Dandelion* 1, no. 1 (2010): 5.

3 Gordon, "Revelling in Genre," 364.

4 See, for example, China Miéville, "Weird Fiction," in *The Routledge Companion to Science Fiction*, eds. Mark Bould et al. (London: Routledge, 2009), 510–16.

5 Due to limited space, I focus on the first of Jones's novels, *White Queen* (London: Vista, 1991), and the second in Baxter's series, *Timelike Infinity* (London: HarperCollins, 1992).

6 Jessica Langer, *Postcolonialism and Science Fiction* (Basingstoke: Palgrave Macmillan, 2011), 125.
7 Homi K. Bhabha, *The Location of Culture* (Abingdon: Routledge, 1994), 162.
8 Joseph Conrad, *Heart of Darkness* (1899; repr., ed. Paul O'Prey, London: Penguin, 1973), 67.
9 Bhabha, *The Location of Culture*, 162.
10 See, for example, the essays in Howard J. Booth and Nigel Rigby, eds., *Modernism and Empire: Writing and British Coloniality, 1890–1940* (Manchester: Manchester University Press, 2000), and John Rieder, *Colonialism and the Emergence of Science Fiction* (Middletown, CT: Wesleyan University Press, 2008).
11 See Kelly Hurley, "The Modernist Abominations of William Hope Hodgson," in *Gothic Modernisms*, eds. Andrew Smith and Jeff Wallace (Basingstoke: Palgrave Macmillan, 2001), esp. 132–6.
12 Robert J. C. Young, *White Mythologies: Writing History and the West*, 2nd edn (1990; repr., London: Routledge, 2004), 186.
13 Ibid.
14 See Young, *Colonial Desire: Hybridity in Theory, Culture and Race* (London: Routledge, 1995), esp. 6–19.
15 Gordon, "Revelling in Genre," 364.
16 Olaf Stapledon, *Star Maker* (1937; repr., London: Gollancz, 1999), 226.
17 Ibid., 220.
18 Ibid.
19 Ibid., 225.
20 Ibid., 227.
21 Ibid., 247.
22 Quoted in Robert Crossley, *Olaf Stapledon: Speaking for the Future* (Liverpool: Liverpool University Press, 1994), 191.
23 Naomi Mitchison recounts her friendship with Stapledon, as well as her knowledge of classic and contemporary SF, in her essay "Wonderful Deathless Ditties," *Foundation* 21 (1981): 27–34.
24 Stapledon, *Star Maker*, 25.
25 Stapledon, "Mysticism, from *Philosophy and Living*" (1939; reprinted in *An Olaf Stapledon Reader*, ed. Robert Crossley (Syracuse, NY: Syracuse University Press, 1997), 187.
26 Stapledon, *Star Maker*, 191.
27 Mitchison, *Memoirs of a Spacewoman* (1962; repr., London: New English Library, 1976), 20.
28 Stapledon, *Star Maker*, 27.
29 Ibid., 26.

30 Ibid., 48.
31 Ibid., 50.
32 Ibid., 54.
33 Ibid.
34 Ibid., 58.
35 For a critical self-reflection on the role of apocalypse in her earlier fiction, see Gwyneth Jones, "*Kairos*: The Enchanted Loom," in *Edging into the Future: Science Fiction and Contemporary Cultural Transformation*, eds. Veronica Hollinger and Joan Gordon (Philadelphia: University of Pennsylvania Press, 2002), 174–89.
36 Brian Attebery, "'But Aren't Those Just … You Know, Metaphors?': Postmodern Figuration in the Science Fiction of James Morrow and Gwyneth Jones," in Hollinger and Gordon, 100.
37 As Jones comments, the ambiguity of the Aleutians is constituted by the degree to which their biological Otherness, despite their humanoid appearance, is complemented by their cultural sameness with the humans. Their non-verbal language, for example, complements the extent to which the subjectivity of women and the colonized has been historically defined by their enforced silence. See Jones, *Deconstructing the Starships: Science, Fiction and Reality* (Liverpool: Liverpool University Press, 1999), 115–16.
38 Jones, *White Queen* (1991; repr., London: Vista, 1998), 193.
39 Stephen Baxter, *Timelike Infinity* (London: HarperCollins, 1992), 248.
40 Ibid., 251.
41 Ibid.
42 Ibid., 35.
43 Ibid.

# Bibliography

Attebery, Brian. "'But Aren't Those Just … You Know, Metaphors?': Postmodern Figuration in the Science Fiction of James Morrow and Gwyneth Jones." In *Edging into the Future: Science Fiction and Contemporary Cultural Transformation*, edited by Veronica Hollinger and Joan Gordon, 90–107. Philadelphia: University of Pennsylvania Press, 2002.
Baxter, Stephen. *Timelike Infinity*. London: HarperCollins, 1992.
Bhabha, Homi K. *The Location of Culture*. Abingdon: Routledge, 1994.
Booth, Howard J. and Nigel Rigby, eds. *Modernism and Empire: Writing and British Coloniality, 1890–1940*. Manchester: Manchester University Press, 2000.
Conrad, Joseph. *Heart of Darkness*. 1899. Reprint, edited by Paul O'Prey. London: Penguin, 1973.
Crossley, Robert. *Olaf Stapledon: Speaking for the Future*. Liverpool: Liverpool University Press, 1994.

Gordon, Joan. "Hybridity, Heterotopia, and Mateship in China Miéville's *Perdido Street Station*." *Science Fiction Studies* 30, no. 3 (2003): 456–77.

Gordon, Joan. "Revelling in Genre: An Interview with China Miéville." *Science Fiction Studies* 30, no. 3 (2003): 355–73.

Hurley, Kelly. "The Modernist Abominations of William Hope Hodgson." In *Gothic Modernisms*, edited by Andrew Smith and Jeff Wallace, 129–49. Basingstoke: Palgrave Macmillan, 2001.

Jones, Gwyneth. *Deconstructing the Starships: Science, Fiction and Reality*. Liverpool: Liverpool University Press, 1999.

Jones, Gwyneth. "*Kairos*: The Enchanted Loom." In *Edging into the Future: Science Fiction and Contemporary Cultural Transformation*, edited by Veronica Hollinger and Joan Gordon, 174–89. Philadelphia: University of Pennsylvania Press, 2002.

Jones, Gwyneth. *White Queen*. 1991. Reprint, London: Vista, 1998.

Langer, Jessica. *Postcolonialism and Science Fiction*. Basingstoke: Palgrave Macmillan, 2011.

Miéville, China. "Weird Fiction." In *The Routledge Companion to Science Fiction*, edited by Mark Bould, Andrew M. Butler, Adam Roberts, and Sherryl Vint, 510–16. London: Routledge, 2009.

Mitchison, Naomi. *Memoirs of a Spacewoman*. 1962. Reprint, London: New English Library, 1976.

Mitchison, Naomi. "Wonderful Deathless Ditties." *Foundation* 21 (1981): 27–34.

Rieder, John. *Colonialism and the Emergence of Science Fiction*. Middletown, CT: Wesleyan University Press, 2008.

Stapledon, Olaf. *An Olaf Stapledon Reader*, edited by Robert Crossley. Syracuse, NY: Syracuse University Press, 1997.

Stapledon, Olaf. *Star Maker*. 1937. Reprint, London: Gollancz, 1999.

Venezia, Tony. "Weird Fiction: *Dandelion* meets China Miéville." *Dandelion* 1, no. 1 (2010): 1–9.

Wells, H. G. *The First Men in the Moon*. 1901. Reprint, edited by Patrick Parrinder. London: Penguin, 2005.

Wells, H. G. *The War of the Worlds*. 1898. Reprint, edited by Patrick Parrinder. London: Penguin, 2005.

Young, Robert J. C. *Colonial Desire: Hybridity in Theory, Culture and Race*. London: Routledge, 1995.

Young, Robert J. C. *White Mythologies: Writing History and the West*. 2nd edn. London: Routledge, 2004.

# 8

# Josephine Baker's contemporary afterlives: Black female identity, modernist performance, and popular legacies of the Jazz Age

*Asimina Ino Nikolopoulou*

"*Unless we arbitrarily terminate modernism's allowable tomorrows, the movement is unending.*"
—HOUSTON BAKER JR., *MODERNISM AND THE HARLEM RENAISSANCE*

An eccentric exile, diasporic transplant, and instant entertainment sensation in interwar Paris, Josephine Baker is veiled in the modern moment that engendered and animated her provocative performance. Arguably the first to "twerk" to entertain, Baker became the locus of fervent debate for her performances of femininity and black identity. By juxtaposing the enfranchised visibility that she enjoyed in Europe to the discriminatory practices of Jim Crow America, Baker's presence crystalized the racial politics of her era in a transatlantic context. To this day, her kinesis and self-reflective oeuvre continue to provide stimulating sights and spaces for the exploration of gender and race *vis-à-vis* modernist aesthetics.

Her trajectory across the Atlantic as well as the dynamism of her movement render Baker's oeuvre a formative moment for the contestation of blackness and femininity in the context of modernity and a curious space for examining the primitivist tropes Baker utilized to craft her dance performance. While those tropes are significant in their powerful articulation of racial and colonial scopic regimes, Baker's contested agency as well as her sartorial self-fashioning problematizes iconic depictions of black femininity. To read Baker's body as a willful terrain of resistance may indeed be too hopeful for the representational practices that she conjured in her performance. However, in order to understand Baker's positionality as an entertainment sensation, a Jazz Age protagonist, and a civil rights activist, it is important to consider the worlds she traversed as a performer and as a citizen.

## Becoming La Bakaire: Josephine's early performance and aesthetic fabrications

To announce Baker's performance as emancipatory, one needs to address the representational conundrum of her iconic self-making. Baker did not rely on readily available stereotypes to amuse and entertain, but rather on the impact that their appropriation instigated in the historical moment that contained her. Refusing to abide by the sensational imagery of Venus Hottentot or the piety of the Mammy figure as proliferated in the American national imaginary, Baker recontextualized black female performance and invented a distinct genre, a composite performance of rich intertextual allusions and innovative kinetic storytelling. Her success depended on the breakdown of representational categories, as her iconic and simultaneously iconoclastic performance provoked rupture and an elusive oscillation between available subject positions.

Rupture was indeed a theme of Baker's early life. Her upbringing was quite frugal, as her father abandoned the family shortly after her birth. Her mother soon remarried and had several other children, while Josephine worked throughout childhood to support her family—initially in short-term menial jobs and later by dancing in local venues or in street performances. By 1919 she was touring as a performer having left Missouri behind, and in 1923 she reached New York City, where she appeared on Broadway shows and at The Plantation Club. During this time, Baker, growing exasperated with the curtailed freedom of the black population in the United States, kept an eye on the booming prominence of Jazz in the music scene of interwar Paris. Finally, in 1925, she decided to follow the lead of the growing number of black artists who had fled to Europe. This transatlantic journey was a turning point for her. By October 1925, she was already dancing in the *Revue Nègre* at the Théâtre des Champs-Élysées minimally clad in a feather skirt. The audience was taken by her *Danse Sauvage* performance and Baker became an instant sensation in Parisian nightlife.[1]

Her inaugural performance in Paris simultaneously amazed and appalled audiences and critics alike. Baker opened the show with a comic number, featuring abrupt plastic movement and accentuated facial expressions. Bending her knees and rolling her eyes, Baker offered a spectacle that was received as primitive, belonging to a realm outside the confines of civilization. The initial commotion escalated to uproar in the final number, which featured Baker carried on stage by her Antillean partner, Joe Alex, as prey on his back. This was not a performance of subtle libidinal undertows; instead, as Baker's seemingly lifeless body came to life with the beating of the drums, the sexual prowess of her kinesis provoked decidedly mixed reactions. In an analysis of audiences' perceptions of black performers in interwar Paris, Karen C. C. Dalton and Henry Louis Gates, Jr. record that "when the curtain fell, some applauded wildly, others booed in derision ... But defenders and detractors alike shared one reaction: shock."[2] Thus, the only common ground uniting audience members was an intense confusion.

Contemporaneous reviews reflect this deep ambivalence. Pierre de Regnier, writing for the local press, summarized Baker's shattering of representational categories with a series of questions that aimed to illuminate the conundrum and rich sensorium her performance engendered:

> Is this a man? Is this a woman? Her lips are painted black, her skin is the color of a banana, her hair, already short, is stuck to her head as if made by caviar, her voice is high-pitched, she shakes continually, and her body slithers like a snake ... The sounds of the orchestra seem to come from her ... Is she horrible? Is she ravishing? Is she black? Is she white? ... Nobody knows for sure. There is no time to know. She returns as she left, quick as a one-step dance, she is not a woman, she is not a dancer, she's something extravagant and passing, just like the music.[3]

This paradoxical molding of representational categories indicates the unnerving spectacle that Baker offered. Jean-Claude Baker and Chris Chase identify the spectacle as being at once "barbaric ... naughty ... a return to the customs of the old ages," yet simultaneously novel and protean.[4] As Jennifer Anne Boittin argues in *Colonial Metropolis: The Urban Grounds of Anti-imperialism and Feminism in Interwar Paris*, Baker was "read as a woman who managed to mold her image around the (African) primitive and the (American) modern."[5] Through the contestation of gender roles and cultural affiliations, Baker's performance allowed her to assume a subject position less rigid than the one that American race politics afforded her, but one still imbricated with the colonial regime that France operated by. Simply put, Baker supplanted entertainment value with provocation. But why exactly was her spectacle so astonishing? Was it her dance, which Baker and Chase describe as "a silent declaration of love, by a simple forward movement of her belly, with her arms raised above the head, and the quiver of her entire rear"?[6] Or was it her oscillation between the primordial and the unprecedented, the awe-inspiring and contempt-probing element that dramatized the conflicts of colonialism for the audience? While some have read Baker's performances as voluntary evocations of colonial mythologies, her self-reflexive aesthetics are perhaps most appropriately viewed as reflections of modernism's investment in the rupture of the past and the fragmented experience of the contemporary moment.

Scholarly debate has long focused on Baker's performance regarding its proliferation, or conversely, its contestation of racial stereotypes. As Anne Cheng notes in *Second Skin: Josephine Baker and the Modern Surface*, to this day "views of Baker remain tethered to the vexed poles of vilification and veneration."[7] The assumption underlying the debate is that Baker was complicit in the proliferation or contestation of these stereotypes by the wanton manipulation of her image alongside or against the American national imaginary. While the debate is often reduced to a question of agency, the matter is more nuanced due to the scopic regimes at play in Baker's performance. Indubitably, Baker's political convictions and her anti-racist agenda were prominent. During the Second World War and while Paris was under German Occupation, Baker contributed to the Resistance by camouflaging intelligence materials as musical scores, and she was awarded two of the highest military honors after the war, the Croix de Guerre and the Legion of Honor with the Rosette of the Resistance. Later on, during the Civil Rights Movement, Baker returned to the United States to participate in the fight for equality, marching side by side with Martin Luther King, Jr. and desegregating venues in which she performed. Her personal life was also imbued with a passionate commitment to equality. At Les Milandes, the estate she bought in the South of France, Baker raised a family of twelve adopted children from diverse ethnic and racial backgrounds. In his exploration of this little-understood part of Baker's life, Matthew Pratt Guterl asserts that these acts "were not mere trifles, not just clever attempts to reclaim the spotlight; they were also remarkable, unprecedented political acts, conceived after a lifetime of thoughtful experimentation by a superstar who could be held down by no rule and no social convention."[8] The "rainbow tribe," as Baker referred to her family, along with all of her other social justice initiatives, were a means to bolster her anti-racist agenda against the stifling confines of segregation in the United States.

Could a woman as decisively engaged in political discourse be unaware of the imagery and affect her performance instigated? This would be an interesting question to address to a performer such as Baker, but it might not be very useful or fair. All such inquiries remove the performer from her historical moment and its cultural production and tend to reveal far more about the speaker's own biases and discursive blind spots than they do about the performer herself. In this context, it is much more pertinent to think about whether it is Baker's agency that confounds us or what her work reveals about modernism in a transatlantic and colonial context.

## Imperial fantasies, colonial embodiments, and the rise of modernity

Baker's arrival in Paris coincided with the advent of a new era, during which fascination with colonial tropes and post-First World War politics created an elusive terrain of racial and national mythologies. As Boittin points out, Baker capitalized upon this ambivalence, as her body became the locus for the enactment of colonial desire and the stimulus for the production of nostalgic colonial rhetoric. According to Boittin, Baker enabled through her embodiment of the *"vogue nègre,"* "a good starting point for understanding the links that Parisians—colonial or Other—established between the cultural production of images of blacks and the politics of race and gender consciousness in the imperial nation state."[9] Boittin goes a step further to suggest that Baker was indeed cognizant of the functions her performance and persona as a "colonial woman" served and audiences too were aware of the colonial dynamic at play, effectively making their "reactions to performances of colonialism" barometers for "how Paris was reacting to empire."[10] In this terrain where both the performance and the reception of it are informed by colonial tensions and newly emergent modernist aesthetics, Baker's oeuvre oscillates between primitivism and modernity. Although the two concepts appear to connote opposite historical trajectories, primitivism alluding to the past and modernism pointing towards the future, breaking down the two in terms of their representational practices yields surprisingly accordant results.

In the primitive elements of Baker's performance, her nakedness, abrupt movement, and exaggerated facial expressions, a set of aesthetic characteristics emerged that did not pertain to an obscure exoticized legacy from the past, but rather to a forthcoming cultural moment—one that emphasized the ruptured, fragmented mediation of human emotion in the post-First World War era. In *Primitive Modernism: Black Culture and the Origins of Transatlantic Modernism* (1988), Sieglinde Lemke writes that Baker's primitive aesthetic was employed to "rejuvenate and to redeem" her audience: "The audience yearned for something lacking in modern European culture. Baker, in turn, gave them what they needed. She took off her clothes, crawled on the floor, engaged in a frenzied, apparently spontaneous gush of energy, and staged 'the primitive.'"[11] This effort to "rejuvenate" and "redeem" is emblematic of a key modernist preoccupation, the drive to "make it new" as a means of addressing the cultural malaise of the interwar years. Similar to other diasporic proponents of modernism, who departed from high modernist aesthetics and embraced their own version of modernist innovation, Baker resorts to the vexed historicity of colonialism and utilizes its tropes and visual rhetoric to dismantle the legacies of subordination that rendered her body an aesthetic aberration. Her regressive performance therefore doubles as a transgression into new territory, a move that aims to appropriate the mechanisms that produce cultural meaning and to affirm her race and gender position.

Baker's affective pull was so powerful that soon an array of other modernist artists flocked to see her performances. Ernest Hemingway, Pablo Picasso and E. E. Cummings, among others, found inspiration in Baker's sweeping performance. Her sight was compelling, and her deft weaving of blackness, femininity and the legacy of colonialism offered other artists significant insights on how modernism was experienced from a transatlantic and diasporic standpoint. More than that, as Carole Sweeney writes in *From Fetish to Subject: Race Modernism and Primitivism* (2004), Baker was an "erotic and exotic figure par excellence for the modernist artist seeking a neat metaphor to express the affiliations and tensions between the modern and the primitive."[12] As such, her figure and intertextual play, between modernism and primitivism, turned her into a muse for her contemporaries.

Baker's resonance in the artistic production of her time (and beyond) problematizes the inherited legacies of primitivism, modernism, and black female identity. Cheng contends that it would be misguided to use "Baker's modernity as a means of refuting the charges of atavism so frequently leveled at her image" because such an approach ignores the fact that "Modernism and Primitivism are intertwined, at times even identical phenomena."[13] For Cheng, objectification and desire are integrally related to the reception of Baker's performance and "the idealization of black female agency" as well as to "the phenomenon of European Primitivism":[14] "At the moment when La Baker was invented on stage we see not the affirmation or the denial of Modernist Primitivism but the failure of its terms to inscribe its own passions."[15] These passions, namely the exercise and imposition of colonial desire upon Baker's body and the fascination with her attires and self-fashioning, indicate an alternate mode of ontology, focusing on skin, epidermis, and surface.

With the advent of technologies associated with the visual, such as photography and cinema, the ocular gained prominence as a means of deciphering the world. As previously demonstrated, modernism, as a cultural and artistic movement, is fascinated with surfaces, porous and impenetrable, perceived and read, greeting them with both conviction and mystification alike. Baker's nudity becomes an aberration in this context, hence her iconic skin is associated with primitivism; however, as her performances and self-fashioning suggest, Baker's nudity is a remarkably layered construct. It is the contrast between the flimsy materials she is clad with and "the eccentric communion with other epidermises" that assigns Baker's body both a prismic and a catalytic function in the context of modernity.[16] Baker, who, in Cheng's words, "[wears] her nakedness like a sheath,"[17] remains in the national imaginary someone whose protean metamorphoses are enabled not only by her artistic prowess, but also by the fabrics and props that adorn her: feathers, banana skins, miniscule items of clothing made of tulle and sequins.

The audience's fascination with Baker's bare skin is driven by the legacy of colonialism and the racial politics of the era. The physical boundary that the skin represents between the self and the world surrounding it resonates powerfully with the segregational practices of Jim Crow and with the desire to cross into new territory. In *Bad Modernisms* (2006), Douglas Mao and Rebecca Walkowitz point out that "early twentieth century writers were … preoccupied with border crossings such as cosmopolitanism, synesthesia, racial masquerade, collage and translation."[18] Baker's performance arguably becomes a site for the demonstration of such tropes, a self-reflexive commentary on the politics and mores of her time. For as Josephine Baker gained stardom and unprecedented fame in Europe, across the Atlantic the Harlem Renaissance evolved into a cradle for the revival of black culture. Removed from the plantation economies of the South and fueled by the incomplete promise of emancipation, Harlem fostered a community vibrant and dynamic, moving towards a new black aesthetic in art. Similarly, Baker's performance promoted a modernist agenda that revisited and revised stereotypes of black womanhood in spite of appearing regressive.

Modernism at least in its literary expression, is associated with specific attributes that high modernist texts are thought to possess. Fragmentation, stream of consciousness, elevated diction, and obscurity, are only few of the characteristics of Anglo-Saxon modernist production. In the same way that writers of color have approached modernism from different standpoints, illuminating their own experiences, Baker infuses her performance with modernist elements that do not abide by the rigid confines of Anglo-Saxon modernism. Mao and Walkowitz argue that "modernism [appears] always in oscillation between a cultural authenticity that can be exposed as artifice and an artifice legible as authenticity."[19] This is a pair of classifications that seem especially well suited to Baker's art.

# Towards a new optics: Revolutionizing black female identity and performance

Discussing Baker's artifice or authenticity without falling into essentialist traps is a rather arduous task. If we accept the contention that "modernism was shaped by a host of exclusions and embattlements pertaining to gender," as Mao and Walkowitz maintain, I would also like to argue that Baker's status as a black woman complicates the performance and reception of her art.[20] Mao and Walkowitz suggest that "women's growing economic independence and the predominantly female audience for genres legible as 'bad by middlebrow and modernists alike,'" were formative to the development of modernist art forms.[21] Considering Baker's case in an intersectional light, I would also like to add that it is precisely the move towards financial independence that allowed her, as a black female performer, to develop her *oeuvre*. Unlike Virginia Woolf, and other white female modernists, whose art was enabled by "a room of [their] own," Baker's performance became an emancipatory site as a result of her very visible labor and the exposure of her body in several nude and seminude iterations. As a result, Baker's liberation from the confines of racism was the outcome of her visibility and her subsequent recognition by her contemporaries and future audiences alike as a cultural and artistic culprit of modernism.

It was indubitably her affluence, attained through hard labor, which allowed Baker to enjoy exceptional privileges as a black woman at the time. Going back to our discussion of agency then, how do we manage the fraught relation between the iconic imagery that afforded Baker substantial liberties, while simultaneously entrapping black femininity in representational limbo? A way to approach the topic would be to consider Linda Hutcheon's concept of modernist parody as "an imitation characterized by inversion that often involves, as John Fowles has said, 'both a homage and a kind of thumbed nose' to 'an obvious previous iconography.'"[22] This hopeful reading of iconography as empowering and dismantling, iconoclastic rather than iconomorphic, allows us to consider Baker's performance from a new modernist standpoint. It would not be hard to argue that parody is indeed part of Baker's multifarious performances. From *danse sauvage* onward, Baker's on-stage numbers as well as her appearances on film included potent self-reflexive moments.

An intertextual reading of her playfulness with fashioning a black female subject yields surprising, often paradoxical, results. Alwina's character, played by Baker in *Princess Tam Tam*, for example, illustrates the parody dynamic embedded in Baker's work by mirroring the story of exoticism and Otherness, while highlighting the sheer delight of the communion of authenticity and artifice in Baker's dance. Mao and Walkowitz point out that it is precisely this function of modernism that keeps it relevant in the contemporary moment:

> Encounters with "difficult" artifacts or performances, whatever elation or frustration they may otherwise engender, hold always a capacity to hearten inasmuch as they seem to confirm how intelligence, complexity, and curiosity have been alive in the world (and draw life again from just such confrontations between perplexed audience and elusive object). Could it be then, that the new-old appeal of modernism lies partly in a consolation of this sort, emerging from its very negatives? If so, we will not be surprised to find modernism holding special allure in times when the future of thinking seems uncertain, when anti-intellectualism seems

ascendant, when resistance to all but the simplest positions and solutions has arrogated to itself the mantle of good.[23]

Examining Baker's controversial performances in the contemporary moment gives us impetus for thought, especially if we consider them as the point of departure in a genealogy of black female performers revered in the public sphere.

In order to examine Baker's lasting legacy in contemporary performance, and what I want to suggest as the development of a new optics, it is important to consider how modernist aesthetics differ depending on the means of their production. Critics such as Houston Baker, Jr. and Carla Kaplan have argued for the diverse articulation of modernism in texts outside of the Anglo-Saxon mainstream. Both theorists contend that along with the orthodoxies of high modernist texts diversified versions of modernism by minority writers are essential to modernism as a movement. Looking for a means of expression that does not abide by an Anglo-Saxon high modernist rubric, or by what critical race theorists refer to as the politics of respectability, Houston Baker traces the black modernist aesthetic back to the late nineteenth century. He argues that the interest of black "spokespersons" at the time, in particular Booker T. Washington and W. E. B. Du Bois, was to express through their discourse both their heritage and the malaise they experienced under the violence of Jim Crow in the South. These figures, Baker notes, created a "'mastery of form' and 'deformation of mastery,' respectively, [which] set the contours of a field of African-American phonics that marks the birth of Afro-American modernism."[24] Specifically, he argues that what appeared at the time as "the deformative sounds of Afro-Americans are the group phonics and common language of the masses, sounds that are traditionally labeled 'substandard,' 'nonsensical,' or 'unlearned' by white speakers."[25] These modes of expression also proved to be formative categories for expressing black identity in America.

Similar to the "deformative sounds" that constitute the new phonics, a form of new optics has been engendered by the performances that pertain to the black aesthetic tradition. Houston Baker argues that in the nineteenth century minstrel shows were the predominant representational prism through which blackness was presented in the national imaginary. He writes that minstrelsy was "a perduring legacy and strategy of representation when blacks appear in white discourse. It [offered] a form of appropriation, a domestic space for taking, hearing, and containing the black Other. Only by assuming a posture relative to this space could turn-of-the-century, Afro-American spokespersons become effectively articulate."[26] Josephine Baker's performance was widely criticized for the minstrelsy elements she employed; yet, if we extend Houston Baker's contention for the emergence of a new phonics through the mastery of form and the deformation of mastery to encompass a new optics, engendered through the same principles, then Josephine Baker's parody becomes a powerful repurposing of black cultural tradition, laden with emancipatory potential.

Josephine Baker's performance exists within a compound of movements and aesthetics, which paradoxically increase its legibility as an innovative modernist moment inasmuch as they threaten to take it apart. The entropy engendered by the indexicality of Baker's performance as it relates to minstrel shows and racial stereotyping of iconic scale addresses precisely the differences between Baker's cultural background and the backgrounds of her modernist contemporaries. In the meantime, performing in France, rather than in Harlem, has led to Baker being considered a minor contributor to the African-American modernist tradition in spite of her success and visibility in the public sphere. Her fame and iconicity inevitably become carriers of her own belittlement as an active agent in the struggle for racial equality. This problem is one that the Harlem Renaissance itself has had to face. Addressing this issue, Houston Baker argues that "Only by reconstructing or re-membering a discursive history of Afro-America and its socioeconomic and sociopolitical motivations and objectives can one see Harlem and its success as articulations that carry a population not away from querulous literary ancestors, but up from slavery."[27] Similarly, it is important to consider how Josephine Baker's performance functioned as a countermodernist moment for the cultural production of the era.

Like Du Bois and Washington, Josephine Baker simultaneously mastered the form and deformed the mastery of white hegemony. However, her skillful veering from masterful artist to instigator of representational mayhem happens outside of the Mecca of emergent black agency. This could be the reason for her notorious displacement outside of black modernity, for as Baker crossed the Atlantic, she performed a regressive representational leap in the public imagination. The attribution of her fame and success to her primitivist performance was a vehicle for her discreditation—as an agentic performer and as a black female capable of complex political engagement.

One could even argue that the fascination with what Josephine Baker appears to express through a surface level reading, her skin, attire, and performance, is the impetus behind the varied playful metamorphoses of her exterior. Cheng notes that situating Baker in the various forms of modernist display, such as photography, film, architecture and the stage itself, reveals "alternative stories about racialized skin, narratives that compel a reconceptualization of the notions of racialized corporeality, as well as of idealized modernist façades. It is on the surface of this most organic, sensual and corporeal of icons that we will find the most unexpected and intense residue of modern synthetics and the imagination that accompanied them."[28] Baker's performance is therefore revelatory and empowering for the black subject, as it contests dominant modernist narratives with an alternative story that is not precluded by preconceived notions tethering African-American modernist expression to the success of the Harlem Renaissance. Instead, it opens up black modernist expression to encompass an array of practices, performances, and aesthetic choices dissociated from high modernist characteristics. Houston Baker accounts for such a possibility, arguing that "perhaps the eternally modern in Afro-American discursive and intellectual history is not so much signaled by the single 'Harlem Renaissance,' as by a more inclusive 'renaissancism' defined as everpresent, folk or vernacular drive that moves always up, beyond and away from whatever forms of oppression a surrounding culture next devices."[29]

Confronting Baker's modernist legacy in the contemporary moment requires a radical repositioning of spectators' views on the aesthetics of her practice and the politics of her era. If we read Baker's performance as an emancipatory act, a means of articulating her resistance against the racial scripts that circumscribed her social and professional life in the context of Jim Crow, then Baker becomes a Jazz Age advocate against racial inequality and gender discrimination. Her self-reflexive performances thus bring to the forefront the marked characteristics of social malaise as reflected on the periphery of white Anglo-Saxon modernism and make palpable the pitfalls of the ocular regimes constituting the American national imaginary and its notions of gender and race.

Indubitably, Baker has left a lasting legacy. Her trajectory emboldened black women to forge their own paths of artistic prowess, and oftentimes the new generation of black women performers paid tribute by emulating her aesthetic both in fashion and in artistic practice. What Baker offered them was not a vision of verisimilitude, but rather freedom from the confines of representation. The impulse to identify an emerging artist with Baker's legacy is a natural outcome of her continued relevance as a pioneering black icon. In the recent past, black female artists, including Rihanna, have been noted as entertainers whose artistry evoked, even cited, Baker's performance. However, the comparison, which focused on their physique and sartorial choices, aimed less at connoting a genealogy of black female performers, and more at indicating that these were exceptional cases of black female dominance within a field marked as optically and aesthetically white.

# Baker's resonance in the contemporary: Beyoncé's articulations of freedom and black female identity

If one switches focus from contemporary performers' physique to the sociopolitical commentary they seek to articulate, Baker's legacy becomes particularly relevant to the work of Beyoncé Knowles, especially *Lemonade*.

As Terri Frances notes in her short piece, "What does Beyoncé See in Josephine Baker?," Beyoncé's engagement with Baker's *oeuvre* has reshaped her performance and marked a shift in her representational practices as she "strategically sampled" Baker's style, sartorial and otherwise, to "remix[] her 1920s aesthetics for contemporary audiences."[30]

Beyoncé's career arguably follows a similar trajectory to Baker's contested performances as a black female dancer. Both of their bodies have been rendered iconic by similar entertainment industries, which might not resemble one another in infrastructure due to their distance in time, yet inevitably evoke the same corrosive visual rhetoric against the female black body. Both performers reveled as protégées of the entertainment industry before taking a stance against its politics, and both became increasingly more vocal as they reached international acclamation. Beyoncé's polemic stance against contemporary politics of black disenfranchisement and dispossession first appeared in "Formations," a single track distributed in February 2016. This track was followed by *Lemonade*, a musical album accompanied by an hour-long film (including bonus sections) that bound the narrative of the music together through poetry, cameo appearances by notable black women, and intertextual references to black culture and history. Released in April 2016, or "dropped" overnight, Beyoncé's *Lemonade* did not simply interject with commentary in a conversation already taking place; rather it framed the shape of the discussion, created its contours, and allowed for questions to be asked. In "Formations," the single that preceded the album, Beyoncé appears on top of a police car sinking in a flooded street in New Orleans. The question that echoes as the tune starts, "What happened at the New Orleans?" sets the tone for the agenda underlying the performance featured. Profuse indexicality and a vast array of citational markers allow the audience to navigate the performance, while visual clues alluding to African-American history abound: Martin Luther King's portrait in a newspaper, the unfulfilled promise of his dream, references to the Black Panther movement, a boy in a hoodie fearlessly dancing in front of armed police officers.

Shortly after the album's release, dithyrambic critiques emerged praising Beyoncé for her engagement with the blurry topographies of violence and desire that circumscribe black bodies in the national imaginary. Media venues and popular culture sites credited the performer with producing an album that was a testament to her blackness, while others more attuned to the essentialist undertows of such praise parodied the audience's attachment to Beyoncé's presumably white aesthetic. Critics who felt less enamored with the outcome focused their scrutiny on what they perceived as a blatant commodification of black history and pain. In "Moving Beyond Pain," bell hooks criticized the overtly stylized outcome of the music video as "certainly not radical or revolutionary," but rather as a "visual extravaganza—a display of black female bodies that ... is all about the body as commodity."[31] hooks's main critique stems from the ways in which the music industry puts pain center stage as the inescapable fate of black communities. Instead, she argues that the vision we should sustain is one of optimal and consistent well-being against the cultivation of tropes that engulf the black community in perpetual mourning. Although hooks's observations on the practices of the music industry and of its constitutive criteria for profit are accurate, it is important to consider, much like in Baker's situational performances in interwar Paris, that Beyoncé is articulating an emancipatory vision that is significant for its resonance *vis-à-vis* post-racial rhetoric in the contemporary moment. Upon closer examination, the music video becomes a terrain in which the unfulfilled promise of freedom and the underlying script of precariousness are presented, contested and recorded afresh without perpetuating imagery that further violates the black body.

What is noteworthy in this filmic representation of Beyoncé's work is the way in which the video evokes imagery associated with African-American historicity and cultural legacy without entrapping the black subject into precarious empathy. The black body is not presented suffering, it is not shown in abjection or agony, it rather beams with forcefulness and purpose in demanding the recognition of past atrocities and the termination of police brutality and systemic discrimination. To call attention to what is palpably evident for black communities but not to the ostensibly post-racial society of the contemporary moment, intruding visual clues interspersed in the *mise-en-scène* create a layered construct much like Baker's layering of epidermis after epidermis, surface after surface. The plantation, the Master's house, water excessively filling up space (be it an urban landscape or a bedroom), tight bodices, narrow corridors, and grim colors accentuate the imagery of confinement. Through their sensory abundance, they succeed in representing the narrative void, the historical omissions purposefully ornamented to indicate the haunting that lingers in the present moment. In the same way that Baker ornamented her naked body to connote the lasting impact of colonialism and to make visible the exoticizing fantasies inscribed upon her flesh, the visual world of *Lemonade* uses the ornate as a means to bring to the forefront what lies beneath the ornamentation and the excess. It is again reality in its rawest iteration that this constructed layering unmasks, each layer an ornate reminder of the bare and the omnipresent, the afterlife of slavery and the enduring discriminatory tactics that embalm black life in circles of precariousness.

Times have arguably changed. Beyoncé is supposedly not performing in an era of lived palpable discrimination like Baker was. Jim Crow laws do not impose segregation, Beyoncé does not have to demand the desegregation of the venues in which she performs. A more profound desegregational practice is, however, imperative to decolonize the national imaginary from the vitriolic views of racial hierarchies established during slavery and perpetuated from Reconstruction to the present day—all of which form a prism through which the world is perceived. In the same vein that interwar Paris dealt with the end of colonialism and the trauma of the First World War during the time Baker performed her numbers, the United States is now facing issues that have crucial impact on the lives of its most vulnerable citizens of color. Police brutality, mass incarceration, and systemic injustice strategically undermine the sustainability of black communities while the existence of a black President appears to justify those who claim that we currently live in a post-racial society. Beyoncé's work in *Lemonade* brings these concerns to the forefront.

Embracing black aesthetics and African-American culture, Beyoncé paradoxically evokes iconic images to perform an iconoclastic function. Walking through the streets with a bat in her hands, she smashes the rigid confines of a world that entraps black identity in stereotypical iterations. The self-reflexivity of her performance, another shared characteristic with Baker, connotes her awareness of the dynamic function of the icon, and its deft manipulation turns her former means of oppression into a powerful tool for the communication of her message. By reshuffling the meanings associated with her iconic persona, Beyoncé contributes to an emancipatory modernist discourse, as her body contests iconic renderings of the black femininity and charts new, global territories for black female self-fashioning and identity through the entertainment industry.

# Notes

1 For further information about Josephine Baker's life and times, see Bennetta Jules-Rosette's *Josephine Baker in Art and Life: The Icon and the Image* (Chicago: Chicago University Press, 2007), Lynn Harney's *Naked at the Feast: A Biography of Josephine Baker* (New York: Dodd, Mead, 1981), and Phyllis Rose's *Jazz Cleopatra: Josephine Baker in Her Time* (New York: Doubleday, 1989).
2 Karen C. C. Dalton and Henry Louis Gates, Jr., "Josephine Baker and Paul Colin: African-American Dance Seen through Parisian Eyes," *Critical Inquiry* 24, no. 4 (1998): 915.
3 Quoted in Jean-Claude Baker and Chris Chase, *Josephine Baker: The Hungry Heart* (New York: Cooper Square Press, 1993), 5.
4 Ibid., 6.
5 Jennifer Anne Boittin, *Colonial Metropolis: The Urban Grounds of Anti-Imperialism and Feminism in Interwar Paris* (Lincoln: Nebraska University Press, 2010), 3.
6 Baker and Chase, *Josephine Baker*, 6.
7 Anne Anlin Cheng, *Second Skin: Josephine Baker and the Modern Surface* (New York: Oxford University Press, 2011), 3.

8 Matthew Pratt Guterl, *Josephine Baker and the Rainbow Tribe* (Cambridge: Harvard University Press, 2014), 9.
9 Boittin, *Colonial Metropolis*, 2.
10 Ibid.
11 Sieglinde Lemke, *Primitivist Modernism: Black Culture and the Origins of Transatlantic Modernism* (Oxford: Oxford University Press, 1998), 100.
12 Carole Sweeney, *From Fetish to Subject: Race Modernism and Primitivism, 1919–1935* (Westport, CT: Praeger, 2004), 121.
13 Cheng, *Second Skin*, 4.
14 Ibid., 5.
15 Ibid.
16 Ibid., 8.
17 Ibid., 1.
18 Douglas Mao and Rebecca Walkowitz, "Introduction: Modernisms Bad and New," in *Bad Modernisms*, eds. Douglas Mao and Rebecca Walkowitz (Durham: Duke University Press, 2006), 2.
19 Ibid., 12.
20 Ibid., 8.
21 Ibid.
22 Linda Hutcheon, *A Theory of Parody: The Teachings of Twentieth-century Art Forms* (Urbana: University of Illinois Press, 1985), 33; This critique is indebted to Sianne Ngai's discussion of Hutcheon, modernism, and parody in *Bad Modernisms* (147).
23 Mao and Walkowitz, "Introduction," 16.
24 Houston A. Baker, Jr. "Modernism and the Harlem Renaissance," *American Quarterly* 39, no. 1 (1987): 93.
25 Ibid., 94.
26 Ibid., 93.
27 Ibid., 95.
28 Cheng, *Second Skin*, n.p.
29 Baker, Jr., "Modernism and the Harlem Renaissance," 96.
30 Terri Frances, "What does Beyoncé See in Josephine Baker?: A Brief Film History of la Diva, La Bakaire," in "Josephine Baker: A Century in the Spotlight," ed. Kaiama L. Glover, special issue, *The Scholar and Feminist Online* 6, no. 1–2 (2007–8): 2. http://sfonline.barnard.edu/baker/francis_01.htm.
31 bell hooks, "Moving Beyond Pain," The bell hooks Institute, Berea College, May 9, 2016. http://www.bellhooksinstitute.com/blog/2016/5/9/moving-beyond-pain.

# Bibliography

Baker, Houston A., Jr. "Modernism and the Harlem Renaissance." *American Quartely* 39, no. 1 (1987): 84–97.
Baker, Jean-Claude and Chris Chase. *Josephine Baker: The Hungry Heart*. New York: Cooper Square Press, 1993.
Boittin, Jennifer Anne. *Colonial Metropolis: The Urban Grounds of Anti-Imperialism and Feminism in Interwar Paris*. Lincoln: Nebraska University Press, 2010.
Cheng, Anne Anlin. *Second Skin: Josephine Baker and the Modern Surface*. New York: Oxford University Press, 2011.
Dalton, Karen C. C. and Henry Louis Gates, Jr. "Josephine Baker and Paul Colin: African-American Dance Seen through Parisian Eyes." *Critical Inquiry* 24, no. 4 (1998): 903–34.
Frances, Terri. "What does Beyoncé See in Josephine Baker?: A Brief Film History of la Diva, La Bakaire." In "Josephine Baker: A Century in the Spotlight," edited by Kaiama L. Glover, special issue of *The Scholar and Feminist Online* 6, no. 1–2 (2007–8). Available online: http://sfonline.barnard.edu/baker/francis_01.htm.
Guterl, Matthew Pratt. *Josephine Baker and the Rainbow Tribe*. Cambridge: Harvard University Press, 2014.
Harney, Lynn. *Naked at the Feast: A Biography of Josephine Baker*. New York: Dodd, Mead, 1981.
hooks, bell. "Moving Beyond Pain." The bell hooks Institute. Berea College. May 9, 2016. Available online: http://www.bellhooksinstitute.com/blog/2016/5/9/moving-beyond-pain.
Hutcheon, Linda. *A Theory of Parody: The Teachings of Twentieth-century Art Forms*. Urbana: University of Illinois Press, 1985.
Jules-Rosette, Benneta. *Josephine Baker in Art and Life: The Icon and the Image*. Chicago: Chicago University Press, 2007.
Kaplan, Carla. "Making it New: Constructions of Modernism." In *A Companion to American Literature and Culture*, edited by Paul Lauter, 40–56. Malden, MA: Wiley-Blackwell, 2010.
Lemke, Sieglinde. *Primitvist Modernism: Black Culture and the Origins of Transatlantic Modernism*, 100. Oxford: Oxford University Press, 1998.
Mao, Douglas and Rebecca Walkowitz. "Introduction: Modernisms Bad and New." In *Bad Modernisms*, edited by Douglas Mao and Rebecca Walkowitz, 1–18. Durham: Duke University Press, 2006.
Ngai, Sianne. "Black Venus, Blonde Venus." In *Bad Modernisms*, edited by Douglas Mao and Rebecca Walkowitz, 145–78. Durham: Duke University Press, 2006.
Rose, Phyllis. *Jazz Cleopatra: Josephine Baker in Her Time*. New York: Doubleday, 1989.
Sweeney, Carole. *From Fetish to Subject: Race Modernism and Primitivism, 1919–1935*. Westport, CT: Praeger, 2004.

# 9

# A hitchhiker's guide to modernism: The futuristic Fordisms of Aldous Huxley, Brian O'Nolan, and Douglas Adams

*Andrew V. McFeaters*

"Then the silence deepened. But, as we listened to the old canal muttering its feeble prayers and the creaking bones of sickly palaces above their damp green beards, under the windows we suddenly heard the famished roar of automobiles."
—FILIPPO TOMMASO MARINETTI, "THE FOUNDING AND MANIFESTO OF FUTURISM" (1909)

On March 24, 1933, Aldous Huxley wrote a letter to his friend, Mary Hutchinson, during his journey through Mexico. He had already been through Trinidad, Belize, Guatemala, and Antigua, and during this extended trip he shared through correspondence with friends his observations about local cultures, political developments, and ancient ruins. As if dramatizing Bernard and Lenina's vacation in the Savage Reservation in *Brave New World*, published only months before, Huxley attempted to make sense of the so-called New World through his European sensibilities:

Have had a delightful time here, Mayan ruins, Spanish churches and altars with Indian primitives, and the most astonishing Indian life in the highlands—huge populations of Mayan stock living up there with all their costumes, and practicing the most amazing mixture of pagan and Catholic religion. They go from the church to the altar in the woods and burn incense impartially in front of Christ and old Maya idols. Most peculiar.[1]

In spite of Huxley's lifelong criticisms of the modern world, his accounts during this trip do not escape an Anglocentric bias. Although his attitudes better reflect "savage" John's cross-cultural curiosity rather than Lenina's visceral prejudices at the sight of the viviparous, his reflections are tinged with an imperialistic gaze at the primitive Other. At times his letters seem to echo Marlow's tale in Joseph Conrad's *Heart of Darkness*, mapping culture and nature through positions which, in spite of shifting sympathies and doubts, presume a superior cultural and material history.

Huxley does not seem surprised, however, at witnessing some signs of modernization during his sojourn. On April 10th, he wrote to Mary Hutchinson from Oaxaca:

Got here from the Pacific Coast, where we landed 12 days ago: stayed on a coffee plantation in the mountains, then we set out on mule back across the Sierra, 11,000 ft high, slept in an Indian house; rode on again with ever sorer bottoms, and at last reached a road and an old Ford; which took us to all but civilization; then another Ford to a train—and here we are at Oaxaca; a lovely place, with marvelous pre-Columbian ruins at Monte Alban.[2]

The appearance of Ford automobiles in remote terrain was not that unusual. By 1933, Ford automobiles were common in much of the world; yet, one can imagine Huxley raising an eyebrow, as if witnessing the ideological and material underpinnings of his fictional World State, wherein Fordism transforms society, replacing centuries of cultural traditions with a sociopolitical structure consumed by mass production, immediate gratification, and a superficial culture industry. In *Brave New World*, Lord becomes Ford, as signified by the Christian cross becoming the letter "T" from the Model T. Ford becomes the surrogate father to all, the viviparous, nuclear family being replaced through eugenic mass production, and Big Ben becomes Big Henry, embodying a sense of time purged of history.

Aldous Huxley is not the only writer who felt and portrayed the affects and effects of Fordism in the world. Brian O'Nolan, who typically penned novels under the name Flann O'Brien and wrote an *Irish Times* column as Dublin Everyman, Myles na Gopaleen, references Henry Ford and Fordism throughout his writing. Henry Ford stands colossal, not merely as an innovator in automotive mass production, but also as an evangelical social engineer committed to spreading a way of life. For O'Nolan, Ford would transform another kind of place historically characterized as a savage reservation: Ireland. Ironically enough, and counter to his satirical views on Fordism, O'Nolan traded in his Morris for a Ford Anglia after the Second World War.[3] By this time, Ford cars had been in production in England and Ireland for several years, largely supplementing a gap in production created by a British manufacturing industry refitted for the war effort. As early as 1925, Great Britain had manufactured its 250,000th Ford automobile.[4] Well before the 1920s, Great Britain had been viewed as an important target for American automotive expansion. In fact, Ford's automotive invasion began in 1909 with its first transatlantic branch appearing on Shaftesbury Avenue in London. As the *New York Times* proclaimed, "Ford cars for 1910 will be sold in practically every quarter of the globe where civilization exists and motor cars can be run."[5]

The spread of Fordism was represented by many writers and is evident in works that depict the Jazz Age and preceding decade, like E. L. Doctorow's *Ragtime* (1974) in which Henry Ford appears as a major character: "Henry Ford had once been an ordinary manufacturer. Now he experienced an ecstasy greater and more intense than that vouchsafed to any American before him, not excepting Thomas Jefferson. He had caused a machine to replicate itself endlessly."[6] Its influence is also shown in Ishmael Reed's *Mumbo Jumbo* (1972) as an expression of Western, imperialist consumerism: "Deluxe Ice Cream, Coffee, 1 cent Pies, Cakes, Tobacco, Hot Dogs and Highways. Highways leading nowhere. Highways leading somewhere. Highways the Occupation used to speed upon in their automobiles, killing dogs pigs and cattle belonging to poor people. What is the American fetish for highways?"[7] Ford's growing production had a direct impact on highway development. These novels do more than depict the early twentieth century; they signify the ongoing effects of Fordism in the decades in which they were written. The near absence of Ford automobiles in F. Scott Fitzgerald's *The Great Gatsby* (1925) is a reminder that Henry Ford's target consumers were everyday people. Gatsby was the antithesis of a Ford consumer. Henry Ford paid his employees well—a practice initially scoffed at by competitors—and by doing so helped to create a class of workers who could afford to purchase the products they created. America's infrastructure grew because its people grew.

As if fulfilling a prophecy of one of the Ford Motor Company's most famous ad campaigns—"There's a Ford in your future"[8]—Douglas Adams's *The Hitchhiker's Guide to the Galaxy* imagines the final frontier of Fordism: space. The alien visitor in *Hitchhiker's Guide* assumes the name Ford Prefect in an attempt to blend in with what he believes is the most dominant species on Earth: automobiles. The Machine Age reaches its foregone conclusion when humanity and machine are one and the same.

*Hitchhiker's Guide*, which began as a radio show on BBC Radio 4 in 1978, would be adapted in novel form, as a television series, as a graphic novel, as a computer game, and, finally—after previous attempts—as a film. In his futuristic allusions to Fordism, Adams perpetuates this recurrent trope of modernity. Henry Ford, the man, his company, and the transformative globalization that came with his manufacturing practices, occupies the central image of modernity, which, among other repercussions, represents the blurring of humanity with technology, a narrative that continues to permeate reality and imagination today. More than this, Fordism, as a modern archetype of technological transformation, represents the road to the future, a science fiction portending possible realities imagined variously as utopian or dystopian.

# Henry Ford's brave new world

Ford himself would play a role in defining Fordism for critical reception. Mass production is defined in the thirteenth edition of *Encyclopedia Britannica* as:

> the focussing upon a manufacturing project of the principles of power, accuracy, economy, system, continuity and speed ... And the normal result is a productive organization that delivers in quantities a useful commodity of standard material, workmanship and design at minimum cost. The necessary, precedent condition of mass production is a capacity, latent or developed, of mass consumption.[9]

The definition, printed in advance by the *New York Times*, was penned by Henry Ford, and as Richard Snow points out in *I Invented the Modern Age: The Rise of Henry Ford* (2013), before people called it "mass production," they called it "Fordism."[10] Henry Ford did not invent mass production, nor did he invent the automobile. He did, however, refine, accelerate, and expand the process at an unprecedented, global scale with the purpose of producing a basic, durable product affordable to the average consumer. Fordism, Bob Jessop writes in "Thatcherism and Flexibility: The White Heat of a Post-Fordist Revolution" (1991), "involves the consumption of standardised, mass commodities in nuclear family households and provision of standardised, collective goods and services by the bureaucratic state."[11] The critique against Fordism had less to do with the products of Fordism than with the practices and conditions of production in the factory. As Evelyn Cobley writes in *Modernism and the Culture of Efficiency: Ideology & Fiction* (2009), "The Ford Motor Company was contradictorily both a testament to the American entrepreneurial spirit and an emblem of the dehumanization of individuals and the homogenization of society."[12] On the one hand, British manufacturers toured Ford's American factories to better understand his astonishing success in the market place; on the other hand, some viewed the repetitive, fragmentary, and easily replaceable labor of these factory workers as demeaning, alienating, and dehumanizing. Humans became cogs in the larger machine of the factory and became indistinguishable from the machines themselves. Cobley points out that the "admiration for Ford's achievement was already tainted by sympathy for the plight of the alienated workers who were dwarfed by the machines controlling them."[13] This was a major point of conflict between Ford's utopian vision and Huxley's dystopian vision of Ford.

Huxley was in part moved to write *Brave New World* after reading Henry Ford's autobiography, *My Life and Work* (1922), a book that would appear among Mustapha Mond's possessions in the novel. Huxley discovered the autobiography in a ship's library during his travels in Asia in 1926.[14] He later quotes from its pages in his 1931 essay "Sight-Seeing in Alien Englands" when discussing Ford's belief that workers without intellectual needs or potentials are content to do repetitive work, a belief Huxley found repugnant for its premise and conclusion. Tracing the evolving role that Ford played in the genesis of Huxley's novel, Jerome Meckier points out that Huxley connected the factory developments in England to Ford's innovations in production. Huxley toured the manufacturing and chemical factories of Joseph Lucas and Sir Alfred Mond, where he "witnessed mass production on British soil."[15] Sir Alfred Mond obviously supplied material for Huxley's Mustapha Mond, but Ford would be the founder of the World State. Huxley is among the authors that Cobley addresses in her cultural critique of the influences of Henry Ford and Frederick Winslow Taylor. She writes:

> *Brave New World* dramatizes overlapping but not necessarily converging understandings of the social ramifications of Henry Ford's obsession with efficiency. As part of the novel indicates, Huxley associated efficiency with the technical efficiency of the machine. In this sense, efficiency is blamed not only for its reifying impact on individuals and its homogenizing social tendencies, but also for its elevation of efficiency as a value or an end in itself.[16]

In reality, the motivation behind adopting Fordist manufacturing methods obviously were economic. The economy itself could be construed as a colossal machine, with each of its parts, including labor, as a cog or lever capable of being adjusted in order to maximize growth. America's economic growth during the 1920s was surely a sign of the success of its methods.

For many Europeans, American practices of Fordism presented a possible solution to Europe's economic slump. Publications like Bernard Austin and W. Francis Lloyd's *The Secret of High Wages* (1926) laud American manufacturing practices. Austin and Lloyd, British engineers, derived research during their visit to America. In June of 1930 the *New York Times* featured an article by Harold Callender titled "Ford's Methods Give Europe Hope for Her Industry." Callender boldly declares, "To Europeans Ford is a symbol of a sort of second Industrial Revolution."[17]

As early as 1923, critics voiced concern over Ford's methods, as evidenced by the Conference of Industrial Welfare held at Balliol College in Oxford that year. According to the *New York Times*, the general concern was that the changes in production "would deprive people of initiative and would tend to become 'soul killing, like the Ford works.'"[18] Responding in earnest, a Miss Mathias declared, "What we want is a robot, not a man. We don't want men of intelligence if we are going to Fordize industry." The ideological conflict hinges on different notions of progress and freedom: progress in economic growth and modernization versus enlightenment principles on equality and individual rights. Interestingly, Callender's article compares Ford to some unlikely bedfellows: "[Ford] is regarded as personifying the America of today somewhat as Gandhi may be said to personify Young India, and Lenin revolutionary Russia."[19] The conflict between Marxism and Fordism is obvious enough, but, as the article hints, Gandhi was also in tune with the global consequences of Fordism.

With the advent of the Great Depression in the 1930s, many viewed the preceding years of economic growth and technological advancement through disillusioned eyes. In November of 1931, Callender wrote another article, "Gandhi Dissects the Ford Idea." The article offers a fascinating portrait of Ford and Gandhi and sets up its discussion as if recounting an epic wrestling match between the two pacifists: "Mr. Ford and Mr. Gandhi, though they are about as different as two men could possibly be in background and habits of thought, are both prophets and preachers ... Each is an active evangelist, offering the world a gospel of freedom."[20] While Ford's vision imagines technology as the means towards greater freedom, Gandhi sees the unequal distribution of modernization as a global divide between two classes. Callender quotes Gandhi from an interview in London: "This mass production is possible because these nations are able to exploit the so-called weaker or unorganized races of the world."[21] For Gandhi, Fordism produced an exploitive system wherein both factory laborers and their pre-industrial competitors lose rather than gain freedoms. Insofar as it extends from Western nations, it becomes an extension of imperialist practices. For largely non-industrialized nations like India and, to some extent, Ireland, whose economic disadvantages were inseparable from a history of colonization, Fordism, in spite of its potentials for economic growth, represented political and cultural problems. It transplanted the center of imperialism from Britain to America.

# Brian O'Nolan's American nightmare

Images of Ford's influence appear in Brian O'Nolan's early novels, marginally in *An Béal Bocht* (1941), overtly in *At Swim-Two-Birds* (1939), and elliptically in *The Third Policeman* (finished in 1940 but published in 1967). In *An Béal Bocht*, Irish peasants initially flee at the sight of motor cars. *At Swim-Two-Birds*, shortly after referencing Aldous Huxley, claims that "Slaveys ... were the Ford cars of humanity,"[22] and the novel imagines the eugenic production of human beings. *The Third Policeman* portrays an underground industrial complex that manufactures the material and sociopolitical realities of the Irish parish above. It is in O'Nolan's unfinished and posthumously published novel, *Slattery's Sago Saga* (1973), that Fordism, along with its impact on Ireland, is most developed.

Although the ending of *Slattery's Sago Saga* will never be known, it is clear that O'Nolan's fictional Ireland was in store for material and cultural transformations not experienced since the Great Famine. Crawford MacPherson, wife to Ned Houlihan, who left Ireland to build an oil empire in America, has come to Ireland to wholly replace its potato crop with sago. This would entail a transformation of Ireland's agrarian economy and an erasure of cultural traditions, and MacPherson is willing to manipulate government policies and practices to make her vision a reality. Ironically, MacPherson is not motivated by money or by the pursuit of agrarian stability; rather, she abhors the immigration of the Irish to America, seeing them, notwithstanding her husband, as a criminal and destructive force. The unfinished novel concludes with cargo shipments of sago just arriving to Ireland and with a letter from Ned to the protagonist and adopted son, Tim, detailing his business and political plans in America. The letter reveals the extent to which business tycoons influence politics and describes his Ford-like expansion and diversification of industries, showing no regard for national and cultural differences. The novel communicates an anxiety that Ireland would become one more American territory through Fordist transformation.

*Slattery's Sago Saga* begins with a reference to Henry Ford that demonstrates a familiarity with the litigious developments that permeated his lifelong business dealings. Beyond the overt references to Ford found in *Cruiskeen Lawn* and the novels, O'Nolan's personal library also shows an interest in Ford.[23] Roger Burlingame's biography *Henry Ford* (1957) is part of O'Nolan's personal library maintained at Boston College. *Slattery's Sago Saga* reveals that the Houlihans had early dealings with Henry Ford:

> [Ned Houlihan's] money had been mostly inherited as a result of a fortune his father amassed from automotive and petrol-engine inventions. Indeed, it was a family tradition that Constantine Houlihan, B.E.,

had been shamelessly swindled by Henry Ford I but that, through his invention of a primitive computer nourished with a diet of stock-market minutiae, the resourceful engineer from Bahola, Mayo, had managed to get together a sum even bigger than that of which he had been deprived.[24]

Burlingame's biography covers the suit for patent infringement that George B. Selden took out against Henry Ford and other auto manufacturers, likely providing material for O'Nolan's backstory on Houlihan. The dispute took years to resolve, but in 1911 the court sided with Henry Ford: "The Selden patent did not apply to any of the cars then being manufactured, [bringing] a sigh of relief to every motor-maker."[25] Henry Ford would later get involved in legal disputes with other manufacturers and, notoriously, with the *Chicago Tribune*. Ford was a symbol of ruthless business practices as much as of innovation and leadership. In *Slattery's Sago Saga*, it is Crawford MacPherson, whose first name is not mere coincidence, who imports these practices into Ireland, and her presence echoes Henry Ford's own dealings in Ireland. Ford built his first Irish factory in Cork in 1932 (from a foundry founded in 1917), where he claimed family origins. MacPherson's business plan extends well beyond Cork. Tim reports to his neighbor, Doctor Baggeley, that MacPherson has a "plan to change the whole face of Ireland."[26] He continues, "She wants to replace the potato here by sago, which gives even more starch and is far hardier. Sago is grown on trees. She wants to have forests of sago trees all over Ireland. She wants to buy up all the farming land and make sago compulsory."[27] The conversation veers into South American practices, and Baggeley mentions, "Brazilian Indians [who] discovered that roasting the tubers of cassava would disperse the hydrocyanic acid in the milky white sap."[28] Baggeley is intrigued by MacPherson's plan, foreseeing that "this new big thing ... will change radically the history of Ireland and later the whole social tilt of Western Europe."[29] MacPherson also mentions South America as one of her sources for sago.[30] For Henry Ford, South America was one more resource and market for expansion.

As a satirist for the *Irish Times*, O'Nolan was well aware of Ford's business enterprises across the world. Among Ford's mammoth projects was the development of what would later be called Fordlandia, a rubber-extraction project in the Amazon basin. The project was not only famous for its ambitious scale, given the difficulty of building in dense jungle, but also for its importation of an American lifestyle. Greg Grandin's *Fordlandia* (2009) details the rise and fall of Ford's South American venture. Ford was already infamous for his determination to control the lifestyles of his workers inside and outside of his American factories. Taking his money could come at a cost to individual freedom. He would apply that same zealousness to Fordlandia, which he purchased in 1928. Fordlandia would eventually refer to the Americanized village of Boa Vista, but originally "referred ... to the entirety of Ford's 2.5 million acres."[31] Grandin chronicles the overtures made by Brazil's business sector, the cost and setbacks of Ford's project, and the employment, exploitation, and Americanization of tribal communities. Fordlandia was more than an American company in Brazil. It was the American lifestyle imported into Brazil, including a school that would disseminate American values and practices.[32] In the mid-1930s, Ford built a town, Belterra, which "looked like a squared midwestern town [with] Model Ts and As [rolling] down its straight streets, which were lined with fire hydrants, sidewalks, streetlamps, and white-and-green worker bungalows, with neat lawns and front gardens."[33] Although Ford would eventually abandon Fordlandia due to its exorbitant cost to his company, Fordlandia would come to portend previously unimaginable heights of globalization, an era where companies would influence national and international policies and transplant history and culture through capitalist ideology. If the assumption is that companies must continuously grow in order to be competitive, then new frontiers for growth must be sought. Crawford MacPherson's vision of Ireland exemplifies this expansionist business model, as does Huxley's World State; but it is Douglas Adams who takes it to its logical extension once all terrestrial frontiers have been exhausted.

## Douglas Adams: There's a Ford in your future

In the introduction to *The Ultimate Hitchhiker's Guide to the Galaxy*, which comprises the five novels that make up the series, Douglas Adams recounts the ideational beginnings and cross-media growth of his futuristic world. The galactic guide, as a repository for travel tips and historical trivia, mimics the popular travel guides used by tourists:

> At this point the title *The Hitchhiker's Guide to the Galaxy* suddenly popped back into my mind from wherever it had been hiding all this time. Ford [Prefect], I decided, would be a researcher who collected data for the *Guide*. As soon as I started to develop this particular notion, it moved inexorably to the center of the story, and the rest, as the creator of the original Ford Prefect would say, is bunk.[34]

The basic storyline is that Ford Prefect is marooned on Earth for longer than he had expected, thus compelling him to immerse himself in the culture until an opportunity to leave the planet arises. He assumes the name Ford Prefect because it initially seemed logical to conclude that automobiles are the dominant species. As *The Hitchhiker's Guide to the Galaxy* progresses, the reader learns that the most intelligent species on Earth are mice, who are trans-dimensional life forms, and dolphins, who attempt, unsuccessfully, to alert humanity to its impending destruction. Humans take third place. The fact that such a technologically-driven species should take third place implies that technology and progress are not always synonymous.

Adams's reference to Henry Ford's infamous claim that "history is bunk" alludes to Henry Ford's aforementioned suit against the *Chicago Tribune* for libel. In 1916, the *Chicago Tribune* had labeled Ford an "anarchist" for his position on the border tensions between America and Mexico. The trial exposed Ford's ignorance on a variety of subjects and drummed up a previous *Chicago Tribune* interview in which Ford declared, "History is more or less bunk. It's tradition. We want to live in the present and the only history that is worth a tinker's damn is the history we make today. That's the trouble with the world. We're living in books and history and tradition. We want to get away from that and take care of today."[35] The speech had been whittled down to "history is bunk," and it is echoed by Mustapha Mond in Huxley's *Brave New World*,[36] discussed in Brian O'Nolan's copy of Burlingame's *Henry Ford*, and reflected in Brian O'Nolan's *Slattery's Sago Saga*. Although Adams's series demonstrates that most of humanity's ideas are bunk, the phrase is directly referenced in *The Restaurant at the End of the Universe*, in which Zaphod utters, "Time is bunk" in response to Ford Prefect's realization that they have traveled too far into the past.[37] It appears again in *Life, the Universe and Everything*, in which the reader learns through the *Encyclopedia Galactica* of the complications of time travel, namely that "history is being polluted."[38] The encyclopedia reads, "One rationalization of this problem states that time travel was, by its very nature, discovered simultaneously at all periods of history, but this is clearly bunk," and the novel continues, "The trouble is that a lot of history is now quite clearly bunk as well."[39] The embodiment of this phrase is best captured at the beginning of the first novel when Arthur Dent, the human protagonist and Ford Prefect's friend, suffers two losses. First his house is bulldozed by the local council to make way for the construction of a bypass. Directly after this, Earth is destroyed by aliens to make way for a hyperspatial expressway. The world-building enterprises in Huxley and O'Nolan's novels have expanded into the next frontier, and Earth and its history are demolished to make way for progress. In fact, Earth's existence in the universe is barely recorded by Ford Prefect's encyclopedia. The entry for Earth reads: "Mostly harmless," which had been amended by Prefect from "Harmless."[40] Paralleling the Fordist philosophy that increased efficiency determines the rationale for all policy and practice, Earth, having no use-value, becomes disposable. All material and labor become exchangeable and disposable in order to serve the greater good: production.

As it turns out in the *Hitchhiker's Guide to the Galaxy*, Earth was actually an organic computer designed to find the question to an answer discovered by another computer which was itself intended to find the meaning of life and the universe. The initial answer was "42," which makes sense to the computer but not to the beings who were looking for an answer that would reflect their metaphysical and epistemological needs. Beyond the series' absurdist humor, which has led to its enormous success as a multimedia franchise, Adams's galactic vision is one of bureaucratic ineffectuality, neoliberal economics, and ruthless and expansive industrial imperialism. The most glaring example of these trends and policies is embodied by the hidden planet Magrathea, which President Zaphod Beeblebrox seeks on his stolen spaceship *Heart of Gold*.

Magrathea is a planet that manufactures luxury planets for the universe's elite. As such, it represents a manufacturing phase that extends from Fordism, namely post-Fordism, which diversifies and customizes products to suit niche consumers representing different economic conditions and needs: the market in which manufacturers produce several models of a car to cater to expressions of status and lifestyle. Adams first parodies the history of imperialism: "Far back in the mists of ancient time, in the great and glorious days of the former Galactic Empire, life was wild, rich and largely tax free. Mighty ships plied their way between exotic suns, seeking adventure and reward among the farthest reaches of Galactic space."[41] This age of galactic imperialism leads to disparities in wealth and resources:

> Many men of course became extremely rich, but this was perfectly natural and nothing to be ashamed of because no one was really poor—at least no one worth speaking of. And for all the richest and most successful merchants life inevitably became rather dull and niggly, and they began to imagine that this was therefore the fault of the worlds they settled on ... And thus were created the conditions for a staggering new form of specialist industry: custom-made luxury planet building.

The boom of planet-customization is soon followed by a depression, as if in parody of the Gilded Age, and the business goes dormant until Zaphod and his crew rediscover the legendary planet. In contrast to the novel's quips on theories in astrophysics and mathematics, the forces of production, consumption, expansion, and demolition form the rationale and backdrop for the adventures of Arthur, Ford, Beeblebrox, and Trillian. Adams's novels, *The Hitchhiker's Guide to the Galaxy* (1979), *The Restaurant at the End of the Universe* (1980), *Life, The Universe and Everything* (1982), *So Long, and Thanks for All the Fish* (1985), and *Mostly Harmless* (1992) anticipate and reflect an era of Thatcherism and Reaganomics, and this is likely part of the series' enduring multimedia success, with its latest permutation found in Garth Jennings' 2005 film adaption of the first story.

## Back to Ford's future

While post-Fordism was an outgrowth of Fordism, it was antithetical to Henry Ford's vision of a single, mass-produced and affordable product for the betterment of all. Regardless, Ford, in all his permutations, personifies modernity and the irreversible march of progress for all of these writers. Fordism, likewise, is a recurrent trope in science fiction as a vehicle through which to explore dystopian and utopian possibilities. In a 1927 review of Fritz Lang's *Metropolis*, the film critic Frank Vreeland wrote the following for the *New York Telegram*: "[The] super efficient master ... bears in the person of a German impersonator a haunting suggestion of Henry Ford."[42] Vreeland is remarking on the character, Joh Fredersen, played by Alfred Abel. The film famously blurs the lines between humanity and machine through the invention of "The Machine Man," whose metallic exterior uncannily transforms into the form of Maria, played by Brigitte Helm. The purpose of the machine is to subvert the political organization of the working class who slave away in an industrial underworld. When the machine is first unveiled by the inventor, played by Rudolf Klein-Rogge, Fredersen cannot turn away from its seductive powers. The scene blends laboratory and occult imagery, revealing a transformative moment of modernization. There is no way to turn away; there is no way to turn back. There is only forward. Likewise, Henry Ford, from the unveiling of his first Model T Ford to the expansion of his factories and evangelical vision, continues to reverberate as the face of modernity in ever new frontiers.

## Notes

1 James Sexton, *Selected Letters of Aldous Huxley* (Chicago: Ivan R. Dee, 2007), 283.
2 Ibid., 284.
3 Anthony Cronin, *No Laughing Matter: The Life and Times of Flann O'Brien* (New York: Fromm International Publishing Corporation, 1998), 156.
4 "Britain Has 250,000th Ford," *New York Times*, April 18, 1925.
5 "Four New Ford Branches," *New York Times*, October 3, 1909.
6 E. L. Doctorow, *Ragtime* (1975; repr., New York: Random House, 2007), 135.
7 Ishmael Reed, *Mumbo Jumbo* (1972; repr., New York: Scribner, 1996), 135.
8 David L. Lewis discusses the ad campaign's success in *The Public Image of Henry Ford* (Detroit: Wayne State University Press, 1976), stating that it "became the immediate post-war era's best-known automobile slogan," 382.

9 Henry Ford, "Henry Ford Expounds Mass Production." *New York Times*, September 19, 1926.

10 Richard Snow, *I Invented the Modern Age: The Rise of Henry Ford* (New York: Scribner, 2013), 9.

11 Bob Jessop, "Thatcherism and Flexibility: The White Heat of a Post-Fordist Revolution," in *The Politics of Flexibility*, eds. Bob Jessop, Hans Kastendiek, and Klaus Nielson (Aldershot: Edward Elgar, 1991), 136–7.

12 Evelyn Cobley, *Modernism and the Culture of Efficiency: Ideology & Fiction* (Toronto: University of Toronto Press, 2009), 38.

13 Ibid., 41.

14 Nicholas Murray, *Aldous Huxley* (New York: Thomas Dunne Books, 2002), 181.

15 Jerome Meckier, "Aldous Huxley's Americanization of the *Brave New World* Typescript," *Twentieth Century Literature* 48, no. 4 (2003): 427.

16 Cobley, *Modernism and the Culture of Efficiency*, 288.

17 Harold Callender, "Ford's Methods Give Europe Hope for Her Industry," *New York Times*, June 8, 1930.

18 "British Assail Ford System of Production as Soul Killing," *New York Times*, September 16, 1923.

19 Callender, "Ford's Methods."

20 Harold Callender, "Ghandi Dissects the Ford Idea," *New York Times*, November 8, 1931.

21 Ibid.

22 Flann O'Brien, *At Swim-Two-Birds* (1939; repr., Normal, IL: Dalkey Archive Press, 1998), 43.

23 I discuss in further detail Ford's impact on Brian O'Nolan in "Reassembling Ford: Time is Money in Brian O'Nolan's Brave New Ireland," *The Parish Review* 3, no. 1 (Fall 2014): 33–42. The issue is specifically devoted to O'Nolan's personal library as an archive for genetic study.

24 Flann O'Brien, "Slattery's Sago Saga," in *The Short Fiction of Flann O'Brien*, eds. Neil Murphy and Keith Hopper (Champaign: Dalkey Archive Press, 2013), 96.

25 Roger Burlingame, *Henry Ford* (Chicago: Quadrangle Books, 1954), 183.

26 O'Brien, *Slattery's Sago Saga*, 113.

27 Ibid., 114.

28 Ibid., 115.

29 Ibid., 116.

30 Ibid., 104.

31 Greg Grandin, *Fordlandia* (New York: Metropolitan Books, 2009), 126.

32 Ibid., 193.

33 Ibid., 321.

34  Douglas Adams, *The Ultimate Hitchhiker's Guide to the Galaxy* (New York: The Random House Publishing Group, 2002), xiii.
35  Wheeler, Charles M., "Fight to Disarm His Life's Work, Henry Ford Vows," *Chicago Tribune*, May 25, 1916.
36  Aldous Huxley, *Brave New World* (1932; repr., New York: Harper Perennial, 2006), 34.
37  Adams, *Ultimate Hitchhiker's*, 248.
38  Ibid., 389.
39  Douglas Adams explored the time-travel genre in his writing for the popular television series, *Doctor Who*. He wrote the four-part series, *The Pirate Planet*, which was aired in the fall of 1978. Neil Gaiman writes in *Don't Panic: Douglas Adams & The Hitchhiker's Guide to the Galaxy* (London: Titan Books, 2009) that "Douglas has sent off the pilot script for *Hitchhiker's* to the *Doctor Who* script editor earlier in the year, hoping to get a commission out of it to do some scripts. The commission came through; unfortunately, it came through at the same time that the six episodes of *Hitchhiker's* were commissioned, which meant that as soon as Douglas Adams had finished the first four episodes of *Hitchhiker's* he had to write the four episodes of a *Doctor Who* story, *The Pirate Planet*" (37).
40  Adams, *Ultimate Hitchhiker's*, 44.
41  Ibid., 78.
42  Frank Vreeland, "Metropolis," *New York Telegram*, March 7, 1927.

# Bibliography

Adams, Douglas. *The Ultimate Hitchhiker's Guide to the Galaxy*. New York: The Random House Publishing Group, 2002.
"Britain Has 250,000th Ford." *New York Times*, April 18, 1925.
"British Assail Ford System of Production as Soul Killing." *New York Times*. September 16, 1923.
Burlingame, Roger. *Henry Ford*. Chicago: Quadrangle Books, 1954.
Callender, Harold. "Ford's Methods Give Europe Hope for Her Industry." *New York Times*, June 8, 1930.
Callender, Harold. "Gandhi Dissects the Ford Idea." *New York Times*, November 8, 1931.
Cobley, Evelyn. *Modernism and the Culture of Efficiency*. Toronto: University of Toronto Press, 2009.
Cronin, Anthony. *No Laughing Matter: The Life and Times of Flann O'Brien*. New York: Fromm International Publishing Corporation, 1998.
Doctorow, E. L. *Ragtime*. 1975. Reprint, New York: Random House, 2007.
Ford, Henry. "Henry Ford Expounds Mass Production." *New York Times*, September 19, 1926.
"Four New Ford Branches." *New York Times*, October 3, 1909.

Gaiman, Neil. *Don't Panic: Douglas Adams & The Hitchhiker's Guide to the Galaxy*. New updated edition. London: Titan Books, 2009.
Gopaleen, Myles na. "Cruiskeen Lawn." *Irish Times*, April 14, 1947.
Grandin, Greg. *Fordlandia*. New York: Metropolitan Books, 2009.
Huxley, Aldous. *Brave New World*. 1932. Reprint, New York: Harper Perennial, 2006.
Jessop, Bob. "Thatcherism and Flexibility: The White Heat of a Post-Fordist Revolution." *The Politics of Flexibility*, edited by Bob Jessop, Hans Kastendiek, and Klaus Nielson, 135–61. Aldershot: Edward Elgar, 1991.
Lewis, David L. *The Public Image of Henry Ford*. Detroit: Wayne State University Press, 1976.
Meckier, Jerome. "Aldous Huxley's Americanization of the *Brave New World* Typescript." *Twentieth Century Literature* 48, no. 4 (2003): 427.
*Metropolis*. Dir. Fritz Lang. Perf. Gustav Fröhlich, Brigitte Helm, and Alfred Abel. Universum Film, 1927.
Murray, Nicholas. *Aldous Huxley*. New York: Thomas Dunne Books, 2002.
O'Brien, Flann. *At Swim-Two-Birds*. 1939. Reprint, Normal, IL: Dalkey Archive Press, 1998.
O'Brien, Flann. "Slattery's Sago Saga." In *The Short Fiction of Flann O'Brien*, edited by Neil Murphy and Keith Hopper. Champaign: Dalkey Archive Press, 2013.
Reed, Ishmael. *Mumbo Jumbo*. 1972. Reprint, New York: Scribner, 1996.
Sexton, James. *Selected Letters of Aldous Huxley*. Chicago: Ivan R. Dee, 2007.
Snow, Richard. *I Invented the Modern Age: The Rise of Henry Ford*. New York: Scribner, 2013.
Vreeland, Frank. "Metropolis." *New York Telegram*, March 7, 1927.
Wheeler, Charles M. "Fight to Disarm His Life's Work, Henry Ford Vows." *Chicago Tribune*, May 25, 1916.

PART THREE

# Resonances of Popular Modernism in the Twenty-First Century

# 10

# Smokescreens to smokestacks: *True Detective* and the American sublime

## Caroline Blinder

Nic Pizzolatto's *True Detective* (thus far encompassing seasons one and two), a seemingly bleak and relentless view of the American South and Southern California, appears to lend itself to a postmodern reading of the detective genre.[1] After all, if the nihilistic oft-quoted commentary by season one's detective Rustin Cohle (played by Matthew McConaughey) and season two's gangster Frank Semyon (played by Vince Vaughn) are anything to go by, Pizzolatto's dialogue is primarily marked by an incredulity towards master-narratives; a firm belief that behind the façade of American democracy lies a series of conspiratorial and often violent attempts to abuse the American people.[2] However, the fact that the series consistently references not only the disenfranchised inhabitants of Mississippi and immigrant workers of Southern California but also the American landscape itself indicates that something more fundamental is afoot. It is, in fact, within the representation of the natural landscape in the two seasons of *True Detective* produced thus far, and their references to geo-politics, the abuse of natural resources and an attendant pollution consistently marked as both psychological and ecological, that we can trace a distinctly modernist aesthetic. This aesthetic is not only configured along the lines of various classical narrative models, from the Gothic in season one to Greek tragedy in season two, it centers the figure of the detective—as in most twentieth-century detective fiction—as an emblem for modern alienation and its often tragic resolution.

To read both seasons in this context enables some understanding of why season one was universally acclaimed while season two has been seen as a comparative failure. While the near universal acclaim of season one seemed to rely on the empathy created for the two main protagonists—detectives Rustin Cohle and Martin Hart (played by Woody Harrelson)—and the audience's desire for them to retain their position as "true detectives" uncompromised by the surrounding corruption, season two was critiqued as too bleak, too relentlessly dark. Much of the criticism of season two arose out of the show's unwillingness to render a satisfactory narrative resolution to the crimes committed, while paradoxically, the success of season one relied on something similar—namely a focus on the internal psychology of the protagonists rather than the solving of the crime. If the complex interior psychology of the characters created the foundation for a story of redemption and resurrection in season one, season two failed to create the catharsis necessary for the tragic elements of the plot to cohere.

Such readings, nonetheless, take as their starting point the use of characterization and dialogue; leaving the question of what importance—if any—the highly-stylized use of landscape plays in the respective seasons. A major question thus remains unanswered: what is the purpose of the much commented-on opening credits, which act more like introductory segments in their own right? And to what extent do they influence the ways in which the subsequent narratives operate? As this chapter will examine, the use of landscapes in these sequences not only enables the subsequent locations to stage the emotional and moral journeys of the detectives, they allow for a social and political reading that places *True Detective* in a longer lineage of modernist work.

## Detection and the American sublime

It is no coincidence that the seasons' intro segments rely heavily on the work of two American landscape photographers: Richard Misrach and David Maisel, both of whom have been instrumental in reinvigorating the epic qualities of American landscape photography towards the sublime. While Misrach and Maisel approach the American landscape from a post-industrial vantage point, they share certain concerns that clearly speak to and aid in rendering the moral trajectories of the detectives. Known initially for a series of large format photographs documenting the changes brought to bear on the environment by various man-made factors such as urban sprawl, industrialization, the testing of explosives and nuclear weapons, and petrochemical manufacturing in particular, Richard Misrach's concerns have always been aesthetic, political and ecological simultaneously. Likewise, David Maisel's most famous project

*Black Maps*, a series of aerial photographs of environmentally impacted sites, including images of open-pit mines, cyanide fields, military testing, and urban sprawl, are both stunningly beautiful nearly abstract renditions of ecological disasters and political comments on the state of the nation. Thus, rather than see the palimpsest of photography and characters that characterize the intros as referential in a postmodern sense, the alignment between landscape and human form in *True Detective* can be viewed as a highly political gesture. By taking the sublime nature of the post-industrial landscape in *True Detective* as a cipher for modernism's use of detective fiction to critique the status quo, the very setting of the program becomes a form of societal indictment. In this respect, *True Detective* takes its title seriously by positing that there are "false" and "true" investigations, good and evil, and that the detective genre is a genuinely modernist model for the investigation of both.

Usually the figure of the detective, in a modernist context, is seen as the protagonist whose attempts at deciphering and unravelling crime are either exercises in restoring the status quo or paradoxically—as in the case of *True Detective*—proofs that the status quo cannot be disrupted. In *Crime Stories: Criminalistic Fantasy and the Cult of Crisis in Weimar Germany* (2009), Todd Herzog argues that the theorizing of detective fiction in modernist terms traces back to the critical philosophy of post-Marxists such as Walter Benjamin, Bertolt Brecht and Siegfried Kracauer, for whom detective fiction perfectly synthesized "mass-market versions of elite modernist works."[3] As Herzog points out, detective fiction "attempted to come to terms with difficult issues of modernity by posing important questions about the place of the subject in the world ... and the dysfunctionality of reason and causality."[4]

In this sense, *True Detective* fits into a reading of the detective genre in modernist terms in which the element of suspense lies squarely within the interior psychology of the detectives. The "dysfunctionality of reason and causality" established in both seasons one and two is squarely placed within the interior psyche of the detectives and as unalterable as the pollution that permeates the landscape. If detective fiction is partly about questioning modernity, the place of the detective "as subject in the world," as Herzog puts it, is largely what the series capitalizes on. Nonetheless, the use of discernibly regional landscapes, moving away from the urban detective and the mean streets of New Orleans and L.A., allows *True Detective* to use the tropes and conventions of film noir and to do so within a landscape that is both hyper-real and sublime. According to Natasha Egan's *Black Maps: American Landscape and the Apocalyptic Sublime—David Maisel* (2007), Maisel's "work is sublime across the definitions of the word, because his pictures draw from nature and possess a beauty whose power inspires awe and anxiety, yet they operate through abstraction where the subject is concealed and evokes fear."[5]

This is rendered throughout *True Detective* in the way that the cinematography uses both Maisel's abstract imagery and Misrach's more recognizable Southern landscapes; the presence of the industrial/apocalyptic/ toxic sublime becomes a cipher for wider insidious and corruptive forces. In this way, the dual use of the sublime is ever present, on the one hand reliant on the sublime aspects of nature, and on the other able to conceal the toxic forces embedded within it. It is the consistent referencing to the presence of toxicity and pollution within a seemingly innocuous landscape that brings the alienation and discomfort of the principal characters into focus. If their past and present environment systematically marks the characters, the effects of geo-political damage tangibly mark the transgressions charted in the show. As such, they are part of a wider modernist critique of the effects of American capitalism; a critique that visibly links the pollution of the areas in which they are set with wider systemic economic and social misuses.

This referencing to what Jennifer Peeples defines as the "toxic sublime" nonetheless fell under the radar of most reviews.[6] Largely because of the confluence of the fantastical and the Gothic, both seasons were seen in populist terms as another postmodern version of noir, rather than something seeking to insert itself into a longer lineage of modernist detective fiction.[7] However, in *True Detective*, the modernist credentials of the detectives are proven by their place in the landscape. Thus the persistence of the sublime, as a metaphor for the detective's attraction to and horror of that landscape, is paramount. If the sublime in Misrach's photographs of the Mississippi Delta and Maisel's aerial shots of California (see Figure 10.1) are emblematic of the rampant capitalism that the detectives labor under, it is also a sign of our continued attraction to the American landscape as a transformed and transformative place. Both seasons are as such characterized by the struggle between aesthetics, rendered most visible in the depiction of landscape, and ethics rendered primarily through the moral choices of the main characters. Likewise, both narratives work effectively along the lines of modernist dystopias; focusing not on the ultimate triumph of humanity and government, but presenting instead a society marked by the suffering caused by greed, an evil which in this case is visualized both as a form of sexual and geo-political abuse.

# Landscape and vision

Nic Pizzolatto, credited as the chief writer and creator, has been open about his methodology. Less intent on the persuasive nature of the crime solving, he is more concerned with how we correlate existential and theological issues to narrative myths that both indicate *and* range beyond national specificity.[8] A paradox is thus at play in *True Detective* in which the specificity of the landscapes, unmistakably American and regional, are nonetheless staging grounds for a series of sublime moments that are meant to take on more universal implications. According to David Nye in *The American Technological Sublime* (1994), "The human relation to this new nature is not, as Barthes suggests, that of beauty or romance, it is that of power ... providing a spectacular perch from which to contemplate the manufactured world as a total environment. As though one were above or outside it."[9]

While *True Detective* consistently duplicates this sense of "being above or outside" the "manufactured world," Maisel's aerial views (see Figure 10.1) nonetheless render the colors of toxic spills and serrated landscapes as both beautiful and terrifying. In season one it is Misrach's endless delta highways that punctuate the individual scenes providing a bird's eye view of the endless flat landscape traversed by the detectives, a landscape seemingly coming from and going nowhere.

Instead of the usual maze of film noir dead ends—this vision of the sublime casts the industrial landscape as at once forlorn, abstract and overpowering. In season two the final shoot-out between detective Ray Velcoro (played by Colin Farrell) and the corrupt law enforcement takes place in a landscape directly in opposition to the industrialized suburbs

FIGURE 10.1 *Richard Misrach*. Pipeline and River Road. Donaldsville, Louisiana. 2010. © Richard Misrach, courtesy Fraenkel Gallery, San Francisco.

FIGURE 10.2 *Frank Semyon in the desert.* True Detective. *Season 2, episode 8. Directed by John Crowley. Written by Nic Pizzolatto. Aired August 9, 2015. Home Box Office, 2016. DVD.*

of L.A.—a verdant primordial-looking forest. Similarly, Frank Semyon's protracted death takes place in a desert devoid of any human markers, as if to graphically outline the impossibility of escape in environmental terms. As Semyon wanders Christ-like towards his death and possible redemption, the landscape becomes the complete antithesis of the urban sprawl that he has desperately sought to rule over. In this respect, *True Detective* shares more with the politics of such neo-noirs as Roman Polanski's *China Town* (1974) and John Boorman's *Point Blank* (1967) than it does with contemporary cable drama.[10]

As in Boorman's *Point Blank*, the existentialist alienation of the detective is created primarily through the atmosphere of the locations. The reception of season two and the criticism leveled at the incomprehensible plot assumed that the stories of the four main protagonists would be resolved in a way that gave them some agency, even if posthumously. However, the fact that the culprits are left unpunished is foretold by the inevitability of the economic expansion that sets the various crimes in motion. As the settings themselves become more expansive and the built environment takes over the entire region, the environment becomes more alienating, spiraling outwards rather than inwards to shelter the detective. Most establishing shots in *True Detective* show the detectives in movement across vast terrains, the upper part of the frame constantly about to engulf the lower part as though to remind us of the insignificance of the detectives themselves. In this way territory rather than something contested or successfully mastered seems to disappear out of shot, evaporating into images of endless freeways and

FIGURE 10.3 *Still from* Point Blank. *Directed by John Boorman. 1967. Reissued, Warner Home Video, 2005. DVD.*

unfettered horizons. It is no coincidence that when Hart and Cohle finally encounter the murderer in season one, it is in a jungle-like place inhospitable to human habitation.

If things are hiding in plain sight in season one, darkness and artificial lighting take over in season two as places become subsumed in a vast suburban conspiracy. Nightclubs and darkened bars are juxtaposed with the pulsating lights of cars and buildings but even the freeways seem to be perpetually wearing off into darkness. It is no coincidence that both seasons incorporate the figure of the veteran in order to reference a state of toxicity whose effects are tantamount to a form of post-traumatic stress disorder. Detective Woodrugh suffers in part due to his suppressed homosexuality and in part due to his past involvement in Iraqi war crimes; the two causes deliberately collapse into one another. Similarly, the soundscape adds to the oblique, but fairly consistent, referencing of a post-Vietnam/post-Iraq environment. The hum of choppers can be heard as the detectives move in in the last episode of season one, and if evil is endemic to the American landscape, it is because of a violent history of both external and internal colonization. The temple-like structure where the final confrontation takes place is replete with obscure writing and signs, totems and sacrificial offerings. While the piles of victims' clothes that the detectives encounter are reminiscent of Nazi gas chambers, the fact that the site is an abandoned underground cathedral seems a fitting reminder of the connection between religion and ideology in American history—a history now rendered through abuse and sacrifice.

The uncanny similarity of Rustin Cohle in season one to Christ on the Cross, as he undergoes a near death experience and a moment of religious epiphany, adds to this connection.

Speaking to Rustin after he awakens in the hospital, Hart says, "it occurs to me that you are un-killable."[11] Cohle's return from the dead allows the

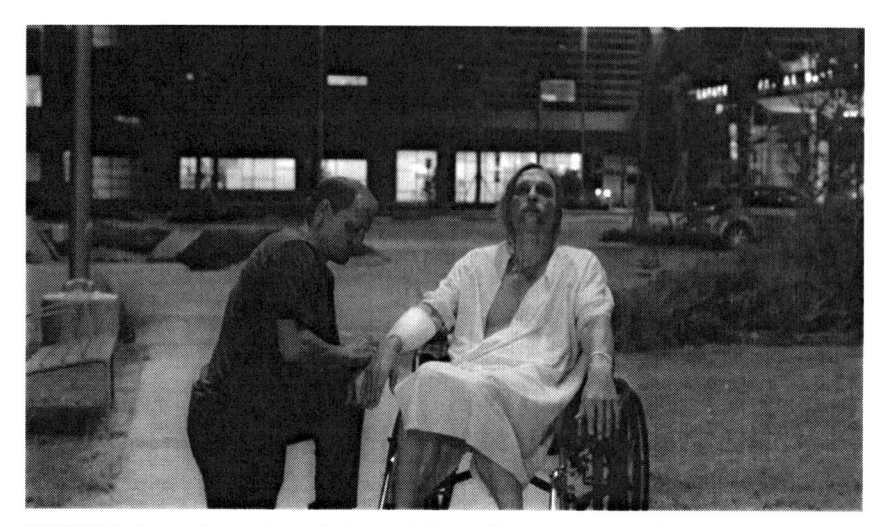

**FIGURE 10.4** *Detectives Cohle and Hart.* True Detective. *Season 1, episode 8. Directed by Cary Joji Fukunaga. Written by Nic Pizzolatto. Aired March 9, 2014. Home Box Office, 2015. DVD.*

series to end with an actual resurrection and the realization that, as Hart says, "there's only one story, the oldest."[12] From the beginning of season one, Cohle has unknowingly established himself as the prophetic figure, "vision is meaning" he states in an early episode in an attempt to counter his partner's pragmatism and complacency.

The concept that "vision is meaning" provides another way to link the visual sublime of *True Detective* to the resurrection of the detective in moral terms. The politics of violence in *True Detective* is in this sense not only incorporated into the various ways that the detectives navigate the landscape. It is entirely governed by their movements within that landscape and their interpretation of the various signs that they encounter. Similarly, a lack of borders accentuates the feeling that there is no discernible gravitational pull, which is then incorporated into the aerial perspective of the cinematography through the use of Misrach and Maisel's photographs. In Misrach's work in particular, icons and signs emerge out of seemingly mundane and inconsequential settings, making the staging areas for various spectacles of violence, both human and ecological, appear as somehow sacred.

The superimposition of Misrach's images of vacant lots and industrial sites into the opening credits of season one, provides a sense of something palpably hyper-real and simultaneously fantastic. Creating a nearly tangible sense of elemental change through color and mist, the Christ-like figure of Rustin Cohle also suffers from psychedelic flashbacks. These flashbacks draw his eye upwards in a gesture reminiscent of pietas—the ultimate

FIGURE 10.5 *Richard Misrach.* Night Releases. Mississippi River Corridor, Louisiana. *1998.* © *Richard Misrach, courtesy Fraenkel Gallery, San Francisco.*

gesture of devotion—not dissimilar to Misrach's camera eye swooping upwards into a polluted and yet sublime sky.

In both seasons the upward glance of the protagonist is shown at crucial moments as though to indicate the almost visceral presence of the sublime. In the last episode of season two, Ray Velcoro looks upwards in a gesture of supplication at the sky seconds before he is shot in the forest, a perspective that aligns us and the camera with an almost God-like point of view.

As in Maisel's cosmic views of California, this territory provides a place where the fear or even fantasy of extinction seems palpable. In both seasons the extinction of communities, displaced people, migrant workers, the trafficking in children and prostitution, etc., encircle the detectives as permanent fixtures of an environment where sacrificial behavior renders an economy so horrific it is beyond linguistic comprehension.[13]

The home of the "Yellow King," the ringleader, cult-murderer in season one, is replete with stereotypical Southern Gothic tropes: whimpering dogs, collections of broken dolls, and a serial killer quoting classical literature while engaging in incest. However, it seems crucial that the killer's hidden home is away from the wide expanse of Misrach's endless horizons, thus allowing for the decrepit lair to operate as an antithesis to the corporate structures that now embody both the police station and the corrupt reverend's church organization. Capitalism, or rather the exchange of bodies for ritualistic and sexual purposes, is here mirrored in a perverse ancient ritual of child sacrifice. The absence of any familial bonds provides another perverse mirroring of the tearing asunder of families due to economic destitution. If the pollution of the Mississippi Delta area is causing cancer, an internal invisible disease, the murder and abuse of children, now mimics the expenditure and infection of natural resources on another grotesque scale.

In this sense, the two seasons share an interest in dramatizing versions of primitivism, one a return to something barbaric and pre-industrial, the other a move into something corporate and faceless. Nonetheless, they also share an interest in rendering at least the possibility of corporeal transcendence within the psyche of the detectives. As in so many other high-modernist/hard-boiled narratives, the first episode of season two ("The Western Book of the Dead"), foretells the immanent dissolution of the characters by setting them in a long line of failed attempts at civilizing America. In the office of the gangster/night club owner Semyon, an image of a Roman-style mosaic of a mythical serpent wrestling with a crocodile references the hostile takeover of Semyon's downward spiraling empire by other gangsters. The discrepancy between Semyon's crass business ways and his desire to be part of a progressive, enlightened form of capital venture is mirrored in his house. Both the interiors and the manicured external grounds are paradigms of modernist architecture, and yet the floor to ceiling glass partitions and doors seem to signal vulnerability rather than a desire for transparency.

Semyon's role in season two is crucial in this respect. If season one posits the backwards regionalism of a traumatized south as the landscape of Cohle and Hart's redemption, the industrialized urban sprawl of season two may be the very thing that prevents the detectives from being similarly "redeemed." Compared to Misrach's eerie parking lots and stagnant waters, Maisel's aerial shots—although they show an abstracted version of L.A.—may simply be too beautiful, too sublime, to be genuinely critical in political terms.

## The non-place as psychosphere

If we return to the opening credits of *True Detective*'s first season where human forms containing landscapes—factories, truck stops, highway overpasses, deserted play-grounds, and ruined towns—are depicted in

FIGURE 10.6 *Image of Detective Hart merged with Richard Misrach's Night Releases, from opening credit sequence of* True Detective. *Season 1. Aired January–March 2014. Home Box Office, 2015. DVD.*

undulating shapes and sizes, the human shapes in season two are more abstract. In Maisel's oversaturated photographs, colors bleed in and out of forms that render them distinctly organic. Max Kozloff articulates some of the dangers of this aestheticization in relation to Misrach:

> Everything that appears in his work is perceived as if from an indefinite mental space of our own. Yet in the end ... the spectacle ... visualized in the melted colors of a kind of pastoral sublime, overwhelms our understanding of its evil. This work is too deliberately ingratiating to be critical.[14]

For Pizzolatto the ability to render "a kind of pastoral sublime that overwhelms our understanding of its evil" is nonetheless the very thing that allows the necessary space for the detectives' redemption and resurrection."[15] In this sense, the images become entries into a space both post-apocalyptic and revelatory in various ways. According to Pizzolatto, "If landscape is a character for me ... the aim is to try to capture a certain psychosphere ambiance of the place ... The [characters] inhabit a poisoned dystopia. It's literally toxic ... These stories take place in areas where the revelation has already happened. The apocalypse has come and gone, and no one's quite woken up to that fact."

FIGURE 10.7 *Image of Detective Cohle, from opening credit sequence of* True Detective. *Season 1. Aired January–March 2014. Home Box Office, 2015. DVD.*

It is no coincidence that a proliferation of images in both seasons center around hubs, transport intersections, and points of exchange. As in the use of one of Maisel's most iconic photographs, from the series *Oblivion* (2004), the knot of freeways creates a center where there is none, allowing a cross to emerge or—according to Pizzolatto—render a revelation in figurative terms where one might least expect it. Like Misrach's limitless horizons in season one, Maisel's California resists visualization precisely because of the endless nature of its various systems, from freeways to other forms of infrastructure. As Alan Rapp puts it in "Cities of Forgetting," Maisel's project is an "ultimate typology of nonplace."[16]

For Maisel himself, the project appears to be articulated in more humanist terms: "I think that these kind of sites correspond to something within our own psyches ... maybe these are all self-portraits. There's something—we collectively as a society have made these places, that's my take on it. And so, they really do reflect us. And so, it's not 'them' making these places, it's us."[17] Maisel's sense of agency and the fact that humanity is governed in ways both tangible and intangible by its surroundings is partly what inspired Pizzolatto to use the Maisel images in the first place.

In an online interview regarding the making of the award-winning title sequence, the director Patrick Clair also accentuated the use of the photographs as a way to superimpose the landscape onto the psyche of the characters:

FIGURE 10.8 *David Maisel's* Oblivion 2N *used to introduce* True Detective *series title. From opening credit sequence of* True Detective. *Season 2. Aired June–August 2015. Home Box Office, 2016. DVD.*

FIGURE 10.9 *David Maisel's* The Lake Project 1, *200l superimposed on opening credit sequence of* True Detective. *Season 2. Aired June–August 2015. Home Box Office, 2016. DVD.*

One way that I like to do it is to just be really super-literal. So when I was first on the phone with Nic for season one, he said, "What we're trying to do is to use the landscape of Louisiana, the way that it's poisoned, the way that it's broken, the way that it's polluted, to show how these people are poisoned and broken and polluted." So I kind of interpreted that in this really straightforward way. I was like, "Oh, why don't we make portraits out of broken landscapes?" And they can be broken portraits with poisoned landscapes.[18]

Maisel's sense of our imaginative abilities, fears as well as desires, as directly marking the territory that we visualize thus becomes Pizzolatto's canvas. Despite the political and industrial misuse of particular regions and places, the aesthetic of the series is still primarily there to facilitate the outplaying of the detective's existential crisis as well as potential epiphany in a modernist sense. According to Pizzolatto,

At its simplest level, everything I've ever written about, including this and season one, is about love. We transpose meaning onto a possibly meaningless universe because meaning is personal. And that question of meaning or meaninglessness really becomes a question of: What do you love? Nothing? Then you've got a good shot at a meaningless existence. But if you love something—how do you love within the necessities of life and the roles you have to play?"[19]

Pizzolatto's decision to turn season two away from the "buddy format" of two detectives traveling together and into a detective story in the manner of *Oedipus Rex* seems one way to outline an essentially modernist model for the detective story. By invoking "love" as the operative term for how we—as humans—apply meaning to what we cannot understand, Pizzolato turns the postmodern paradigm into a modernist one in which the search for connection rather than disconnection becomes paramount. In this version, according to Pizzolatto, "the detective is searching and searching and searching, and the culprit is him ... That's why detectives are great engines for stories. They go everywhere. A detective story is really just the way you tell a narrative—you start with the ending. At the end, this person is dead. Now I'm going to go back and piece together the story that led to it ... It's about the final un-knowability of any investigation."[20] This sense of "un-knowability" is paradoxically accentuated by the inclusion of the photographic material. At the aptly called Panticapaeum Institute (a reference to an ancient Greek City destroyed by the Huns), another oblique reference to L.A. as a city on the brink of extinction is provided in the form of a Latin inscription: "*irae autem tacere, in die novissimo,*" loosely translated as "wrath and then silence on judgment day."

FIGURE 10.10 *First shot from episode 1 of* True Detective. *Season 2. Directed by Justin Lin. Written by Nic Pizzolatto. Aired June 21, 2015. Home Box Office, 2016. DVD.*

Like Cohle in season one, Semyon and Velcoro's deaths are fated from the beginning just as Semyon's memory of being incarcerated in the basement as a child becomes a cipher for a sense of continuous entombment. Nonetheless, despite these rather heavy-handed markers for hubris and tragedy from the beginning of season two, the settings and landscapes are what predominantly direct the events. More importantly, the use of Maisel's imagery is also a reference to the use of Misrach in season one. The very first shot in season two is tellingly not of the customary "scene of the crime" but of the actual crime at the heart of the narrative, namely the deliberate polluting of the ground water in areas earmarked for development. As the camera pans across the sticks that mark the sites of pollution in an otherwise pastoral field, the overall look is more akin to the graves of unknown soldiers, a tacit alignment as in season one between geopolitical misuse, ecological contamination and human sacrifice. Conveniently, Maisel's use of heavy reds (originating not in filters or digital manipulation but in the toxic nature of the spills photographed) warns us of the bloodshed to come—in the same way that the industrial sublime of his Oblivion series renders the city abstract through a variety of grids and lights, not unlike the motherboard of a computerized landscape. As Frank Semyon points out, the only "true" history is the one "paid for"; the only true history of California—in other words—is one of money.

# Conclusion

When asked about his influences, Pizzolatto returned to the issue of geography rather than plot: "I tend to be influenced by places as much as anything ... You look around and notice details and it starts to form a world and then you find characters to inhabit this world."[21] Pizzolatto's statement that once you've formed a world "you find characters to inhabit [it] "is a reminder of how much the narrative trajectory of the characters in *True Detective* relies on the environment they occupy. It may be that the success of season one can be attributed—in simple terms—to the audience's familiarity with the South as a suitable location for an essentially Gothic narrative. Certainly the regional stereotype of the murderous inbred backwater inhabitant, the revivalist con artists and so forth, allows for a landscape that may be unsettling but not so much that it discredits Cohle's resurrection at the end. When asked, following the success of season one, whether he ever contemplated killing off his two main protagonists, Pizzolatto responded:

> It was something I considered, but the trajectory of their arcs and where the journey took them was much more interesting to me with them left alive and altered in some way ... The only other ending I considered, but [it] was never put on the page, was something more mysterious, where you're not sure what happened to them. In the end, I felt that was too diffuse and moved us away from the hard realism of the show. The macabre aspects of it are grounded in a reality, this kind of poisoned dystopia.[22]

This continuing fascination with a "poisoned dystopia" is clearly in evidence in season two as well. This is all the more reason to applaud Pizzolatto for refusing to duplicate season one's redemptive ending. If the burned out eyes of the city manager in season two is just one of many metaphors for the blind refusal to face an already devastated civilization (Southern California), the fact that the female detective Bezzerides (played by Rachel McAdams and at various points also called Antigone and Athena) is the only one left alive to testify adds to the relentless tragic trajectory of season two.

If Cohle and Hart enter the sacrificial site, the "poisoned dystopia" of the South and get out again, Bezzerides' entry into the underworld in the brothel episode of season two indicates a much more brutal collapse between bodies as commodities, commodities as transactions, and in the end all economic transactions as potentially corruptive. Maisel's photographs, despite their ephemeral qualities, are the perfect backdrops for such transactional narratives. In interviews, Maisel speaks of how he is fascinated visually with "the unfolding of secret synchronicities" that occur when he views landscapes from above.[23] In this context, the similarities between the attempted high speed California central rail corridor in season two and the soon to be defunct Mississippi oil corridor in season one lies as much in their sublime qualities, what we intuit from afar, as it does in the political and economic context on the ground.[24]

Above all, in order to form a useful space for the detectives to occupy, the use of Misrach and Maisel's photographs sets the tone for a narrative in which the landscape is paramount as an active participant and not simply a backdrop. The fact that the proper boundaries between things become increasingly blurred in the process, both visually and through an industrial re-colonization, does not automatically make *True Detective* a postmodern rather than a modern opus. If Pizzolatto struggled in season two to tie the various characters' problems to one overriding sensibility, this in its own way renders the series more modernist in its aims. In both *True Detectives*, the photographs offer us visions of the results of an ingrained capitalist paradigm, intent on cannibalizing whatever natural resources it needs. Nonetheless, in the end any genuine sense of catharsis and redemption in *True Detective* has to rely on the landscape that facilitates it; a landscape mired in both the horror and beauty of the sublime.

# Notes

1 *True Detective*, season 1 was first aired on HBO January 12, 2014. Directed by Cary Joji Fukunaga, written by Nic Pizzolatto. *True Detective*, season 2 was first aired on HBO June 21, 2015. Directed by Justin Lin, Janus Metz, Jeremy Podeswa, John Crowley, Miquel Sapochnic, and Daniel Attitas, written by Nic Pizzolatto, episodes 4 and 6 co-written by Scott Lasser.

2 As coined by Jean-François Lyotard in his Introduction to *The Postmodern Condition: A Report on Knowledge*, trans. Geoff Bennington and Brian Massumi (1979; repr., Manchester: Manchester University Press, 1986), xxiv–xxv.

3 Todd Herzog, *Crime Stories: Criminalistic Fantasy and the Cult of Crisis in Weimar Germany* (London: Berghahn Books, 2009), 25.

4 Ibid.

5 Natasha Egan, "The Mining Project: Eliciting Anxiety in the Presence of the Sublime," in *Black Maps: American Landscape and the Apocalyptic Sublime*, ed. David Maisel (London: Steidl, 2007), 63–89.

6 Jennifer Peeples, "Toxic Sublime: Imaging Contaminated Landscapes," *Environmental Communication: A Journal of Nature and Culture* 5, no. 4 (2011): 373–92.

7 The "classic" hardboiled novels by Dashiell Hammett and James M. Cain in particular contain numerous references to industrial contaminants and their effects on the psyches of detectives and criminals alike.

8 Nic Pizzolatto's *Galveston* (2010), a Southern noir novel, charts very similar territory with an alcoholic ex-detective on the run as its main protagonist.

9 David Nye, *American Technological Sublime* (Cambridge, MA: MIT Press, 1994), 106.

10 An oblique reference to *Point Blank* is provided in episode 2 of season 2 when Semyon stays home with his wife to watch anything "with Lee Marvin" in it.

11 *True Detective*, season 1, episode 8, directed by Cary Joji Fukunaga, written by Nic Pizzolatto, first aired January–March 2014 (Home Box Office, 2015), DVD.

12 Ibid.

13 For more on the aestheticization of such narratives and how they function as allegories for wider capitalist systems of exchange, see Michael Szalay, "Pimps and Pied Pipers: Quality Television in the Age of Its Direct Delivery," *Journal of American Studies* 39, no. 4 (2015): 1–32.

14 Max Kozloff, "Ghastly News From Epic Landscapes," *American Art* 5, no. 1–2 (1991): 123.

15 In these statements, from a longer 2015 *Vanity Fair* Interview, Pizzolatto compares the material from his first foray into detective fiction in his novel *Galveston* (2010) with *True Detective*. Rich Cohen, "Can Nic Pizzolatto, *True Detective*'s Uncompromising Auteur, Do It All Again?," *Vanity Fair*, July, 2015.

16 For the Oblivion Series, Maisel used a high-speed, black-and-white film to impart graininess and then used the negatives themselves to make the images. As cited in David Maisel, *Black Maps: American Landscape and the Apocalyptic Sublime* (London: Steidl, 2007), 14.

17 Interview with Paul Moakley of *Time Magazine*, "Uncharted Territories: Black Maps by David Maisel," March 27, 2013.

18 Patrick Clair, interview by Will Perkins, eds. Lola Landekic and Will Perkins, *Art of the title*, January 14, 2014. http://www.artofthetitle.com/title/true-detective.

19 Cohen, "Can Nic Pizzolatto."

20 Ibid.

21 Cohen, "Can Nic Pizzolatto."

22 Ibid.

23 Natasha Egan, "The Mining Project," 75.

24 The California high-speed rail project also shares much of the iconography of an actual historical project, namely President Barack Obama's plans for the building of a high-speed rail network.

# Bibliography

Clair, Patrick. Interview by Will Perkins, edited by Lola Landekic and Will Perkins. *Art of the Title*, January 14, 2014. Available online: http://www.artofthetitle.com/title/true-detective.

Cohen, Rich. "Can Nic Pizzolatto, *True Detective*'s Uncompromising Auteur, Do It All Again?" *Vanity Fair*, June 11, 2015.

Egan, Natasha. "The Mining Project: Eliciting Anxiety in the Presence of the Sublime." In *Black Maps: American Landscape and the Apocalyptic Sublime*, edited by David Maisel, 63–89. London: Steidl, 2007.

Herzog, Todd. *Crime Stories: Criminalistic Fantasy and the Cult of Crisis in Weimar Germany*. London: Berghahn Books, 2009.

Kozloff, Max. "Ghastly News from Epic Landscapes," *American Art 5*, no. 1–2 (1991): 108–31.

Lyotard, Jean-François. *The Postmodern Condition: A Report on Knowledge*, translated by Geoff Bennington and Brian Massumi. 1979. Reprint, Manchester: Manchester University Press, 1986.

Maisel, David. *Black Maps: American Landscape and the Apocalyptic Sublime*. London: Steidl, 2007.

Misrach, Richard and Kate Orff. *Petrochemical America*. New York: Aperture, 2010.

Moakley, Paul. "Uncharted Territories: Black Maps by David Maisel." *Time Magazine*, March 27, 2013.

Nye, David. *American Technological Sublime*. Cambridge, MA: MIT Press, 1994.

Peeples, Jennifer. "Toxic Sublime: Imaging Contaminated Landscapes." *Environmental Communication: A Journal of Nature and Culture 5*, no. 4 (2011): 373–92.

*Point Blank*. Directed by John Boorman. 1967. Reissued, Warner Home Video, 2005. DVD.

Szalay, Michael. "Pimps and Pied Pipers: Quality Television in the Age of Its Direct Delivery." *Journal of American Studies* 39, no. 4 (2015): 1–32.

*True Detective*. Season 1. Directed by Cary Joji Fukunaga. Written by Nic Pizzolatto. Aired January–March, 2014. Home Box Office, 2015. DVD.

*True Detective*. Season 2. Directed by Justin Lin, Janus Metz, Jeremy Podeswa, John Crowley, Miquel Sapochnic, and Daniel Attitas. Written by Nic Pizzolatto, episodes 4 and 6 co-written by Scott Lasser. Aired June–August, 2015. Home Box Office, 2016. DVD.

# 11

# Of modernist second acts and African-American lives: F. Scott Fitzgerald, *The Wire*, and the struggle against lockdown

*Walter Bosse*

Originally airing on HBO from 2002 to 2008, *The Wire* is a sprawling police drama that explores the dynamic and conflicted interplay between various social and institutional forces within a specific post-industrial geography. The show's creator, David Simon, drew from his many years of experience as a crime reporter for the *Baltimore Sun* in presenting viewers with a Dickensian vision of the twenty-first-century city.[1] The show plumbs the depths of Baltimore's blown-out urban spaces and takes measure of its criminals, police, union workers, schoolteachers, political officials, and media representatives. However, astute viewers recognize that the show is relevant well beyond Baltimore's city limits. As Anmol Chaddha and William Julius Wilson point out in their study of the series and its portrayal of urban inequality, "the fundamental principles depicted in *The Wire* certainly parallel changing conditions in other cities, especially older industrial cities in the Northeast and Midwest."[2] The prevailing narrative across all five seasons traces the profound impact of the War on Drugs in American society.

Throughout the series, police officers and detectives contend with major players in Baltimore's various drug organizations. This primary conflict between police and dealers repeatedly emphasizes how public policy in the late-twentieth and early-twenty-first centuries counterintuitively transformed and distorted policing practices in U.S. cities. The very title of the show directly references the practice of wiretapping, a contentious form of surveillance that prioritizes "drugs on the table" over and above substantive structural improvements to the culture of a city. Police in *The Wire* contrive to secure warrants for wiretaps, which they then use to collect enough evidence to justify raids that may or may not yield a significant volume of illegal substances. This recurring process points up perhaps the major argument within the show's central narrative: namely, the administrative push to apprehend high quantities of drugs perpetuates a vicious circle of criminal activity, compromises policing practices, and precludes the possibility of real systemic change.

Furthermore, the show's highly attentive focus on race illustrates that the disciplinary measures within this vicious circle overwhelmingly constrain and determine the lives of the city's black inhabitants. African-American characters in *The Wire*—be they dealers, inmates, stick-up artists, or addicts—all occupy what Houston A. Baker, Jr. describes as "tight places" in American society.[3] In his *Turning South Again: Re-thinking Modernism/ Re-reading Booker T.* (2001), Baker theorizes that "modernism's emphasis falls on the locative—where one is located or placed."[4] Baker traces an historical and material genealogy from the holds of slave ships, to the carceral spaces of plantations, to post-Reconstruction chain gangs, and argues that the contemporary realities of ghettoization and mass imprisonment can be seen as legacies of modernism's tight places in the twenty-first century. The crime drama thus portrays administrative protocols such as the War on Drugs as not only corrupt and counterintuitive, but also as contemporary vestiges of institutional and ideological projects "that have perennially sanctioned shackling the black body, its lockdown in America."[5]

Within each individual season, *The Wire* explores different facets of Baltimore's systems and institutions and, in doing so, demonstrates the precarious structural connections between action in the streets and society as a whole. Season one focuses exclusively on police efforts to stymie the Barksdale gang; season two explores the waning influence and culture of the working class; season three involves the role of city government and political attempts to redress the material, social, and cultural decline of Baltimore; season four mourns the decay of public education; and season five reflexively examines the function and responsibility of the media. Chaddha and Wilson rightly acknowledge that the systemic vision of the show "captures the attention of social scientists concerned with a comprehensive understanding of urban inequality, poverty, and race in American cities."[6] Indeed, its sophistication as an imaginative text and its compelling use of narrative have also attracted the attention of literary and cultural studies scholars who examine and theorize the workings of power and ideology within cultural productions.[7]

This chapter thus emphasizes the literary and sociopolitical value of *The Wire* as a twenty-first-century text that actively appropriates and utilizes earlier works of literature to confront contemporary societal problems. More specifically, it explores the current paradigm of mass incarceration—another consequence of the War on Drugs—*vis-à-vis* a moment of radical intertextuality involving F. Scott Fitzgerald's 1925 novel, *The Great Gatsby*. In episode six of the show's second season, Simon pulls Fitzgerald's novel into the space of the prison in order to dramatize a critique of the American "justice" system. Law scholar Michelle Alexander points to the numbers to emphasize the incredible impact of the drug war on prison populations: "In less than thirty years, the U.S. penal population exploded from around 300,000 to more than 2 million, with drug convictions accounting for the majority of the increase."[8] She goes on to cite the fact that America imprisons more of its racial and ethnic minorities than any other country in the world, and that the legally stigmatic aftermath of incarceration creates a black undercaste "locked out of mainstream society."[9] Simon uses Fitzgerald's early-twentieth-century narrative about class (im)mobility to reflect upon and excoriate the staggering probability of incarceration facing African-American men in the twenty-first century.[10] The inmates' engagement with the text demonstrates Simon's belief in the sociopolitical value of cultural productions, and it does so by locating the institution of American letters squarely within the nation's prison-industrial complex. Reading the inmates reading Fitzgerald illuminates both the living legacy of American modernism and the living hell of American prisons.

## "The past is always with us": Reading *The Wire*, reading *Gatsby*

The fictional worlds of Fitzgerald continually reappear in contemporary media, and literary scholars frequently note the cultural relevance of such adaptations.[11] However, *The Wire* does not necessarily *adapt* the narrative of *The Great Gatsby* in this instance; rather, the show actively *appropriates* the book, features it as an object of study, and subjects it to a transformative analysis in the hands of prison inmates. It is no coincidence that Simon chose such an authoritative and widely recognized text from the realm of American modernism for the inmates to read and interpret. In their discussion of the book, the inmates reveal what Michel de Certeau in *The Practice of Everyday Life* identifies as "the clandestine forms taken by the dispersed, tactical, and makeshift creativity of groups or individuals already caught in the nets of 'discipline.'"[12] Reading actively from the confines of the penitentiary, they use a core modernist text to evaluate their marginality.

*The Great Gatsby* makes its appearance midway through an episode titled "All Prologue." The very title of the episode suggests that Simon overtly positions it in direct relation to the literary world. The episode occurs during season two, which follows the ongoing machinations of the Barksdale gang as established in season one. Season two also explores the working-class struggles of union stevedores in Baltimore's port area. The scene in question, however, takes place neither in the streets nor on the docks, but in a Maryland state penitentiary. It opens with the inmates already engaged in an active discussion about the book. At only one minute and forty-six seconds, the scene is rather brief. However, what it lacks in duration it makes up for in critical density. The camerawork is simple and the dialogue is measured and thoughtful. Occurring halfway through the episode, the scene provides a meditative, introspective pause that briefly suspends the bustling action taking place outside of the prison walls. Approximately a dozen inmates sit seminar-style around a long table; the civilian instructor is seated at one end and D'Angelo Barksdale—played by Lawrence Gilliard, Jr.—is positioned at the other.[13] Prior to his incarceration, Barksdale had occupied a middle-management position in his uncle's drug operation, dealing out of a low-rent housing district known as The Pit. Circumstances led to his arrest in the first season, and he was sentenced to a twenty-year maximum term in prison. Barksdale and most of the other prisoners in the scene are African-American. Each wears a blue prison uniform and holds his own copy of *The Great Gatsby*—the Scribner trade paperback edition bearing the cover illustration by Francis Cugat and the cover design by Cherlynne Li. The camera focuses steadily on each respondent when he contributes to the discussion.

Although Barksdale contributes the lengthiest and most insightful commentary in the scene, there are others in the group whose responses precede his. As the scene begins, one of the unnamed inmates is in the middle of a remark about the novel: "It's fucked because the man [Jay Gatsby] got to where he needed to be, and she wasn't even worth it. Daisy wasn't nothin' past any other bitch anyway, you know? He did all that for her, and in the end, it doesn't amount to shit."[14] Practicing a reader-response approach to the novel, this first inmate discusses the text in a way that reveals his own values, beliefs, and biases. Of course, his response tells us more about him than it does about the fictional world of West Egg. Not only does his reading perpetuate sexist views that fault a woman (Daisy Buchanan) for the fall of a man, it also validates and valorizes Gatsby's ascension to wealth and power. His response legitimates Gatsby's illicit entrepreneurialism and fails to acknowledge that the protagonist plays a central role in his own downfall. He fully sympathizes with Gatsby, as evidenced by his use of the term "the man" in talking about the character. In contrast, he describes Daisy as a typical "bitch," ignoring the fact that her character has an older—and thus more tenacious—claim to the cultural capital of high society. As the camera captures his response, the inmate's delivery of this remark sounds much like a complaint; he wears a troubled look and offers this commentary up to the instructor as if seeking an explanation for the way things end in the book.

Of course, the Prohibition-era context of *The Great Gatsby* and the title character's illegal business practices provide direct parallels to the contemporary War on Drugs in *The Wire* and to various characters' efforts to climb the social ladder by any means necessary. The illegal importation of contraband is in fact a primary issue for the stevedores in season two and can be seen as another direct link to Gatsby's business ventures. These parallels demonstrate Robert McParland's claim that "novels of the 1920s continue to offer us predicaments that are relevant to our own time."[15] Indeed, the criminality of Gatsby's character and the contextual circumstances of Prohibition solidify specific connections between the 1925 novel and the twenty-first-century show. The first inmate identifies with and expresses sympathy for Gatsby perhaps because that character behaved according to the same logic that calls forth criminal activity on the streets of Baltimore. Like Gatsby, the drug offenders in the prison attempted to use resources at their disposal to generate an income and possibly transcend the lower stratum into which they were born. All are punished accordingly.

This first inmate's sympathy for the fallen Gatsby offers one way of measuring the enduring relevance of modernism within *The Wire*. The speakeasy culture of bathtub gin and smuggling are analogous to the criminal behaviors that play out on the crack-addled streets of Baltimore. The system of Prohibition created the cultural and political conditions that engender Gatsby's success; however, the rigid classist ideology of West Egg guarantees his failure. Gatsby's downfall occurs as a consequence of his inability to perceive the difference between measurable financial wealth and upper-class status. As Peter L. Hays rightly puts it, "[p]art of Gatsby's tragedy—besides his idealization of Daisy—is his belief in the American myth of a classless society, that his newly acquired wealth has made him the equal of Tom Buchanan."[16] The first inmate re-enacts Gatsby's disillusioned belief. Interestingly, the language of monetary gains and losses pervade his response when he says, "she wasn't even *worth* it" and "it doesn't *amount* to shit." He is bewildered and irritated that the protagonist—a self-made man—is destroyed at the end of the narrative. He so fully believes in the staying power of capital gain and in the accompanying rhetoric of bootstrappery that he cannot fathom why Fitzgerald would allow for Gatsby's death when that character finally "got to where he needed to be." The inmate, like Gatsby, seems duped by the American myth of self-making. Despite living behind bars, he fails to recognize the physical and ideological constraints that define his world and prescribe his limitations.

The instructor takes the inmate's response and reframes it in the form of a question for the group, and he uses an often-quoted line from Fitzgerald to do so: "Fitzgerald said that there were 'no second acts in American lives.' Do you believe that?"[17] The first person to answer is a different unnamed inmate who points out the obvious: "Man, shit, we locked up. We best not believe that, right?" This is, of course, the expected reply. Taken out of context, the quote carries rather bleak connotations, and the instructor clearly wants the inmates to disagree with the notion that there are no second chances or alternative life paths in store for them. The second inmate phrases his reply as a rhetorical question—"We best not believe that, right?"—and he laughs and throws up his hands when he says it, eliciting laughter from the group generally. Although the question in the second inmate's reply is rhetorical, it nonetheless illustrates his inability to answer definitively in the form of a declarative sentence. He is uncertain about his own subjectivity and uses humor to veil that anxiety.

Barksdale, however, is neither amused nor satisfied with the reply to the instructor's question. As the others laugh, he sits with his arms crossed and retains a dour expression: "He's sayin' that the past is always with us. Where we come from, what we go through, how we go through it. All that shit matters. I mean, that's what I thought he meant."[18] Intrigued and likely surprised by the insight of Barksdale's response, the instructor encourages him to continue. Barksdale sits up straight and becomes visibly more engaged as he explains:

> Like at the end of the book, you know, boats and tides and all. It's like you can change up. You can say you somebody new, you can give yourself a whole new story, but what came first is who you really are. And what happened before is what really happened. And it don't matter that some fool say he different because the only thing that make you different is what you really do, what you really go through. Like, you know, like all them books in his library. Now he frontin' with all them books, but if we pull one down off the shelf ain't none of the pages ever been open. He got all them books and he ain't read nary a one of them. Gatsby, he was who he was, and he did what he did, and because he wasn't ready to get real with the story, that shit caught up to him. I think, anyway.[19]

In the course of his response, Barksdale focuses on the fact that Jay Gatsby performs an identity and fails—that despite his great wealth he is unable to manufacture an enduring new subject position within the world. Barksdale attributes Gatsby's failure and ultimate demise to a kind of critical naïveté about the rigid constraints of class and the risks involved in acting outside of one's prescribed station. For Barksdale, Jay Gatz's "second act" as Jay Gatsby falls flat, namely because his new, self-made narrative is a disillusioned one. As he puts it, Gatsby "wasn't ready to get real with the story" and, as a consequence, he grossly underestimates the fallout.

Of course, readers of all ages and backgrounds commonly recognize conflicts in *The Great Gatsby* that revolve around the disjunction between

FIGURE 11.1 *D'Angelo Barksdale (Lawrence Gilliard, Jr.) offers critical insight about F. Scott Fitzgerald's* The Great Gatsby *during a prisoner-education course.* The Wire. *"All Prologue." Season 2, episode 6. Directed by Steve Shill. Written by David Simon and Ed Burns. Aired July 6, 2003. Home Box Office, 2008. DVD.*

appearances and reality. Classroom discussions of the novel often explore the tension between Gatsby's past and the narrative present, and students quickly acknowledge that Gatsby's personal ambition must contend with larger social forces. However, Barksdale's reading is remarkable insofar as its imprisoned context actively transforms the novel's meditation on class mobility into an outright recognition of *caste* and social immobility. His interpretation demonstrates the "iterability" of language and text and illustrates *The Great Gatsby*'s "ability to function in new contexts with new force."[20] Jay Gatsby's primary struggle is with the ideological boundaries that ultimately compromise his ability to act according to his own designs. Barksdale, however, represents a group of individuals whose boundaries are concrete, enforced and reinforced by political and juridical machinery. In her explanation for why she uses the term "caste" to describe the material impact of the prison on black social life, Michelle Alexander offers the following:

> Today it is perfectly legal to discriminate against criminals in nearly all the ways that it was once legal to discriminate against African Americans. Once you're labeled a felon, the old forms of discrimination—employment

discrimination, housing discrimination, denial of the right to vote, denial of educational opportunity, denial of food stamps and other public benefits, and exclusion from jury service—are suddenly legal. As a criminal, you have scarcely more rights, and arguably less respect, than a black man living in Alabama at the height of Jim Crow. We have not ended racial caste in America; we have redesigned it.[21]

Thus, when Barksdale says, "the past is always with us," he invokes much more than an existential reflection about personal history. The statement acknowledges that specific conditions of modernity—such as Jim Crow segregation in the U.S.—are still prevalent in different iterations in the twenty-first century. It is important to recognize that Alexander's use of the term "mass incarceration" applies both to prisoners actively serving time and ex-convicts who have been released. It signifies a system that involves penitentiaries as important features of its disciplinary praxis, but which also includes "the larger web of laws, rules, policies, and customs that control those labeled criminals both in and out of prison."[22] There are only a few scenes that actually take place within the walls of a prison in the entire series of *The Wire*. Most of the show's action unfolds on the streets, in police department offices, and in courtrooms, but Alexander would argue that these spaces are certainly active in perpetuating the prison-industrial state of mass incarceration. Viewed accordingly, *The Wire* can be seen as a study of mass incarceration across a variety of discrete spaces in the contemporary American city.

Because Simon's appropriation works to emphasize the literal immobility of human beings, the intertextual exchange between *The Wire* and *The Great Gatsby* presents a seemingly grim view of subjectivity in the face of institutional forces. The rhetoric of Barksdale's interpretation emphasizes this overdetermined sense of the world. His insistence that "what came first is what really happened" can indeed be viewed as fatalistic, as a deterministic refusal to allow for new possibilities, changes, or hope. In the context of the show, this effect is accentuated by the fact that Barksdale is murdered in prison at the end of the episode in which this scene takes place.[23] Such gravity is appropriate though, considering Simon's effort to dramatize the "real story," what Alexander would call life in the undercaste.

However, the acts of perceiving and interpreting offer something of value here. Like a well-trained student, Barksdale uses textual evidence to substantiate his ideas. The specific moments that he refers to in *The Great Gatsby* help to theorize the appropriation and establish a point of strength in the activity of reading. In a fascinatingly reflexive turn, he describes Gatsby's fraudulent performance of identity via a scene early in the novel when the narrator, Nick Carraway, his love interest, Jordan Baker, and an unnamed minor character are looking at Gatsby's books in his library. Barksdale refers to the following passage from *The Great Gatsby*:

He waved his hand toward the book-shelves.
"About that. As a matter of fact you needn't bother to ascertain. I ascertained. They're real."
"The books?"
He nodded.
"Absolutely real—have pages and everything. I thought they'd be a nice durable cardboard. Matter of fact they're absolutely real. Pages and—Here! Lemme show you."
Taking our skepticism for granted he rushed to the bookcases and returned with Volume One of the 'Stoddard Lectures.'
"See!" he cried triumphantly. "It's a bona fide piece of printed matter. It fooled me. This fella's a regular Belasco. It's a triumph. What thoroughness! What realism! Knew when to stop too—didn't cut the pages. But what do you want? What do you expect?"
He snatched the book from me and replaced it hastily on its shelf muttering that if one brick was removed the whole library was liable to collapse.[24]

Within the novel, the revelation that Gatsby has not read any of his books galvanizes Carraway's growing suspicion of the protagonist. Indeed, Barksdale also appears to critique him heavily on this front. He fixates on the objects of literature in his interpretation, repeating the word "books" three times: "Like, you know, like all them books in his library; now he's frontin' with all them books, but if we pull one down off the shelf, ain't none of the pages ever been open. He's got all them books, and he ain't read nary a one of them." The scene in the prison with Barksdale and his fellow inmates can thus be viewed as a polarized version of Gatsby's library. Whereas the wealthy, white, and ostensibly "free" Gatsby has a great, high-ceilinged room of unopened, uncut, and unexplored books, the imprisoned black readers in *The Wire* are huddled around their dog-eared Scribner-edition paperbacks. In this reversal, and in Barksdale's emphasis on "books" in his response, the object of the work of literature materializes as an explicit point of appropriation.

This reinforces the argument that *The Great Gatsby* does not simply serve as a passing allusion and that there is far more at stake than a thematic connection. Barksdale focuses on the books in Gatsby's library at the same time that the camera angle methodically captures all of the inmates with their books in their hands. Under the direction of Steve Shill, the camera slowly pans around the room as Barksdale talks. His peers and the instructor are engrossed, held fast by the power of his reading. The visible impact of Barksdale's discourse on the text can be seen in the awestruck looks of his fellow inmates. This suggests the value and potential of reading and interpreting. In this sense, Barksdale's engagement with the text demonstrates de Certeau's claim that "[r]eading thus introduces an 'art' which is anything but passive" as he makes *The Great Gatsby* "function in a new register."[25] From perhaps one of the most repressive margins on the American landscape, Barksdale takes hermeneutical control over the terms of the text. His use of a modernist masterpiece enables him to engage the cultural ephemera of the mainstream, and in doing so, to project his own subject position and voice.

## Conclusion: The importance of (re)telling a good story

*The Wire* thus raises questions about the relationship between aesthetics and politics. When asked about the role of his own social consciousness within his work as a writer and producer, Simon slightly downplays the idea that political activism is a primary motivator for his craft:

> Everybody grafts onto me a motive because just telling a story is never enough for people. So I'm either civic minded and socially responsible and passionate about those things (which I don't feel unpassionate about). But I never expected the world to get fixed. I came from a place [the *Baltimore Sun*] where you tell a story and if it's shocking enough they pass a law and they make it worse. Telling a good story is the end in itself. And if something magical happened and they say we all watched *The Wire* and we're going to end the drug war because this is a disaster, then great. But it's never the expected result and not the intention. It was just a good story.[26]

Of course, viewers are free to reach their own conclusions about the sociopolitical inclinations of the show. However, Simon's reflections are significant because they revisit some of the central cultural debates that occurred during the modernist era, debates that dealt with the role of art in shaping a more just and integrative society.

Within Barksdale's interpretation of an early-twentieth-century work of art, multiple legacies of modernism unfold on the screen at once. Certainly, Barksdale's reading confirms the relevance of Fitzgerald's novel to specific realities in the twenty-first century. His incarcerated subject position conjures a vision of black life that also questions definitive claims to historical progress in the black public sphere. For Baker, African-American modernism occurs in the performance of blackness against tight institutional spaces such as "enslavement, peonage, tenantry, urban ghetto banishment, differential mandatory sentencing, death row."[27] Modernism is indeed very much alive in *The Wire*, though the implications of its endurance within the contemporary moment remain troubling, to say the least.

Although Simon professes that the telling of a "good story" is more important than any sociopolitical agenda, the inmates' engagement with *The Great Gatsby* reveals that art is always and already shot through with sociopolitical potential. Interestingly, critic Ronald Berman formulates a view of Fitzgerald's artistic ethos in the mid-1920s and describes the young author's social and artistic sensibilities in a way that parallels Simon's view of his own: "There are certainly public values in Fitzgerald—they are in fact vitally important to his work. But he was at this point in his intellectual life equally concerned with the idea of perception. In *The Great Gatsby* he asks not only what America *is* like but what it *looks* like."[28] Embedded within the narrative of *The Wire*, the modernist novel signifies new realities in the hands of the prison inmates whose own milieu represents what America looks like for a vast segment of the country's population.

# Notes

1. The adjective "Dickensian" is in fact a prevalent signifier in season five of *The Wire*, when a newspaper editor uses the term repeatedly to describe his efforts to capture a specific vision of the city. It is worth noting this reference because it attests to the literary awareness of the show and to Simon's consciousness of its relation to other cultural productions. Viewers have recognized that *The Wire* has a narrative quality much like a novel. Given the show's probing portrayal of social conflict and its serial form, there are indeed many connections between *The Wire* and Charles Dickens's social realism.
2. Anmol Chaddha and William Julius Wilson, "'Way Down in the Hole': Systemic Urban Inequality and *The Wire*," *Critical Inquiry* 38, no. 1 (2011): 164.
3. Houston A. Baker, Jr., *Turning South Again: Re-thinking Modernism/Re-reading Booker T.* (Durham: Duke University Press, 2001), 15.
4. Ibid., 69.
5. Ibid., 89.
6. Chaddha and Wilson, "Way Down in the Hole," 164.
7. For a recent discussion of *The Wire*'s engagement with and continuation of core modernist issues, see Nicholas Brown's chapter, "The Plain Viewer Be Damned: Or, Modernism on TV," *The Contemporaneity of Modernism: Literature, Media, Culture*, eds. Michael D'Arcy and Mathias Nilges (New York: Routledge, 2016), 178–89. In his chapter, Brown reconsiders the modernist claim to aesthetic autonomy *vis-à-vis* the genre of contemporary television and its move away from the network model.
8. Michelle Alexander, *The New Jim Crow: Mass Incarceration in the Age of Colorblindness* (New York: The New Press, 2012), 6.
9. Ibid., 7.

10  In his exploration of the criminal justice system and social inequality, Bruce Western points out that the "basic brute fact of incarceration in the new era of mass imprisonment is that African Americans are eight times more likely to be incarcerated than whites." *Punishment and Inequality in America* (New York: Russell Sage Foundation, 2006), 3.

11  For a recent and particularly enlightening study of a film adaptation of Fitzgerald's fiction, see Scott Ortolano, "Changing Buttons: Mainstream Culture in Fitzgerald's 'The Curious Case of Benjamin Button' and the 2008 Film Adaptation," *The F. Scott Fitzgerald Review* 10, no. 1 (2012): 130–52.

12  Michel de Certeau, *The Practice of Everyday Life*, trans. Steven Rendall (Berkeley: University of California Press, 1984), xv.

13  Lawrence Gilliard, Jr. is the only credited actor in the scene, as D'Angelo Barksdale is one of the show's main characters in seasons one and two.

14  *The Wire*, "All Prologue," season 2, episode 6, directed by Steve Shill, written by David Simon and Ed Burns, aired July 6, 2003 (Home Box Office, 2008), DVD.

15  Robert McParland, *Beyond Gatsby: How Fitzgerald, Hemingway, and Writers of the 1920s Shaped American Culture* (Lanham, MD: Rowman & Littlefield, 2015), xvii.

16  Peter L. Hays, "Class Differences in Fitzgerald's Works," in *F. Scott Fitzgerald in Context*, ed. Bryant Mangum (Cambridge: Cambridge University Press, 2013), 217.

17  Simon and Burns, "All Prologue." It is worth noting that this line appears in several different places in Fitzgerald's body of work. The author included it among some working notes in the manuscript version of *The Last Tycoon*, a novel that remained unfinished at the time of the author's death. It also appears in an essay titled "My Lost City" that Fitzgerald composed in 1932. For further insight on the interesting history of this quote, see Audie Cornish's interview with scholar Kirk Curnutt, "Fitzgerald Might Disagree with His 'No Second Acts' Line," npr.org, May 8, 2013, http://www.npr.org/2013/05/08/182337919/fitzgerald-might-disagree-with-his-no-second-acts-line.

18  Simon and Burns, "All Prologue."

19  Ibid.

20  Jonathan Culler, *On Deconstruction: Theory and Criticism after Structuralism* (Ithaca, NY: Cornell University Press, 1982), 135.

21  Alexander, *The New Jim Crow*, 2.

22  Ibid., 13.

23  Interestingly, he is killed in the prison library, yet another nod to the textual and contextual relevance of literature within *The Wire*.

24  F. Scott Fitzgerald, *The Great Gatsby* (1925; repr., New York: Scribner, 2003), 50.

25  De Certeau, *The Practice of Everyday Life*, xxii, 32.

26  Peter L. Beilenson and Patrick A. McGuire, *Tapping into* The Wire: *The Real Urban Crisis* (Baltimore: The Johns Hopkins University Press, 2012), xv–xvi.
27  Baker, *Turning South Again*, 37.
28  Ronald Berman, *Translating Modernism: Fitzgerald and Hemingway* (Tuscaloosa: The University of Alabama Press, 2009), 32.

# Bibliography

Alexander, Michelle. *The New Jim Crow: Mass Incarceration in the Age of Colorblindness*. New York: The New Press, 2012.
Baker, Houston A., Jr. *Turning South Again: Re-thinking Modernism/Re-reading Booker T*. Durham: Duke University Press, 2001.
Beilenson, Peter L. and Patrick A McGuire. *Tapping into* The Wire: *The Real Urban Crisis*. Baltimore: The Johns Hopkins University Press, 2012.
Berman, Ronald. *Translating Modernism: Fitzgerald and Hemingway*. Tuscaloosa: University of Alabama Press, 2009.
Certeau, Michel de *The Practice of Everyday Life*. Translated by Steven Rendall. Berkeley: University of California Press, 1984.
Chaddha, Anmol and William Julius Wilson. "'Way Down in the Hole': Systemic Urban Inequality and *The Wire*." *Critical Inquiry* 38, no. 1 (2011): 164–88.
Culler, Jonathan. *On Deconstruction: Theory and Criticism after Structuralism*. Ithaca, NY: Cornell University Press, 1982.
Fitzgerald, F. Scott. *The Great Gatsby*. 1925. Reprint, New York: Scribner, 2003.
Hays, Peter L. "Class Differences in Fitzgerald's Works." In *F. Scott Fitzgerald in Context*, edited by Bryant Mangum, 215–23. Cambridge: Cambridge University Press, 2013.
McParland, Robert. *Beyond Gatsby: How Fitzgerald, Hemingway, and Writers of the 1920s Shaped American Culture*. Lanham, MD: Rowman & Littlefield, 2015.
Western, Bruce. *Punishment and Inequality in America*. New York: Russell Sage Foundation, 2006.
*The Wire*. "All Prologue." Season 2, episode 6. Directed by Steve Shill. Written by David Simon and Ed Burns. Aired July 6, 2003. Home Box Office, 2008. DVD.

# 12

# Don Draper's identity crisis and *Mad Men*'s modernist masculinity

## *Camelia Raghinaru*

> "*The causes may vary—insofar as causes are suggested at all—but the same theme of manhood in jeopardy appears again and again in the texts and images of early High Modernism.*"
> —GERALD IZENBERG, MODERNISM AND MASCULINITY

In *Mad Men* advertisement functions as the conjuring of desire and its fulfillment. It also ties to questions of identity. Don Draper's obsessive questions are "Who is Donald Draper?" and "What do women want?" His answer to the latter question entangles his masculine identity with desire because, according to him, women essentially want to get closer to men like him. Don Draper places himself at the center of that desire. He succumbs to the allure of the illusion he is creating—as consumer and consumed—and consequently oscillates between power and powerlessness. (One of the accusations he brings against his boss is that he is complicit in the game of power and powerlessness inherent in the chain of command of the mid-managerial job they are performing.) Power itself is an illusion, created by the fascination advertisement exerts by its mere allure, without the backing of a particular product. Ad men deal in image, appearance, and illusion, and invariably Don Draper is described as a magician of words, a master craftsman who wields his magic by the sheer power of his charisma. Drawing from Jacques Lacan and Alenka Zupančič's theories about castration and desire, this chapter reads Don Draper's masculinity as desiring, vulnerable and dominating because of his status as a castrated modernist subject.

## Modernism and masculinity

Tracing the construction of masculinity from the medieval chivalric age that combined physical capacity for combat with the idealization of women and spiritual service to the vassal lord and Christ the Lord, Gerald Izenberg argues that some of the same traits survived in modernity, with the ideal bourgeois male combining a standard of aggressiveness and self-discipline put in the service of market forces and the political public arena.[1] In many ways, the male–female polarization is even more intense than before, since "the separation of the spheres was not simply a fact of economic life but the intentional results of men's desires to keep women out of the affairs of business in order to preserve male autonomy."[2] This bourgeois ideal was already in crisis by the end of the nineteenth century due to the decline of middle-class male economic roles, technological developments, and the weakening of masculinity in a consumer society. The ambiguity of modernist masculinity consists in an opposite pull toward the feminine: as a re-appropriation of female wholeness in order to rejuvenate masculine creativity versus a fear of traditional feminine stigmas, such as passivity, weakness and dependency.[3]

While modernism does not speak in one voice, modernist literature collectively records the instability of masculinity. Natalya Lusty notes that modernism is gendered "as a site of masculine emotional trauma and corporeal fragmentation,"[4] and this psychic wound is important in the context of castrated masculinity discussed in this paper. Male hysteria related to PTSD adds anxiety and vulnerability to the list of Victorian ideals of masculinity, namely courage, rationality, and objectivity.[5] Modernists tended to compensate with calls to hyper-masculinity, such as Marinetti's militarist manifesto of 1909, which states, "We wish to glorify war—the sole cleanser of the world—militarism, patriotism, the destructive act of the libertarian, beautiful ideas worth dying for, and scorn for women."[6] As Lusty explains, the invocation of an apocalyptic present opens "a primal scene of both aesthetics and politics for male modernism."[7] In this politicized view, women and the passivity and idealization of romantic love are derided and ridiculed. Rita Felski's study on the contradictions of gender in modernity reveals that even though modernists seem to be aware of the complexities of gender, their sympathies lie with a masculine view of women as "sacrificial victims" and burdens on men's quest for self-development.[8]

When undertaking the presentation of modernist masculinity, scholars like Sarah Cole focus on two extreme poles: from the "glowing, glistening, vibrant body of aestheticist dream"[9] to the wounded, debilitated body post-war—both positions and everything in between are repositories for ideology.[10] Thomas Strychacz explains that masculinity at the end of the nineteenth century was defined by its vulnerability in the context of the corporate economy: "As anomie became a more common experience than entrepreneurial agency, values of competition and independent effort that once were thought to pertain to individual men began to seem largely symbolic. Hegemonic constructions of manhood responded by reconfiguring and imaginatively consolidating the power of individual men."[11] Thus, competitiveness, ambition, and combativeness became reinscribed as codes of manliness well into the twentieth century.[12] For the modernist generation, the Hemingway ideal, a fetish of primitive, brutal instinct, wary of culture and reverting to a pre-cultural heroic code, becomes generative of a type of originary masculinity, a return to a state of nature.[13] D. H. Lawrence, whose work was foundational to modernist ideals of masculinity, links belligerence to masculine prowess. He sees the regeneration of emasculated men depending upon the return of femininity to domestic spaces, a move that would free men from the stifling confinements of family and possessions.[14] If modernism is indeed gendered as male, woman is defined as the representative of passive tradition against which the newly emerging autonomous male must define himself and attempt to transcend.

If *Mad Men* is seen as an attempt to commemorate the past and our nostalgia for it, it does so by commemorating a particular manifestation of the 1960s upper-middle-class white male. This is achieved by projecting the anxieties of individual protagonists onto a public commentary that mixes sentimentalism and nostalgia with an uncomfortable reminder of the temporal proximity of gender hierarchy, sexism, homophobia, and racial discrimination. The present is consequently destabilized as the viewers seek to project their current anxieties about gender and race onto the past. Thus, we see female characters like Joan and Peggy challenge us to ask whether we today are free from violence and discrimination against women. Critics point out a perverse impulse at play in our fascination with the show, as if contemporary audiences long for a time when it was acceptable to be sexist and racist, thus subverting our implicit superiority and confidence in the present. At the very least, it makes us aware that our supposed superiority has more to do with technological and medical advances that we use to conceal moral failures. Ultimately, in portraying Don Draper as the focus of the series, the show makes a point about midcentury wounded masculinity that is still seeking its home. This follows from Don's use of the Odyssey concept of gnostos, which reunites the meanings of wounding, nostalgia and homecoming, and which he uses to develop the conceit for the Kodak carousel commercial.[15]

In *Mad Men*'s advertisement world of the 1960s the insignia of power has become intangible and unrecognizable to the eyes of tradition. As Peter Campbell's father puts it, Peter has nothing to show for himself in terms of a solid career. In his job as an advertisement junior executive, it is as if he is trading in thin air. He is, in fact, trading in glamour—that is, in symbolic power. The "Mad Men" of advertising enjoy not power in the traditional sense, but rather the insignia of power that is bestowed upon them by their moneyed customers and their tangible and marketable product (the steel magnate, the tobacco industry, the department store owner, etc.). There is, therefore, a gap between product and its image, and this gap is filled by the advertisement executives. Their existence in this gap determines the nature of their masculinity—a modernist masculinity that seeks the enjoyment that is made possible precisely by this distance. What gives them power is the ability to manufacture desire and become objects of desire themselves. Don Draper's charisma is what makes him a good ad man, but it is precisely because he is desirable in the first place, as an attractive product to be consumed, that he is the man for the job. He enjoys the state of his symbolic function to the point of becoming lost in it. He is a figure of power due to the proliferation of copycats like Peter Campbell. The effect is almost tragicomic—each Mad Man despises the other's symbolic authority, but at the same time craves and respects it in order to maintain the logic of the illusion and his own role in it. Ultimately, however, this leads to disillusionment, because reality must be repressed for the illusion of power to prevail. Don Draper treads the fine line between repression and awareness of repression, and this delicate balance is at the heart of masculine gender performance in the 1960s.

## Don Draper's identity quest

The question of who Don is—his mysterious past and subsequent self-invention—structures the series. However, who Don *is not* is even more important. Don is both a fantasy self—the lone-wolf male that seduces his audience—and also a gap or distance from this self, created by the subversion or castration of that fantasy self—the man dependent on alcohol, women and the privileges of his race and gender at a particular moment in his national history. Don is the failed autonomous, self-reliant American legend. It is clear throughout the series that women are always there to prop Don up, to enable his alpha-male fantasy, and to spur him on to new adventures by mirroring his perfect fantasy for him. Even though women are not presented as subversive emasculators (on the contrary, their servile submission is what makes postmodern audiences cringe), their constant support nonetheless undercuts and castrates Don's invulnerable masculinity, cutting it down to the size of mere desire—the fantasy to which Don himself is both a slave and a stage of display. Thus, Nicky Falkof states that "Don Draper calls up an ideologically inflected vision of American manhood simultaneously repeated and deconstructed, revealed as fiction even as it struts its way across the screen."[16] Given that desire separates the subject from its object, while allowing the subject enjoyment in that very gap, Don himself aspires to be Don Draper (quite literally as Dick Whitman) as he plays his part in this fantasy. The fantasy in turn creates Don Draper—the empty, fluid, fictional subject. Fantasy and subject are inextricably linked, and yet completely separate.

Critics point out Don Draper's fragile masculinity as a weakness, but I argue that this very weakness and emptiness functions as the locus of power at the core of hegemonic masculinity. The core of power is empty, but power is predicated on this very emptiness and the tacit agreement the audience makes about both ignoring and accepting this site of vulnerability and enabling it with various props. Power is at its most effective when it reveals its vulnerability. Our satisfaction at watching Don's persona unravel does not diminish our fascination with Don Draper's exercise of masculinity. The more he unravels and weakens, the more he distances himself from his aura, and that strengthens the hold of the fantasy on us and himself. The appeal is not about being the fantasy, but always falling short of it, and that reinforces the power of the fantasy, as well as Don's status as enjoying and desiring subject. The tension is not between the failure of the masculine ideal and its success, but in the failure of masculinity *as* its success. Consequently, with every failure, Dick Whitman becomes more and more like the "Don Draper" fantasy he aspires to fulfill: in the wake of his divorce he marries Megan, his younger secretary; in the wake of his expulsion from Sterling Cooper, because of alcoholism, he regains his grip on his creative power; and at the end of the show, in veritable comedic fashion, he is restored to his initial splendor, even as in the final season he seems precariously positioned to succumb to alcohol again.

## Castration as gap and enjoyment

In *The Odd One In* Alenka Zupančič links castration directly to enjoyment. Castration is the cut that creates the gap separating the subject's body from its own enjoyment, while simultaneously binding one to it. Far from being solely an "operator of lack,"[17] castration in the Lacanian sense is also a marker of surplus, a "coincidence between 'no more enjoyment' and 'more enjoyment.'"[18] It is only in this space, that is both gap and surplus, that enjoyment emerges. The theory of enjoyment as castration applies also to symbolic roles of power, or what Zupančič calls "insignias." If the insignia of an official role is taken away, that stripping of power is akin to a type of symbolic castration. Power, like enjoyment, has the status of appendix, or surplus, exterior to the body. As such, it belongs to the realm of loss of control. The displacement of enjoyment is a matter for comedy, claims Zupančič. Characters who lose their enjoyment are essentially comic characters, invulnerable and indestructible in their own happiness.[19]

It is only because of the separation between Subject and its *jouissance* that enjoyment ensues. In this sense castration is the pre-condition for enjoyment: "Castration is what introduces a gap into the very logic and dynamics of (human) enjoyment, a gap on account of which enjoyment never directly coincides with itself ... but inevitably raises the question of how we relate to our own enjoyment."[20] The autonomy of enjoyment from its subject makes possible the fear of castration as a fear of loss of enjoyment. It also explains why enjoyment "can walk away" from the id in any direction and realize itself in unexpected or unusual activities.[21] Fear of castration is fear of losing control over this independent part of one's being. Thus, castration and enjoyment are linked as double sides of the same coin. Enjoyment comes as "always-already a consequence of castration" because we perceive enjoyment as something that appears as detachable, that we fear will be taken away from us;[22] something that is not an organic part of ourselves, but belongs to us in a gap or interval. Consequently, the source of human comedy is the "(dis)location of enjoyment."[23] (The miser losing his treasure chest, for example.) Comic characters are engaged simultaneously in enjoying and guarding/fearing the loss of their object, forever radically and dangerously exposed to loss and vulnerability. And yet, Zupančič claims, more astounding is these characters' invulnerability. Inexplicably, in comedy they are not inevitably crushed by the loss of the object of their obsession.

Jacques Lacan's seminar *The Formations of the Unconscious* analyzes Jean Genet's comedy *The Balcony* and its setting of the bordello as a "house of illusions,"[24] much like a parable of the Madison Avenue office. Just as the brothel is a place of illusions and a product of the sublimation of the ego, so the office is "accompanied by an eroticization of the symbolic relationship[s]" between men and women.[25] In Genet's play, customers who frequent the brothel don disguises and costumes of symbolic authority (i.e., that of a bishop, judge, general, and statesman) in order to enjoy briefly the symbolic power of their position. Similarly, on Madison Avenue, the suits and the glasses of liquor, the inner sanctum of the office vs. the outside desk of the secretary, the telephone, the couch, etc. are the equivalent of the symbolic vestments of power, yet not actual power. The bordello, in its constant state of degradation, is a mirror of the larger culture, Lacan argues, and it embodies for us the disguises and perversions of "relationships which are supposed to be sacred and fundamental to man and to the world."[26]

Don's relationships with women are modeled by the archetypal relationships of the brothel he witnesses from a young age. Accordingly, season six pictures Don either witnessing sexual transactions or being essentially raped by a prostitute as an underage boy. The sexual relationships he witnesses or participates in are abusive, predatory, and mercantile. In another instance, season five depicts the sexual encounter/business transaction between Herb and Joan and anticipates Don's veiled rape by Aimee. Joan becomes a transaction object in what Pete calls a business proposal and she calls prostitution. In this sense, the events of season six provide a symmetric role reversal, in which an underage Don becomes an object of transfer from the position of sick child mothered by prostitute Aimee to sexual object manipulated into non-consensual sex.

In questions of desire and *jouissance*, castration is an essential act for Lacan because it symbolically cuts the subject from fantasy. In the process of castration, fantasy becomes all the more valuable and desirable, placed in a special relationship to the subject. Don Draper's castration happens on multiple levels: when he cuts himself off from his real identity as Dick Whitman and from his brother, Adam, he severs all connections to reality and transfers his entire existence onto a symbolic, fabricated plane where nothing is really his (wife, kids, job, social position) because Don Draper no longer exists. He was killed in the Korean War, as Peter Campbell points out to Bert Cooper. Thus, castration separates Don from reality and enables him to possess the desired fantasy of social success in a symbolic way that to him is more real than his own rejected reality. Dick Whitman has been castrated at birth, if we count the symbolic arsenal of class, familial legitimacy, and social stability as phallic. But in a sense, Don is orphaned at birth and illegitimate on multiple levels. His conception is illegitimate, adulterous, and unrecognizable, as a result of the sexual transaction in a whorehouse. His legitimacy is tenuously restored at his quasi-adoption by his natural father. He describes himself as a "whore child" to the visiting hobo, however, aware of his tenuous position in his father's house. From a young age, therefore, Dick is aware of his social and familial deprivation—his symbolic castration of the insignia of power, as a lower-class foundling in rural Illinois with no social or economic prospects.

Perhaps his facility in accepting his makeshift reality enables Dick to make the second and more decisive move toward self-reinvention when he adopts the identity of Don Draper. As Lacan notes, castration itself originates at the end of a series of "displacements, of transpositions,"[27] all of which can be traced back to the fear of the father. Don's relationship with his father is uncertain at best. Though his natural father, he is more intransigent, unyielding and unkind than his stepmother, and his father's accidental death frees Don to escape the limiting setting of the farm and enlist in the army. To the extent that desire of the Other is barred, the Subject will recognize his forbidden, and therefore unsatisfied, desire, and will have its most authentic encounter with it. Castration, therefore, mediates desire for the Subject. Don Draper is an archetypal man in that he has already experienced his castration of symbolic phallic power from birth. As Lacan puts it, "man is never virile except by an indefinite series of proxies,"[28] and he is in constant search for his phallus.

In the wake of the culture wars of the 1960s, masculinity was predicated on the loss of the Father, the Law, and all patriarchal illusions of the late modernism of the pre-1950s conservative era. Advertising as a field was largely responsible for popularizing and glamourizing this new vulnerability and propagating enjoyment as loss. Zupančič argues that castration is the phallic model of modernity.[29] Castrated symbolic power is the means of exercising public power. The vulnerability of the new masters prevents us from grabbing and castrating them. Comedy is about the clumsy masters and their ridiculous forms of power. The naked realism of a figure of power is a lure. It imitates the weak point of power with symbolic efficiency in such a way that oppression remains undisturbed. In the case of contemporary corporate power, we know and accept its inconsistencies, but love the moment it presents itself as castration. Instrumental vulnerability is its mode of domination: Even though we know that the figure of power may be corrupt, stupid, or weak, we recognize that the law speaks through him. Thus, knowledge itself is crucial to the function of power and the public display of power. Democracy doesn't need the costumes and insignias of power because the best instrument against democracy is democracy itself.[30]

## Don Draper and women

Lacan's statement that "the woman does not exist" points to a symbolic lack, Zupančič argues.[31] For the woman to exist as Real, rather than Symbolic, is to threaten the fabric of patriarchal society. Symbolically, women exist in a network of relations as mothers, wives, sisters, and daughters: "This abundance of symbolic identities disguises the lack that generates them. These identities make it obvious not only that the woman does indeed exist, but also that she is the 'common denominator' of all these symbolic roles, the substance underlying all these symbolic attributes."[32] The woman's lack of being is not simply explained as her being possessed by a man. It is rather about the way a woman determines the man's being, rather than his having.

In the Madison Avenue office, the fate of women as secretaries is similar to that of women in traditional societies. They stop existing when their symbolic relationship to a man ends. They exist only as secretaries, or when they marry their bosses, as wives, or mothers of the boss's offspring. Peggy and Joan break this mold in ways that reveal the existence of a new woman who asserts herself independently from her Symbolic relationship to men.

To accomplish this, both Peggy and Joan have to deny the Symbolic: Peggy as a mother to an unacknowledged son, Joan as a perceived sex object.

In contrast to the women in the office, Don Draper is not primarily a husband, son, father, or brother. On the contrary, he represses violently those roles as soon as they try to confine him. He perceives himself as a man, in a society in which woman does not exist. When woman as non-mother, sister, or wife appears, Don Draper is also displaced as self-reliant, and he has to justify his relationship to others to clarify his meaning. Because all these relationships are symbolic, and "pure woman and "pure man" are entities obscured by the Symbolic, they are frightful conditions to contemplate. Under patriarchy, woman resists representation. For Zupančič, she is the "'not-all' under the formulation of a feminine 'not-all,' that is, the proposal that there is no whole, no 'all' of woman, or that she is not One."[33] However, once the conditions of patriarchy are under attack and masculinity undergoes a type of fluid dissolution, man resists representation as well.

In Don's character the show makes a comment on masculinity as a product of class and financial status. It is only because Don has lived his borrowed life solely with an eye toward acquiring the accoutrements of a well-groomed, successful, moneyed masculinity that he gets to be Don Draper, the face of executive advertisement. As a young Dick Whitman looking into the world of adult masculinity, he tries to decipher it as if acquiring a foreign language. The most important lesson he learns growing up in the brothel is that masculinity defines itself through and against women, in a sort of game of mastery and seduction, where women are both the locus of warmth and affection and also the battleground for the forging of masculinity. The relationships at the office are an exact replica of the relationships in the brothel, with men wielding the power and women offering themselves in submissive pliancy in exchange for their livelihood. Thus, Don's sexual affairs are part of a script of social ascendancy and boost his sense of masculinity.

The show makes a comment on masculinity in relation to social class as well as economics. As a pubescent boy, Dick Whitman looks into the world of working-class masculinity just as later, as a young man, he peers into middle-class masculinity—with the eyes of an outsider looking in and mimicking the rules. He learns to perform masculinity. His sexual affairs are part of the script. Sex is not so much about enjoyment as it is about acquisition. His marriage to Betty is about acquiring the fitting wife of an executive. His divorce from Anna is about making possible the right marriage. Don does not have a core as Don Draper, as he does not have a core as Dick Whitman. Void of a solid, preformed identity, he makes an interesting case study for masculinity because he constructs his gender as if by prescription. He is a collage of practices, and he is not aware of Betty's unhappiness because he himself is not happy or unhappy—he's just a façade. Don attempts to answer the question of what women want by trying to embody the answer himself: "[T]hey want a cowboy. He's quiet and strong. He always brings the cattle home safe."[34] But this is the answer of the ad. It is a fantasy, not reality; it is made to sell himself as a poster boy of masculinity, just like he invents love to sell nylons. In asking "What do women want?" Don asks a deeper question about his relationship to women. Consequently, Don gravitates toward women like him. Midge, the future drug addict, is a woman who possibly has everything or nothing because she lives in the moment and adheres to the maxim "Nothing is everything."[35] Consistently in the show the male gaze is tethered to women as if men would sink were they not able to be moored on the shore of femininity. There is anxiety in this, as if men have to constantly prove themselves to women and to their own standards of masculinity. Betty's psychoanalyst is a metaphor of stolid masculine silence, uncomprehensive, against which the female drama plays constantly. He is another empty suit among the many in the office. Don's awareness is greater than that of the others, though, and this frees him to reinvent himself. He has no anxiety about his self-fashioned identity, only about not losing his social place. His anxiety is about class because he knows better than anyone that economics is the only identity worth having.

# Castration as a form of domination in the twenty-first century

*Mad Men* resorts to a mythically constructed category of masculinity in the contexts of domesticity and the workplace. This alludes to the endurance and dominance of the fiction of masculinity that reproduces itself, even though, as Sally Robinson asserts, "individual men never easily measure up to [the] impossible standard of pure masculinity."[36] But because of rewards or punishments, in case of violation of the unwritten codes of masculinity, the gender construct is seductive and coercive at the same time. In attempting to disrupt the monolithic approach to masculinity, we have to reinvent new ways of embodiment for masculine desire that respond to the ever shifting social landscape that those desires construct and play against.[37] This new way of reconceptualizing masculinity takes into account the dynamic started by modernism, that Judith Halberstam places "between embodiment, identification, social privilege, racial and class formation, and desire, rather than the result of having a particular body."[38]

*Mad Men* depicts the dissolution of the monolithic conception of gender in its opening sequence of the male silhouette falling from the skyscraper, while the office space around him implodes. The fall is graceful, and it incorporates staples of the quickly vanishing patriarchal world of domesticity (mainly referencing marriage and the nuclear family revolving around the working husband and the decorative domestic housewife). The fall is ambiguous—it could capture a downfall or the end of an era and the beginning of another. After all, modernism and its dictum "Make It New" rebuilds the new world on the ruins of the old, in the wake of the destruction of tradition. The fable of the "Emperor's New Clothes," referenced by Harry in relation to Bert Cooper's modernist office art, hints at the discomfort produced by reinvention. Anxious, vulnerable, and displaced, the softening of the new male is the new macho, and Don Draper adapts yet again, a product of multiple self-fashionings.

Zupančič casts the trope of gender fluidity in terms of a void of power.[39] Costumes dress up the symbols of power, the "nothing" that constitutes symbolic power. They are the "clothing of the void," masquerading as fetishisms and insignia of power. According to Zupančič, a fetish is the thing one notices last before realizing the void of power. The men in the bordello dressed up as figures in power enjoy not power, but its insignia. Therefore, we return to the idea of distance and gap in enjoyment—the distance from power via the insignia that supplies the proof of our ascension to power. When others find enjoyment in dressing up in the insignia of the judge, it validates the judge as an authority figure. The comic effect comes from the shift of perspective, and it is almost sinister. The restoration of a different typology of power after the revolution (and the fall from grace of the Chief of Police) forces the figures of masquerade to come out of the closet. The restoration of power is based on the cynical knowledge of all parts involved of how things really stand. Each side despises the other's symbolic authority but at the same time respects it due to necessity.[40]

Zupančič argues that disillusionment is the political game capitalism plays, not despite, but precisely because of, our disillusionment. What is repressed is not knowledge, but rather repression itself. A type of cynical, disillusioned knowledge of how things really stand can be a form of not knowing. In this context, awareness of repressed content is the mechanism of social repression. *Mad Men* captures this contradiction of American capitalism during what Melanie Hernandez and David Thomas Holmberg call a "moment of cultural rupture, an overt denunciation of paternalistic social values that hatched a turbulent counterculture backlash."[41] By portraying the logic of enjoyment as a strange mix of childishness and power, authoritarianism (in its gendered and racial forms as well) no longer needs to disguise itself. In a democracy, no costumes are needed because inequality wears no costume. The more power the masters/bosses possess, the more casually they dress, in order to avoid the ridicule that comes with costume. The new kind of mask/costume claims a lack of pretense of the plain, useful clothes. This marks a change in the function of the costume. The emperor's new clothes are designed for him to appear naked. Nakedness is the most fashionable costume as no-costume. The logic of the new image is different. The image can be disgraced, but not the original.[42]

# Notes

1. Gerald Izenberg, *Modernism and Masculinity: Mann, Wedekind, Kandinsky through World War I* (Chicago: University of Chicago Press, 2000), 6.
2. Ibid., 7.
3. Ibid., 18.
4. Natalya Lusty, "Introduction: Modernism and Its Masculinities," in *Modernism and Masculinity*, eds. Natalya Lusty and Julian Murphet (Cambridge: Cambridge University Press, 2014), 4.
5. Ibid., 5.
6. Filippo Marinetti, "The Futurist Manifesto," in *Critical Writings: New Edition*, ed. Günter Berghaus, trans. Doug Thompson (New York: Farrar, Straus and Giroux, 2008), 14.
7. Rachel Blau DuPlessis, "'Virile Thought': Modernist Maleness, Poetic Forms and Practices," in *Modernism and Masculinity*, eds. Natalya Lusty and Julian Murphet (Cambridge: Cambridge University Press, 2014), 22.
8. Rita Felski, *The Gender of Modernity* (Cambridge: Harvard University Press, 1995), 2.
9. Sarah Cole, *Modernism, Male Friendship and the First World War* (Cambridge: Cambridge University Press, 2007), 8.
10. Cole, *Modernism, Male Friendship*, 8.
11. Thomas Strychacz, *Dangerous Masculinities: Conrad, Hemingway, and Lawrence* (Gainesville: University Press of Florida, 2008), 77.
12. Ibid.
13. Ibid., 89.
14. Ibid.
15. Ong Yi-Ping, "'Smoke Gets In Your Eyes': *Mad Men* and Moral Ambiguity," *MLN* 127, no. 5 (2012): 1025.
16. Nicky Falkof, "The Father, the Failure, and the Self-Made Man: Masculinity in *Mad Men*," *Critical Quarterly* 54, no. 3 (2012): 36.
17. Alenka Zupančič, *The Odd One In: On Comedy* (Cambridge, MA: MIT Press, 2008), 192.
18. Ibid., 192.
19. Ibid., 194.
20. Ibid., 192.
21. Ibid.
22. Ibid., 193.

23  Ibid.
24  Jacques Lacan, *The Formations of the Unconscious*, The Seminar of Jacques Lacan, 1,449–1,450, Book V, trans. Cormac Gallagher from unedited French typescripts, -272, http://www.valas.fr/IMG/pdf/THE-SEMINAR-OF-JACQUES-LACAN-V_formations_de_l_in.pdf, 272.
25  Ibid., 236.
26  Ibid., 237.
27  Ibid., 278.
28  Ibid., 336.
29  Alenka Zupančič, "Power in the Closet (and Its Coming Out)" (lecture, University of California, Irvine. April 11, 2015).
30  Ibid.
31  Alenka Zupančič, "Kant with Don Juan and Sade," in *Radical Evil*, ed. Joan Copjec (London: Verso, 1996), 113.
32  Ibid.
33  Joan Copjec, *Imagine There's No Woman: Ethics and Sublimation* (Cambridge, MA: MIT Press, 2004), 6.
34  *Mad Men*, "Ladies Room," season 1, episode 2, directed by Alan Taylor, aired July 26, 2007 (Lionsgate Entertainment, 2008), DVD.
35  Ibid.
36  Robinson, "Pedagogy of the Opaque," 150.
37  Judith Halberstam, "The Good, the Bad, and the Ugly: Men, Women, and Masculinity," in *Masculinity Studies and Feminist Theory*, ed. Judith Gardiner (New York: Columbia University Press, 2002), 354.
38  Ibid., 354.
39  Zupančič, "Power in the Closet."
40  Ibid.
41  Melanie Hernandez and David Thomas Holmberg, "'We'll Start Over Like Adam and Eve': The Subversion of Classical American Mythology," in *Analyzing Mad Men: Critical Essays on the Television Series*, ed. Scott F. Stoddard (Jefferson, NC: McFarland and Company, 2011), 41.
42  Zupančič, "Power in the Closet."

# Bibliography

Cole, Sarah. *Modernism, Male Friendship and the First World War*. Cambridge: Cambridge University Press, 2007.
Copjec, Joan. *Imagine There's No Woman: Ethics and Sublimation*. Cambridge, MA: MIT Press, 2004.
Blau DuPlessis, Rachel. "'Virile Thought': Modernist Maleness, Poetic Forms and

Practices." In *Modernism and Masculinity*, edited by Natalya Lusty and Julian Murphet, 19–37. Cambridge: Cambridge University Press, 2014.

Falkof, Nicky. "The Father, the Failure, and the Self-Made Man: Masculinity in *Mad Men*," *Critical Quarterly*, 54, no. 3 (2012): 31–45.

Felski, Rita. *The Gender of Modernity*. Cambridge: Harvard University Press, 1995.

Goodlad, Lauren. "The Mad Men in the Attic: Seriality and Identity in the Narrative of Capitalism Globalization," *Modern Language Quarterly* 73, no. 2 (2012): 201–35.

Halberstam, Judith. "The Good, the Bad, and the Ugly: Men, Women, and Masculinity." In *Masculinity Studies and Feminist Theory*, edited by Judith Gardiner, 344–68. New York: Columbia University Press, 2002.

Hernandez, Melanie and David Thomas Holmberg. "'We'll Start Over Like Adam and Eve': The Subversion of Classical American Mythology." In *Analyzing Mad Men: Critical Essays on the Television Series*, edited by Scott F. Stoddard, 15–44. Jefferson, NC: McFarland and Company, 2011.

Izenberg, Gerald. *Modernism and Masculinity: Mann, Wedekind, Kandinsky through World War I*. Chicago: University of Chicago Press, 2000.

Lacan, Jacques. *The Formations of the Unconscious*. The Seminar of Jacques Lacan, 1957–1958, Book V, translated by Cormac Gallagher from unedited French typescripts. Available online: http://www.valas.fr/IMG/pdf/THE-SEMINAR-OF-JACQUES-LACAN-V_formations_de_l_in.pdf.

Lusty, Natalya. "Introduction: Modernism and Its Masculinities." In *Modernism and Masculinity*, edited by Natalya Lusty and Julian Murphet, 1–18. Cambridge: Cambridge University Press, 2014.

*Mad Men*. "Ladies Room." Season 1, episode 2. Directed by Alan Taylor. Aired July 26, 2007. Lionsgate Entertainment, 2008. DVD.

Robinson, Sally. "Pedagogy of the Opaque: Teaching Masculinity Studies." In *Masculinity Studies and Feminist Theory*, edited by Judith Gardiner, 141–60. New York: Columbia University Press, 2002.

Strychacz, Thomas. *Dangerous Masculinities: Conrad, Hemingway, and Lawrence*. Gainesville: University Press of Florida, 2008.

Yi-Ping, Ong. "*Smoke Gets In Your Eyes: Mad Men* and Moral Ambiguity." *MLN* 127, no. 5 (2012): 1013–39.

Zupančič, Alenka. "Kant with Don Juan and Sade." In *Radical Evil*, edited by Joan Copjec, 105–25. London: Verso, 1996.

Zupančič, Alenka. *The Odd One In: On Comedy*. Cambridge, MA: MIT Press, 2008.

Zupančič, Alenka. "Power in the Closet (and Its Coming Out)." Lecture, University of California, Irvine. April 11, 2015.

# 13

# A century of reading time: From modernist novels to contemporary comics

*Aimee Armande Wilson*

Finding new ways to depict time propelled many of the experiments with literary form that characterize modernism. Frequently, these experiments were aimed at portraying the tension between time as represented on a clock and time as experienced in the human psyche. To achieve this end, drastic changes to the form of the novel were necessary because its basic organizational pattern is linear, characterized by a constant push forward that is similar to the clock's inevitable march into the future.[1] Experiential time, however, is full of stops, starts, reversals, and leaps forward. Time seems to speed up when we are enjoying ourselves, and trips to the dentist make the minutes crawl by; experiential time is anything but evenly meted out like the hour marks on a clock face. Gertrude Stein's continuous present, Marcel Proust's involuntary memory, and James Joyce's use of repetition are some of the best-known examples of modernist attempts to disrupt the novel's linear progression into the future.

In contrast to the novel's linear orientation, paintings are often understood to be oriented radially, or in a manner that presents the entire work simultaneously.[2] In other words, radial orientation causes the viewer to contemplate that which is *above*, *below*, or *beside*, rather than only what comes *before* and *after*. It is a critical commonplace to argue that modernist literature attempted to break down this division between linear and radial orientation by adapting painting techniques for literature. What is not frequently observed is the way in which comics, too, combine the linear organization of novels with the radial orientation of images (significantly, the genre of comics as we know it came into being in the late nineteenth and early twentieth centuries).[3] In "Time and Free Will: Bergson, Modernism, Superheroes, and *Watchmen*," Eric Berlatsky argues that the genre of comics "is both a 'time-art' in the manner of literature (as one must spend time sequentially reading word by word and panel by panel), and a 'space-art' capable of being viewed in a single moment."[4] Berlatsky's essay analyzes the similarities between comics and canonical modernist literature as regards Henri Bergson's notions of space and time. I have no interest in recapitulating or critiquing Berlatsky's perceptive argument, but rather seek to build on the idea that comics are a spatial and temporal medium from a reader-response perspective.

Although comics retain much of the linear orientation of novels—with the storyline driving the reader forward—the radial orientation of each panel invites the reader to linger in the image until his or her curiosity is satisfied and take in the various parts of the image in whichever order he or she chooses. This orientation is reflective of and conducive to the reversals, gaps, and pauses that characterize psychological time. In this way, then, comics replicate—and even amplify—*in the reading experience* the tension between clock time and psychological time that so often appears in modernist works. The linear–radial orientation of comics can therefore be read as an addition to the panoply of modernist techniques that interrupt the linear progression of clock time with time as felt by the individual.

Of course, not all comics are self-aware of the tension caused by this linear–radial orientation. *The League of Extraordinary Gentlemen* (1999–), by Alan Moore and Kevin O'Neill, is an exception and therefore a particularly illustrative case study because it plays with the difference between clock and psychological time in both form and content. The series is, in Thomas Mann's terms, a "tale of time"—one operating on the basis of time passing (which all tales are)—as well as a "tale about time," one dealing directly with time and its impact on characters.[5] Of particular interest to my argument is the third volume in Moore and O'Neill's series, titled *Century*. The volume is divided into three chapters: "1910," "1969," and "2009" (note that the titles themselves draw our attention to clock time). *League* brings together fictional characters in a deliberate pastiche of time periods, genres, and nationalities. Characters include Orlando, the gender-bending protagonist from Virginia Woolf's *Orlando: A Biography* (1928), and Mina Murray, a reprisal of Bram Stoker's character from *Dracula* (1897), as well as the Invisible Man, Dr. Jekyll/Mr. Hyde, Allan Quatermain, and James Bond, to name just a few. These characters form a vigilante group engaged in combating threats to England.

Although most characters stem from Victorian texts, the series nevertheless draws characters from an array of time periods, both in terms of the periods in which the characters' narratives are set and the publication dates of the books in which they star. Adding to this temporal dislocation, many of the characters in *League* are immortal. As this fact should make clear, Moore's depictions of these famous personages are not always faithful to the original, but the connections are unmistakable. For example, Orlando is referred to as "the new Vita" in *Century: 1969*, an allusion to Vita Sackville-West, the person on whom Woolf's Orlando is based.[6] In terms of form, *League* is similar to other comics in that it engages the tension between clock and psychological time by virtue of its linear–radial orientation. In terms of content, the series is distinct from most comics in that it engages a modernist conception of time, most directly through the character of Orlando. I will address the linear–radial orientation of comics before discussing the ways in which clock time is personified in *League*'s Orlando; doing so encourages us to see the ways in which clock time— usually thought to be an objective, public dimension of time—is actually quite subjective.

## Versions of time

William Faulkner famously said, "the past is never dead. It's not even past,"[7] and his works manifest this sentiment via myriad techniques that fold the past into the future. Faulkner was not alone in his focus on time, of course. As Randall Stevenson states:

> Modernist writing generally ... gave up, amended or abbreviated the chronological sequence, the vision of life as a series, which had conventionally structured the novel in the nineteenth century. The progressive, sequential development of the *Bildungsroman*, for example—tracing its central figure's life, step by step, over many years from birth to maturity—is at a considerable remove from the work of Joyce or Woolf, following their protagonists through only single days in *Ulysses* (1922) or *Mrs. Dalloway* (1925).[8]

This sequential progress of the novel was difficult to interrupt because, as noted earlier, the organizational paradigm of the novel is linear, a "sequential design mirror[ing] a temporal order" that progresses persistently forward.[9]

Modernists attempted in many ways to interrupt the linear organization of the novel: to make readers feel as though time had slowed down or gone in reverse; to, in effect, make the reading experience of a novel more like time as experienced in a character's psyche. The most obvious technique used to achieve this end is the simple addition of words to amplify the importance and richness of a character's thoughts. Virginia Woolf, for example, takes some four pages to describe Mrs. Ramsay's stream of consciousness while she measures the length of a knitted sock against her son's leg in *To the Lighthouse* (1927). As Erich Auerbach states of this scene and others similar to it, "the road taken by consciousness is sometimes traversed far more quickly than language is able to render it."[10] A second technique used by writers to interrupt clock time is defamiliarization, to use Viktor Shklovsky's term. He writes, "The technique of art is to make objects 'unfamiliar,' to make forms difficult, to increase the difficulty and length of perception because the process of perception is an aesthetic end in itself and must be prolonged."[11] This method forces readers to slow down to orient themselves to the world of the novel (as in the Benjy section of *The Sound and the Fury*, 1929). The forward pull of the linear narrative is slowed by the reader's desire for comprehension. A third favored method is repetition to create a sort of circularity, to fold the past of the novel into the present and the future; Molly Bloom's yeses in the final chapter of *Ulysses* are an obvious example.

Many of these formal experiments with time were, of course, directly inspired by the theories of Henri Bergson. Particularly influential in this regard was his notion that time as delineated on the clock (*temps*) does not represent time as experienced in the individual psyche (*durée*); the former being quantitative, objective, and public, while the latter is qualitative, subjective, and private. An example from Bergson's *Time and Free Will* should illuminate the way in which he distinguishes these versions of time:

> Whilst I am writing these lines, the hour strikes on a neighbouring clock, but my inattentive ear does not perceive it until several strokes have made themselves heard. Hence I have not counted them; and yet I only have to turn my attention backwards to count up the four strokes which have already sounded and add them to those which I hear. If, then, I question myself carefully on what has just taken place, I perceive that the first four sounds had struck my ear and even affected my consciousness, but that the sensations produced by each one of them, instead of being set side by side, had melted into one another in such a way as to give the whole a peculiar quality, to make a kind of musical phrase out of it ... In a word, the number of strokes was perceived as a quality and not as a quantity.[12]

Bergson's distinctions between *temps* and *durée*, public and private, objective and subjective time remain prevalent in critical discussions about time and modernism. Nevertheless, not all modernists who dealt with time were directly influenced by Bergson (some were openly critical), and Bergson was not the only intellectual discussing time in the early years of the twentieth century.

Indeed, discussions about time were so common that Stephen Kern calls the years between 1880 and 1918 "the culture of time and space."[13]

One need not have read Bergson to be aware of his ideas, or the ideas of other theorists of time such as G. E. Moore, William James, and Bertrand Russell. Modern life alone led some people to generate questions about the nature of time; factors such as "technological changes, scientific theories, new conditions of work and daily life, [and] the increasing shift of populations to cities,"[14] all contributed to an emerging sense that orderly, artificial timekeeping systems were, at best, inaccurate representations of time as the individual experienced it and, at worst, an impersonal force that steamrolled the individual into submission to modern ways of life. This threat is embodied in the linear organization of literary works. As a result, for writers hoping to depict the tension between clock and psychological time that people live with on a daily basis, the novel can only go so far. The radial orientation of images is more permissive of the individual's experience of time because images do not push readers/viewers to move in one direction (forward).

## Images and narrative drive

Thierry Groensteen argues that the individual panel in a comic "has the power to hail the reader, momentarily frustrating the 'passion to read' that drives the images so as always to be in the lead."[15] Indeed, panels interrupt the narrative drive into the future because the reader is momentarily halted, called upon to move his or her eyes up, down, left, or right, sometimes repeating the movement, sometimes reversing it, and often moving in directions that are the exact opposite of the left-to-right, top-to-bottom motion that signifies forward progress in Western novels.

To be sure, an artist might draw a panel in a way that directs the reader's gaze, causing most people to look first, say, at a road in an image by making this road large and in the center of the panel; by following the road, the reader's eye might then be drawn to animals on the side of the panel, and then to the trees just beyond the animals. But readers do not have to follow this set pattern when viewing a panel. A reader might notice the trees first and the road last. As A. A. Mendilow states, viewers of visual arts are "free to concentrate on any part of any size for any length of time and in any order, according to his own desire and not owning to any inherent necessity in the medium of sculpture or painting."[16] Significantly, this idiosyncratic variation does not impede the viewer's ability to understand the portion of the narrative expressed within an individual panel of a comic. Certainly, readers of Western comics expect to move from top to bottom and left to right on the page (though this pattern is often varied), but within each panel the reader is given latitude to move in alternate directions. Virginia Woolf, too, acknowledged the fact that "the formal railway line of sentence" runs counter to human consciousness: "people don't and never did feel or think or dream for a second in that way; but all over the place, in your own way."[17] Radial orientation, by contrast, opens a space for reader autonomy, for individual experience, that is more akin to the psychological experience of time. Therefore, the presence of radially oriented panels within the broader linear structure of a comic as a whole amplifies the tension between psychological and clock time that so many modernists (Woolf included) strove to develop in their novels.

By virtue of this linear–radial orientation of comics, the reading experience is distinct from that of watching a film or seeing a painting. Movies, on the one hand, display images at a pre-determined narrative pace. Federico Fellini explains that "comics, more than film, benefits from the collaboration of the readers: one tells them a story that they tell to themselves; with their particular rhythm and imagination, in moving forward and backward."[18] In essence, the particular formal properties of comics allow, even require, the reader to experience the narrative at his/her own pace. Novels, of course, allow the same sort of individual pacing, but are still oriented linearly and so cannot achieve the same degree of tension between clock time and psychological time as comics. On the other hand, paintings are oriented radially but do not have the narrative drive which pushes readers constantly forward and thereby emulates clock time. Groensteen makes a similar point when he argues, "the comics image is not that of painting" due to the sequentiality of comics' images; in other words, the position of panels within a larger system makes comics different from other art forms.[19]

Indeed, a narrative composed of text and images is an ideal way to create tension between clock time and the individual's psychological experience of it. Jacques Raverat seems to have anticipated this idea when, in a letter to Virginia Woolf, he argued that writing was "essentially linear"; Quentin Bell summarized his thoughts, stating that Raverat claimed the only way a writer could achieve the simultaneity enjoyed by painters would be through "some graphic expedient such as placing the word in the middle of a page and surrounding it radially with associated ideas."[20] The combination of images and narrative sequence means that comics combine both the linear, clock-like orientation of novels and the radial orientation of images, with the panels repeatedly breaking up the flow of the narrative. The result is a reading experience that emulates the tension between clock time and psychological time.

Achieving this reading experience is due in no small part to a defining feature of comics: the gutter. Gutters divide panels into discrete units, each one thereby seeming to occupy a distinct moment in time. Scott McCloud has shown that time in comics is actually much more complicated—that it is more accurate to think of each panel as "occupying a time slot"[21]—but that readers nevertheless *perceive* the progression of panels to represent the progression of time, the unfolding of events in roughly chronological order. As McCloud says, "in learning to read comics we all learned to perceive time spatially, for in the world of comics, time and space are one and the same."[22] The first panel in a comic is understood to occur before the last one. Because of the gutter, each panel is distinct from the one before and after it, while also having a position in relationship to these other panels. Gutters function, then, to divide a narrative in a manner that is similar to the way a clock face divides hours and minutes into units that are whole onto themselves.

Although most comics have a fairly uniform system of gutters throughout a series, illustrators frequently play with gutters to achieve a narrative purpose. This is particularly true of pages and panels Benoit Peeters classifies as "rhetorical," or those in which "the panel and the page are no longer autonomous elements; they are subordinated to a narrative which their primary function is to serve. The size of the images, their distribution, the general pace of the page, all must come to support the narration."[23] Other types of panels balance narrative and artistic purposes. For instance, an illustrator might depict a particularly forceful punch by allowing the panel's action to spill over the border and into the gutter. This spillover is a visual manifestation of a character's pain and dizziness in the moment. If we read gutters as I am arguing, as divisions marking the passage of clock time, the disruption of the gutter in this example can be read as representing psychological time because it depicts an experience strong enough to knock the character out in two ways: to make him or her unconscious as well as out of sync with clock time. This simple device of breaking gutter borders is thereby a subtle, but effective, way to illustrate the tension between clock time and psychological time.

A more complex example occurs in *League*. In this case, illustrator Kevin O'Neill heightens the tension between clock and psychological time by *not* breaking gutter borders. *League* features a character known as the Prisoner of London, so named because he can time travel at will but cannot leave the geographical borders of London.[24] The appearance of the Prisoner of London always occurs over a series of panels (generally between 3 and 4), each panel depicting London at different times. For example, in *Century: 1969*, the first panel in a series of three depicts London under attack by Martians (a reference to events in the first chapter of *Century*, set in 1910); this panel is followed by one set in the fictional world of George Orwell's *1984*; the final panel is set in the present moment of the series, 1969.[25] Although each panel expressly depicts a different time period, the Prisoner's presence in each panel is nearly identical: he stands in the same position, faces the same direction, in the same clothing.

The Prisoner's static presence in the panels heightens the continuity that already exists between panels, that is, the narrative drive that impels readers to develop chronological connections between panels. Nevertheless, each panel is oriented radially, which competes with the forward drive of the narrative. The reading experience is thus one of repeated shuttling between forward progression through the panels and idiosyncratic movement within each panel as readers attempt to understand the relationship between the Prisoner and the plot. In characteristically modernist fashion, Moore and O'Neill make readers work hard to understand the Prisoner's relationship to other characters and his role within the narrative because time does not operate in the manner we expect.

## Form and content

On a few occasions in *League*, characters seem to slip entirely out of clock time and exist in psychological time only (but only seem to, as I will later explain). One such occasion occurs toward the end of *Century: 1969*. Mina Murray, Allan Quatermain, and Orlando are fighting a supernatural villain named Oliver Haddo (based on a character created by W. Somerset Maugham). Mina encounters Haddo on a drug-fueled trip on the "astral plane." The importance of this climactic battle is mirrored in the panels of the book: a single image taking up three-quarters of a two-page spread. This over-large panel is the culmination of a gutter breakdown that began several pages earlier. While most panels in this series have regular, 90-degree borders, in the pages leading up to the image depicting the battle, the borders grow increasingly wavy and objects begin breaking through them: first, a man steps just over the border and into the gutter, then a knife pierces the edge of a panel, and finally Haddo, in the figure of a green monster, obliterates the black line surrounding panels as his body becomes the border of the panel. This progressive gutter dissolution represents the decreasing hegemony of clock time for Mina while also showing the increasing effects of the hallucinogenic drug.

Panels demonstrating Mina's experience are occasionally interrupted by ones depicting action occurring to other, sober, characters. When this happens, the gutters between the panels become regular, 90-degree angles again. This change is, of course, intended to depict the difference between sober and drugged characters. Nevertheless, the gutter distortions do not function only on the level of content. The change also alters the reading experience. As divisions between panels break down, so too does the forward pull of the narrative for readers: the order in which we are supposed to read the panels becomes less directed, more open to individual choice until we encounter the large, three-quarter-page panel that invites readers to experience their own psychological time alongside Mina.

Arguably, comics have the potential to be more successful than novels in depicting the tension between psychological and clock time by virtue of the genre's form. The following scene from Faulkner's *As I Lay Dying* (1930) will help elucidate the point:

> "Where's Jewel?" pa says. When I was a boy I first learned how much better water tastes when it has set a while in a cedar bucket. Warmish-cool, with a faint taste like the hot July wind in cedar trees smells. It has to set at least six hours, and be drunk from a gourd. Water should never be drunk from metal.[26]

This interior monologue continues for nearly a full page. When Darl finally answers Anse's question—"'Down to the barn,' I say. 'Harnessing the team'"[27]—readers are often caught by surprise because the focus of the narrative is anything but Jewel's location. Presumably only a few seconds elapse between Anse's question and Darl's response, but readers must take a minute or more to read the page of interior monologue.[28] This discrepancy accounts for readers' surprise while also making them aware of the difference between Darl's psychological time and the clock time in which characters exist collectively.

As successful as Faulkner's method of depicting psychological time is, the genre he employs is still linear, which means the narrative retains the forward push of clock time even as Faulkner attempts to interrupt it with the more idiosyncratic experience of psychological time. In other words, readers can only get a limited experience of Darl's psychological time because we must continue to receive the narrative in an inexorably forward, linear movement. The content may toggle between psychological and clock time, but the form is always linear. In comics, both form and content may alternate between the two versions of time.

## Public and private time

Returning to Mina's trip on the "astral plane," it is significant that her experience is not a pleasant one. In truth, it is a dangerous, harrowing event. Haddo comes close to destroying Mina's soul, and her body—which remains inert in the physical world—is sexually assaulted. This encounter with Haddo occurs because he is able to breach the boundary of her subjective experience and intrude on her psychological time. Although this breach is possible within the narrative because of the hallucinogenic drug Mina took, the events are suggestive for other circumstances. Indeed, this reading of Mina's psychological time raises questions about the extent to which psychological time is private, as it is usually understood to be.

Clock time regulates everyone in the same way: an hour lasts sixty minutes no matter who you are or what you are doing. Furthermore, clock time is generally a system agreed upon by a governing body to regulate its people and its business. These properties lead critics to refer to clock time as public. The private nature of psychological time would seem to be self-evident. Psychological time is, after all, the passage of time as perceived by an individual, based on his or her subjective experiences. These public and private versions of time are usually understood to be mutually exclusive. Paul Ricoeur, in his seminal study *Time and Narrative*, argues that public "monumental" time and private "mortal" time are "irreconcilable";[29] there exists an "insurmountable fissure ... between the monumental time of the world and the mortal time of the soul."[30]

*League*'s depiction of Haddo within Mina's psychological experience of time brings the private nature of psychological time into question. Indeed upon consideration, it becomes clear that psychological time is not private at all. For example, we often perceive the passage of time in the same way as others. Just think how often someone's complaint about time passing slowly in a meeting is met by groans of agreement from co-workers. Furthermore, when we experience time passing more slowly or more quickly than clock time, we still exist in and are subject to the public sphere. That is to say, our experience of psychological time is mediated by the concurrent actions of the people, events, and objects surrounding us; class drags by for a student *because* the professor is a boring lecturer, and it conversely speeds up when lectures are lively. Indeed, a field of psychology has recently emerged around this and similar sensations. Called embodied cognition, researchers in this field study the ways in which a person's subjective time is affected by the emotions of the people around him or her.[31]

Conversely, *League* suggests ways in which clock time has private, subjective aspects. To explain, consider the fact that the modernist sense of clock time as impersonal and potentially hazardous to individual psychology is markedly different from depictions of clock time in other eras. As Adam Barrows argues, Victorian literature usually depicts clock time as a tool to help people tame threats and points to Stoker's *Dracula* as an exemplary text. For example, Mina says that "the 'whole connected narrative' of *Dracula* is produced ... by 'knitting together in chronological order every scrap of evidence they have' and passing it among the hunters to be studied as 'evidence.'"[32] The final product of this knitting, according to Barrows, "translates into a uniform typewritten font the individual idiosyncrasies of handwriting style or vocal pattern, a translation that ... 'excludes all particularities in favor of a general equivalence.'"[33] Homogenous clock time is central to the protagonists' ability to thwart Dracula.

Modernist texts, in contrast, are much more skeptical or even fearful of clock time. Barrows explains this fear by placing clock time in historical context:

The period during which Greenwich Mean Time became accepted, nation by nation, as Universal Time, spans the period in English literary history typically associated with high modernism ... Greenwich, by the early twentieth century, had entered modernist consciousness as a powerful symbol of authoritarian control from a distance and of the management of diverse populations.[34]

This context helps explain why, in Woolf's *Orlando*, clock time is dangerous. Chimes marking the hour are "awful and ominous"; they strike "remorselessly," "violently assault" Orlando, and "hurtle through her like a meteor."[35] As Mark Hussey states, "Clock time threatens an individual's sense of continuity" because it takes no account of the lived experience of time."[36] It is important to note that Woolf's *Orlando* positions clock time as an element external to Orlando. Clock time is a public force that threatens the individual.

By the twenty-first century, however, clock time has lost much of its punch. We may feel hampered by clock time, but it hardly seems like a violent threat. In accordance, *League* transforms clock time into the character Orlando. Rather than the clock being an external entity—a machine whose sounds intrude upon Orlando's psychological time—Orlando's voice becomes the chimes of the clock. In this series, Orlando regularly refers to historical events experienced over the course of his/her very long lifetime. These references to events function as the chiming clock, reminders of the passage of time.

For example, at the beginning of *Century: 1969*, Orlando remarks that Dover, where the group's ship landed, is not far from London: "We built a road straight there when I landed here with Caesar. Or was it Agricola? Actually, I led the Romans to London, having helped Brutus found the city when ..." Mina interrupts, stating, "Lando, shut up ... Although you're right about the road."[37] Mina's reaction is typical. The other characters are generally indifferent to or annoyed by Orlando's rather arrogant reminders that he/she has lived longer than any of the others. Yet their annoyance also stems from the fact that Orlando is a wildly inaccurate clock. He/she is often confused about where and when events happened. No one could stop Dracula by Orlando's memory of events, but neither is anyone haunted by clock time.

## Conclusion

By personifying the clock, *League* encourages readers to see the ways in which it is private, subjective, and irregular. Even if clock time measures out history in regular intervals, humans nevertheless relate to it through our experiences; in other words, our relationship to clock time is always mediated by personal experience. The union of text and image in comics emulates the private/public character of clock time by asking readers to constantly shift between the linear pull of the narrative and the radial orientation of the panels. This linear–radial orientation of comics thereby carries on modernist experiments with time in powerful, if not always intentional, ways.

The legacy of modernism in the twenty-first century is sometimes easy to spot: novelists' persistent experiments with form, the unquestioned presence of free verse in poetry, or even the continued salience of Freudian concepts in Anglo-American literature. In other ways, the legacy of modernism is harder to find, particularly in the world of pop culture where many of the traits that traditionally characterize modernism—allusiveness, defamiliarization, alienation, and so forth—might seem to preclude the crowds and the money that are thought to be necessary for pop culture success. Yet as this essay has shown, paying attention to time in the hugely popular *League* series helps illuminate modernism as a red thread running all the way into the twenty-first century, and surprisingly—but decisively—into the world of comics.

# Notes

1. Ann Banfield makes this argument via Jacques Raverat and Roger Fry. Others have noted the linear, time-based organization of writing, among them Gotthold Ephraim Lessing, Joseph Frank, and A. A. Mendilow. Ann Banfield, "Time Passes: Virginia Woolf, Post-Impressionism, and Cambridge Time," *Poetics Today* 24, no. 3 (2003): 472–3.
2. Ibid.
3. Scott McCloud, *Understanding Comics: The Invisible Art* (New York: Harper Perennial, 1994), 18.
4. Eric Berlatsky, "Time and Free Will: Bergson, Modernism, Superheroes, and *Watchmen*," in *Understanding Bergson, Understanding Modernism*, eds. Paul Ardoin, S. E. Gontarski, and Laci Mattison (New York: Bloomsbury Academic, 2013), 262.
5. Quoted in A. A. Mendilow, *Time and the Novel* (New York: Humanities, 1972), 16.
6. Alan Moore and Kevin O'Neill, *The League of Extraordinary Gentlemen. Century: 1969* (Marietta, GA: Top Shelf, 2011), n.p.
7. William Faulkner, *Requiem for a Nun* (1951; repr., New York: Vintage, 2011), 73.
8. Randall Stevenson, *Modernist Fiction* (Lexington, KY: University Press of Kentucky, 1992), 87.

9   Banfield, "Time Passes," 473.
10  Erich Auerbach, *Mimesis: The Representation of Reality in Western Literature*, trans. Willard R. Trask (Princeton, NJ: Princeton, 2003), 537.
11  Viktor Shklovsky, "Art as Technique," in *Literary Theory: An Anthology*, ed. Julie Rivkin and Michael Ryan (Malden, MA: Blackwell, 2004), 18.
12  Henri Bergson, *Time and Free Will: An Essay on the Immediate Data of Consciousness*, trans. F. L. Pogson (1889; repr., New York: Harper, 1960), 127–8.
13  I am indebted to Banfield for this observation. Banfield, "Time Passes," 473.
14  Ibid.
15  Thierry Groensteen, *The System of Comics* (Jackson, MS: University Press of Mississippi, 2007), 26.
16  Mendilow, *Time and the Novel*, 25.
17  Quoted in Quentin Bell, *Virginia Woolf: A Biography* (New York: Harcourt, 1972), 338.
18  Quoted in Groensteen, *System*, 11.
19  Ibid., 7. Groensteen nevertheless argues that comics should be thought of as a primarily visual art form. He states that scholars of comics must "renounce" the idea that "comics are essentially a mixture of text and images, a specific combination of linguistic and visual codes" (3). I incline to David Carrier's argument, which positions comics as a composite art form, a combination of text and language, on the basis of the speech balloon as a defining characteristic. For more, see Carrier, *The Aesthetics of Comics* (University Park, PA: Pennsylvania State University Press, 2000), 4.
20  Bell, *Virginia Woolf*, 338.
21  McCloud, *Understanding Comics*, 97.
22  Ibid., 100.
23  Benoit Peeters, "Four Conceptions of the Page," trans. Jesse Cohn, *ImageTexT: Interdisciplinary Comics Studies* 3, no. 3 (2007): para. 19.
24  The Prisoner of London is based on a character from Iain Sinclair and David McKean's *Slow Chocolate Autopsy*.
25  Moore, *League of Extraordinary Gentlemen*, n.p.
26  William Faulkner, *As I Lay Dying* (1930; repr., New York: Vintage, 1985): 10–11.
27  Ibid., 11.
28  My reading of the scene is influenced by Auerbach's reading of *To the Lighthouse* in *Mimesis*.
29  Paul Ricouer, *Time and Narrative*, vol. 2, trans. Kathleen McLaughlin and David Pellauer (Chicago: University of Chicago Press, 1985): 107.
30  Ibid., 110.
31  See, for example, Sylvie Droit-Volet, "How Emotions Colour our Perception of Time," *Trends in Cognitive Sciences* 11, no. 12 (2007).

32  Quoted in Adam Barrows, "'The Shortcomings of Timetables': Greenwich, Modernism, and the Limits of Modernity," *MFS: Modern Fiction Studies* 56, no. 2 (2010): 283.
33  Ibid.
34  Ibid., 263.
35  Virginia Woolf, *Orlando: A Biography*, ed. Maria DiBattista (1928; repr., Orlando, FL: Harcourt, 2006): 45, 224, 236.
36  Mark Hussey, *The Singing of the Real World: The Philosophy of Virginia Woolf's Fiction* (Columbus, OH: Ohio State University Press, 1986), 122.
37  Moore, *League of Extraordinary Gentlemen*, n.p.

# Bibliography

Auerbach, Erich. *Mimesis: The Representation of Reality in Western Literature*, translated by Willard R. Trask. 1953. Reprint, Princeton, NJ: Princeton, 2003.
Banfield, Ann. "Time Passes: Virginia Woolf, Post-Impressionism, and Cambridge Time." *Poetics Today* 24, no. 3 (2003): 471–516.
Barrows, Adam. "'The Shortcomings of Timetables': Greenwich, Modernism, and the Limits of Modernity." *MFS: Modern Fiction Studies* 56, no. 2 (2010): 262–89.
Bell, Quentin. *Virginia Woolf: A Biography*. New York: Harcourt Brace Jovanovich, 1972.
Bergson, Henri. *Time and Free Will: An Essay on the Immediate Data of Consciousness*, translated by F. L. Pogson. 1889. Reprint, New York: Harper, 1960.
Berlatsky, Eric. "Time and Free Will: Bergson, Modernism, Superheroes, and *Watchmen*." In *Understanding Bergson, Understanding Modernism*, edited by Paul Ardoin, S. E. Gontarski, and Laci Mattison, 256–80. New York: Bloomsbury Academic, 2013.
Carrier, David. *The Aesthetics of Comics*. University Park, PA: Pennsylvania State University Press, 2000.
Droit-Volet, Sylvie. "How Emotions Colour our Perception of Time." *Trends in Cognitive Sciences* 11, no. 12 (2007): 504–13.
Faulkner, William. *As I Lay Dying*. 1930. Reprint, New York: Vintage, 1985.
Faulkner, William. *Requiem for a Nun*. 1951. Reprint, New York: Vintage, 2011.
Frank, Joseph. "Spatial Form in Modern Literature: An Essay in Three Parts." *The Sewanee Review* 53, no. 4 (1945): 643–53.
Groensteen, Thierry. *The System of Comics*. Jackson, MS: University Press of Mississippi, 2007.
Hussey, Mark. *The Singing of the Real World: The Philosophy of Virginia Woolf's Fiction*. Columbus, OH: Ohio State University Press, 1986.
Lessing, Gotthold Ephraim. *Laocoon: An Essay on the Limits of Painting and Poetry*, translated by E. C. Beasley. London: Brown, Green, and Longmans, 1853.

Maugham, W. Somerset. *The Magician*. London: Heinemann, 1908.
McCloud, Scott. *Understanding Comics: The Invisible Art*. New York: Harper Perennial, 1994.
Mendilow, A. A. *Time and the Novel*. New York: Humanities, 1972.
Moore, Alan and Kevin O'Neill. *The League of Extraordinary Gentlemen. Century: 1969*. Marietta, GA: Top Shelf, 2011.
O'Sullivan, James. "Time and Technology in *Orlando*." *ANQ: A Quarterly Journal of Short Articles, Notes, and Reviews* 27, no.1 (2014): 40–5.
Peeters, Benoit. "Four Conceptions of the Page," translated by Jesse Cohn. *ImageTexT: Interdisciplinary Comics Studies* 3, no. 3 (2007): 41–60.
Ricoeur, Paul. *Time and Narrative*, vol. 2, translated by Kathleen McLaughlin and David Pellauer. Chicago: University of Chicago Press, 1985.
Shklovsky, Viktor. "Art as Technique." *Literary Theory: An Anthology*, edited by Julie Rivkin and Michael Ryan. Malden, MA: Blackwell, 2004.
Sinclair, Iain, and David McKean. *Slow Chocolate Autopsy: Incidents from the Notorious Career of Norton, Prisoner of London*. London: Phoenix House, 1997.
Stevenson, Randall. *Modernist Fiction*. Lexington, KY: University Press of Kentucky, 1992.
Stoker, Bram. *Dracula*. 1897. Reprint, London: Vintage, 2013.
Woolf, Virginia. *Orlando: A Biography*, edited by Maria DiBattista. 1928. Reprint, Orlando, FL: Harcourt, 2006.
Woolf, Virginia. *To the Lighthouse*. 1927. Reprint, New York: Harcourt Brace Jovanovich, 1981.

# 14

# Hemingway's console: Memory and ethics in the modernist video game

*Dustin Anderson*

"*Woody Allen dreamt of the interactive novel. Video game designers plan to implement it, perhaps less voluptuously, by putting the player in control of a character who lives not in a maze but in a piece of literature.*"
—SHERRY TURKLE, *THE SECOND SELF: COMPUTERS AND THE HUMAN SPIRIT*

In his concluding essay for the 1933 collection, *The Use of Poetry and the Use of Criticism*, T. S. Eliot speaks directly about every author's desire to reach an audience in a pervasive and lasting way. He claims every poet wants to have some "direct social utility" and every author really wants to be something like a popular entertainer.[1] Eliot's early high-modern sentiments do not initially seem to correlate to a mechanism that is available to the masses, but his final comment on where and how stories should be delivered is certainly popular if not proletarian. He claims the poet "would like to convey the pleasures of poetry, not only to a larger audience, but to larger groups of people collectively; and the theatre is the best place in which to do it."[2] The theater, unlike the novel or the poem, creates a socially interactive space for the audience. It has a vitality that enables it to be accessible to the larger audience—it is not a *flat* text. The performance of the script is dynamic and forces the audience's engagement. It begs more than a response; it demands participation.

Over the course of the twentieth century there have been a number of media innovations that have reconfigured what we consider art, and how we consume it: film, television, online media. Each of these are their own type of evolution from the theater. None of those, however, demand the same type of participation Eliot talks about with the theater. Contemporary narrative-driven video games—often taking the form of Role Playing Games (RPGs) or First-Person Shooter Role Playing Games (FPS/RPGs)— do, however, demand the same type of collaborative participation. Likewise the ambiguous ethical dilemmas of contemporary game series (such as *Call of Duty: Modern Warfare*, *Assassin's Creed*, and *Mass Effect*) harken back to the same ethical issues Ernest Hemingway, William Faulkner, and James Joyce developed in the early twentieth-century novel; moreover, the treatment of time, perception, and memory as interactive processes touch directly on elements of the modernist project these authors created.

Participating in non-linear ethics-based narrative games is an act of collaboration rather than a passive encounter with a text. At the purely formal level, game interaction is closer to Antonin Artaud's Theatre of Cruelty than Tristan Tzara's Dadaist project, but the result is the same: integrated narrative construction from the author and the audience. That collaboration is not far off from the mark Eliot imagines with the theater. The non-linear digital narratives created through video game interaction places the audience in a similar position. The player must make ambiguous ethical decisions on the narrative at hand to direct the response and development of the text. Where modernist authors made their audiences aware of cultural and personal inequities, interactive digital narrative (here in the guise of video games) forces their audiences into a position of both awareness and action. The experimental nature of modernist fiction is a ready-made translation into the judgments players must make in interactive digital narratives.

From the ludological standpoint, we cannot simply unpack games like we would a traditional form of *flat* narrative, like film, television, or print. Instead, these digital texts must be studied as highly formal and structured texts designed for both haptic and intellectual involvement. They are, in some senses, most easily allied with our already established modes of modernist aesthetic discourse, but also offer a development on the types of Friedrich Nietzschean and Henri Bergsonian ethical ambiguities authors like Hemingway, Joyce, Samuel Beckett, and, later, Cormac McCarthy brought forth in their novels.

# Punching the keys: Newer media and older aesthetics

While the admission of video games into the intellectual discourse community remains a controversial topic, let us operate under the premise Steven E. Jones introduces in his 2008 book, *The Meaning of Video Games*: "video games are meaningful—not just as sociological or economic or cultural evidence, but in their own right, as cultural expressions worthy of scholarly attention."[3] Describing the emergence of video games in the Academy, Dexter Palmer finds that digital narratives occupy a very different end of the cultural spectrum from, say, *Ulysses*, and that drawing them into discussion would be "very, very wrong."[4] Exclusive arguments like this one appear to be precisely what Jessica Pressman takes issue with in *Digital Modernism*. Pressman traces the question about the relationship between narrative and digital media (here the database) back to the same text Palmer references: James Joyce's *Ulysses*. Her reading shrewdly connects literary experimentation and new media technologies to highlight the representation of cognition through media including traditional text.

This situation of the video game as *interactive digital narrative* builds on the early New Media treatments of non-traditional texts by scholars like fellow Deleuzean, Richard Dienst and by Espen Aarseth. Aarseth, in *Cybertext: Perspectives on Ergodic Literature*, provides a fascinating complication of the received notion of interactivity in reading practices. Aarseth highlights the most fundamental problem we face in interactive media studies: definition. He claims there are two polarized possibilities in defining the concept of "interactive fiction."[5] On one hand, interactive fiction means nothing (i.e., it is "so trivial to be self-explanatory"), or it must take on a dissatisfying dictionary definition based on the traditional elements of the two component terms. Aarseth seems to build a middle-ground by invoking Peter Bøgh Andersen's earlier description of semiotic interactive aesthetics: a work that integrates the reader's interaction as a vital part of the sign production process.[6] Aarseth notes that this is perhaps the most accurate portrayal of the relationship between the adventure game and its player. Interactive here does not indicate that the reader/player can create a large-scale or fundamental change within the text itself, but that he or she is a prime contributor to the thematic discourse developed by the text. For Aarseth, these "ergodic" literatures ultimately describe systems in which the reader generates the literary sequence through interactivity.

This notion of embracing is subtle, but core to the understanding of the modernist legacy of media production in games. Dienst points back to Marx's *Grundrisse* notes to explain the always ongoing process of new media creation at the heart of modernity even in the baldest economic sense of artistic production. The implied question Dienst draws out of Marx's conclusion—there has always been an "uneven development of material production relative to e.g., artistic development"[7]—is: How can we go about reducing the gap between political economy and culture?[8] The underlying implication that production and circulation (capital or otherwise) are intrinsically related to forms of consciousness and power is in many ways the *how* that interactive digital narratives think in. The act of value-based creative production is not limited to the existing material of the text (i.e., game) itself, but within the form of consciousness that arises from the interaction the player has with the ethical dilemmas posed by the text in order to create both the narrative and the thematic weight or circulation of ideas within the narrative as the text builds or progresses.

In her 2011 *The Language of Gaming*, Ensslin provides the most comprehensive explication of video games' purchase into both the current society and morals and into the intellectual marketplace. Perhaps most germane to the examination of the modernist legacy in video games are the familiar literary and semiotic traditions she includes: ludology, narratology, media studies, and cultural studies.[9] Ensslin also points to the intertextuality that has, at least in part, provided the basis for the success of the video game industry: "they draw on and refer to other texts, discourses and media, particularly from pop culture ... recognising resemblances of characters, settings and events from other texts, situational and discursive contexts and media makes players feel on quasi-familiar territory and can be exploited to evoke tragic, horror, nostalgic, comic and satirical effects."[10] She goes on to define the space in which we find the games discussed below. Although somewhat different from, what she calls, the serious games she explicates in her book, the "paradox of literary games" is fundamental to our understanding of interactive digital narratives as a development of modern aesthetics and themes. Ensslin very astutely identifies the receptive, productive, aesthetic, phenomenological, and social differences between the traditional literary forms and digital mediums, but ultimately brings them together through the concurrent multimodality of traditional unimodal texts.[11] This kind of simultaneity speaks to the modernist aesthetic that interactive digital narratives create by nature rather than design.

Aesthetically, we find a similar drive to the creation, production, and circulation of this art. Video game creators, much like the modernist poets and painters, are, as Ensslin explains, "playing 'with' rather than 'by' the rules in order to evoke critical responses towards gaming."[12] Moreover, she helps to define how the phenomena of interactivity, simultaneously separates and connects video games from and to traditional literary forms: "Clearly, the semantic prosody of video games and gaming as entertainment artefacts and rule-based activity is their inherent expectation of being played rather than read."[13] The deployment of decoding mechanisms, while fundamentally the same, takes on a new valence as they must be, as she says, co-deployed, rather than sequentially deployed. Of texts designed purely to entertain or distract, that co-deployment would be absent. However, only on the most surface level is this true of many iconic modernist texts. The crucial, though often overlooked, effect of modernist literature is the multi-cognitive engagement with elements of the text. Parsing Eliot's intertextual and multivocal situation in "A Game of Chess" in *The Waste Land* is not fundamentally different than the co-deployment of simultaneously decoding the "manuals and quest directives on screen, listening to non-player characters giving instructions and hints, and interpreting the navigational iconicity, symbolism and indexicality of [the] interface design" that Ensslin discusses.[14]

Ian Bogost's discussions of modernist legacies in gaming technology comes from his treatment of what he calls "Encounters across Platforms," which he draws together through treatments of chance encounters in the poetry of Charles Baudelaire and Walter Benjamin's discussions of aura and the work of art created itself in *The Arcades Project*. Bogost deftly deconstructs Benjamin's discussion of Baudelairian motifs, and explains how they act as precursors for what game designers will later call "unit operations."[15] Each of these units, though separate, must function on an interactive continuum. Bogost explains that, as tools, they function differently than the procedural lists that act as denotative divisions: "I am most interested in how Baudelaire creates tools for living modern life—strategies that function procedurally even more than they do lyrically. As a figure in transition across an anonymous urban expanse, the *flâneur*'s role is fundamentally a configurative one."[16]

Bogost's most profound contribution is, unfortunately, not fully developed. While only touching on the role of Henri Bergson in Benjamin's understanding of Baudelaire's creations, Bogost does crack the shell of one of the most fundamentally modernist aspects of the kind of non-linear digital narratives only a video game platform can fully realize: memory. In *How to Talk About Videogames*, Bogost explains that "Benjamin relies on Henri Bergson's *Matter and Memory* as a model for the way Baudelaire represents experience. Under Benjamin's reading of Bergson, experience becomes 'a convergence in memory of accumulated and frequently unconscious data.'"[17] He later returns to Bergson (via Deleuze), albeit briefly, in his introduction of "object-oriented ontology" in 2012's *Alien Phenomenology*: "The inherent partition between things is a premise of OOO [Object-Oriented Ontology], and *lists* help underscore those separations, turning the flowing legato of a literary account into the jarring staccato of real being. *Lists* offer an antidote to the obsession with Deleuzean becoming, a preference for continuity and smoothness instead of sequentiality and fitfulness. The familiar refrain of 'becoming-whatever' (it doesn't matter what!) suggests comfort and compatibility in relations between units, thanks to the creative negotiations things make with each other"[18] (emphasis mine).This object-oriented ontology might draw game theorists more closely together with modernist artists than anything else.

The rejection of human privileging is in part what the surrealists attempt to convey by phantasmagorically layering images in order to express a new dialectical experience. While the media is different, the effect viewers, readers, or players experience is much the same between the surrealist page and the game screen. For Benjamin, the kind of ultimate dialectic experience taken for granted in the Romantic world is missing from the modern world. The non-linear digital narrative does not exist between being and nothingness, but as both simultaneously. As Bogost hints at, the player functions much like the *flâneur* of Baudelaire's faux-pastoral landscape both interacting with the thing that *is* and is *not* already there—in this case the text.

In *The Arcades Project*, when Benjamin talks (at great length) about Baudelaire, two things are clear: (1) the Baudelaire is in some way conflicted; that is his approach to modernity is "anticlassical and classical. Anticlassical: as antithesis to the classical period. Classical: as heroic fulfillment of the epoch that puts its stamp on its expression;" and (2) "Baudelaire speaks of his partiality for 'the landscape of romance,' more and more avoided by [modern] painters."[19] This takes shape in the second section of *Les Fleurs du Mal* (*the Flowers of Evil*) as the *flâneur* travels the city streets of Paris and encounters "*Tableaux parisiens*" (Parisian scenes). For Benjamin, Baudelaire is actively writing against the Classical Pastoral tradition, and simultaneously re-creating the Pastoral as a modern phenomenon—not one of lush countryside, but of drunken ("*Le Vin*") and depraved city streets (sexually and otherwise in "*Fleurs du Mal*"), which even contain the antithesis of the natural praise of the Classical Pastoral, through introducing Satanism (as in "*Révolte*"). At times Baudelaire's treatment comes in the form as mere parody, as in "The Sick Muse," where the classical elements are inverted: "Poor Muse, alas, what ails thee, then, today? / Thy hollow eyes with midnight visions burn, / Upon thy brow in alternation play, / Madness and Horror, cold and taciturn."[20] Here he takes a single element, the invocation, and satirically inverts it. However, more often (and interestingly), Baudelaire's treatment of the pastoral is to break and re-shape the genre into something singularly modern.

While the intention might or might not be present in the design of non-linear digital narratives, the effect is the same as Baudelaire's re-made pastoral: the narrative genre is actively deconstructed and reconstituted in a fashion that challenges the existing binary relationship between viewer and text. The level of interaction still includes the suspension of disbelief from the viewer, but the viewer must also actively engage with ongoing ethical decisions shaping the experience of the text. Like the modern novel, re-approaching or replaying these narratives will result in different textual interactions and new ethical dilemmas. Although a large number of non-linear digital narratives could serve as example, I will limit the comparisons to Action Role-Playing games, specifically *Assassin's Creed*, *Call of Duty: Modern Warfare*, and *Mass Effect*. In each of these narratives, we find the same treatment of the ethics of remembering. For many interwar modernist authors, the concepts of time, perception, and memory are intrinsically bound through an understanding of ethical dilemma not as a passive reading experience, but as a creative and interactive process.

## "Would you like to return to your previous checkpoint?": Ethics and modern memory in digital narratives

In the opening cinematic of *Fallout 3*, the narrator, voiced by Ron Perlman, offers a stridently modernist take on violence and human interaction. "War," he says, "War never changes. Since the dawn of human kind, when our ancestors first discovered the killing power of rock and bone, blood has been spilled in the name of everything: from God to justice to simple, psychotic rage." Following the First World War, modernist authors have depicted the ambiguity of moral choice in settings full of blood-dimmed tides. On one hand it might be easier to see the effect of multimodalities native to non-linear digital texts focused on conflict in war poets like Thomas Hardy, Isaac Rosenberg, Siegfried Sassoon, Charles Sorley, Robert Graves, or Wilfred Owen. However, the interactivity of these non-traditional narratives leans more towards the types of experimental narrative constructs found in novels. While a fair number of interwar texts could serve to illustrate the treatment of ethical memory in video games, two novels might best provide separate examples of where the modernist legacy in non-linear digital narratives begins: Ernest Hemingway's *For Whom the Bell Tolls* (1940) and William March's *Company K* (1933).

Like many of the aforementioned texts, Hemingway's *For Whom the Bell Tolls* highlights the ambiguous depictions of the value of human life and the destruction of innocence in the face of war as he portrays the struggle between Falangist, Fascist, and Republican ideologies during the Spanish Civil War. While the novel primarily focuses on Robert Jordan and the band of Republican guerillas, Hemingway deftly includes two small, but stunning portrayals of the conflict between ethics in modernity and traditional morality through two minor characters.

Berrendo is the only Fascist soldier fleshed out to any degree. Berrendo is left in an untenable situation when Mora is killed by El Sordo. He appears as a devout Catholic (reciting Hail Mary both during and after the airstrike), and he is clearly repulsed by the prospect of mutilating the dead soldiers. Neither of those things keep him from doing so, though. With Mora gone, he has no one to report to, yet carries out the decapitation of the guerillas. Likewise, Joaquin, rendered unconscious by the blasts, poses no combat threat to the Fascist soldiers, yet Berrendo executes him anyway. Karkov, on the other hand, occupies the polar opposite end of the conflicted moral spectrum. He takes pride in "educating" Jordan in the true nature of the world, bringing him into the conflict, and seemingly benefiting from the potential publications that Jordan might later make about the nature of the war itself. Karkov functions primarily in flashback in the novel pointing to the role he plays in Jordan's memory as part of the active decision-making process Jordan undergoes. Both Berrendo and Karkov highlight the nature of remembered guilt in strikingly different ways: Berrendo's guilt to come, and Karkov's divorce from guilt in Jordan's memories of him.

The nature of remembered guilt simultaneously works twofold in non-linear digital narratives: passively and actively. Games like *Call of Duty: Modern Warfare 2* and *Mass Effect* highlight the interaction of those two modes. BioWare's 2007 *Mass Effect* offers players vague and ambiguous sets of decision-making options. As Commander Shepard, the players might take any number of paths to achieve the designated objective. No single choice made in the game demonstrates a singular effect. Rather the implications of the multiple decisions made shape the narrator as the game moves forward. The game ultimately ends the same way, but the depictions of the path to that end can change in small or profound ways. The player is made aware of the overall receptions of the character's moral appearance or perception by a sliding scale of Paragon and Renegade alignments. One is built through decisions reflecting diplomacy and tolerance, whereas the other is a much more action-oriented path. There are, however, no black-and-white choices since any decision will have far-reaching consequences. As the narrative progresses the player's past choices dramatically impact the story itself. Much like Jordan, Shepard finds his/herself in a situation of self-sacrifice, and must make a decision with consequences far beyond his own story. Up to the endgame of the narrative, the player has been made witness to a wide range of questionable ethical decisions both on his/her part and on the parts of the Non-Player Characters (NPCs). Characters *can* die; even Shepard can die based on the decisions the player makes.

As opposed to the ambiguity of the *Mass Effect*'s decision tree, *Call of Duty* creates situations of immediacy in the ethical decision-making process. "No Russian," the fourth mission of *CoD: MW2*, has often been referred to as one of the most controversial realistic instances of play in contemporary gaming. The player, in the persona of Joseph Allen, under the alias of a Russian criminal must at least witness the act of terrorism and mass murder carried out by the Non-Player Characters. The player screen resolves to the exit of an elevator while known terrorist Vladimir Makarov instructs the player and other NPCs to speak in "no Russian." After departing the elevator, the NPCs walk through airport security checkpoint at Zakhaev International Airport where the NPC gunmen open fire on the civilians. The controversy of this level is not that the player takes part in a massacre of hundreds of civilians, but that the player can simply not take an active role in the portrayal of terrorism. The player can simply follow the NPCs through the level—the player is forced to walk slowly through the airport as the terrorists execute the civilians and airport personnel—and witness the remorseless killing of innocents. There is little decision-making in this regard, and the player chooses to either actively or passively participate in a reprehensible activity. That concept is nothing new to non-linear digital narratives or to traditional narratives for that matter. The act of reading or later watching Alex "the Large" beat and rape victims in *A Clockwork Orange*, for instance, is not far from the guilt a player should experience within *Call of Duty*. However, the developers of the game include an option to "skip" the level completely. Labelling the level as containing Disturbing Content, the game prompts the player to choose not to play the level at all, or to pause the game and skip the level at any time. As with passively reading the text on a page, there are no penalizations in terms of game completion for skipping the level. Likewise, there is no on-screen guidance to shoot at anyone, civilians or terrorists; the only "objective" for the level is to "Follow Makarov's lead." So, if acts of violence towards collateral parties are nothing new in games, why would the developers of *Call of Duty* offer the player the chance to alter the narrative?

The answer might lie in how a player is positioned to *knowingly choose how to understand* this decision. As the reader progresses through *For Whom the Bell Tolls*, we learn more of how Jordan, through his interactions with Karkov, came to fight for the guerillas. Although Jordan's role of freedom fighter is deeply romanticized in the novel, Hemingway muddies the ethical waters by including Karkov's influence on Jordan. Robert Jordan is as much a terrorist as Berrendo is a defiler of corpses. Jordan is doing what he thinks is right and that belief is reflected in Berrendo's own actions. What Hemingway does in *For Whom the Bell Tolls* is subtly force the reader from a passive receiver of knowledge (or someone simply entertained by the story) to a state of active decision making. When Karkov tells Jordan about writing about these same experiences he will undergo later in the narrative, Hemingway is building a model for us to move into a space of active participation. Katerina Clark describes Karkov's role in the novel as uncovering paired writing projects; Karkov, who discusses writing on his Spanish "adventures," becomes more than just an aspiring novelist. He becomes a potential version of Jordan's "narrative headquarters."[21] She goes on to explain that Karkov is Jordan's own point of orientation to construct meaning for his actions. The reader following Jordan's ruminations about Karkov must come to terms with how they understand Jordan's actions: is he a terrorist, freedom fighter, or some third thing? The act of understanding is not what separates this text from multitudes of war novels, but the participatory ethical decision the reader is made aware of through the narrative very much sets this text apart. Like the player in "No Russian," the reader must choose to participate.

This choice is magnified by the a-sequential nature of the game. The player finds themselves operating a number of characters in disparate environments, all leading towards a similar end. This structure, as paired with themes of violence, existential choice, and memory, harkens back to Marsh's *Company K*. Marsh's novel is as much an experiment in structure as any non-linear digital narrative. The "novel" is made up of over a hundred vignettes told from the point of view of the same number of men in Company K. These vignettes run from the Marine's training to the aftermath of the war itself. Roy Simmonds points to Graham Greene's review of *Company K* in the *Spectator* as an explanation of how March paradoxically creates the most genuine, yet unrealistic portrayal of the ethics of war in novel form:

> His book has the force of a mob-protest; an outcry from anonymous throats. The wheel turns and turns and it does not matter, one hardly notices that the captain of the company, killed on page 159, is alive again a hundred pages later. It does not matter that every stock situation of the war, suicide, the murder of an officer, the slaughter of prisoners, a vision of Christ, is apportioned to Company K, because the book is not written in any realistic convention. It is the only War-book I have read which has found a new form to fit the novelty of the protest.[22]

This same "novelty of the protest" resurfaces in games with immediate results in ethical dilemmas posed to the player like *Call of Duty*, and perhaps more so in narratives where the choices the players makes have a long-lasting and deep impact on the nature of the narrative itself. These choices need not be remembered as the digital narrative forces the player to re-experience them—to create a new memory of those events—and perceive them through the lens of experiences. By no means are these narratives the only two examples of ethical-dilemma focused games. Many narratives like *The Walking Dead* by Telltale or *Papers, Please* investigate even more complicated moral issues without privileging one decision over the other, and certainly not creating a correct path to follow. They do, however, offer insights into how we choose, and how we understand building narratives around the multiplicity of those choices.

The *Assassin's Creed* series stands as another significant non-linear digital narrative that pushes modernist legacies into a singular space of literary engagement. The serialized narrative started in 2007 and follows a group of shadowy conspirators called the Assassins in a millennia-long struggle with the fascist Templars. The narrative is grounded in the premise of recovering memory through DNA; the game itself is structured around re-enacting or playing the memories as if they were a game. The player, initially, takes on the role of "assassin" Desmond Miles, and through Desmond's interactions with a neurological interface called the Animus further takes on the role of Desmond re-living his ancestors' memories as Altaïr Ibn-La'Ahad during the Third Crusade in Masyaf; Florentine native Ezio Auditore da Firenze during the late fifteenth and early sixteenth centuries; and Mohawk Ratonhnhaké:ton (or Connor) during the American Revolution. Later iterations of the series position the player as an anonymous Animus operator exploring the memories of Welsh pirate Edward Kenway during the eighteenth century; Irish turncoat Shay Cormac during the Seven Years' War; Arno Dorian during the French Revolution; and the Frye twins during London's Industrial Revolution. Unlike *Call of Duty*, *Assassin's Creed* features little in the way of discouraging killing, but the ethical dilemmas are not centered around that concept. As a suspension of disbelief, the player operates always already knowing the character (Desmond, Ezio, etc.) will engage in the self-titled activities. The player is rewarded by only engaging with the target NPCs, but not to the point it profoundly affects the narrative. Within the game-world, if Desmond in the guise of his ancestor murders someone he was not supposed to have assassinated, then the game "desynchronizes" and Desmond must begin the memory again.

Where the *Assassin's Creed* series sets itself apart is how it depicts this fluidity and multiplicity of time, identity, perception, and memory. Those very same cognitive issues dominate texts like Faulkner's *The Sound and the Fury* as each narrator demonstrates differing aspects of each of the concepts (or sometimes, like Benjy, multiple aspects simultaneously)—the notions of time and space in this text (for someone like Deleuze) would function as a unifying force imposed by the subject to create a kind of identity. Benjy's situation of himself in these slippages of when and where he is forms the identity that we, as readers, come to understand. This visual conceptualization of time and space is at the heart of modernist works across genres and cultures: in Wallace Stevens's "Sunday Morning" as the narrator's contemplation of the spirit is grafted onto a spectrum of memory and language; in Jean Toomer's *Cane* where identity, memory, and consciousness are always in question; in Albert Camus's *The Stranger* in the existential disabling of free will; in Flann O'Brien's *The Third Policeman* in the issues of mathematics, mechanics, memory, identity at the limit of reason; or, perhaps more evidently, in authors like Beckett and Proust as they deal with the non-spatial or temporal and focus on the virtual memory created during this memory process. However, no other texts attempt to textually demonstrate and depict the representational world of memory introduced by Bergson as fully as Joyce in *Finnegans Wake*. The game within a game within a game developed by Ubisoft does almost the exact same thing, but relies on

3-dimensional models, graphic, and haptic interaction in addition to the multi-layer, non-linear narrative.

While the *Wake* might seem like an active deconstruction of the English language (and is in many ways a political attack on the language), it rather creates a new language to find a means of expression. Given the importance of Giordano Bruno and Giambattista Vico in Joyce's work, it is not surprising to find the destruction of language is marked only by the simultaneous reconstitution of language. The Brunonian Monad is the point at which extreme opposites meet. It is a single surface effect of a greater holistic binding phenomenon. All surface effects are essentially the same; they all represent the meeting of two extreme opposites, but are merely new instance of the same phenomenon. For Joyce, these surface effects appear as events in history. They are manifestations of the same event, or of the same person, in various historical locations, or in various guises. Structurally, Joyce uses the Viconian Cycle series to show this language phenomenon. Vico's cycles are generally understood in parts: the age of gods, the age of heroes, and the age of people, followed by a revolution or *ricorso* that is the instantaneous end of the third age and the re-beginning of the first age; it is a single instant of destruction and creation. The memories the player engages with through Desmond (who is in some cases simultaneously Desmond, Ezio, and Altaïr while also *being* none of those individuals alone) show the same archeological layering of narrative.

By pushing identity to its utmost extant, Joyce is able to simultaneously destroy and re-create identity. By using heteroglossic languages, Joyce shows that identities can all be the same, while displaying their vast differences—as any number of words are identical in several languages, but can mean different things. Joyce's approach is polychronic in such a way that encapsulates all of history by simultaneously showing the same situation again and again, or "the seim anew."[23] That moment, or perhaps the moments Joyce focuses on are when a thing is being destroyed and simultaneously reconstituted: a Joycean *ricorso*. Events in the *ricorso* are always conflated to contain any number of people or geographic locations. The joining of Shem and Shaun, which results in the destruction of two individuals and the creation of a single person (HCE), is the same as Tristan and Isolde (or HCE and ALP) creating the seed of new life; this instance is also conflated with stories like Buckley shooting the Russian General to show monadic moment in a number of locations and times. Desmond, likewise, is created and recreated through the process of overlaying memory with identity. His interaction with the existent representational world of his genetic ancestors changes his identity in a manner best described as a durative becoming. This happens sometimes with single memory overlays, and sometimes with three and four layers of memory. As they stack, they become porous and allow Desmond to move between the narrative tracks of his memories into the hidden places behind them, and perceive new elements of old stories.

This is the identical method Joyce creates through repetition. The situation or even the characters might change, but the manifestation of the crisis remains. Joyce's texts run language out to an extreme, find it inadequate, and begin the system anew. This happens in a number of different ways, not only in *Finnegans Wake*, but also in *Ulysses*, *Dubliners*, and *Portrait*. The repetitious actions and thoughts of one character are manifested in another; for instance, Bloom's metempsychotic imitation of Stephan as Stephan daydreams and then remembering Molly and writing to Martha. Like the surface effects of the Brunonian Monads, Joyce links his characters and histories together by showing them at the same instance of linguistic crisis—he collapses history to show the peoples, languages, and structures of the world as doing the same thing at the same time—the moments of destroying and re-building the languages, narratives, and ultimately traditions. It is the modern drive of creation and experimentation—to show an interconnection, and a wholeness.

The depiction of memory processes Ubisoft develops in a game like *Assassin's Creed* is likely not an allusion to the *Wake* any more than it was directly influenced by the novel. The game's depiction, however, would not be possible without the illustration of synaptic function in narrative form Joyce creates in his final novel. Moreover, it also serves as a touchstone for how games are reshaping what we mean by narrative. They are certainly not replacing the traditional narrative, but in the finest modernist tradition, they are creating new spaces for knowledge and storytelling to exist. If the underlying drive of modernism is to create new approaches to traditional concepts, then these non-linear digital narratives are coming from the same point of origin. These new modes of narrative present us with an experience of difference that frustrates our preconceived categories, and forces us to create new epistemologies.

## Notes

1 T. S. Eliot, *The Use of Poetry and the Use of Criticism* (1933; repr., Cambridge, MA: Harvard University Press, 1986), 154.
2 Ibid.
3 Steven Jones, *The Meaning of Video Games* (New York: Routledge, 2008), 1.
4 Dexter Palmer, quoted in Michael Erard, "The Ivy-Covered Console," *New York Times*, February 26, 2004.
5 Espen J. Aarseth, *Cybertext: Perspectives on Ergodic Literature* (Baltimore: Johns Hopkins University Press, 1997), 50.
6 Ibid., 49.
7 Karl Marx, *Grundrisse: Outlines of the Critique of Political Economy*, trans. Martin Nicolaus (1857–61; repr., New York: Penguin, 1973), 109.

8   Richard Dienst, *Still Life in Real Time: Theory after Television* (Durham: Duke University Press, 1994), 64.
9   Astrid Ensslin, *The Language of Gaming* (New York: Palgrave Macmillan, 2011), 2–3.
10  Ibid., 53.
11  Ibid., 149–51.
12  Ibid., 160.
13  Ibid., 151.
14  Ibid.
15  Ian Bogost, *Unit Operations: An Approach to Video Game Criticism* (Cambridge, MA: MIT Press, 2006), 73–92.
16  Ibid., 75.
17  Ian Bogost, *How to Talk About Video Games* (Minneapolis: University of Minnesota Press, 2015), 78.
18  Ian Bogost, *Alien Phenomenology, or What It's Like to be a Thing* (Minneapolis: University of Minnesota Press, 2012), 40.
19  Walter Benjamin, *The Arcades Project*, trans. Howard Eiland and Kevin McLaughlin (Cambridge: Belknap Press, 1999) J38a, 1:297; J34, 4:290.
20  Charles Baudelaire, *Flowers of Evil and Other Works/Les Fleurs du Mal et Oeuvres Choisies: A Dual-Language Book*, trans. Wallace Fowlie (1857; repr., New York: Dover Publications, 1992), 21.
21  Katerina Clark, *Moscow, the Fourth Rome* (Cambridge: Harvard University Press, 2011), 260.
22  Graham Greene, "Fiction," review of recent fiction publications, the *Spectator*, London, April 7, 1933.
23  James Joyce, *Finnegans Wake* (1939; repr., New York: Penguin, 1999), 215.

# Bibliography

Aarseth, Espen J. *Cybertext: Perspectives on Ergodic Literature*. Baltimore: Johns Hopkins University Press, 1997.
*Assassin's Creed*. Developed by Ubisoft. Created by Patrice Désilets, Jade Raymond, and Corey May. Ubisoft, 2007.
Baudelaire, Charles. *Flowers of Evil and Other Works/Les Fleurs du Mal et Oeuvres Choisies: A Dual-Language Book*, translated by Wallace Fowlie. 1857. Reprint, New York: Dover Publications, 1992.
Benjamin, Walter. *The Arcades Project*, translated by Howard Eiland and Kevin McLaughlin. Cambridge: Belknap Press, 1999.
Bogost, Ian. *Alien Phenomenology, or What It's Like to be a Thing*. Minneapolis: University of Minnesota Press, 2012.
Bogost, Ian. *How to Talk About Video Games*. Minneapolis: University of Minnesota Press, 2015.

Bogost, Ian. *Unit Operations: An Approach to Video Game Criticism.* Cambridge, MA: MIT Press, 2006.
*Call of Duty: Modern Warfare 2.* Developed by Infinity Ward. Directed by Jason West. Activision, 2009.
Clark, Katerina. *Moscow, the Fourth Rome.* Cambridge: Harvard University Press, 2011.
Dienst, Richard. *Still Life in Real Time: Theory after Television.* Durham: Duke University Press, 1994.
Eliot, T. S. *The Use of Poetry and the Use of Criticism.* 1933. Reprint, Cambridge, MA: Harvard University Press, 1986.
Ensslin, Astrid. *The Language of Gaming.* New York: Palgrave Macmillan, 2011.
Erard, Michael. "The Ivy-Covered Console." *New York Times*, February 26, 2004.
Greene, Graham. "Fiction." Review of Recent Fiction Publications. *Spectator*, London, April 7, 1933.
Jenkins, Henry, Brad Seawell, and David Thorburn. *Rethinking Media Change: The Aesthetics of Transition.* Cambridge, MA: MIT Press, 2004.
Jones, Steven. *The Meaning of Video Games.* New York: Routledge, 2008.
Joyce, James. *Finnegans Wake.* 1939. Reprint, New York: Penguin, 1999.
*Mass Effect.* BioWare. Directed by Casey Hudson. Microsoft Game Studios, 2007.
Marx, Karl. *Grundrisse: Outlines of the Critique of Political Economy*, translated by Martin Nicolaus. 1857–61. Reprint, New York: Penguin, 1973.
Pressman, Jessica. *Digital Modernism: Making It New in New Media.* New York: Open University Press, 2014.
Simmonds, Roy S. *William March: An Annotated Checklist.* Huntsville: University of Alabama Press, 1988.
Turkle, Sherry. *The Second Self: Computers and the Human Spirit.* New York: Simon and Schuster, 1985.
Wark, McKenzie. *Gamer Theory.* Cambridge: Harvard University Press, 2007.

# AFTERWORD

Modernism is all around us. Not late modernism, not postmodernism, but modernism. One of the things that we discover in this collection is the myriad ways in which modernist ideas, techniques, and aesthetics are revived, re-used, invoked, or critiqued in the popular culture of the late twentieth and twenty-first centuries. At the same time, these contemporary modernisms are themselves indebted to the popular appropriations of modernism that happened much earlier, in silent cinema, early radio drama, operetta, or gangster flicks.

In her chapter on modernist time, Aimee Wilson quotes William Faulkner's famous pronouncement that "the past is never dead. It's not even past." Taken together, the essays in this collection seem to suggest an adaptation: "Modernism is never dead. It's not even past." But can we reach it and immerse ourselves in it, or do we always experience it through a veil of nostalgia or twenty-first-century knowingness? In his chapter on broadcasting, Adam Nemmers proposes that radio is the modernist medium par excellence, "the only art-form born and matured during the modernist period." Not only this, but radio drama, "freed from technical considerations and the tyranny of the 'visual scene' … could venture anywhere within the human imagination." Yet, according to Nemmers, these days, "radio drama is all but defunct, and radio sets themselves have largely disappeared from households." After reading this, I walked around my apartment counting my radios. Six. I thought back to the three BBC radio dramas I had listened to (live, analogue) in the last week. Have I been left behind in a past century? Or is my attachment to live radio simply another proof of the continuing power of the modernist imagination in the present day? Indeed one of the plays I had listened to was set in a railway carriage in the 1920s. Another was about Noël Coward and E. Nesbit: both popular authors who engaged warily with modernism.

I read on. Soon, it became clear that television must also be taken into account. Television was foreseen in the early twentieth century: Nicholas Daly points this out, using the example of Ivor Novello's "Ruritanian" operetta, *Glamorous Night*. Yet television is not a modernist technology, and I have always felt I could ignore it. Indeed, I have unfortunately not paid attention to *Mad Men*, or *The Wire*, and I have no patience with *Downton Abbey*. Now, however, I am fully persuaded that all these series perform what Scott Ortolano describes so astutely as "a strategic invocation of past modernisms to help the audience confront the modernities of our present moment." Oh dear. I had hoped that I was eschewing nostalgia and sentimentalism by refusing to watch *Downton*. But it turns out that I am simply failing to celebrate the resurgence and reinvention of modernism in popular cultural forms. As Ortolano puts it: "modernism's sense of experimentation, engagement with new technologies, and paradoxical relationships with the past and future have always been in conversation with—and a driver of—mass culture. It is to this important but often unappreciated truth that the essays in this collection are dedicated." Bravo!

Among the technologies of modernity that interest me especially are those of printing and textile manufacture. These come together in Marsha Bryant's chapter on the 1950s men's magazine *Gentry*, which was famous for including fabric samples in its beautifully designed pages. Bryant comments that the magazine's portrayals of the photographer Alfred Stieglitz and the shirt designer Alfred Shapiro "highlight the way each figure brought the artist's hand to mechanical means of making photographic prints and menswear, respectively." She also describes the modernist sculpture and painting that was presented in the art sections of *Gentry*, observing: "Modernism was no longer new in the 1950s. Yet modernist art, design, literature mixed with men's high fashion to make *something else* new in the pages of *Gentry*." This comment could equally be applied to many of the other cultural products discussed in this collection. The modernist moment is past, but modernism still has immense generative power. It can still make new things. At the same time, the physical things that were made by modernist artists and designers, and even by the production lines of the early twentieth century, are a crucial part of modernism's legacy to us. The circulation of modernist stuff in contemporary culture might have been an apt subject for another chapter in this collection. Think, for instance, of the growing popularity of exhibitions of modern design: in London, this culminated in the November 2016 re-opening of The Design Museum in a dramatic renovated space in Kensington. Think, too, of the prices that can be fetched by the sale of couture clothing or art deco objects from the interwar years—a Poiret dress, for example, can sell for up to $50,000 at auction.

*Gentry* purveyed an ideal of affluent, cultured masculine modernity, encouraging well-off middle-class men to aspire to distinction. At the other end of the social scale, the gangsters in the 1930s films explored in Jonathan Goldman's chapter, and the prisoners depicted in *The Wire* and discussed here by Walter Bosse, also aspire to "be somebody." They turn to crime in a bid to escape the restrictions of the low social stratum that they belong to. In both chapters, *The Great Gatsby* is a reference point, because Gatsby is both a criminal and an emblem of (failed) social mobility. These two fine essays, though so different in approach and content, arrive at remarkably similar conclusions. The gangsters and the prisoners were, in Bosse's words, "duped by the American myth of self-making," and the films and TV series rely, in Goldman's phrase, "on a modernist notion of self-objectification."

An alternative, and more triumphant, version of this American mythology is played out in the career of Josephine Baker. She is a figure who has provoked intense debate, particularly about whether she was reiterating or contesting racial stereotypes. As Asimina Ino Nikolopoulou comments in her chapter on Baker and her afterlives: "To announce Baker's performance as emancipatory, one needs to address the representational conundrum of her iconic self-making." Nikolopoulou argues that Baker's provocative performance did indeed disrupt conventional categories and ways of seeing, as well as offering other artists insights into the way modernism was experienced by a black subject. Her legacy in the present moment, according to Nikolopoulou, is especially visible in the work of Beyoncé, whose self-reflexive and citational performance "contributes to an emancipatory modernist discourse, as her body contests iconic renderings of black femininity." In concluding her essay in this way, Nikolopoulou points to one of the primary interventions of this collection as a whole. It offers us ways of reading contemporary artists as contributing to, rather than simply referring back to, modernist discourse. It enables us, as critics, to move away from retrospection and explore modernism from within—as an element of our own twenty-first-century intellectual and aesthetic atmosphere.

Faye Hammill

# NOTES ON CONTRIBUTORS

**Scott Ortolano** is Professor of English at Florida SouthWestern State College. His scholarship explores the cognitive and existential repercussions of consumerism and the future of the humanities. Among other work, he has recently published in *The F. Scott Fitzgerald Review*, *South Atlantic Review*, *The Explicator*, *Women's Studies*, *Terror in Global Narrative: The Aesthetics and Representation of 9/11 in the Age of Late-Late Capitalism* (Palgrave Macmillan, 2016), and *Teaching Hemingway and the Natural World* (Kent State University Press, 2017). He co-edited *Perspectives on the Short Story*, an anthology of short fiction published by Pearson (2012, 2014), and also recently co-edited a special issue of the *South Atlantic Review* focused on sustaining English programs in the twenty-first century.

**Faye Hammill** is Full Professor of English at the Univeristy of Glasgow. She is author or co-author of six monographs, including *Women, Celebrity, and Literary Culture Between the Wars* (University of Texas Press, 2007), *Sophistication* (Liverpool University Press, 2010), *Magazines, Travel, and Middlebrow Culture* (Liverpool University Press, 2015) and *Modernism's Print Cultures* (Bloomsbury Academic, 2016). She founded the AHRC Middlebrow Network in 2008, and her current project on Noël Coward is funded by a British Academy Mid-Career Fellowship.

**Dustin Anderson** is Associate Professor & Director of Graduate Studies in the Department of Literature & Philosophy, and associate faculty for The Center for Irish Research and Teaching at Georgia Southern University. His research crosses developments in literatures and cognitive philosophy, with an emphasis on how the writings of transnational modernists complicate received discourses on cognition and memory. His scholarly work has recently appeared in *Understanding Bergson, Understanding Modernism* (Bloomsbury Academic, 2013), *The Plays of Samuel Beckett* (Bloomsbury Methuen Drama, 2013), and *Samuel Beckett Today/Aujourd'hui*. Anderson has recently directed the 13th International F. Scott Fitzgerald Conference, the ALA Symposium on American Literature and War, and is a regular organizer for the British Commonwealth and Postcolonial Studies Conference.

**Caroline Blinder** is Senior Lecturer in American Literature and Culture at Goldsmiths, University of London. She has published widely on the intersections between literature and visual arts, and her forthcoming monograph, *The American Photo-Text: 1930–1960* (Edinburgh University Press, 2017), traces a series of documentary collaborations between photographers and writers. Other publications include: *New Critical Essays on James Agee and Walker Evans: Perspectives on Let Us Now Praise Famous Men* (Palgrave, 2010), "Fragments of the Future: Walker Evans's Polaroids"—in *Mixed Messages: American Correspondences in Visual and Verbal Practices* (Oxford University Press, 2016), "Ruses and Ruminations: The Architecture of Let Us Now Praise Famous Men" in *The Centenary Edition of Let Us Now Praise Famous Men*, ed. Michael Lofaro (University of Tennessee Press, 2017), "Sitting Pretty: Municipal Chairs in the Photography of Doisneau" in *The Everyday in Modernist Practice* (European Modernism Association, 2012), "Brassaï's Chair, and Henry Miller and The Eye of Paris" in *Text and Image Relations in Modern European Culture* (Purdue University Press, 2011). Her first book *A Selfmade Surrealist—Ideology and Aesthetics in the Work of Henry Miller* was published by Boydell and Brewer in 2000 (Camden House).

**Walter Bosse** is Assistant Professor of English at Brescia University in Kentucky where he teaches courses in literature and writing. He has published articles on Ralph Ellison, Ernest Hemingway, and Charles W. Chesnutt, and his research continues to theorize crosscurrents of aesthetic and sociopolitical influence between black and white modernists in the American tradition.

**Marsha Bryant** is Professor of English & Distinguished Teaching Scholar at the University of Florida, and an Associate Editor for the journal *Contemporary Women's Writing*. She received an NEH fellowship for her recent book, *Women's Poetry and Popular Culture* (Palgrave, 2011). Bryant also wrote *Auden and Documentary in the 1930s* (University of Virginia Press, 1997), and edited *Photo-Textualities: Reading Photographs and Literature* (University of Delaware Press, 1996). Her recent essays have appeared in the journals *Modernism/modernity*, *Journal of Modern Literature*, and *Plath Profiles*, as well as the collections *A History of Twentieth-Century American Women's Poetry*, *Identity and Form in Contemporary Literature* (Cambridge University Press, 2016), and *Approaches to Teaching H.D.'s Poetry and Prose* (MLA, 2011). She has curated exhibitions at the Harn Museum of Art and the Whitney Museum of American Art.

**Kirk Curnutt** is Full Professor and Chair of English at Troy University's Montgomery, Alabama, campus. He is the author of thirteen books of fiction and criticism, including *Brian Wilson* (Equinox, 2012), an entry in

Equinox Publishing's Icons of Pop Music series. He also serves as managing editor of *The F. Scott Fitzgerald Review*.

**Jonathan Goldman** is Associate Professor of English at New York Institute of Technology. He is author of *Modernism Is the Literature of Celebrity* (University of Texas Press, 2011), editor of *James Joyce and the Law* (University of Florida Press, 2017), and co-editor of *Modernist Star Maps: Celebrity, Modernity, Culture* (Ashgate, 2010). His writings on twentieth-century literature and culture appear in *The Cambridge Companion to Ulysses* (Cambridge University Press, 2014), *Cambridge Contexts: Bernard Shaw* (Cambridge University Press, 2015), *James Joyce Quarterly*, *Narrative*, *Novel: A Forum on Fiction*, *The Paris Review*, *The Millions*, and *The Chronicle of Higher Education*.

**Nicholas Daly** is Full Professor of Modern English and American Literature at University College Dublin. He is the author of *Modernism, Romance, and the Fin de Siècle* (Cambridge University Press, 1999), *Literature, Technology and Modernity* (Cambridge University Press, 2004), and *Sensation and Modernity in the 1860s* (Cambridge University Press, 2009), and many articles on Victorian and twentieth-century literature and culture. His *The Demographic Imagination and the Nineteenth-Century City: Paris, London, New York* was published by Cambridge University Press in 2015, and he is currently working on a project on Ruritanian fiction and film, from *The Prisoner of Zenda* to *The Princess Diaries*, and on an edition of *The Scarlet Pimpernel* for Oxford World's Classics.

**Barry J. Faulk** is Full Professor of English at Florida State University, where he teaches Victorian Literature and popular culture. He is co-editor with Brady Harrison of *Punk Rock Warlord: The Life and Work of Joe Strummer* (Ashgate, 2014), the author of *British Rock Modernism* (Ashgate, 2010), and a contributor to *The Edinburgh Companion to T. S. Eliot and the Arts* (Edinburgh University Press, 2016).

**Paul March-Russell** is Lecturer in Liberal Arts and Comparative Literature at the University of Kent. He is the editor of *Foundation: The International Review of Science Fiction* and the SF Storyworlds series (Gylphi Press). In 2016, he was appointed as one of the judges of the Arthur C. Clarke Award and in 2017, with Andrew M. Butler, he is co-organizing a centenary conference on Clarke's life and work at Canterbury Christ Church University. His publications include *Modernism and Science Fiction* (Palgrave, 2015) whilst, most recently, he has contributed on science fiction to *The Cambridge History of the English Short Story* (Cambridge University Press, 2016) and *The Cambridge History of Science Fiction* (forthcoming 2018).

**Andrew V. McFeaters** is Assistant Professor at Broward College. He earned his PhD from Florida State University in 2010, having written his dissertation on James Joyce, Samuel Beckett, and Flann O'Brien. He has published essays in *The Parish Review*, *The Edinburgh Companion to Samuel Beckett and the Arts* (Edinburgh University Press, 2014), *Hypermedia Joyce Studies*, and the *Journal of Post-Graduate Art at University of Brasilia*. His research focuses on the unique contribution of Irish literature to avant-gardism, global literature, and transatlantic modernism in general.

**Adam Nemmers** is a recent graduate of Texas Christian University and an Assistant Professor of English at Lamar University, where he teaches courses in literature and composition. His research touches upon a number of broader nodes of twentieth- and twenty-first-century American Literature. Recent or forthcoming publications include *Yours in Filial Regards* (TCU Press, 2015) and *Transatlantic Anglophone Literatures, 1776–1920* (Edinburgh University Press, forthcoming), as well as essays on Harper Lee, Richard Wright, *An American Tragedy*, *The Sound and the Fury*, and settler colonialism.

**Asimina Ino Nikolopoulou** is Visiting Lecturer of English at Tufts University. She received her PhD in English from Northeastern University and completed an MA in American Studies at Columbia University as a Fulbright Scholar. Her dissertation, *Senses and Sights of Dispossession: Contemporary Tales of the Black Diaspora and the Global South* (2017), examines the affective underpinnings of contemporary narratives of dispossession authored or curated by women of color. Her teaching and publications revolve around race, gender and visuality in a transnational context.

**Camelia Raghinaru** is Associate Professor of English at Concordia University, Irvine. She received her PhD in English from the University of Florida, and her research interests focus on utopian studies, modernism, and popular culture. Her articles on Conrad, Lawrence, Joyce, Woolf, and Breton have been published in various academic journals, including *Studies in the Novel*, [sic], *Forum*, and edited collections, including *Great War Modernism* and *Critical Approaches to Joseph Conrad*. She is currently researching the shift from Victorianism to modernism in Joseph Conrad's work.

**Aimee Armande Wilson** is Assistant Professor of Humanities at the University of Kansas, where she specializes in transatlantic modernism and feminist theory. Her work has appeared in *Modern Fiction Studies*, *symplokē*, and *Genre*. She is the author of *Conceived in Modernism: The Aesthetics and Politics of Birth Control* (Bloomsbury Academic, 2016) and is currently researching the relationships among masculinity, pregnancy, and modernist aesthetics.

# INDEX

Aarseth, Espen J. 249
Adams, Douglas 10, 167–8, 173–6, 178 n.39
Adorno, Theodor W. 3, 45, 57
Africa (African) 134, 141, 151,
African-American 11, 55, 153–62, 203–13, 265
aliens *see* extraterrestrials
American Revolution 257
Anglo *see* British
anti-Semitism 53–4 *see also* Judaism
appropriation 65, 114–15, 117, 119, 150, 157, 204–5, 210–11, 218, 263
*Arcades Project* (Benjamin) 96–8, 105, 251–2
Artaud, Antonin 248
*Assassin's Creed* 248, 253, 256–9

Baker, Houston A., Jr. 149, 157–9, 204, 212
Baker, Josephine 10, 149–62, 265
*Ballet Mécanique* 45, 103–4
Barth, John 4
Baudelaire, Charles 33–4, 96–9, 105, 107, 251–2
Baxter, Stephen 134, 136, 140–4
Beach Boys, The 10, 115–18, 121–5 *see also* Wilson, Brian
Beckett, Samuel 71, 248, 257
Benjamin, Walter 82, 95–107, 185, 251–2
Bergson, Henri 232–5, 248, 251, 257
Bhabha, Homi K. 134–5
black identity 149–62, 203–13
*Brave New World* (Huxley) 10, 165–9, 174
Brecht, Bertolt 69, 72, 185

Britain (British) 1–9, 36, 47–9, 54–7, 59 nn.23, 25, 65–6, 108 n.9, 133, 167, 169–70
  Anglo 10, 89, 96, 103, 155, 157, 159, 166, 242
  England (English) 1–9, 32, 36, 46, 47–9, 54–7, 58 n.7, 100, 106, 167, 169–70, 232, 241, 258
  Edwardian 1, 6, 22, 33, 47–8, 55
  Victorian 47, 53, 55, 98, 134, 218, 232, 240,
  Scotland (Scottish) 138
  Wales (Welsh) 46, 66, 257
*Broom* 104
Burnett, W. R. 85–6

Cagney, Jimmy 86–91 *see also Public Enemy, The*; Powers, Tommy
*Call of Duty: Modern Warfare* 11, 248, 253–7
capitalism (capitalist) 97, 141, 173, 186, 192, 199, 227
castration 218–26
Cather, Willa 89
celebrity (movie star, stardom, fame) 9–10, 21, 48, 79–91, 114–15, 119, 121–2, 155, 158, 167, 172, 233 *see also* icon
Chandler, Raymond 114, 124
Chaplin, Charlie 10, 90, 95–107 *see also* Tramp, the
Christianity (Christian) 136, 166 *see also* religion
cinema (film, movies) 2–3, 9, 30–1, 36–7, 45–8, 55–6, 63, 66–7, 70, 74, 79–91, 95–6, 98–105, 108 n.14, 119, 154, 156, 158,

160–2, 168, 175–6, 185–7, 190, 236, 248, 253, 263–5 *see also* Hollywood
Civil Rights Movement 150, 152
class
  lower class 4, 24, 223
  middle class 11, 24, 33, 37, 218–19, 225, 264 *see also* middlebrow
  upper class 11, 207
  working class 84, 96, 102, 176, 204, 206, 225
clock time 11, 231–42
colonial (colonialism) 134–5, 138–44, 150–5, 161–2 *see also* imperialism; postcolonialism
comedy (comic) 46–8, 55, 100, 106–7, 150, 220, 222, 227, 250
  humor 7, 26, 90, 175, 208
  slapstick 121
comics 11, 231–42, 243 n.19 *see also* graphic novel
computer 168, 172, 174–5, 197
Conrad, Joseph 134, 166
consumer culture (consumer, consumerism) 68, 81–4, 115, 167–8, 175, 217–18
cosmopolitan (cosmopolitanism) 22, 64–5, 70, 155
crime (criminal) 10, 79–91, 102, 108 n.19, 113–19, 124–5, 171, 184–9, 197, 203–4, 207–10, 254, 264
  criminality 91, 207
  gangster 9, 79–91, 92 n.5, 183, 192, 263–5
crime fiction 113–16, 117, 124–5
cubism 19, 25–7, 30
cult 114, 117–18, 120

dada 248
dance 46, 56, 85, 137, 149–62
dandy (dandyism) 22, 29, 34–8
*Danse Sauvage* 150, 156
Darwinian 134, 136–7
Derridean 143
desire 7, 49, 79–80, 83–7, 91, 98, 135, 139–42, 153–5, 160, 184, 192, 196, 217–26, 234–5, 247

detective (private investigator, P.I.) 10, 114, 117, 121–4, 183–99, 203
Dickens, Charles (Dickensian) 101, 106, 203, 213 n.1
Doctorow, E. L. 167
Dora, Miklos (also known as "Miki" and "Da Cat") 115, 118–21
*Downton Abbey* 1–9, 263
drama *see* theater
Du Bois, W. E. B. 157–8
dystopian 168–9, 176

Eco, Umberto 113
Edwardian England *see* Britain, England
Eliot, T. S. 2, 30–1, 95, 105–7, 113–14, 247–8, 251
empathy 7, 138, 161, 184
England (English) *see* Britain
Ensslin, Astrid 250–1
entropy 140, 144, 158
epidermis 154, 161
ergodic 11, 249
escapism (escapist) 1, 3, 53, 56–7
Europe (European) 22, 30–1, 34, 37, 46, 47, 49, 53, 56, 100, 141, 149–50, 153–5, 165, 169–70, 172
everyday *see* quotidian
evolution 26, 135–8, 142–3
exotic (exoticism) 54, 142, 153–6, 161, 175
extraterrestrials
  aliens 64, 68, 133–44, 167, 169, 174
  Martians 134, 137, 140–1, 237

fame *see* celebrity
fascist (fascism) 46, 54, 56–7, 67, 137, 253–6
fashion 19–38, 49, 56–7, 72, 95–8, 102, 114, 122, 150, 154–6, 159, 162, 226–8, 264
Faulkner, William 113, 233, 239, 248, 257, 263
Fellowes, Julian 4
Felski, Rita 3–4, 218
femininity (feminine) 11, 149–50, 154–6, 162, 218–19, 225–6, 265

# INDEX

feminism (feminist) 133, 140, 151
film *see* cinema
fine art *see* highbrow
*Finnegans Wake* (Joyce) 257–9
First World War (The Great War, World War One) 6, 46, 48, 65, 88, 90, 138, 153, 162, 253
Fitzgerald, F. Scott 11, 89, 167, 203–13, 214 n.17
*flâneur (flâneuse, flânerie)* 33, 96–105, 251–2
Ford, Henry (Fordism) 10, 165–76
France (French) 53–4, 151–2, 158
Freudian 134, 242
Fukuyama, Francis 141
Futurism (Futurist) 45, 55, 59 n.17, 63–4, 69, 165 *see also* Marinetti, F. T.

gangster *see* crime
gay *see* sexuality, homosexual (gay)
gender 3, 11, 25, 33, 140–1, 149–62, 218–20, 225–8, 232
*Gentry* 9, 19–38, 264
German (Germanic) 46–7, 54, 71–2, 104, 152, 176, 185, 250
Gershwin, George 45
Gershwin, Ira 47
*Gidget: The Little Girl with Big Ideas* (Kohner) 115, 118
Gilliard, Jr., Lawrence 206–13, 214 n.13 *see also Wire, The*, Barksdale, D'Angelo
*Girl in the Telltale Bikini, The* (Morgan) 117–20
*Glamorous Night* 9, 45–58, 263
  Allen, Anthony (*performed by* Ivor Novello) 49–56
globalization 168, 173
God *see* religion
gothic 183, 186, 191, 198
graphic novel 168 *see also* comics
*Great Gatsby, The* (Fitzgerald) 11, 89–91, 167, 205–13, 264
Great War, The *see* First World War
Greenberg, Clement 3, 19, 28
guru 117, 120
Gypsy 49, 52, 56

Hammett, Dashiell 10, 117, 200 n.7
Harlem Renaissance 3, 13 n.17, 149, 155, 158–9
Hegel, G. W. F. (Hegelian) 136–7, 141
hegemony 57, 134–5, 158, 219–221, 238
Hemingway, Ernest 25, 113, 154, 219, 247–8, 253, 255
Hendrix, Jimi 122
hero (heroic, heroine) 48–9, 53, 87–8, 96–8, 120–1, 137, 143, 219
heterosexual *see* sexuality, heterosexual
highbrow (high culture) 3, 24, 113
  fine art 28–9, 69, 74
high modernism *see* modernism
*Hitchhiker's Guide to the Galaxy, The* (Adams) 10, 165, 167–8, 173–6, 178 n.39
Hitler, Adolf 54, 69
Hollywood 9, 48, 80–91, 95, 101, 103, 105, 107, 115, 126 n.9
homosexual *see* sexuality, homosexual (gay)
hooks, bell 160–1
Horkheimer, Max 2–3
humor *see* comedy
Huxley, Aldous 10, 165–6, 169, 171, 173–4
Huyssen, Andreas 2–3
hybridity 10, 19, 33, 133–44

icon (iconic, iconography) 30, 33, 67, 150, 154–62, 190, 194, 200 n.24, 251, 265 *see also* celebrity
iconicity 67, 158, 251
iconoclastic (iconoclasm) 118, 156, 162
Imagism 30
immobility 205, 209–10
imperialism (imperial, imperialist) 6, 134–7, 153–5, 166–7, 170, 175 *see also* colonial
incarceration *see* prison
indexicality 158, 160, 251
industrial 10, 29, 37, 81, 104, 170–1, 175–6, 184–7, 190, 192,

196–7, 199, 200 n.7, 203, 205, 210, 257
Industrial Revolution 170, 257
*Inherent Vice* (Pynchon) 114, 121–5
intermodernism *see* modernism
intersectional 156
interwar period 53, 64, 66, 69, 149–62, 253, 264
  interwar Paris 149–62
Ireland (Irish) 89, 166–73, 257
Italy (Italian) 63

James, Henry 19
James, William 235
Jazz Age 10, 149–62, 167
Jefferson, Thomas 19, 36, 167
Jim Crow 149, 155, 157, 161, 210
Jones, Gwyneth 134, 140–4
Josephson, Matthew 104
Joyce, James 49, 95, 231, 233, 248–9, 257–9
Judaism (Jewish) 53–4, 89 *see also* anti-Semitism; religion
justice system 11, 205

Kerouac, Jack 115
King Carol II of Romania 53–7, 59 n.22
Knowles, Beyoncé 10, 159–62, 265
Kohner, Frederick 115, 118

Lacan, Jacques 217, 221–4
*League of Extraordinary Gentlemen, The* (Moore and O'Neill) 11, 232–3, 237–42
Lewis, Wyndham 137
Lindbergh, Charles 72
*Little Caesar* (Burnett) (novel) 85–6
*Little Caesar* (film) 79–91
  Rico (*performed by* Edward G. Robinson) 79–91
London 30, 33, 48–9, 55, 65–6, 70, 96, 100–2, 106–7, 108 n.19, 108–9 n.23, 167, 170, 237, 241, 257, 264
London, Jack 155
Los Angeles (L.A.) 113–25, 127 n.27, 185, 188, 192, 196

lower class *see* class
ludology 248, 250
Lupescu, Elena (also Helena) 53–4, 57, 59 nn.20, 22
Lusty, Natalya 24, 218

Macdonald, Ross 114, 116–17, 120, 122, 127 nn.22, 27
*Mad Men* 2, 11, 217–28, 263
magazine 9, 19–38, 68, 70, 74, 84–5, 113, 115, 118, 264
magic 55, 72–3, 100, 102, 212, 217
Maisel, David 184–7, 190–9, 200 n.16
Malibu 115, 118, 127 n.27,
Manson, Charles 114, 118–25
Marinetti, F. T. 45, 63, 69, 74, 165, 218 *see also* Futurism
Martians *see* extraterrestrials
marriage 47, 49, 53, 85, 87, 150, 224–5, 227
Marx, Karl 82–3, 98, 249
Marxism (Marxist) 133–7, 170, 185
masculinity 11, 19, 21–38, 113, 126 n.9, 217–28, 264
mass communication 69, 168
*Mass Effect* 11, 248, 253–4
Maugham, W. Somerset 19, 238
McCarthy, Cormac 248
McLuhan, Marshall 8
media studies 249–50
Melville, Herman 115
*Memoirs of a Spacewoman* (Mitchison) 133, 137–40
memory 45, 71, 74, 124–5, 141, 197, 231, 241, 248, 251, 253–9
*Metropolis* (film) 176
metropolis (metropolitan, metropole) 10, 21, 30, 33, 70, 95–6, 99–106, 114
Mexico 174
middlebrow 59 n.11, 155 *see also* class, middle class
middle class *see* class
Miéville, China 133, 135–6
minstrelsy 157–8
misogyny 86
Misrach, Richard 184–99
Mitchison, Naomi 133–44

mobility 84, 100, 205, 209–10
modernism
  high modernism 3, 65, 70, 217, 241
  intermodernism 53, 59 n.19
  modernisims 2, 9, 11, 133, 155, 263–4
  new modernist studies 2, 8, 12, 13 n.13, 156
modernity 2, 3, 47, 55, 96–8, 104–7, 133, 149, 153–8, 168, 176, 185, 210, 218, 224, 249, 252–3, 264
Moore, Alan 11, 232–3, 235, 238
Morgan, Patrick (*pen name of* George Snyder) 117–20
movie star *see* celebrity
movies *see* cinema
musical 9, 46–8, 55–8, 71, 88, 115, 121–2, 152, 160, 234
Mussolini, Benito 69

new media 7, 55, 57, 249
new modernist studies *see* modernism
newspaper 55, 68, 79, 83–4, 86, 97, 106, 160, 213 n.1
newsreel 55
nihilism 113, 183
noir 10, 91, 113–20, 124–5, 127 n.22, 185–8, 200 n.8
noise *see* sound
non-linear narrative 11, 71, 248, 251–9
Novello, Ivor 9, 45–58, 58 n.10, 263
  *see also Glamorous Night*, Allen, Anthony
Nunn, Kem 114, 118–20, 126 n.9, 127 n.30

O'Neill, Kevin 11, 232, 237–8
O'Nolan, Brian (*wrote under the pen name of* O'Brien, Flann) 10, 165–7, 171–4
O'Brien, Flann *see* O'Nolan, Brian
Offenbach, Jacques (Jakob) 46–7
opera 46–9
  soap 1
  space 142
operetta 9, 45–58, 263

*Orlando: A Biography* (Woolf) 232–3, 241
Other (otherness) 89, 135–42, 146 n.37, 153, 156–7, 166, 223

Paris 22, 26, 46–7, 70, 96–9, 102–5, 149–62, 252
  interwar Paris *see* interwar
Parker, Dorothy 3, 13 n.17
parody 4, 86, 120, 156–8, 160, 175, 252
patriotism 6, 64
performance 10, 47, 57, 68, 81, 85, 89, 104, 149–62, 210, 212, 220, 247, 265
Picasso, Pablo 19, 24, 26–8, 30
Pizzolatto, Nic 183–99, 200 n.8
*Playboy* 21, 24, 33
Poe, Edgar Allan 96, 99
poetry (poetic, poet) 31, 36, 65, 67, 73, 96–100, 160, 242, 247, 251, 253
*Point Blank* 188–9, 200 n.10
pollution 174, 183, 185–6, 191–2, 196–7
postcolonialism 134–5 *see also* colonial; imperialism
postmodernism 3–5, 71, 133, 135, 142, 183, 185–6, 196, 199, 220, 263
Pound, Ezra 30–1, 69
Pressman, Jessica 2, 7, 249
primitivism (primitive) 48, 127 n.22, 149, 151, 153–4, 158, 166, 172, 192, 219
*Princess Tam Tam* (*performed by* Josephine Baker) 156
prison 34, 46–7, 118, 204–13, 214 n.10, 237–8, 256, 264–5
  incarceration 118, 162, 197, 205–6, 210, 212, 214 n.10
  prison-industrial complex 205, 210
private investigator (P.I.) *see* detective
psychological time 232–42
*Public Enemy, The* 80, 86, 88–9
  Powers, Tommy (*performed by* Jimmy Cagney) 86, 88–9
Pynchon, Thomas 10, 114–15, 121–4

queer 33, 36
quotidian 3, 49
  everyday 3–4, 30, 53, 68, 99, 101, 167, 205

racism (the effects of) 135, 149–62, 203–13, 219, 265
  institutional (in the criminal justice system) 203–13
  racial stereotypes and identity 149–62, 265
radio (wireless) 3, 7, 9, 49, 53, 55, 57, 59 n.17, 63–74, 124, 168, 263
realism (realist) 10, 57, 64, 105–6, 137, 141, 198, 211, 213 n.1, 224, 254, 256
Reed, Ishmael 167
religion (religious) 25, 166, 189 *see also* Christianity; Judaism
  God 136, 142
Robinson, Edward G. *see Little Caesar* (film), Rico
romance (romantic) 1, 3, 46–9, 53, 57, 90, 102, 106, 108 n.23, 133, 137, 142–3, 187, 218, 252, 255
Romania 53–4, 57, 59 nn.22, 23, 59–60 n.25
Roosevelt, Franklin Delano 69
Rubenstein, Hal 21–2, 25, 33, 37
Ruritania 45–58, 263
Russia (Russian) 64, 102, 170, 254, 256, 258
  Soviet Union 141

*Scarface* 80, 83–4, 86–8, 90
science fiction (SF) 10, 133–44, 168, 176
scopic regimes 150, 152
Scotland (Scottish) *see* Britain
Second World War (World War Two) 10, 37, 46, 48, 66, 115, 152, 167
Seldes, Gilbert 104–5
sentimental (sentimentalism) 1, 13 n.17, 46, 48, 55, 113, 123–4, 219, 264
September 11 5–6
sexuality 7, 84–7, 115, 138, 140, 142, 151, 186, 189, 192, 223–5, 239, 252
  heterosexual 86–7
  homosexual (gay) 48, 86–7, 189
Shakespeare, William (Shakespearian) 31, 102, 106, 123
Shapiro, Alfred 30–3, 36, 264
silence 65, 72–3, 123, 146 n.37, 165, 196, 226
Simon, David 203–5, 209–10, 212–13, 213 n.1 *see also Wire, The*
slapstick *see* comedy
Snyder, George *see* Morgan, Patrick
sound 45, 64–74, 85, 121, 151, 157, 189, 234, 241
  noise 45, 64, 67, 72
Soupault, Philippe 100–7, 108 n.19, 108–9 n.23
Southern Gothic 191
Soviet Union *see* Russia
Stapledon, Olaf 133, 135–40, 142–3
*Star Maker* (Stapledon) 133, 136–7, 139–40, 143
stardom *see* celebrity
Stein, Gertrude 69, 104, 106–7, 113, 125 n.1, 231
Stieglitz, Alfred 19, 30–3, 36, 264
Stoker, Bram 232, 240
surfing (surfers) 10, 113–25, 126 n.10, 126 n.11
surrealism (surrealist) 22, 99–101, 103–4, 108 n.23, 252

technology (technological) 2, 6–9, 13 n.17, 30–1, 33, 49, 55, 57, 63, 65, 73, 98–9, 107, 141, 154, 168, 170, 174, 187, 218–19, 235, 249, 251, 263–4
telephone 7, 66, 72, 90, 115
television (TV) 1–3, 9, 11, 28, 36, 46, 49, 53, 55, 66, 74, 114–15, 168, 178 n.39, 213 n.7, 248, 263, 265
terrorism 5, 6, 9, 254–5 *see also* War on Terror
theater (theatre, drama) 1, 9, 31, 45–58, 63–74, 88, 102, 106, 150, 188, 203–4, 247–8, 263

# INDEX

*Timelike Infinity* (Baxter) 142–4
Titanic 5, 7
Tracy, Terry-Michael "Tubesteak" 115
Tramp the (*performed by* Charlie Chaplin) 95, 100, 104–7 *see also* Chaplin, Charlie
transatlantic 30, 33, 72, 149–54, 167
*True Detective* 10, 183–99, 199 n.1, 200 n.15
Tzara, Tristan 248

*Ulysses* (Joyce) 47, 49, 233–4, 249, 259
unilinear narrative 136, 231–6, 239, 242, 242 n.1
United States (America, American) 1, 4–5, 10–11, 19, 21–2, 24–5, 28–9, 30–8, 47, 54–5, 57, 65–6, 68, 71, 79, 80–6, 88–9, 91, 96, 99, 101, 103–4, 106–7, 124, 141, 149–152, 157–62, 167–74, 183–9, 192, 203–13, 214 n.10, 220–1, 227, 242, 257, 265
upper class *see* class
utopia 57, 97–9, 116, 136, 168–9, 176

vaudeville 46, 89
Victorian England *see* Britain, England
video games 11, 247–59
Vienna 47, 56
visuality (visual art, visual technologies) 21–2, 26, 31, 55, 66, 70, 73, 86, 88, 96, 98, 153–4, 160–1, 186, 190, 193–4, 196, 199, 235, 237, 243 n.19, 257, 263

Wales (Welsh) *see* Britain, Wales
War on Drugs 203–5, 207
War on Terror 6, 9 *see also* terrorism
Washington, Booker T. 157–8
Washington, George 36
*Waste Land, The* (Eliot) 30, 251
Welles, Orson 67
Wells, H. G. 134–8, 141–2, 144
Wellsian 137, 140, 142, 144
*White Queen* (Jones) 140–4
Wilson, Brian 115, 121–4, 127 n.26, 128 n.43 *see also* Beach Boys, The
*Wire, The* 11, 203–13, 213 n.1, 213 n.7, 263–4
    Barksdale, D'Angelo (*performed by* Lawrence Gilliard, Jr.) 206–13, 214 n.13
wireless *see* radio
Woolf, Virginia 6, 69, 95, 137, 156, 232–3, 235–6, 241
World War One *see* First World War
World War Two *see* Second World War
working class *see* class

*Zebra-Striped Hearse, The* (Macdonald) 116–17, 127 nn.22, 27
Zupančič, Alenka 217, 221–2, 224–7

CPSIA information can be obtained
at www.ICGtesting.com
Printed in the USA
LVOW10*1155130218
566410LV00006B/72/P